The Jewish Body

JEWISH CULTURE AND CONTEXTS

Published in association with the
Herbert D. Katz Center for Advanced Judaic Studies
of the University of Pennsylvania

Series Editors
Shaul Magid, Francesca Trivellato, Steven Weitzman

A complete list of books in the series
is available from the publisher.

The Jewish Body

A History

Robert Jütte

Translated by
Elizabeth Bredeck

PENN

UNIVERSITY OF PENNSYLVANIA PRESS

PHILADELPHIA

Publication supported by a grant from
Jewish Federation of Greater Hartford

Publication of this volume was assisted by a grant from the Herbert D. Katz
Publications Fund of the Center for Advanced Judaic Studies at
the University of Pennsylvania.

The translation of this work was funded by Geisteswissenschaften
International—Translation Funding for Work in the Humanities and Social
Sciences from Germany, a joint initiative of the Fritz Thyssen Foundation,
the German Federal Foreign Office, the collecting society VG WORT,
and the Börsenverein des Deutschen Buchhandels
(German Publishers & Booksellers Association).

Originally published as *Leib und Leben im Judentum* by Robert Jütte.
© Jüdischer Verlag im Suhrkamp Verlag Berlin 2016

Published by
University of Pennsylvania Press
Philadelphia, Pennsylvania 19104-4112
www.upenn.edu/pennpress

Printed in the United States of America on acid-free paper
10 9 8 7 6 5 4 3 2 1

Library of Congress Cataloging-in-Publication Data
ISBN 978-0-8122-5265-1

Contents

Translator's Note

In transcribing Hebrew letters, names, and words, diacritical marks have been omitted, both in keeping with common practice in many English-language lexicons on Judaism and for greater readability; the transcription is phonetic. Transcribed Hebrew terms appear in italics, with the exception of those that are so commonly used they are no longer considered foreign words, such as Sabbath, Kabbalah, and Torah. The names of Hebrew-language authors are spelled as they most often occur in English-language sources. Hebrew book titles in the bibliography are followed by English translations in square brackets. The spelling of Yiddish words is based on Ronald Lötzsch, *Jiddisches Wörterbuch*, 2nd ed. (Mannheim: Bibliographisches Institut, 1992).

Unless otherwise noted, Bible passages are cited from *The New English Bible with the Apocrypha* (New York: Oxford University Press, 1971). Biblical names are spelled as they appear in this edition. Passages from the Babylonian Talmud (BT), Mishnah, and other rabbinical texts with the exception of the Jerusalem Talmud are taken from the Sefaria and Chabad websites. The names of rabbinical texts are spelled as they appear on these websites. Passages from the Jerusalem Talmud (JT), if not otherwise noted, have been translated by the author. Dead Sea Scrolls passages are taken from *Die Texte aus Qumran* (1986; 2001); see bibliography.

A number of the German and Yiddish texts cited are available in English translation; in those cases, the existing translation was used, and the English title appears in the bibliography. For works unavailable in English, the original titles appear in the bibliography, and the translations, unless otherwise noted, are my own.

Introduction

A ssejfer on a hakdome is wi a guf on a neschome.
(A book without an introduction is like a body without a soul.)
—Yiddish proverb

What Separates a Non-Jew from a Jew?

A goy bolts out of bed in the morning, slips on his pants, splashes himself with water, falls to his knees, and stammers his prayers. Then he gets back up, takes a seat and swigs a glass of schnapps, scarfs down a piece of bread, and heads out to the street to do business. Afterward he goes back to his hovel, sits down with his brats and his old lady, eats and drinks like a pig so he can race back out again and cheat the world. In the evening he goes to church, crosses himself like a donkey, comes back to his hovel, stuffs himself again, and crashes.

But a Jew! In the morning he arises from his bed, puts on his garments, washes himself thoroughly, and stands to say his morning prayer. Then he partakes of a small drink of something and a piece of bread and makes his way outside to do business and trading. . . . Later he makes his way back home, sits down at the table with his spouse and little ones, may they enjoy good health, gives the blessing, eats, says grace after meals, and returns to the street to continue doing business. Before nightfall he attends the evening service in the synagogue, returns home, takes his supper, says his bedtime prayers, and lays himself down to sleep.

The goy fritters away his few years like this, croaks, and is tossed into a pit. The Jew, however, lives quietly for as much time as he is granted, then dies and is buried, laid to rest in a Jewish grave.[1]

The reader of these lines, taken from one of the best-known collections of Yiddish anecdotes, proverbs, and humorous tales, *Rosinkess mit Mandlen* (Raisins and Almonds), is surprised at first to read the same story twice. Only the word choice and exaggeration make the life of the one person—namely, the Jew—seem more worthwhile than that of the other. As Sigmund Freud (1856–1939) observed in his book on jokes,[2] Jews often try to turn what is actually an oppressive experience into an ironic situation. Hence the black humor Jewish jokes are known for.

The dual perspective is surprising for a different reason as well. The Jewish conception of history long included the belief that a Jew who lived and lives in the *galut*, or Diaspora, was doomed to a life of trials and tribulations. Yet here we see a completely different, self-confident image. In the anecdote, the moral superiority of the Jew's life is what elevates it above the life of his counterpart, the non-Jew living in mainstream society. The same motif occurs in a Yiddish children's rhyme taught to ultra-Orthodox children in Jerusalem already in kindergarten: "Oj, wie scheyn zu sajn a jid, oj, wie schwär zu sajn a goj!" (Oh, how great to be a Jew, but oh, how hard to be a goy!). I first heard it in the mid-1980s while living and teaching in Haifa; watching a program on Israeli television, I rubbed my eyes in astonishment and wondered what these budding ultra-Orthodox people would ever experience of the world of the goyim in their later lives that were to be devoted to the study of Jewish religious texts. For you can be truly proud of something only if you also know its opposite.

In the opening comparison of a goy and a Jew, the alleged difference between them, underscored by the use of derogatory terms, is most clearly visible in their bodily practices. These include morning routines, hygiene, food intake, physical movement, and sleep, but also the end of corporeality, death. In all of these areas the Jew supposedly surpasses the non-Jew, whose life seems bleak and hardly enviable. The vivid, downright motion-based rhetorical style of the original Yiddish reinforces this impression. But if we "neutralize" both texts by removing the religious shading, we discover that the daily life of the Jew is hardly any different from that of the non-Jew, including their bodily practices.

The insight we gain by reading the Yiddish text against the grain has been given perhaps its most poignant expression and clever staging by none other than Shakespeare. In the famous scene from *The Merchant of Venice*, Shakespeare— who could not have known any Jews personally—has Shylock forlornly exclaim: "Hath not a Jew hands, organs, dimensions, senses, affections, passions; fed with the same food, hurt with the same weapons, subject to the same diseases, healed by the same means, warmed and cooled by the same winter and summer as a Christian?" (3.1).[3] As we know, however, this emphasis on Christians' and Jews' equality under the laws of nature, which also apply to the human body and mind, falls on deaf ears and in the course of the play is contradicted outright.

In fact, at the time (at least in Venice) Jews were physically almost indistinguishable from Christians, as the English traveler Thomas Coryat (ca. 1577–1617) attests. On a 1608 visit to the ghetto in Venice, he is astonished to find that here the English expression "to look like a Jew" has no relation to reality: "I observed some fewe of those Jewes especially some of the Levantines to bee such goodly and proper men, that then I said to my selfe our English proverb: To looke like a Jewe (whereby is meant sometimes a weather beaten warp-faced fellow, sometimes a phrenticke and lunaticke person, sometimes one discontented) is not true. For indeed I noted some of them to be most elegant and sweet featured persons, which gave me occasion the more to lament their religion."[4]

What prompts Coryat to question stereotypes and popular images was for many of his contemporaries more a cause for concern.[5] How could you recognize a Jew at all if not by his physical appearance? This worry goes back to late medieval efforts to identify Jews with the help of clothing regulations (garish colors, colors with negative connotations, and accessories such as the yellow ring sewn to their clothing). It was believed that these made it possible to instantly recognize a Jew, who often did not have the "typical" physical features of a hooked nose or beard.[6] And even after conversion, in Christian circles well into the early modern period there was lingering doubt whether baptism had actually made a new Christian out of a Jew if there was no clear physical "proof." Legends circulated that baptized Jews ostensibly no longer stank, something alleged of their former brethren. And if such wondrous bodily transformations were lacking, then converts had to at least adapt their bodily practices to their new environment. Especially in the Inquisition trials of forcibly baptized Spanish Jews (Marranos), suspicious bodily practices could raise doubts about the credibility of the conversion. One test, for example, involved the "proper" treatment of a corpse.

What to us may at first seem like an anachronism actually still plays a role in modern society. A sizable number of converts try to underscore the shift in their beliefs or religion by altering practices related to the body. Studies have been done in the sociology of religion, for instance, on American Jews who, after leaving their ultra-Orthodox parents' homes, felt the need to emphasize this step with new body techniques (for instance, morning routines, eating patterns throughout the day, style of dress).[7] In these cases it was apparently insignificant whether the person had merely shifted to a less Orthodox denomination or had become an atheist. Other religious communities show similar shifts in behavior following conversion.[8] As yet, however, no historical studies have been done that explore this religious-sociological phenomenon in earlier times.

But why should a historian bother with the body at all, and especially the Jewish one? Does it even have a history?

The need to view the body not just biologically but also as something with a historical dimension has been convincingly argued in recent decades by researchers in body history.[9] Fundamental questions of methodology have been debated, and there is no longer any doubt that the body is a social construct. Body culture studies and, more specifically, body history seek to ask "questions about received notions about the body and bodily practices in an effort to find answers about social construction."[10] This "corporal turn" in historiography has also begun to inform Jewish history. Discussion since the 1990s has focused on how the Jewish body was "constructed" in the course of history, by Jews and non-Jews alike.[11] It has addressed not only images of self and other, but also specific bodily practices that are ascribed to the Jews or play an important role in creating the identity of a religious and cultural community. American Jewish journalist Leon Wieseltier has objected that such research is banal since, after all, every Jew has a body, but his critique misses the point.[12] Wieseltier's essentialism, which presupposes a timeless, ahistorical human *physis*, serves him merely as a way to promote a history of ideas that privileges (what is usually considered progressive) Jewish thinking. To take this approach is to ignore the fact that anti-Judaism and anti-Semitism, but also Jewish self-hatred, are directed first and foremost at the body, not the mind. This somewhat singular and one-sided position has therefore been rightly criticized by American scholars of Jewish studies, who note, for instance, that the body of Jewish religious laws known as Halakhah itself contains many different and detailed regulations concerning "techniques of the body."[13]

Let us recall how the French anthropologist Marcel Mauss (1872–1950), who introduced this expression and incidentally came from a Jewish family, defined the term: "the ways in which from society to society men know how to use their bodies."[14] So, what are the body techniques that Jews have acquired from childhood on from parents and authority figures, and what is Jewish about them?[15] How have these changed in the course of a history of more than two thousand years (most of it spent in exile)? How have these practices affected the non-Jewish outside world? How have they influenced the image of the Jewish body? In this context, the question also arises of how secularization has influenced the body.[16]

Deliberately bracketed here is the relation between body and soul in Judaism. A whole, separate book could be written about the Jewish *neschome* (Yiddish for "soul")—both in the literal and figurative sense. This has to do not least with the broad spectrum of Jewish spirituality, which not only includes multiple terms for the soul, but also contains, in particular, mystical elements. Think of the Kabbalah, for instance, whose central theme is the divine-human union in which the soul plays an intermediary role. Liturgical, philosophical/theological, and even medical aspects would also need to be considered. That would have been far beyond the scope of this book. I have therefore chosen to keep the strict division between body and mind that became part of natural philosophy with René Descartes (1596–1650) and which has been used ever since by many, if not all, Jewish philosophers and physicians.

The primary aim of this book is to answer a variety of questions that are almost exclusively about the body. To do so, I refer to a broad range of Jewish and non-Jewish sources. Its central focus is always the human *physis* in all of its facets, even if the division between body and mind—as noted above—is more of an artificial one used here for practical reasons.

A closer look at traditional body stereotypes serves as an ideal starting point, not only because these are so familiar but also because they remain powerful even today. They range from the so-called "Jewish nose" to the particular smell that Jews are said to have.

The fact that the external appearance can be changed, be it through clothing or particular body techniques (sports, tattoos)—of this there is particularly eloquent testimony in Jewish history. In this connection, the Zionist alternative model of the "muscular Jew" in particular deserves special mention.

The history of gender has also discovered the Jewish body. It addresses topics including the notion popularized in ancient Christendom, especially by the apostle Paul, that Judaism has an ostensibly carnal or bodily orientation and, correspondingly, different sexual practices (for example, in issues concerning procreation and celibacy).

The categories "sickness" and "health" are central to any history of the body. For the Jewish people these terms were and are of key importance, not only in the sense of biological terms for phenomena and processes. They also have a metaphorical meaning—think only of the anti-Semitic concept of Judaism as "illness."[17] But the opposite belief—that due to their religion Jews are particularly concerned about maintaining the health of their bodies—also did and does exist. How Judaism has dealt with these two anthropological constants (sickness and health), which on closer look emerge as largely social constructs, is one of the least-examined areas in Jewish history.

And finally—how could it be otherwise, given this topic?—the end of physicality: death and the transience of human life coupled with the hope of resurrection, which has a different character in Judaism than in Christianity or other faiths. Here, as in other contexts, we can trace connections to ethical issues in contemporary medicine (for instance, brain death, autopsy). The following chapters will approach these issues from an interreligious perspective and explore their historical foundations.

Chapter 1

The Biological Body

The Image of God

The human body, according to Jewish beliefs, reflects not only God (man as the image of God)[1] but all of creation as well. This idea is expressed with particular clarity in a passage of the *Avot de-Rabbi Nathan*, a rabbinical commentary on the Mishnah Avot that has survived in two different versions in the extracanonical addendum to the Babylonian Talmud. Here we read for instance that God created trees in order to bear witness to human bones (*Avot D 'Rabbi Natan* 31). The firmament is connected in a similar way to the tongue, and almost the entire body is interpreted macrocosmically.

The medieval *Sefer Chasidim* (Book of the Pious), a compilation of ethical and liturgical rules of conduct, many in the form of exempla and some with arcane mystical content, goes even a step further and claims that individual body parts can foretell the future. Its author, Rabbi Judah he-Hasid, cites Job 31:4 ("Yet does not God himself see my ways and count my every step?") and gives the following example: just as the number of steps in a person's life is predetermined, so, too, does an itchy hand predict that the person is about to come into money, and an itchy cheek is a sign that the person will soon have reason to weep. God, it is argued here, allows people to foretell the future through the portents of their individual body parts.[2]

A Yiddish proverb goes: "A blind man is sick in the eyes, a dumb man is sick in the mouth, and a fool is sick in all 248 bones" (A blinder is krank oif di ojgen, a schtumer is krank oif dem mojl, a nar is krank oif alle rámach éjwerim).[3] According to Jewish tradition, the human body consists of 248 bones,[4] which the Mishnah divides into the following groups: "Thirty in the foot—six in each toe—ten in the ankle, two in the shin, five in the knee, one in the thigh, three in the hip, eleven ribs, thirty in the hand—six in every finger—two in the forearm, two in the elbow, one in the upper arm, and four in the shoulder. One hundred and one of this [side of the body], and one hundred and one of that. Eighteen vertebrae in the spinal cord: nine in the head, eight in the neck, six in the openings of the heart, and five around its cavities" (Oholot 1:8). It is not known how this count was arrived at. The ancient Hebrews' knowledge of anatomy was based on a number of different sources: analogies between animals and humans; autopsies on non-Jewish cadavers, since in Judaism the dead body may not be harmed; and observations about discovered skeletal remains. The Talmud reports, for example, that the students of Rabbi Ismael "cooked" the corpse of a prostitute condemned to death by the Romans (BT Bekhorot 45a), separating flesh from bones in this way, just as later anatomists in the early modern period did in order to make dry preparations. This is how they came up with the number 252. The Torah scholar explains the apparent contradiction to the Mishnah by noting that a woman has "two door frames and two doors" more than a man (BT Bekhorot 45a). The image is a reference to the primary and secondary sex organs of a woman, which differ from those of a man. The "one-sex model" that American cultural historian Thomas Laqueur claims was the norm in antiquity is thus at odds with Jewish source materials.[5] The Talmud passage quoted here even raises some doubt as to whether the number 248 in reference to the male sex is accurate. The Tosefta, another significant compilation of Jewish oral law, gives only a vague determination by setting the number of bones somewhere between 200 and 280 (Tosefta Ohalot 1:7).[6] Incidentally, the great non-Jewish medical authorities of Greco-Roman times—Hippocrates (ca. 460–370 BCE) and Galen (ca. 126–216 CE)—are similarly cautious: the latter speaks only of "more than 200 bones" in this context.[7] However, medieval physicians in the Islamic world such as Avicenna (ca. 980–1037 CE) also came up with the number 248. They had apparently learned about the Talmudic numbering from Jewish physicians, since in this case their usual source of guidance, Greek medicine, provided no specific details.

Anatomists to the present day still have some trouble naming a precise number. According to our current information, the human skeleton consists of approximately 212 bones. However, individual differences need to be taken into account (some people, for instance, have one additional pair of ribs), so in medical literature the total number can range from 206 to 214. Infants even have more than 300 bones, some of which fuse over the course of time.

The question is: why did Judaism in particular take such an early interest in determining the number of human bones as accurately as possible? One important reason is adherence to the laws of purity. According to the Mishnah, "a human does not impurify [others] until his life leaves him" (Oholot 1:6). Hence, if a corpse is in a covered space such as a tent, whoever enters becomes temporarily impure. "This is the law when a man dies in his tent: everyone who comes into the tent, and everyone who is in the tent, shall be unclean seven days" (Numbers 19:14). But how was someone to act in a case where there were only portions of the corpse? Here the Talmudic basic law applies that something greater than half must be counted as a whole.[8] It was therefore essential to know what constituted the basic totality. Assuming that the human body has 248 bones, the critical number was thus 125 (Oholot 2:1).

The number 248 had more than practical significance in Judaism. It also had a symbolic value, one that is linked to holy scripture. In the Mishnaic period (first to third century CE), rabbinical sages concurred that the Torah contained 613 commandments, of which 365 are negative and 248 positive. The anthropomorphic creature known as the golem (magically created from clay or mud, on most accounts) is described in the Talmud with the words *Rava bara gavra* ("Rava created a man," BT Sanhedrin 65b).[9] In the Kabbalistic interpretation, these three words have numerological significance.[10] In the original, the second word is nothing more than the first one in reverse, and a *gimmel*, the third letter of the Hebrew alphabet, has been added to the third. But when the Hebrew numerals corresponding to these ten letters of these three words are added together their sum is 612, that is, not quite 613. The artificial man created by Rava was thus not identical with God's creation; he was missing one body part.

In the sixteenth century, Jewish authors in Italy and other countries published the practical guidelines to following the 613 commandments and prescriptions collectively known as the *Sefer Hamitzvot*. These include the *Sefer Hareidim* by Elazar Azikri (1553–1600). This book is unusual in that it relates the individual mitzvoth to the body, as announced already on the title page: it "comments and explains the commandments for each limb according to its time."[11] The anonymous author of a different early modern period work, a compilation of Midrashim expositions, likewise related the 613 commandments and prescriptions to the 248 members and 365 desires of the human body. Not included are twelve so-called "ministers," including the five senses and feelings such as anger and mirth. The latter were apparently taken from the "six nonnatural things" (*sex res non naturales*) in Hippocratic-Galenic dietetics that must be kept in balance to insure good health.[12]

The *Sefer Yetzirah*, a key text of early Kabbalah, stresses among other things the importance of the number 12 in body symbolism: "The numbers in the body are the ten and the twelve" (*Sefer Yetzirah* 5:2). According to this count, a person has twelve central organs: two hands, two feet, two kidneys, spleen, liver, gall bladder, small intestines, stomach, and large intestine. God "made them like a dispute, and arranged them like a battle" (*Sefer Yetzirah* 6:1). This description recalls the well-known political fable by the Roman politician Menenius Agrippa (d. 493 BCE) about a dispute among individual body parts over which one is the most important.

The world in miniature (microcosm), according to Kabbalistic interpretations, also reflects the world in its totality (macrocosm), which means that the internal organs, too, are included in the anthropomorphic symbolism of Jewish mysticism. This is particularly true of the teaching about the *sefirot*, the ten divine attributes or emanations in the tree of life (*etz chajim*).[13]

The *sefirot* are interconnected, and Kabbalah uses a number of different images to illustrate their organic relation. In addition to the tree of life, which includes roots, trunk, and branches, we often find the figure of the mythical primordial man, *Adam Kadmon* (Hebrew אדם קדמון).[14] His rather less glorious likeness is the human being, who lacks the three attributes that place *Adam Kadmon* next to God: wisdom, majesty, and immortality.

In contrast, primordial man has all ten *sefirot*. His head consists of a crown— symbol of power—which is linked to wisdom and intelligence. The chest represents beauty and is connected to both the right and left arms, compassion and justice. The third triad consists of the lower body (the foundation), the right leg (strength), and left leg (splendor). The polar opposite of the crowned head is made up of the feet, symbol of the kingdom.[15]

The Jewish natural philosopher Abraham ben Hananiah Yagel (1553–ca. 1624) made the physical image of the ten *sefirot* even more concrete by assigning specific external and internal organs to them. In his version, the head consists of two eyes, two nostrils, two ears, and a mouth. That adds up to seven, which in turn refers to the seven lower *sefirot* that receive light and reflection from the upper ones. The four worlds of emanation (*Atziluth*, Emanation; *Beriah*, Creation; *Yetzirah*, Formation; and *Asiyyah*, Action) are also connected to the human body through their respective *sefirot*. *Beriah*, the second level, contains ten body parts normally hidden from view. Here Yagel includes the heart, lungs, esophagus, trachea, stomach, abdomen, intestines, spleen, and male and female genitals.[16]

According to the teachings of Kabbalist Isaac Luria (1534–72), the first phase of creation is characterized by the contraction (*tzimtzum*) of divine infinite being (*Ein Sof*). This is the prerequisite for the creation of *Adam Kadmon*, the primordial form of all being. Creation then proceeds from him, as divine power in the form of light streams from his bodily orifices and into the world. The second phase of creation begins since the vessels intended to contain the divine light shatter from the impact of *Adam Kadmon*'s light. This event is called *schwirat hakelim*, or "Shattering of the Vessels." The *sefirot* are transformed in this way into five faces, or *parzufim* (Hebrew-Aramaic singular *parzuf* [פרצוף], "face"; plural *parzufim*). One of these faces is called *seir anpin* (Aramaic זעיר אנפין; literally, "short/small face"), which is described as a completely formed male figure with head and body. This includes the duality of left and right that is expressed in a person's two arms, for example. Even more anatomical details are found in the *Zohar*, the most significant work of Kabbalah, which centers the vigor of the male between his two thighs with two kidneys and testicles in between (cf. *Zohar* 3:296a).

While these Kabbalistic notions about the body clearly derive from anatomical knowledge that was the foundation of Greco-Roman medicine and accepted by doctors, theologians, and natural philosophers up until the sixteenth century,

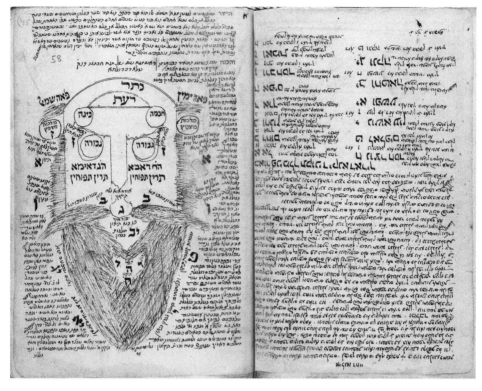

Figure 1. The face of *Adam Kadmon*. Illuminated Hebrew manuscript.
Gross Family Collection, Tel Aviv, MS 151, fol. 58r.

they had little influence on medicine or religion in daily life. They are instead
evidence of how the Jewish faith attempted to fit God's creation into a system
and create connections between mind and body, microcosm and macrocosm.
Moreover, this way of thinking contributed to the view that divine will is at work
in the development of illnesses. The *Zohar*, for example, outlines the importance
of individual organs for a person's general health, and does so in a way that is
largely consistent with medical knowledge at the time (the theory of the four
humors, or temperaments, from antiquity). Its uniqueness lies solely in the
attempt to bring this into harmony with Jewish conceptions about God. If, for
instance, the gall bladder becomes inflamed or infected, according to the Kabbalistic interpretation this could definitely become more serious if the Shechinah did
not protect the sick person like a coastal sand barrier (cf. *Zohar* 3:234a). In
Judaism the term *Shechinah* refers to the "dwelling" or "settling" of Yahweh in
Israel, and thus stands for the presence of God among his people and therefore
also for divine help in case of illness. This, for instance, is the reason that when

visiting the sick, a person customarily sits neither at the head nor the foot of a devout Jew: the Shechinah is said to be at the head of the sickbed, the angel of death at the foot. The Shechinah was also believed to be a kind of divine breath of wind that wafts around all bodily organs, guarding against illnesses (cf. *Zohar* 3:227b). The spleen is another organ whose importance is not only cosmological. The excess of black bile that collects there and leads to melancholia, according to the four humors theory of antiquity, is also interpreted as causative in the *Zohar*. But unlike in the Greco-Roman macrocosm, this imbalance of the humors is not linked with the god Saturn or the planet of the same name, but instead with Lilith, a female demon described in one Jewish legend as the dreaded final angel of the ten unholy *sefirot*.[17] Such Kabbalah-influenced images of the body remained quite popular among Jews well into the early modern period, as evidenced, for example, by the widespread use of amulets that among other things were supposed to protect against Lilith.[18]

Analogies

In the mid-seventeenth century, a number of Jewish physicians strove to share the theory of the four humors that still dominated medicine (together with therapeutic advice based on that theory) with a larger Jewish audience by writing in Yiddish. One of these was Issachar Bär Teller (ca. 1594–1687).[19] His work, like that of other Jewish physicians at the time, no longer shows much Kabbalah influence, and hence no anthropomorphic notions of God in anatomical illustrations.[20] This is also true of Tobias Cohen (1652–1729), who studied in Padua at one of the leading medical faculties in Europe and was even allowed to continue his medical studies at the university in Frankfurt an der Oder, the first Jew to do so.[21] He is still known today as the originator of the "living house" metaphor: a visual comparison of the human body with a house containing different rooms and floors.[22]

Apparently developed as a teaching tool, Cohen's model shows at left a man whose fully exposed upper body allows us to see into the body's interior as in an autopsy. The organs visible are labeled with Hebrew letters. Separated from this image by a scroll bearing a Hebrew text, the right side depicts a four-story house whose attic resembles a human head, that is, clearly anthropomorphic features. Contrary to what has been claimed,[23] it is not absolutely necessary to look to other medical authors or Jewish sources such as the *Midrash Rabbah Genesis* 24.1 to find precursors.[24] The concept of a living house is popular in many cultures,[25] and if that image depicts a house with eyes and ears, it stands to reason that the inside of the house might also be imagined as a collection of human organs. The only remarkable thing is that Cohen's house metaphor aligns him with Jewish tradition, since it draws on the Hebrew Bible-inspired comparison of a person with a city. As proof he cites a passage from Ecclesiastes: "There was a small

Figure 2. Tobias Cohen, *Maase Towia*. Engraving, 1708. Heb 7459.800*, Houghton
Library, Harvard University, Cambridge, MA.

town with few inhabitants, and a great king came to attack it; he besieged it and
constructed great siege-works against it. There was in it a poor wise man, and he
alone might have saved the town by his wisdom, but no one remembered that
poor wise man" (Ecclesiastes 9:14–15). For Cohen's purpose of illustrating
human anatomy and physiology with an easily understood image, however, it
sufficed to use the house as a term of comparison instead of the larger unit of the
city. In addition to the ground floor and attic the individual building has three

floors, exactly like the human body whose key component parts are the head, chest, and abdomen.[26] As this example shows, Judaism contained not only the widely known image of the "living house" but also its reverse, the metaphor of a living organism as a building.

We cannot speak of a specifically Jewish view of the body in this case, even though the learned doctor does try to bring then-current medical ideas into harmony with Jewish tradition and does so without allowing theological interpretations to get the upper hand as they do in the *Zohar*, for instance. Cohen, who practiced in Constantinople and Jerusalem, saw himself as a doctor first and therefore committed to the medical science of his time. The few religious references in his work may have resulted from his visit to a Polish Talmudic school prior to starting his medical studies in Padua. His work also represents those Jewish doctors and natural philosophers of the premodern period who either rejected or ignored the strict separation of body and mind in the Cartesian model still used today. That would change only in the nineteenth century under the influence of scientific medicine.

Today we also remember another Jewish doctor—and namesake—solely because of the physical model he popularized. This model, however, fits very neatly into the Cartesian worldview.[27] Its creator lived a good 250 years later. His name: Fritz Kahn, MD (1888–1968). Between 1922 and 1931 he published a popular five-volume medical work entitled *Das Leben des Menschen* (The Life of Man). In it he takes the lay reader on a spectacular journey through the human body. Kahn became best known for the poster *Der Mensch als Industriepalast* (Man as Industrial Palace), which he designed for his book *Das Leben des Menschen*.[28]

It shows a cutaway view from the head down to the digestive tract, not in the style of an anatomical diagram, but instead as an illustration of a glass palace with (work)rooms and pipes, conveyor belts and laboratories. The physiological processes in the body are not remotely controlled. Homunculi work everywhere in the different chambers of the human body, using control panels to direct the electrical processes and chemical reactions taking place in the body's interior. Kahn did not draw himself but instead hired illustrators who helped him depict the human being as machine, showing the circulation of the blood as a system of pipes, the sequences involved in sight and hearing as circuitry, and the digestive process as mechanical-chemical production. The mental aspect, the connection between body and mind, is absent.

Kahn popularized his machine model just as reductionist thinking in medicine was coming under heavy criticism. At the height of his success as one of Germany's best-known popular scientists, he had to flee because he was a Jew. He lost his medical license, and his books were burned. To the National Socialists, who were eager to establish a "New German Medicine," Kahn apparently represented

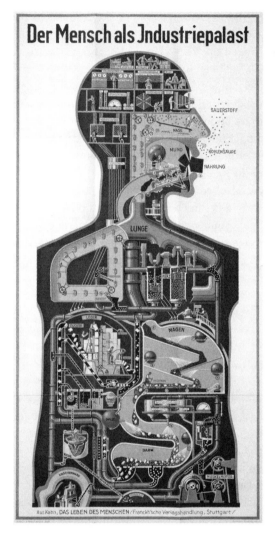

Figure 3. Fritz Kahn, *Der Mensch als Industriepalast*. Poster, 1926. National Library of Medicine, Bethesda, MD.

the negative stereotype of the Jewish doctor par excellence. Around the turn of the twentieth century, when Jewish physicians were pioneers in many fields of scientific medicine, making groundbreaking discoveries and enjoying phenomenal success with their treatments, it was difficult for anti-Semitic propaganda to dispute the medical abilities of Jews. The National Socialists therefore accused Jewish doctors of rationalism, lack of empathy, and strong business acumen. The completely industrialized image of the human body that made Kahn and his poster world famous fits this image well. In the United States, the country that finally offered him refuge after a long odyssey, his achievement met with greater appreciation: in 1943 the *New York Times* published a review of his book *Man in Structure and Function* (a translated and revised edition of *Das Leben des Menschen*) that contained the following praise:

> The last sections are on the nervous system, the skin and sensory organs—eye, ear, nose—and sex life. In this last it is gratifying to see that Dr. Kahn's exegesis differs from the school physiologies used by the sage of Baltimore in which 'all of the abdomen south of the umbilicus was represented by a smooth and quite uneventful surface.'
>
> The text is accurate, detailed, adequate, albeit somewhat plodding. Perhaps it is as well that it should be because its principal purposes [sic] is to furnish an explanation of the illustrations.
>
> ... They have the qualities of the wonderful exhibits in the Deutsche Musee [sic] in Munich. I pray nightly that the R.A.F. will spare that. They may have Cologne Cathedral and Potsdam and the Brandenburg Gate and the castles on the Rhine so far as I am concerned if only they leave the Deutsche Musee [sic] intact.[29]

Kahn is credited with having made complex biological and physical processes comprehensible to a large lay audience. As the German newsmagazine *Der Spiegel* notes: "He was far ahead of his time—decades before scientific programs became popular and Hollywood produced the first films about journeys into the human body."[30] A similar wish to illustrate an idea had motivated Tobias Cohen several centuries earlier when he created the image of the human body as house. In contrast to Fritz Kahn, Cohen's work long remained limited to Jewish circles since even today his book is available only in Hebrew. The fact that it was reprinted multiple times (in 1715, 1728, 1769, and most recently in 1850) nonetheless testifies to how highly regarded his medical compendium remained among readers of Hebrew even well into the nineteenth century.

Body Stereotypes

Certain physical features and character traits ascribed to the Jews, most with negative connotations, have a long tradition as anti-Jewish stereotypes. In some cases, they date back as far as the late Middle Ages, and they are fully developed in the early modern period. These attributes include the allegedly rank odor exuded by Jews (*foetor judaicus*),[31] certain physiognomic peculiarities (beard, dark skin, hooked nose), and behaviors supposedly inherited and/or determined by character, such as libido, avarice, miserliness, and deceitfulness.[32] At the beginning of the eighteenth century, Frankfurt high school professor Johann Jacob Schudt (1664–1722) informed his readers that—contrary to what Shylock argues in his famous soliloquy—it was indeed possible to tell the difference between a Jew and a Christian: "the *character* or distinguishing feature of the Jews is in part the body / in part the disposition / in part the way of life / by which we can quickly tell a Jew from a Christian."[33] The (in)famous Jew hater does not leave it at a vague description of distinguishing features, but instead goes into detail: "among physical characteristics I count not only the strange beard-pulling of the men / and the women's covering of their heads / . . . but [also] the very way the face is *formed* / so that the Jew protrudes forward / with nose / lips / eyes / also color and entire body *posture*."[34] Personality traits Schudt mentions include self-importance, ingratiating behavior, garrulousness, false subservience, malice, craving for recognition, and hunger for profit. He considers even their distinctive way of speaking—meaning Judeo-German—an additional distinguishing feature. Here, the term "language" means not only a sociolect that is an identifying feature of a group but also a character trait. Even before Schudt, the Hebrew scholar Johann Christoph Wagenseil (1633–1705) had expressed doubt that identifying markers for Jews (such as the yellow ring) were really necessary, since it was easy to tell Jews from Christians by their behavior and their bodies.[35] Toward the end of the eighteenth century, even in educated circles of Enlightenment thinkers the belief persisted "that Jews carry with them the mark of their fatherland the Orient to all four corners of the globe." That was at least the opinion of the writer Jakob Michael Reinhold Lenz (1751–92), as cited by Johann Caspar Lavater (1741–1801) in the highly regarded *Physiognomische Fragmente* of 1787. Lenz explains further: "I mean their short, black, curly hair and brown facial color." Lavater, who carried on a lively correspondence with Lenz, then adds: "I also count a pointed chin and large lips with a clearly drawn center line as part of the national character of the Jewish face."[36]

The belief that the Jewish body must be different thus has a long tradition: it is not a conclusion drawn for the first time in nineteenth- and early twentieth-century biologistic theories of race. American Judaic scholar Howard Eilberg-Schwartz aptly characterizes the Jews as "the people of the body," since to this day it is primarily bodily stereotypes that shape the image of the Jew.[37] At the same time, Eilberg-Schwartz notes the double meaning of the term. There can be little doubt that Judaism is itself very body-oriented; we need only look at the 613 commandments an observant Jew should follow in accordance with tradition. In one rabbinical Talmud commentary, for example, we read: "Ben Azzai says, 'Anyone whose body was stricken [with some disease], because of his wisdom it is a good sign for him. [And] anyone whose wisdom was stricken [with some disease], because of his body it is a bad sign for him'" (Tosefta Berakhot 3:5).

The embodiedness (*Körperlichkeit*) often closely linked to Jewishness turns out to be a double disadvantage, as many examples from its over-two-thousand-year history of persecution and defamation show. First, Jews were criticized for having deficient bodies (the missing foreskin due to circumcision, for instance, but also their susceptibility to certain illnesses and physical abnormalities). And second, Jews were accused of placing too much emphasis on matters of the flesh, in contrast to Christianity, which prided itself on its spirituality.[38] The Christian teaching of original sin plays a role in this connection: it is responsible for the corruption of the body and the soul and can be overcome only through baptism, that is, through acceptance of the true faith. Jewish historian Irven M. Resnick gives the following persuasive explanation of how ever since the Middle Ages stereotypes concerning the body have figured in Christians' perceptions of Jews: "As the principles of physiognomy become systematized and more broadly accepted in medieval culture, Jews will be consistently depicted with physical deformities and associated with disease and illnesses that somehow reflect a persistent sinful state, seeing that they remain throughout their lives subject to original sin and its consequences, which Christians overcame through the sacrament of baptism."[39] The apostle Paul plays a fundamental role in this Christian understanding of the body, setting up the opposition between "flesh" (Greek *sarx*) and "spirit" (Greek *pneuma*) and then using it to distinguish Judaism from Christianity.[40] Church fathers, including Origenes (ca. 185–254 CE) and John Chrysostom (ca. 349–407 CE), refer to Paul in their writings, where they not only mention circumcision as a distinctive characteristic but also discuss in detail the carnal lust of Judaism in contrast to Christian morality.[41] Evidence of an enduring perception of circumcision above all as physical difference or even flaw can be found in the surgical procedures to "repair" or restore this loss that date back to antiquity.[42] We find additional proof in the files of the Spanish Inquisition, which show that doctors examined boys in order to see if their *converso* parents had not secretly had them circumcised after all.[43]

To better understand how stereotypes function it is useful to look at the theory of culture developed by Homi Bhabha. Bhabha's description of stereotyping in colonial discourse can also be applied to Christian-Jewish relations if these are viewed as an ongoing, protracted overreach of the Christian system into the Jewish lifeworld. In the context of colonialism, stereotypes, according to Bhabha, contribute to the "fixity" or unchanging character of the imbalance of power, which also entails characterizing otherness in terms of physical inferiority and degeneracy. But unlike other theories about stereotypes, Bhabha's approach also contains what he calls the process of ambivalence. In his view, classic concepts of the stereotype "operate a passive and unitary notion of suture which simplifies the politics and 'aesthetics' of spectator-positioning by ignoring the ambivalent, psychical process of identification which is crucial to the argument."[44] As in colonial discourse, which is permeated by stereotypes, the process of stereotyping Jews' physical features might be described as "the polymorphous and perverse collusion between racism and sexism."[45] The Jewish body is defective, yet at the same time Jews are ostensibly immune to certain diseases, including epidemic ones. The Jewish man is considered "feminized" on the one hand, but regarded with sexual envy on the other. While Jewish historiography has been dominated by a normative ideological critique of such stereotypes, Bhabha is interested in their effectiveness, and especially in how power is inscribed into the symbolic modes of representation of such stereotypes. He discusses "strategies of discriminatory power" that are not unique to the discourse of race but instead are reflected in all forms of ambivalence, "whether racist or sexist, peripheral or metropolitan."[46] According to Bhabha a stereotype is a reciprocal phenomenon that involves both sides.

This applies, for instance, to the notion prevalent in the early modern period that a male Jew always has a (full) beard. Halakhic regulations about trimming the beard in a particular way certainly contributed to this stereotype, which even today seems to be confirmed by Orthodox Judaism.[47] When these relaxed somewhat from the early eighteenth century onward, the authorities stepped in. The Königsberg (Kaliningrad) Jewish Regulations of 1748 stated: "forthwith no Jew who is married, and old enough to grow a beard, may have it shaven off entirely as Christians do, but rather, so that he may be recognized, must retain a mark of it."[48]

Given the prevalence of anti-Semitic body stereotypes, especially in the first half of the twentieth century but also still with us in the twenty-first, it is important not to be too quick to see direct connections between things considered essential characteristics of the Jews at the end of the Middle Ages and in the early modern period and biological markers that became associated with the Jewish body in later times. As art historian Peter K. Klein notes in an essay about traditions of anti-Semitic visual stereotypes: "both existed—the uninterrupted continuity of anti-Jewish prejudices and stereotypes, but also ruptures and radical shifts in the relations between non-Jews and Jews."[49]

Nose

Of the many distinguishing physical traits mentioned by Schudt and other early modern writers, it was the face above all that purportedly made it possible to recognize a Jew. In a bilingual conversation between a Christian and a Jew about belief in the Messiah (Basel, 1539), the cosmographer, Hebrew scholar, and historian Sebastian Münster (1488–1552) tells how a Christian obviously well versed in theology addresses a Jew he meets on the street in Hebrew. The Jew is astonished at having been identified as such and asks his conversation partner how he had known. The Christian replies: "I can tell by the look of your face that you are a Jew. For you Jews have a particular countenance, different in form and figure from the rest of humanity, which has often surprised me: namely, you are black and ugly and not white like most people."[50] In the Hebrew translation, incidentally, the distinguishing feature "white" is followed by an additional criterion, "beautiful" (*jafim*).

The traditional sign for "Jew" in German sign language—the index finger imitating the shape of a crooked nose—is no longer considered politically correct. In the United States and England it has also not been used for some years. Instead, the hand is drawn from the chin to the chest—symbolizing the beard worn by devout Jews. Even to this day, this particular shape (the "hooked nose") is indeed considered typically Jewish, even though anthropological studies done already in the late nineteenth century determined that it is common in other populations as well. According to that research, three-fifths of all Jews had a straight "Roman" nose and 14 percent had a crooked one. In contrast, 30 percent of all Bavarians were said to possess a "Jewish nose."[51] Be that as it may, belief in this stereotype remains widespread to this day. National Socialist (NS) propaganda has apparently left deep traces in the collective consciousness of the Germans. When Sander L. Gilman, author of an essay on this topic still well worth reading,[52] was once asked if there was such a thing as a Jewish nose, he quipped in reply: "I have never yet met a Jew without a nose."[53] As young Jewish author Lena Gorelik recently wrote in a highly personal commentary on a much-discussed special exhibit of the Jewish Museum in Berlin, the list of the ten most popular prejudices begins with: "Jews have hooked noses." Which prompts the following comment: "Basically, everything that Jews make jokes about is true. My nose definitely looks strange. Perhaps not quite the classic hooked nose we know from Nazi caricatures, but still too long. Shorter than those of most people in my family, but just too long. Oh well, I also have protruding elephant ears that complement this nose beautifully."[54]

In the vast literature on the history of anti-Semitism we find repeated assertions that the representation of the Jewish nose in word and image is a modern phenomenon, even though "by the end of the eighteenth century the concept of a national Jewish physiognomy, and in particular one of the nose, had been developed and disseminated."[55] In Spanish illuminated manuscripts of the thirteenth and fourteenth centuries, Jews, in contrast to Old Testament figures like Moses, are already depicted with crooked noses and red beards.[56] Similar findings are true of England: a miniature contained in an English document of 1233 and today housed in the London Public Records Office shows a Jew with three faces, each with a protruding nose. Klein notes this image's striking resemblance to a clearly anti-Semitic postcard from around 1939,[57] and as an art historian he concludes: "the beaked or hawk nose was thus a firmly established stereotype of the 'Jew' already at that time [that is, thirteenth century]; it did not just become a physiognomic cliché in modern times."[58]

Figure 4. A caricature of Isaac of Norwich by an anonymous scribe in an English document, 1233, detail. The National Archives, London.

Sieht man Dich seitwärts, vorne, hinten,
So kann man gar nichts and'res finden

Als das, was nicht zum leugnen ist,
Dass Du — ein richt'ger Jude bist.

Figure 5. "A real Jew"—"Ein richt'ger Jude." K. Krejčik , anti-Semitic postcard, circa 1939. Berlin, private collection. © Bildarchiv Foto Marburg.

In notable contrast, Hebrew or Yiddish illuminated manuscripts from the Middle Ages show Jews with only beards and cone-shaped Jewish hats, not hooked noses. The hooked nose found only in images of Christian provenance from the thirteenth century on is clearly "a visual construct"[59] with negative connotations, since at the time the devil, too, was shown with such a nose. This view is shared by Irven M. Resnick, whose work on Christian perceptions of Jews in the High Middle Ages shows that these representations have theological underpinnings. He notes that the beaked nose "was judged a deformity: in the Old Testament priests with a large or crooked nose were ineligible for Temple service (Lev. 21:18)."[60] In my view the argument advanced by Sara Lipton is more convincing, namely, that only beginning in the twelfth century was a moral meaning inscribed in Jewish faces, including the use of hooked noses. Lipton holds that initially this sign was still too unstable to clearly signal Jewish identity and therefore needed to be accompanied by other signs such as beard and hat.[61] It was only in the thirteenth century that the "hook-nosed, pointy-bearded Gothic Jewish caricature" developed,[62] a caricature that from then on could stand on its own as an iconographic sign.

Theories vary about how such attributions came about. Historian Cecil Roth (1899–1970) believes that such distorted images had been inspired by the physiognomy of individual Jews.[63] In contrast, Bernhard Blumenkranz (1913–89), an expert on the medieval history of the Jews, maintains that it is not how Jews actually looked that is important, but how Christians saw them.[64] Art historian Peter K. Klein, cited above, sees neither a problem of description or perception in these stereotypes and instead views them as an ideological construct with theological roots. In my opinion, however, none of these explanations get at the heart of the matter. In daily life, unmistakable signs were needed to tell a Jew from a Christian. The special clothing required by the Fourth Lateran Council of 1215 for all Jews and Saracens, whose main purpose was to prevent any sexual involvement with Christian women, was not enough of an identifying marker,[65] and the Jewish badges required in certain cities and regions from the thirteenth century on could be easily concealed.[66] Therefore, what was needed were "visible identification marks" for the invisible enemy, to borrow a phrase from historian Valentin Groebner.[67] In the Christian-Jewish context this meant a distinctive physical feature that could be readily seen, since it was impossible to tell offhand if someone was circumcised or not. As the medieval theologian Rupert von Deutz (ca. 1070–1120) ironically notes, things would have been different had God chosen a different body part for circumcision: the nose, for instance, the eyes, the ears, or the lips.[68]

To identify an enemy of Christianity, it was necessary to find a material sign (Latin *signum*) that was permanent and could not be concealed. This is where physiognomy and also posture came into play—an unmistakable form of identification found even in the Bible: "You can tell a man by his looks and recognize good sense at first sight. A man's clothes, and the way he laughs, and his gait, reveal his character" (Ecclesiasticus 19:29–30).

Even in the Middle Ages people did not go so far as to brand Jews on the face, a common practice with criminals and heretics.[69] This was unnecessary, since the ostensibly "typical" nose already distinguished the Jew from the crowd and made him visible to all.[70] The Jewish German writer Heinrich Heine (1797–1856) recalls this several centuries later in his *Reisebilder* (*Pictures of Travel*) when he poses the rhetorical question: "Or it may be that these long noses are a sort of uniform whereby Jehovah recognizes his bodyguards even if they have deserted?"[71] Here Heine anticipates the discourse of racial biology used by Jewish and non-Jewish anthropologists from the mid-nineteenth century on. At issue here is the question: to what extent did an unmistakable physical sign still exist for Jews, since by now their skin color had lost much of its distinctive character?[72] The nose lent itself to this—or as Australian Jewish social scientist Joseph Jacobs (1854–1916) put it: "Nose—this feature is the one usually regarded as distinctive of the Jew, and it is also considered anthropologically important."[73] Neither baptism nor climate could diminish this feature. Anti-Semites were not alone in this conviction; even voices in the Jewish camp pointedly expressed this view, including philosopher and proto-Zionist Moses Hess (1812–75), who states in *Rome and Jerusalem* (*Rom und Jerusalem*, 1862): "Jewish noses cannot be reformed, nor black, curly Jewish hair be turned through baptism or combing into smooth hair. The Jewish race is a primal one, which has reproduced itself in its integrity despite climactic influences."[74]

Toward the end of the nineteenth century there was ample statistical evidence that it was "hard to speak of a 'Jewish' or 'Semitic' nose,"[75] in view of the fact that this ostensibly typical nose shape was common, and sometimes even more prevalent, in other populations as well. Yet at the time, even Jewish anthropologists saw the sense in looking for a characteristic facial feature among Jews. They focused not on the length of the nose, but instead on the shape of the nostrils. The above-mentioned Joseph Jacobs unwittingly provided anti-Semites with the appropriate image of a typically Jewish nose, one that later appeared repeatedly in National Socialist propaganda and caricatures. According to Jacobs, to draw a Jewish nose you simply need to draw the number 6 with a long curving tail on a piece of paper. The effectiveness of this simple drawing instruction can be seen more than fifty years later when Ernst Hiemer (1900–1974), a teacher and the editor in chief of the Nazi propaganda weekly *Der Stürmer*, published the infamous anti-Semitic children's book *Der Giftpilz* (The Poison Mushroom; illustrated by Fips). Seventy thousand copies were printed already in the year it was first published. Here the reader learns: "First of all you can recognize a Jew by his nose. The Jewish nose is hook-shaped. It has the shape of a 6. That's why we call it 6-shaped. Many non-Jews have the same kind of hooked nose. But in their cases the noses curve upward, not downward. That has nothing to do with the Jewish nose."[76] Hiemer also published among other things a compilation about Jews in proverbs (1942), where we read for example: "Jews in the country and on the road do not always have curly hair and crooked noses. The worst are those you cannot recognize and who like to call themselves Germans!"[77]

This stereotype was so powerful that even warnings like the following from prominent racialist anti-Semite Houston Stewart Chamberlain (1855–1927) went

Figure 6. Fips (that is, Philipp Rupprecht), "The Jewish nose. . . ." Color print, from Ernst Hiemer, *Der Giftpilz* (Nuremberg: Der Stürmer, 1938).

basically unheeded: "nose alone is no reliable proof of Jewish descent."[78] Carl Ludwig Schleich (1859–1922), a Berlin doctor and surgeon not otherwise known to be an anti-Semite, sounded the same note when he stated: "I do not count the often-mocked Jewish nose among invariable Semitic criteria, since even the bridges of Aryan noses can be more pronounced without there being even a hint of anti-Semitism. Take for instance Moltke's nose on Begas's classical bust in the National Gallery! The curvature is enormous, yet there is nothing Jewish about it."[79]

Such doubts and words of caution barely registered in popular literature or even the work of Thomas Mann (1875–1955),[80] who as we know was married to a woman of Jewish ancestry. In both cases—as in caricature, a genre that relies heavily on exaggeration and one-sidedness—we repeatedly find the stereotype of the "Jewish nose." The same still applies to some literature of the second half of the twentieth century, though in this particular case it is found primarily in the works of Anglo-American Jewish writers.[81] In his novel *Nemesis*, for example, Philip Roth describes the Jewish Dr. Steinberg as follows: "His nose was his most distinctive feature: curved like a scimitar at the top but bent flat at the tip, and with the bone of the bridge cut like a diamond—in short, a nose out of a folktale, the sort of sizable, convoluted, intricately turned nose that, for many centuries, confronted though they have been by every imaginable hardship, the Jews had never stopped making."[82] And in *Goodbye, Columbus*, published several decades earlier (1959), Roth already makes reference to something ("I had my nose fixed") that a small number of Jews had been doing since the latter part of the German Empire: having cosmetic surgery, or, more precisely, rhinoplasty, known more commonly as a nose job.[83]

The wish of many assimilated Jews at the time of the German Empire to assume a new identity by means of an operation was already parodied fairly early on in the anti-Semitic grotesque *The Operated Jew* (*Der operirte Jud'*) by Oskar Panizza (1853–1921).[84] The character Itzig Faitel Stern, whom the author gives every imaginable physical deformity, has a wealthy Jewish father who pays for expensive surgeries so that his son may lose his Jewish appearance, or "Jewey-ness." Yet the obvious choice of a nose operation remains undone, since apparently the orthopedic corrections to Itzig's "Jewish gait" alone require all the skills of a fictional Heidelberg surgeon. This body part, however, really needed it: "Itzig Faitel's countenance was most interesting. It is a shame that Lavater had not laid eyes upon it. An antelope's eye with a subdued, cherry-like glow swam in wide apertures of the smooth velvet, slightly yellow skin of his temples and cheeks. Itzig's nose assumed a form which was similar to that of the high priest who was the most prominent and striking figure of Kaulbach's painting 'The Destruction of Jerusalem.' "[85] Just thirty years later came a Jewish response—it, too, in the form of a grotesque. The author was Salomo(n) Friedlaender (1871–1946), who wrote under the pseudonym Mynona. At the center of this pastiche about assimilated Jewry is the aristocratic family Reshok ("kosher" spelled backward), which is trying to hide every trace of its Jewish ancestry. Physical features, too, have disappeared. The counts now all have an Aryan appearance: "thin lips, Prussian chins, proud necks, and fabulously slender builds."[86]

At the very time Panizza published his satirical short story, a new era in nasal surgery was dawning. Significantly, a pioneer in this field was a Jewish surgeon practicing in Berlin at the turn of the twentieth century, Jacques Joseph (1865–1934).[87] Because of his specialty he was also known in Jewish circles as "Nose Josef" or "Nosef," and he became famous primarily because the rhinoplasty he performed left no visible scar. His first patient in 1898 was probably not a Jew, but the case still typifies the hope that a nose correction would lead to social acceptance. This patient wanted Joseph to transform his "actually completely healthy but noticeable nose, given its size and shape, into an unremarkable one."[88] In addition, he told the doctor "that his nose had long been the source of great chagrin. No matter where he stood or walked, everyone stared at him, and he had often been the target of ridicule, both direct and indirect (indicated through gestures). He had consequently become almost melancholy, had withdrawn almost completely from any social life, and now fervently wished to be free of his disfigurement." The operation succeeded, the patient was satisfied, and Joseph could present his success to his peers in a highly respected publication. In 1902, or four years after the first operation, the Berlin surgeon had already performed ten nose reduction operations. Two years later he treated forty cases, and in 1907 the total was up to two hundred. Beginning in 1904 Joseph performed the operation intranasally, thereby avoiding any visible scarring. He also developed a new surgical instrument called a raspatorium—a coarse file used to prepare the lower part of the nasal passage—still used today in plastic surgery and known as "the Joseph raspatory." The steady stream of patients, including more than a few Jews, brought him wealth and with it also envy, as we see in the satirical essay by Egon Erwin Kisch (1885–1948), "Das Haus zu den veränderten Nasen" (The House of Altered Noses): "The professor first needs to know how rich a person is," the so-called "racing reporter" says of Joseph.

> He is then paid accordingly for the operation . . . , and he needs to know the type, since that is what he uses afterward to construct the nose. "Would you like a pert nose or an intelligent one, a coquettish or an energetic one?" Each person can order the nose he or she would like to have. The professor hands patients an album with hundreds of photographs of former patients before and after the operation. You look through the album and select the nose you want. "Good," says the professor, and grasps you by the nose. He covers it with his hand and fingers and shows you how you will look afterwards. "Come to my private clinic at 22 Bülow Street early tomorrow morning."[89]

Other sources indicate that Joseph sometimes treated patients free of charge. Among them were Jews who could not afford the operation, as we learn from a report by Adolphine Schwarz, a Jewish patient who had corrective surgery performed on her nose in January 1933 after her older brother had done the same.[90]

Today, particularly in the United States, hundreds of thousands of "Jewish noses" are still corrected. Jewish girls in particular no longer follow Barbra Streisand's decision to keep her natural nose and often receive a rhinoplasty as a bat mitzvah present at the age of twelve.[91] In 2007 American filmmaker Gayle Kirschenbaum made a short film called *My Nose* about her experience as a fifteen-year-old, when her mother brought her to a cosmetic surgeon. There she was presented with a collection of "desirable noses," but Kirschenbaum rejected the idea of surgery and kept her allegedly Jewish appearance. In doing so she pushed back against the trend of the time: as she documents in the film, American high school and college yearbooks from the 1950s and 1960s included many examples of "before and after" pictures. This desire for a change of identity lives on even in contemporary American films such as *A Serious Man* by the Coen brothers (2009). At the center of the film is Larry Gopnik, who leads a peaceful life in a small Jewish community in the Midwest. He is a loving husband, caring father, and successful professor until things start to go wrong in his life. His wife asks for a divorce so that she can live with her new lover; his son has problems with school and drugs; and his daughter steals from him in order to pay for a nose job.

Just how firmly entrenched the stereotype of the Jewish nose remains in people's minds even sixty years after the Shoah can be seen in more than the Berlin Jewish Museum exhibit mentioned above. In 2010 in the newspaper *Der Westen*, a reader named Ludwig wrote the following online comment about an article on former Social Democratic Party politician Oskar Lafontaine: "There are some people who are just 'sleazy scoundrels.' Nothing more. Lafontaine is a prime example. He has used all of his power to harm Germanness. His pointy Jewish nose shows it. Everything against Germany!"[92]

Lips

Like the typical nose, lip shape was singled out as a characteristic feature of the Jews, and not just beginning in the nineteenth century. Schudt mentions this peculiarity, and bulging lips appear in anti-Jewish imagery already in the thirteenth century.[93] The grimacing face of the English Jew Aaron, son of Leo, that was added to a 1277 manuscript features both a hooked nose and protruding lips.[94] A late medieval crusade panel in the parish church of St. Bartholomew's in Oberbergkirchen, Bavaria (by a Salzburg master circa 1450), identifies the blind Roman captain Longinus as a "Jew" by means of Hebrew characters, a beard, bulging lips, and a snoutlike nose. At the time, overly large lips are not yet a racial characteristic; they merely indicate a negative character trait of the person in question. That person does not necessarily have to be a Jew, but this physical sign is quite often associated with Jews since it fits the image of the devious, devilish murderer of Christ.

Giambattista (or Giovanni Battista) della Porta's (1535?–1615) standard work on physiognomy (1586) strongly influences the belief held in the entire early modern period that a person's external appearance, and especially facial features, can be used to draw conclusions about character traits. Porta does this by comparing humans with animals: a person who resembles a donkey (including its alleged character traits—namely, stupidity or lack of erudition) would typically have a thick protruding upper lip and a long protruding nose.[95] The accompanying illustration of a donkey's head and similarly shaped head of a man in profile recalls early modern representations of Jews. The author suggests that a rough man can be recognized by his large head and thick-lipped prominent mouth, whose lower lip protrudes even farther than the upper one. The bridge of the nose seen in profile has either no inward curve or a thick protrusion starting at the brow.

Porta's most important successor, Charles Le Brun (1619–90), likewise relies on the comparison between donkey and human in his work. It includes a similar profile image, different only in that it contains greater detail. Whoever has lips like a donkey, the image suggests, can be no "noble" human.[96]

In the eighteenth century, Lavater in his *Physiognomische Fragmente* makes lips into a key signifier of character: "like the lips, so too the character. Firm lips, firm character. Soft, quick-moving lips, soft, mercurial character."[97] Fleshy lips reveal that the person "struggles with sensuality, indolence, and reveling." That Lavater was thinking of Jews in particular in this connection is clear from what he adds to Lenz's disparaging remarks about Jews (quoted above): "I also count a pointed chin and large lips with a clearly drawn center line as part of the national character of the Jewish face."[98] Unsurprisingly, Lavater's physiognomic teachings were eagerly adopted in nineteenth-century anti-Semitic discourse by writers such as Panizza, whose comments on the Jewish *ponim* (face) were noted above. This same body stereotype is found in the anti-Semitic leaning *Bayreuther Blätter* at the turn of the twentieth century: "It is not without good reason that there is talk of a Negro aesthetic in art that does not owe its start to chance, but rather, to the seeds of Negro blood sown everywhere among us by Judaism. . . . The thick lips and woolly hair of so many Jews prove that in their earlier homeland they absorbed Negro blood."[99] This distorted image also appears in so-called "spa anti-Semitism." In 1921, the Austrian National Socialist weekly *Deutscher Volksruf* incited against Jews who came to summer resorts in the Salzburg area: "A foreign people has made itself comfortable here, recognizable by Semitic hook nose, Mongolian slit eyes, Negroid bulging lips and Negroid bushy hair."[100] Postcards sold in German spas on the North Sea and the Baltic show Eastern European spa guests with hooked noses and overly large lips.[101]

Isolated Jewish voices, which tried to draw attention to anthropological research, could do little to change the popular stereotype. Writing in the *Israelitisches Familienblatt* in 1929, Heinz Caspari (1900–1994) advised his fellow Jews not to avoid those spas and baths known for their anti-Semitism, but instead to do just the opposite, namely, disprove popular notions about body images by appearing on the beaches and promenades: "They [the residents] would be utterly astonished to find that 'the Jews' are not all or even overwhelmingly afflicted with crooked noses, Negro ringlets, puffy lips and sagging bellies."[102] In a piece for the journal *Der Jude* (ed. Martin Buber, 1878–1975), Arnold Zweig (1887–1968) also pushes back against this prejudice: "Even though ethnologists have statistically determined a very small percentage of so-called 'Jewish noses' (those drooping curved and thickened noses) among Jews, and though anyone in the eastern centers of Jewish masses could see this with his own eyes at any time, the anti-Semite draws the 'typical Jew' with a bulbous nose, bulging lips, crooked legs, massive hands and feet, slit eyes behind pince-nez, and a belly."[103]

Even Thomas Mann was not immune to such a stereotype, as several early stories and even *The Magic Mountain* show. In "Der Wille zum Glück" (The Will to Happiness, 1895) the Jewish characters are generally small and unappealing, stocky and squat, with black eyes, enlarged lips and prominent noses.[104] Far more spiteful descriptions can be found in the works of openly anti-Semitic authors such as Artur Dinter (1876–1948), whose trash novel *Die Sünde wider das Blut* (The Sin Against Blood, 1918) tells how a blond Germanic man produces children with a blond woman, but eventually discovers that she is half Jewish and that her father has an "ugly, inert, curved nose" as well as "a bulging mouth with a drooping lower lip."[105] The novel *Gottes Rune: Ein Buch von Glaube und Treue* (God's Rune: A Book of Faith and Loyalty, 1938) by Hannes Kremer (1906–?), an example of "SA Literature" (literature of the *Sturmabteilung*, the Nazi party's paramilitary wing), characterizes Judaism as follows: "Suddenly a snarling grimace. Right nearby. Jacob awakens and senses that he is pale and gray. Eyeball to eyeball with the face of the mob. He knows it well. It is broad, bony, coarse, pouting lips, menacing glances from deceitful slits, a flattened nose."[106]

Hidden in these anti-Semitic tirades by writers with National Socialist leanings (who are justly forgotten today) is the Third Reich's official theory of race. It draws on pseudoscientific studies such as Hans F. K. Günther's *Rassenkunde des deutschen Volkes* (Race Science of the German People), which states: "the lips are usually larger and puffier than among non-Jewish European peoples. The lower lip often protrudes in a characteristic way, sometimes so far that it almost appears to droop downward, which gives the face something reminiscent of the lips of a camel."[107] Not surprisingly, these claims are unsupported by any references to anthropometric studies done by researchers on race. Over the centuries, the image of the large-lipped Jew had become so engrained in the consciousness of the population that it required no scientific proof.

The enduring power of this body stereotype can be seen in, but also beyond, anti-Semitic caricatures in the Islamic world that look as if they could have been modeled on propaganda from *Der Stürmer*. In February 2014, a caricature that appeared in the *Süddeutsche Zeitung* and referenced the business practices of Facebook founder Mark Zuckerberg created quite a stir in the German press.

His company was depicted as a kraken with a lascivious, devious expression and squinting eyes, a large mouth with thick lips, and a protruding oversized crooked nose. *Der Spiegel* columnist Georg Diez was not the only person who was reminded of all-too-familiar depictions of Jews,[108] and the newspaper's editors later apologized for this journalistic lapse.

Skin Color

Together with the nose, an additional stereotype made its appearance early on in written and visual sources: the reputed swarthiness of the Jews. As far back as the twelfth century, the unusual skin color is considered a distinguishing feature, and, as noted above, this external characteristic of a Jew was emphasized by Schudt.

The catalog of signs used to describe "others" from the late Middle Ages on includes the color black. When "gypsies" made their first appearance in Western Europe in the early fifteenth century, chroniclers described them as "black like the Tartars" (*nigri ut tatari*) or an "ugly black people."[109] This description prompted Johann Christoph Wagenseil, one of the most prominent early modern Judaic scholars, to wonder if the gypsies might be of Jewish descent. That view, however, is countered in *Zedlers Universal-Lexicon* of 1749, where we read that the skin color of the Jews, which from the waning of the Middle Ages onward was usually described as dark, was nevertheless not black.[110] Jewish tradition took a similar view, as a Mishnah tractate on leprosy shows: "R. Ishmael says: The children of Israel, I am their atonement! They are like a box-tree, not black and not white, but intermediate" (Negaim 2:1).[111]

In the Middle Ages, the stereotypical notion that Jews had darker skin than Christians was so widespread that Jewish scholars felt compelled to offer an explanation. The *Sefer Nizzahon Yashan* (or *Nizzahon Vetus*), one of the most remarkable late medieval apologetic texts by a Jew, answers the question why most non-Jews are supposedly white and attractive, while the majority of Jews have dark skin and are flawed, in the following way: "Answer them," the anonymous author advises his fellow Jews, "that this is similar to a fruit; when it begins to grow it is white but when it ripens it becomes black, as in the case of sloes and plums. On the other hand, any fruit which is red at the beginning becomes lighter as it ripens, as is the case with apples and apricots. This, then, is testimony that Jews are pure of menstrual blood so that there is no initial redness. Gentiles, however, are not careful about menstruant women and have sexual relations during menstruation; thus, there is redness at the outset, and so the fruit that comes out, i.e., the children, are light."[112] The *Sefer Yosef ha-Meqanne* from approximately the same time (thirteenth century) contains a similar argument. Rabbi Nathan, speaking with someone who has been baptized, compares the white blossoms of a plum tree with the reddish blossoms of an apple tree: "Similarly, we [Jews] come from a pure and white seed; therefore our face is dark. You [Christians], however, come from a red seed, from menstruant women; therefore your complexion is fair and rubicund" (*Sefer Yosef ha-Meqanne*, 104).

Several centuries later Eastern Jews still do not necessarily see dark skin as a flaw, even if the ideal of beauty continues to be white skin, as we learn from a Yiddish folk song: "Black you are, black, as a gypsy, I thought you would always be mine; you are black, but with grace,—for others you may be homely, but for me you are handsome."[113] This song collection also includes the familiar equation of black and gypsy ("Schwarz, schwarz, schwarz / Schwarz binstu [sic], wi a Zigainer"),[114] a topos also found in Christian-influenced texts about Sinti and Roma.

Only toward the end of the eighteenth century do we find the view that Jews actually do have darker skin appear in works by several Jewish authors. For Abraham ben Elijah (1766–1808), a son of the Vilna Gaon, dark skin was even a positive sign since it was due to the fact that Jews had not mixed with other peoples.[115] The famous rabbi Jonathan Eybeschütz (ca. 1690–1764) likewise describes the Jews as *kushim* (blacks), though it is not entirely clear if he means their complexion in the sense of the four humors theory rather than their skin color.[116] The context allows for a metaphorical interpretation, since the Altona scholar also cites a Bible verse in this context—one that includes a moral: "can the Ethiopian change his skin or the leopard his spots? Then also you can do good who are accustomed to do evil" (Jeremiah 13:23). It is nonetheless worth noting that in this passage Eybeschütz indicates he is familiar with the then-popular climate theory, which he refers to here directly. The majority of Jewish Enlightenment thinkers, or *maskilim*, actually did still believe this theory, which held that dark skin was not innate, but instead developed in response to environmental influences. It is the theoretical underpinning of the famous statement by the Amsterdam Jew Isaac de Pinto (1717–87) in a letter to Voltaire: "a Portuguese Jew from Bordeaux and a German Jew from Metz look like two completely different beings! It is therefore impossible to speak of the behavior of Jews in general without going into greater detail and considering individual circumstances; the Jew is a chameleon that adopts all the colors of the different climates in which he lives, the different peoples with whom he has contact, and the different governments under which he lives."[117] An influential Christian supporter of this theory was the French naturalist Georges-Louis Leclerc de Buffon (1707–88), who links the wide variety found in the Jewish people to climate theory: "It has been pretended that the Jews, who came originally from Syria and Palestine, have the same brown complexion they had formerly. As Mission, however, justly observes, the Jews of Portugal alone are tawny. As they always marry with their own tribe, the complexion of the parents is transmitted to the child, and thus with little diminution preserved, even in the northern countries. The German Jews, those of Prague, for example, are not more swarthy than the other Germans."[118]

After the discovery of America there was speculation in Jewish scholarly circles about whether one of the lost tribes of Israel might turn up in the New World, and Native American tribes became a topic of interest. Menasseh ben Israel (1604–57), who took part in this debate, shared the belief of many Jewish scholars that Jews had originally had fair skin, which they lost in exile as an additional punishment. At the same time, however, he saw no connection to the red-skinned Indians: "the *Indians* are of a browne colour, and without beards; but in the new world, white and bearded men were found, who had never commerce with the *Spaniards*; and whom you cannot affirme to be any other than *Israelites*."[119]

In non-Jewish circles well into the early modern period the idea prevailed that the Jews' swarthiness was God's punishment for their obduracy and their responsibility for the death of Jesus Christ. Only a person who was baptized could be washed clean by the baptismal water and lighten the color of his skin. The French diplomat and philosopher Isaac de La Peyrère (1596–1676), for instance, argued that the Jews would no longer have "that black and sunburned color" ("cette couleur noire & bazanée") after baptism, since this was a sign of their exile and of the just punishment for their transgressions. Henceforth they would have a light skin tone that would gleam like the feathers of a white dove.[120]

Valentin Groebner correctly points out that, as a general rule, references to red or black skin in early modern sources cannot be interpreted using modern dermatological terminology, since these are references to body rather than skin color: "skins not only exhibited degrees of color, but they could be charged with shades of meanings adopted from astrology, the doctrine of bodily fluids, and cosmology, as required."[121] Which is to say: the exterior mirrors the interior, and together with it the person's character or temperament (in the sense of ancient Greco-Roman humorism). Up until—and even during—the early modern period, gypsies, slaves, and even the German papal guards were described as "black." A person's color also indicated invisible character traits, especially in the case of a foreigner or "other." Decoding was done with the help of so-called "complexion books" such as *Kunst der . . . Physiognomey* (1523) by Johannes Indagine (1467–1537). This genre enjoyed great popularity beginning in the sixteenth century, since it provided the reader with "a useful natural art" that could be used to "identify different people with ease by the marks on their bodies."[122] As Groebner puts it, the medieval doctrine of complexion, that is, the combination of the four bodily fluids and their consequences for health and character, had been "effectively physiognomized."[123] Thus, Lenz's late eighteenth-century reference to the dark-skinned faces of Jews as an identifying feature is not an example of proto-racist thinking; instead, it suggests behaviors like deceitfulness and unchaste conduct that were seen as Jewish character traits as far back as the Middle Ages.

Jews were not only classified as people with dark skin or faces and assigned to a specific catalog of signs. There were supposedly even "red Jews," a term that is used in German-language texts dating back to the late thirteenth century. In the medieval doctrine of colors, red usually has negative connotations.[124] Red is the color of the enemies of Christ, and *Rotwelsch* is the underworld slang of deceitful beggars. Judas Iscariot is depicted not only with reddish hair and robe, but sometimes also with reddish skin that marks him as the betrayer of Christ. But as Rebekka Voß notes, red Jews are "a prime example of 'counter-history' as formulated by Amos Funkenstein."[125] Funkenstein uses the term to describe a subversive, polemical reversal of prevailing attitudes. In the Yiddish version of this early modern legend, the color red gets a positive reinterpretation, one that refers to King David, who the Bible says was "handsome, with ruddy cheeks and bright eyes" (1 Samuel 16:12). We can even see something of this counter-history in a mid-eighteenth-century explanation by Friedrich Albrecht Augusti (1691–1782), a Jewish convert, for why Ashkenazi Jews called the ten lost tribes of Israel "red Jews": "By Red Jews they [the Jews] definitely understand the inhabitants [of the land] beyond the river Sambation, to whom they give this name, which is highly esteemed and glorious among them, both on account of the red and lively color of their face, and of the precious purple clothes, which they wear as the sign of a free people, in order to distinguish them from all other [Jews] living in miserable exile."[126] In the Yiddish version of this legend the reversal is even more pronounced: red stands not for weakness or inferiority, but for the Jew who in the eyes of Christians may appear small and weak, but who will triumph in the end. Here once again we see how stereotypical attributes can be internalized by a marginalized group, reinterpreted as something positive and consequently perceived as "confirmation of their moral (and religious!) superiority."[127]

In the discourse on race in the nineteenth and early twentieth centuries the skin color of the Jews also played an important role since, in the words of American Jewish anthropologist Maurice Fishberg (1872–1934), it belongs to those traits which are "constant in a race and depend on heredity."[128] Climate theory, which in the eighteenth century was still the accepted explanation for differences in skin color among populations, gave way to race theory, which held that geographical milieu was of no importance in accounting for differences in skin color.[129] The so-called "black Jews" in India were no longer explained in terms of the country's greater amount of sunlight, but as follows: "[they] do not have the same ethnicity as their co-religionists in Europe."[130] An early thinker along these lines was British anthropologist James Cowles Prichard (1786–1848), who in 1813 published his acclaimed *Researches into the Physical History of Man*. Here he asserted that "true" Jews had fair skin and that in the course of human history this had remained "permanent."[131] The thesis concealed religious motives: for the Quaker-turned-Evangelical, the notion that Jews were not white was difficult to

Figure 7. Jews with "typical" physical features. Color engraving from Dietrich Schwab,
Detectum Velum Mosaicum Iudaeorum nostri temporis . . . (Mainz: Schwab, 1619).
© Historical Museum, Frankfurt. Photo: Horst Ziegenfusz.

square with his worldview, which saw black-skinned people as morally inferior
and primitive. Prichard relied on reports by a Scottish traveler to India named
Claudius Buchanan (1766–1815), who had met both light-skinned and "black
Jews" in Cochin. He describes the latter as a "mixed race," which in the eyes of the
indigenous people would place them in a low caste. An argument clearly based on
racial biology is presented several decades later by British physician and anato-
mist Robert Knox (1791–1862) in his influential work *The Races of Men*
(1850).[132] Knox no longer counted the Jews as members of the white race, assert-
ing instead that they had an "African look."[133] In doing so he was thinking not so
much of the skin color as of physiognomy.

When Karl Marx (1818–83), who was familiar with then-current theories of
race in England, failed yet again to get money from Ferdinand Lassalle (1825–
64), he wrote to his friend Friedrich Engels (1820–95) on July 30, 1862:

The Jewish Nigger Lassalle, who fortunately departs at the end of this
week, has luckily again lost 5,000 taler in a fraudulent speculation. The
fellow would rather throw his money into the muck than lend it to a
"friend," even if the interest and capital were guaranteed. In addition, he
acts on the notion that he must live like a Jewish baron or baronized
(probably by the countess) Jew. . . .

It is now completely clear to me that he, as is proved by his cranial
formation and [curly] hair—descends from the Negroes who had joined
Moses' exodus from Egypt (assuming his mother or grandmother on the
paternal side had not interbred with a *nigger* [in English]). Now this union
of Judaism and Germanism with a basic Negro substance must produce a

peculiar product. The obtrusiveness of the fellow is also *Nigger*-like [in English].[134]

In July of 1937, the SS organ *Das Schwarze Korps* published an article by physicist Johannes Stark (1874–1957) called "'White Jews' in Science" defaming German physicist Werner Heisenberg (1901–76) as a *Gesinnungsjude*, or "Jew in spirit."[135] "Black" Jews, in contrast, were thus the "real" Jews. Incidentally, the term "white Jews" used in reference to assimilated Jews appears already in the first half of the nineteenth century in the work of Hartwig Hundt-Radowsky (1780–1835), a leading figure of radical anti-Semitism.[136] In the long run, not even the most committed National Socialist–leaning racial biologists could ignore the fact that most of the Jews they knew had light skin, even if the stereotype suggested otherwise. For this reason, most tried to steer clear of making categorical statements that might give the lie to their own theory. For example, in his manual on racial theory that was later quite popular in the Third Reich, Günther makes only the following statement of the Jews: "their skin color is *usually* darker than in nations of primarily northern races."[137]

Beard

As visual sources prove, ever since the thirteenth century Jews can be identified by not only their "unusual" noses or dark skin but also their (long) beards, whereas Christian men in these illustrations are clean-shaven. The beard is often red, most likely alluding to the beard of Judas. We see the decidedly negative connotations of a red beard in *Wendunmuth* (1563), an entertaining collection of stories by Hans Wilhelm Kirchhof (1525–1605): in one story, a courier gives an innkeeper a large sum of money for safekeeping, then quickly asks to have it back, explaining: "your face and red beard show that you have not much good about you."[138] The notion that people with red hair or beards are inferior actually dates all the way back to antiquity,[139] and for this reason, the association of a red beard with the Jews becomes a motif still commonly used in the early modern period. Thomas Jordan (ca. 1612–85), an English actor and poet, includes the following rhyme in "Forfeiture," a ballad from 1664:

> His beard was red; his face was made
> Not much unlike a witches.
> His habit was a Jewish gown,
> That would defend all weather;
> His chin turn'd up, his nose hung down,
> And both ends met together.[140]

In contrast, Muslim men often dye their beards red to show their observance of the prophet Muhammad's prohibition against dying hair black.[141] The account (*hadith*) of Jabir Ibn Abdullah is worth mentioning in this connection; according to this text, the founder of Islam is supposed to have said: "One should not conclude from these words that it is obligatory for every Muslim to dye his white hair red. It is a command which implies simply an approval and permissibility. The Jews and Christians strictly refrained from dyeing their white heads and white beards."[142]

Even unconnected to the color red a Jewish beard had negative connotations that stigmatized the wearer. We still see this for example in a late eighteenth-century almanac for both doctors and laypeople, where, in a fictional conversation about beard styles between a certain M. and a doctor, the doctor asserts: "here no one has a beard but the goat, the Jew, and the stinking Capuchin monk."[143] In the 1780s, Enlightenment thinker and writer Johann Pezzl (1756–1823) described the Jews in Vienna in this way: "their necks exposed, the color of a Black, their faces covered up to the eyes with a beard, which would have given the High Priest in the Temple chills, the hair turned and knotted as if they all had the 'plica polonica'" (an allegedly Jewish disease of the hair).[144] It is therefore not surprising that in modern times the Jewish beard as a powerful stereotype could even become the common name for a plant species of the saxifrage family (*Saxifraga stolonifera*). This unusual name presumably comes from the appearance of the plant's blossoms, since the drooping white flower petals resemble whiskers. Even earlier, toward the end of the eighteenth century, henbane roots were also likened to the beard of a Jew: "long hairs that look like a Jewish beard sprout from the fruit knot."[145]

In Roman times, no author mentions the beard or any other physical feature to describe a Jew.[146] How then could the so-called Jewish beard become a distinctive feature, since having a beard was a common practice in many different populations and became the fashion time and time again?[147] In the twelfth and thirteenth centuries when this stereotype developed (as visual sources document), clergy members were clean-shaven, unlike their Eastern Orthodox counterparts.[148] Jews, in contrast, traditionally wore beards and not only because of the commandment against shaving. According to Halakhah, having a beard signaled that a young man was legally an adult.[149] In biblical times the Israelites had beards (see 2 Samuel 10:4); in the same book of the Old Testament we read how Joab grasped Amasa's beard and kissed it as a sign of respect (2 Samuel 20:9). The Talmud likewise indicates that from early on a beard was a Jewish man's ornament (BT Bava Metzia 84a). The beard had to be groomed (Psalm 133:2), but shaving it off completely was not allowed (Leviticus 19:27), at least not with a blade or knife; other forms of shaving (scissors or depilatories) were nonetheless allowed. At a rabbinical meeting in Mainz in the early thirteenth century it was decided "that no one shall cut his hair in non-Jewish fashion, or his beard with a razor or in such manner as approximates the effect of a razor."[150] Primarily in communities of observant Jews, and especially in Hasidic circles, a full beard in addition to the obligatory sidelocks, or *pejes*, was a sign of piety.[151] When making a promise in Yiddish, Eastern Jews make it more emphatic by adding the words "as I wear a beard and *pejes*" (wie ich trug burd ün pejess).[152]

The strong influence of the Kabbalah on the Eastern tradition of the full beard is noted by Salomon Maimon (1753–1800), a follower of Kant who in his youth had also studied the *Zohar*.[153] These studies led him to reflect on two contradictory concepts: the tree of life on the one hand, and God's beard on the other, a beard "in which the hairs are divided into numerous classes with something peculiar of each, and every hair is a separate channel of divine grace."[154] Several years later the chief rabbi summoned him to discuss his appearance and behavior, which were reputedly not in keeping with Jewish customs: "you do not wear a beard; you do not go to the synagogue."[155] Maimon cleverly defended himself by, among other things, citing relevant passages in the Talmud, which he obviously knew well.

We know for a fact that in the Middle Ages, Christians who converted to Judaism let their beards grow.[156] In this connection it is interesting to note that the Christian clergy seen through Jewish eyes was likewise reduced to an external characteristic—namely, the tonsure and/or lack of beard. In Hebrew and Yiddish the term for a priest is *galach*, meaning "the shaven one."

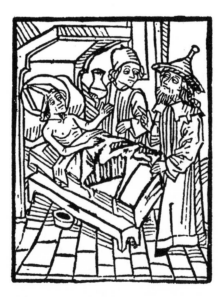

Figure 8. Saint Basil of Caesarea and the Jewish doctor Ephraim. Woodcut from *Plenarium* (Augsburg: Hans Schobser, 1487).

There are cases from the Middle Ages, but also even in the early modern period, in which a Jewish court punished a male Jew for any number of different offenses (including sexual offenses and failure to keep the Sabbath) by forcing him to shave his hair or beard.[157] On the other hand, a Jew who had disfigured another Jew's beard during a physical altercation could be severely punished by a rabbinical court.[158] Even so, this and other reports do not allow us to draw the more general conclusion that Jews everywhere in medieval Europe voluntarily grew full beards as a sign of piety (like Rabbi Judah the Pious) or to distinguish themselves from heathen priests (the reason given by Moses Maimonides, for example). Christian iconography in particular, which shows Jews almost exclusively with beards, gives a distorted image and one that bears little resemblance to daily life in medieval Ashkenaz, the Rhineland valley and neighboring French region settled by the Ashkenazim.[159] In the Orient, however, Jews had early on adopted the regional custom of having a full beard, especially since there in contrast to Central and Western Europe it was not a sign of in- or exclusion. Just the opposite: a Christian pilgrim or Jew doing business there among Arabs and Saracens did well to look like the locals and follow their lead in treating the beard with respect.

During the High Middle Ages, full beards and mustaches were scorned in circles of the Roman Catholic Church. "A full beard, if red or braided," writes medievalist Helmut Hundsbichler "signals a lack of Christianity."[160] However, a long beard did not necessarily have negative connotations; otherwise emperors and kings such as Frederick Barbarossa would not have grown one. Unlike secular rulers, popes—with very few exceptions—remained clean-shaven on into the early modern period.[161] An edict by Emperor Frederick II (1194–1250) is worth noting in this connection: announced on a court day in Messina in 1221, it required male Jews to wear a blue shirt, but also a beard so that they might be identified more easily.[162]

In places like fourteenth-century Nuremberg where a long beard had been the exclusive privilege of Christians for some time, a 1343 ruling required Jews to remove their beards at least every four weeks so that they could be distinguished from Christians.[163] Yet in the late Middle Ages among Christian men, including those of high social rank such as emperors and kings, a beard was the exception rather than the rule. Then, at the beginning of the sixteenth century, first the nobility and then also the citizenry discovered the beard as status symbol.[164] Especially at court, a beard was considered elegant and a sign of virility, as we know from Baldassare Castiglione's Book of the Courtier (1528). At that time, when the full beard replaced beardlessness as the latest fashion, the stereotype of the Jewish full beard was already so well established that this distinctive feature remained part of the discourse, even though its importance in daily life had decreased. Yet, when at the start of the early modern period several Augsburg city councilmen let their beards grow, it still caused a stir, as humanist Max Welser (1558–1614) notes in his town chronicle. Welser writes that prior to this sudden shift in fashion, a long beard "was an indication that the wearer was either doing it as a prank or must have been up to some mischief."[165] A Florentine chronicle from the same period also mentions this fashion phenomenon: "and in addition, people at this time [1532] began to cut their hair, which everyone had previously worn long, down to their shoulders . . . and now they started to wear beards, whereas earlier not a single person existed who would have had a beard."[166] Barely two hundred years later, beard fashion had shifted yet again, and not just in Germany.[167] Once again it was the nobility that set the fashion trend. Willibald Kobolt (1676–1749), a learned Benedictine priest, noted in his treatise *Die Groß- und Kleine Welt* (1738): "at the present time there is nothing more common / than cutting off one's hair and beard: it is no longer considered an adornment / to have long hair and a beard / instead a person is regarded as poorly groomed / if his hair has not been shed / and his beard has not been cut back to his skin."[168] In an influential 1716 commentary on the Golden Bull of Charles IV, Halle professor of state law Johann Peter Ludewig (1668–1743) explained the loosening of the rules about wearing Jewish emblems as follows: "Jews are now recognizable by their beards, since secular Christians have not had beards for some fifty years now."[169] Kassel city councilman Johann Wilhelm Christian Gustav Casparson (1729–1802) likewise saw no point in continuing to force Jews to wear a badge on their clothing, writing in 1785: "I do not know why their men should be given an additional marker in addition to their beards and Oriental facial features."[170] Thus at the close of the seventeenth and start of the eighteenth century, the full beard as a means of distinguishing Jews from Christians was reestablished as a tangible sign. We find proof of this, for example, in a list containing profiles of mixed-denomination robber bands. Westphalian criminal records of 1752 make reference to a Jew named Jössel, "otherwise called Joseph . . . of medium stature, handsome face and because he had no beard, not recognizable as a Jew."[171] At this time, therefore, it once more made sense to require Jews to have traditional-style beards, as the aforementioned Königsberg (Kaliningrad) Jewish Regulations of 1748 show. The situation was comparable in Habsburg countries.

Under Empress Maria Theresa (1717–80), the Jews were not only temporarily exiled from Prague in 1744 but also forbidden to shave their beards like Christians. A report sent to the empress from the Lower Austrian government in 1778 contained this critique: "for some time now a number of both the local and foreign Jews, mainly among their younger and less important people, have dared to set aside their formerly accepted and generally recognizable head covering and garments, and instead adopt not only clothing commonly worn by Christians that differentiated them from Jews, but even that of the nobility."[172] The Lower Austrian government was, however, prepared to compromise. They did not insist that

Jews in the future would have to have beards, apparently realizing that few would comply; but Jews should definitely be forbidden to have either a braided or wrapped hairstyle, since these were permitted only among the nobility.

Only with emancipation was the law revoked that required Jews to wear both an identifying symbol and a beard.[173] At the same time, representatives of the Jewish Orthodoxy lost the power to banish Reform Jews who demonstratively shaved their beards, something that still occurred in the Altona Jewish community in 1781.[174]

At the beginning of the nineteenth century things had developed to the point that a Christian supporter of Jewish emancipation could address a Jewish public in a work called *Mein erstes Wort wider die Juden mit und ohne Bart* (My First Word Against the Jews With and Without Beards).[175] Two years before converting to Protestantism, Heinrich Heine wrote from Berlin on April 1, 1823, to Immanuel Wohlwill (1799–1847) in Hamburg: "We no longer have the strength to wear a beard, to fast, to hate, and through that hatred to endure. This is the motive for our Reformation."[176] Here Heine is alluding to more than the goals of the Jewish Enlightenment or Haskalah. His call to turn away from the traditional way of life in Judaism has a specific political background—namely, the setback for Jewish emancipation in the place he had earlier lived and studied. He continues in the letter to Wohlwill: "Pardon my bitterness; the blow from the revoked edict has not affected you . . . I too lack the strength to wear a beard, to hear people taunt me for 'Jewish mumbling' [*Judenmauscheln*], to fast, etc." Heine is referring to the Napoleonic Jewish Emancipation Edict of 1812 that was partially revoked twelve years later in Prussia. The poet, who like many of his coreligionists was ultimately baptized, makes it clear how difficult he thought their external appearance (notably, he mentions only the beard) made it for Jews to achieve the integration into Christian mainstream society that they aspired to.

In the nineteenth century, even Eastern Jewry could not completely insulate themselves from the disappearance of a distinctive external appearance, since several decades earlier they had received rabbinical permission to use hair removal creams.[177] While on the streets of Vilnius and elsewhere Jewish teachers and seminarians of a state school at first still wore beards and black caftans, members of the next generation were already clean-shaven and had trimmed their hair. Instead of the traditional outer garment they wore trousers or a frock coat.[178] The great Yiddish literary figure Isaac Bashevis Singer (1902–91) writes in one of his stories of Jewish bookkeepers brought from Lithuania to Poland because Russian-speaking skilled workers are needed. "These strangers, who were beardless and wore Gentile clothes, considered themselves enlightened, but the town found them heretical."[179] Resistance to such changes definitely existed, since in some cases these changes had also been imposed on the Eastern Jews from without. When in 1845 an edict ordered Russian Jews to give up their traditional

clothing together with their beards and sidelocks, the Hasidim in particular protested. They were prepared to pay fines and special taxes rather than depart from
the traditional ways of their fathers.[180] As late as 1871 the journal *Der Israelit*
mocked the "barbaric laws" governing Russia and the kingdom of Poland,[181] laws
that curbed the patriotism of the Jews by forbidding them to wear "Jewish traditional clothing," which also included a beard.

To be forced to shave one's beard, which happened time and time again
during the many pogroms of the czarist empire, for instance, was considered
particularly humiliating. But since it was the result of an arbitrary act, fellow
Jews tended to accept it as simply a blow dealt by fate.[182] Anyone who shaved
his beard of his own free will, however, was banished from the community. Even
in 1927 Joseph Roth (1894–1939) noted in an essay from *The Wandering Jews*:
"most devout Jews are unsparing in their condemnation of the man who shaves
his beard—the clean-shaven face serving as the visible sign of breaking with the
faith. The clean-shaven Jew no longer sports the badge of his people."[183] Even
so, the assimilated Austrian writer and journalist had no illusions that shaving
would outwit Jew haters: "even that isn't enough for him to escape anti-
Semitism."

One way to deal with this anti-Semitic discrimination focused on the Jew's
external appearance is through humor. Tzvi Ratwisch, a caftaned Galician Jew
with a long beard and *pejes*, complains to Sami Salmonowitz:

"Anti-Semitism is getting worse and worse! Yesterday I was riding in the
streetcar with two officers who never stopped complaining about the Jews."

"So, what did you do?"

"Well! I made sure not to let on that I'm a Yid!"[184]

The beard's importance in shaping Eastern Jewish identity in particular can
be seen in another joke that humorously targets the particular dangers facing
Jewish immigrants in a foreign, non-Jewish environment, but at the same time
reveals the threat to the very core of Judaism: a young Polish Jew who has emigrated to America returns several years later to his old home for a family visit.

"What happened to your beard?" his mother asks in alarm.

"Nobody has a beard in America, Mom."

"But you do still keep the Sabbath, don't you?"

"Mom, business is business. In America people work even on the Sabbath."

"Do you at least eat kosher?"

"Mom, it is really hard to eat kosher in America."

The old woman hesitates a second, then blurts out: "So tell me one thing. Are
you still circumcised?"[185]

At least the founder and most prominent supporter of Zionism Theodor
Herzl (1860–1904) did not break with the tradition of having a beard. His lush
black beard became an icon of sorts for the national trend in Judaism.[186] Writer

and Kafka confidant Max Brod (1884–1968) recounts in his memoirs that three things had helped him rediscover his Jewish identity: an Eastern Jewish theater troupe's performance in Prague; Martin Buber's three speeches about Judaism; and a photo he first saw in the room of his friend Hugo Bergmann (1883–1975). "I noticed the picture of a melancholy, serious man who looked very imperious indeed—a king with an Assyrian beard, a demigod, in modern dress." Brod did not know who it was and asked his friend, who responded: "Theodor Herzl." The name meant nothing to him, so he asked, "And who is Theodor Herzl?" "The founder of Zionism."[187] Brod at the time had at least heard something about that.

The symbolic weight of Herzl's beard even before World War I is reflected in an anecdote that was frequently told in Zionist circles at the time. At a banquet in Herzl's honor given in 1900 by British Zionist Sir Francis Montefiore (1860–1935), a high-ranking British diplomat sardonically remarked to David Wolffsohn (1856–1914), who later succeeded Herzl as president of the Zionist Congress and also had a full beard: "I believe the success of Zionism rests solely on the exquisite beauty of Dr. Herzl. If Dr. Herzl removes his beard, Zionism is dead." To which Wolffson supposedly replied: "Possibly, but I assure you, Zionism will grow right back."[188]

Probably the most famous portrait of Herzl with his luxurious black beard was done by Hermann Struck (1876–1944), one of the founders of the *misrachi* movement of religious Zionism. Struck emigrated to Palestine in 1923 and there became a member of the Bezalel Academy of Art and Design in Jerusalem. As a volunteer recruit during World War I, he, too, had a neatly groomed full beard, as his Berlin friend Sammy Gronemann (1875–1952) reports: "He still had his impressive black Herzl beard. A rumor was circulating that the beard had died in the war, and it was hard to imagine what a hue and cry would have gone up among the daughters of Judas had the rumor proven to be true—and by the way, not just among the daughters of *Judas*!"[189]

Anti-Semitic propaganda appropriated the contrast between the clean-shaven assimilated Jew and the bearded Eastern Jew early on. In 1869, for instance, the *Fliegende Blätter* published a caricature with the caption, "Physiognomic Studies on the Brühl in Leipzig During the Fair." In the foreground are "typical" Eastern Jews, characterized by their beaked noses, covered heads, and full beards. Behind them is a row of men who are also clearly flagged as Jews but who have no beards, or in some cases just a mustache.[190] A flier from the Weimar Republic shows the formerly proud and fierce Germania in a state of frozen shock. She registers neither the chains of the Treaty of Versailles, the broken sword, nor the crown that is lying on the ground. The two people on either side of her also go unnoticed: the clean-shaven Jew representing Western capitalism and happily rubbing his hands together as the other figure, recognizable as an Eastern Jew by his beard and hat, puts money into a bag.[191] The (in)famous NS propaganda film *Der ewige Jude* (The Eternal Jew, 1940, dir. Fritz Hippler [1909–2002]) also draws on this anti-Semitic visual tradition, making it clear right at the start that Jews know how to disguise themselves very well and do not openly identify themselves as such. Filmic techniques are therefore used in an effort to strip away the mask and reveal the true face of Judaism. It is found in Eastern Jewry. The viewer sees figures with long dark hair and beards, haggard faces, head coverings, and sidelocks. The message: "the civilized Jews we know from Germany give us an incomplete picture of their racial uniqueness. This film shows original footage from the Polish ghettos; it shows us Jews as they look in reality, before they hide behind the mask of civilized Europeans."[192]

To make those few Jews still living in Germany after 1938 look more like the stereotypical Eastern Jew, the government as of June 26, 1941, no longer issued them ration cards for soap and shaving soap; the apparent goal was to make it possible to recognize a Jew by his beard.[193] This recalls the statement of Theodor W. Adorno (1903–69) and Max Horkheimer (1895–1973) that anti-Semites adjust the Jew "until he resembles the image."[194] When the regulation took effect in Dresden on February 6, 1942, Victor Klemperer (1881–1960), who was married to a Christian woman, wrote in his diary: "In the new soap coupons issued today (always for four months) there is, for the first time, no shaving soap for Jews. Is there such a shortage—do they want to reintroduce the medieval Jew's beard now by force? I still have a small hoarded reserve. I hope it will not be noticed during a house search. I hope being clean-shaven will not make one suspect."[195] There were at least rumors of this anti-Jewish measure in other cities, too, as reports by the Security Service of the Reichsführer's SS from Bielefeld indicate for August 1941.[196]

When German soldiers followed by the infamous *Einsatzgruppen* marched east at the start of the war in 1939, they came upon a male Jewish population that for the most part had retained the traditional style beard. Anti-Semitic stereotypes already familiar from the incendiary *Der Stürmer* and other National Socialist propaganda instantly became concrete. One German working as a police officer in Poland wrote to his brother: "and then we really cleaned up among the Jews; we clubbed away so that today both my hands still hurt. But it was sorely needed, since the Jews and the Polacks make our lives really hard. We cut off rabbi beards by the dozens."[197] In the small Ukrainian town of Korets the German occupiers forced rabbis to cut off each other's beards and cut the shape of a cross into the hair on their head to make the shame even greater.[198] A German former policeman who had been stationed in Sosnowiec, Poland, in early 1940 later testified: "a few of my comrades cut the beards of many Jews off with a razor blade. . . . I was busy doing something right nearby as the person in question used a razor blade to remove a Jew's beard and cut him so badly that you could see his esophagus."[199] A survivor of the ghetto in Łódź recalled in his memoirs how Germans lit an elderly Jewish man's beard on fire.[200] German soldiers frequently even made a joke out of forcibly shaving off beards by taking souvenir photos,[201] as seen in the impressive visual documentation of the Wehrmacht exhibit (1995–99 and 2001–4). Despite such repeated abuse from German soldiers and SS members, apparently very few Orthodox Jews voluntarily shaved their beards in the hope of avoiding public display and humiliation. It also usually didn't work.[202] As we read in an eyewitness account from the Łódź ghetto, devout men who for religious reasons were unwilling to sacrifice their beards, sometimes tied cloths around their heads in desperation "as if they had toothaches."[203]

In view of these traumatic experiences in the Shoah, it is not surprising that the Israeli Supreme Court used the general principle of human dignity as a basis for deriving the specific right to grow a beard.[204] Certain restrictions do apply, however, to members of the Israeli armed forces (IDF). In 2016, observant soldiers filed hundreds of appeals against the introduction of even stricter rules concerning beards in the army. Rabbi Shlomo Aviner, chief rabbi of the West Bank settlement Bet El, even compared the new regulations with those of Nazi Germany. In doing so he referred to a well-known photo from the time of the Shoah that shows German soldiers forcing one Jew to cut off the beard of another. According to the new IDF rule, soldiers must obtain permission to have a beard from their commanding officer, not the army rabbi as in the past.[205]

Hair Color

"Why do Jews often have dark hair? (I am not a Nazi!!!) When I see Jews on TV, I see that they often have dark hair. Jews are of course not races (for God's sake!!!). And I am also not a Nazi!"[206] This "naive" question, posted to an online advice column by a "MissSpeedy123" in 2011, sheds light on the long tradition of a physical stereotype that assigns Jews a specific hair color (usually black). Like the Jewish beard, almost always depicted as red, the hair color of the Jews was also associated with this stigmatizing color on into the early modern period. Here, too, the model was the "betrayer" Judas Iscariot, who in Christian iconography since the Middle Ages is usually shown wearing a red robe or with red hair and/or a red beard. It is not just the resemblance between their names that links the Jewish people with Judas already in the Middle Ages. Augustine of Hippo (354–430 CE) among others played a part by likening Judas to the Jews in his influential writings.[207] In theological discourse up into the twentieth century, Judas often stands as a representative of the Jewish people as a whole,[208] an equation that the fundamentally anticlerical National Socialists used for their own purposes.[209] A different equation has also proven influential in this connection, namely, one involving the Edomites (Genesis 36:10–19), whose tribal designation derives from the Hebrew אֱדוֹם (*adom*, "red"). While Christians saw themselves as the people of the new covenant and hence the "true Israel," the biblical name Edom was linked to the chosen people of the Old Testament, the Jews. However, in rabbinical sources since the time of the Bar Kochba uprising against Roman occupation, "Edomite" is used as a synonym for Rome. Esau was thus one of the founders of the capital city of the Roman Empire.[210] Here, too, the non-biblical connotation is clearly negative. In addition, the legend of the "red Jew" mentioned earlier in a different context helped further reinforce the image of the red-haired Jew.[211] Even so, in the early modern period we do find isolated voices objecting to the stigmatization of redheads; one was that of baroque writer Hans Jakob Christoffel von Grimmelshausen (1621–76).[212]

It was only in their interpretation of the color red that insider and outsider views differed. While in Judaism this color (אדומי) had predominantly positive connotations due to King David's reddish hair (1 Samuel 17:42), in Christian tradition it symbolized negative traits. Red beards and red hair in particular were considered signs of falsity and deviousness, as we see, for instance, in the Middle High German Arthurian romance *Wigalois*: "Both his hair and his beard were fiery red, and I hear that such people are false-hearted."[213]

It is therefore not surprising that after their expulsion from Spain, baptized Jews or *conversos* were described as redheads during Inquisition trials, where physical attributes were mentioned in order to underscore the wickedness of their deeds (such as desecrating the host).[214] This is reflected in Spanish baroque literature such as the picaresque novel *El Buscón* (1626) by Francisco Gómez de Quevedo (1580–1645). Here a recent Christian convert known for his avarice and his cruelty is negatively "flagged" for the reader by his red hair. The situation is similar in early modern England, where at first Jews were allowed to return only on an individual basis. In early performances of Shakespeare's *Merchant of Venice*, the actor playing Shylock appeared onstage in a red wig that identified him as a Jew.[215] The same stereotype occurs in German literature as well, though not until the nineteenth century, where in Gustav Freytag's 1855 novel *Soll und Haben* (*Debit and Credit*) we read the following description of the Jewish owner of a feudal estate: "Indeed, young Itzig was by no means a pleasant apparition, pale, haggard, red-haired, and shabbily clothed as he was."[216]

In the second half of the twentieth century this cliché occurs even in works by American Jewish authors, though it is usually used ironically, as in *Tuesday the Rabbi Saw Red* (1973), the aptly titled detective novel by Harry Kemelman (1908–96). While working as an adjunct professor at a Boston college, hobby investigator and rabbi David Small shares an office with a certain Professor John Hendryx who is later mysteriously murdered. When the rabbi-detective asks his office mate one day about the popularity of his colleague Professor Fine, Hendryx replies:

"I don't know how popular Roger Fine is. He's a good-looking fellow, so I suppose the girls go for him. That red hair—" He broke off. "Somehow I don't think of red hair in connection with your people. Do you suppose there was some hanky-panky between his mother or grandmother and some Russian or Polish soldier?"

"If so," said the rabbi quietly, "it was probably involuntary, during a pogrom. But actually there is a genetic strain of red hair among our people. King David was supposed to be red-haired."[217]

The fictional Professor Hendryx, described here as not exactly a friend of the Jews, was not the only one who had trouble with the notion of red-haired Jews, especially King David. Richard Wagner's son-in-law Houston Stewart Chamberlain chided Martin Luther (1483–1546) for describing David as "brownish" (*bräunlich*) in his translation of the Bible (though Luther may well have meant reddish-brown). It was Chamberlain's firm belief that the resplendent slayer of Goliath had been of Indo-Germanic descent and must therefore have had blond hair.[218]

In the early modern period, red gradually gives way to black as the imagined color. The Jewish convert Antonius Margaritha (ca. 1492–1542) explained the purported fact that the majority of Jews had black hair by noting that boys began covering their heads already at the age of seven; their hair "choked under the hats" in this way and darkened as a result.[219] English headmaster John Greenhalgh (1615–74) wrote in 1662 to the Reverend Thomas Crompton (1635–99): "They [the Jews] are all generally black, so as they may be distinguished from Spaniards or native Greeks, for the Jews' hair hath a deeper tincture of a more perfect raven black."[220] In a German wanted list from 1715, the Jewish men profiled in the warrants for arrest had both red and black hair.[221] By several years later, the color black dominated in these documents as the hair color of the Jews. For late eighteenth-century figures like Lenz and Lavater it was a given that the majority of Jews had black curly hair. The 1819 *Handbuch der Entbindungskunst* (Manual for the Obstetric Art) by renowned Göttingen obstetrician Friedrich Benjamin Osiander (1759–1822) qualifies this description slightly by noting that Jewish mothers give birth to children with either "very black or fox-red hair," but then adds: "genuinely black hair" occurs only in "Orientals, Jews, Africans, and South Americans."[222]

Even in Jewish circles this stereotype goes unquestioned at first, as a commentary in the *Allgemeine Zeitung des Judenthums* indicates: "In the midst of German blue eyes, blond hair, and fair-skinned faces, the Jew displays his religious affiliation in his black locks, in his glowing eyes."[223] With the rise of anthropology based on racial characteristics around the middle of the nineteenth century, statistics can be found that aim to either prove or disprove this statement. The 1886–87 report by Rudolf Virchow (1821–1902) on the color of German schoolchildren's skin, hair, and eyes ("Gesamtbericht . . . über die Farbe der Haut, der Haare und der Augen der Schulkinder in Deutschland") includes information on tens of thousands of Jewish children.[224] Of these, 54.39 percent had brown hair, 11.46 percent had black hair, 32.03 percent were fair-haired, and 0.42 percent had red hair. Other contemporary statistics reflect a similar hair color distribution among Jews in most European countries, though the percentage of black-haired individuals was generally even higher: Poland had the highest (96 percent), and England the lowest (73.8 percent).[225]

Where nature had determined otherwise, people had the option of dyeing their hair blond in order to avoid racial stereotypes. Jewish women and occasionally also men chose this option as early as the late empire. Committed Zionist Arthur Ruppin (1876–1943) chided his fellow Jews in 1918 for often emphasizing a person's blond hair in wedding announcements and sometimes even adding the phrase "not Jewish-looking" to the description.[226] In the 1920s when new chemicals came on the market that made long-term hair color change possible, many Jewish women were apparently among the customers in what were now professional beauty parlors.[227]

For race researchers with National Socialist sympathies, the statistical finding that Jews apparently included not only people with black hair but also a sizable number of blond men and women was an annoying fact that could not simply be argued away. In his *Rassenkunde*, reprinted many times and probably the most widely used textbook on ethnogeny, Hans F. K. Günther states: "In terms of color, the hair of the majority of Jews is dark, either brown or black. Yet there are a noticeably large number of red-haired Jews, and blond hair also has such strong representation in the Jewish people that in southern European surroundings, Jews are occasionally more fair-haired than their non-Jewish environment."[228] Such distinctions were not allowed by the inflammatory weekly *Der Stürmer*. A 1937 article emphasizes both black and red hair as innate characteristics of all Jews, whereas—according to the author—only an Aryan could be blond.[229] Founder of the ariosophical "Bund der Guoten" Kurt Paehlke (1875–1945), who during the Weimar Republic wrote under the pseudonym "Weisshaar" (Whitehair) and early on enjoyed the esteem of later Reichsführer-SS Heinrich Himmler (1900–1945), did not see things quite so strictly. For Paehlke, a person's degree of blondness was not a decisive factor in joining the league he had founded, an association with several thousand members. Under certain circumstances even Jews could become members, assuming they had completely overcome their "Jewish essence."[230] Also noteworthy in this connection is that Paehlke incorporated Jewish mysticism into his racially motivated visions of human breeding.

The NS henchmen who carried out Hitler's Final Solution by ultimately committing mass murder had little interest in such ariosophical notions. In addition to physical traits that were familiar and repeatedly stressed in anti-Semitic writings (first and foremost, the hooked nose), the black hair that ostensibly made Jews instantly recognizable was something they focused on when conducting raids. The group leader of a German mounted police unit who was present during the mass shooting of Jews in Pinsk notes how irritated he had been to discover under the mountain of corpses the body of a blond girl "who did not look at all Jewish."[231] To elude their captors, both Jewish men and women tried to cover and hide their black hair or even dye it blond. German businessman Berthold Beitz (1913–2013), who during the Third Reich witnessed how the Jews of Drohobych were driven to the forest of Brodnica and killed, remarked that some of the children were blond: "their hair was quite plainly dyed, they were so white-blond. I assume that the Jew responsible had deliberately dyed their hair so light."[232] Together with his wife Else, Beitz famously saved hundreds of Jews from extermination. In occupied Poland the demand for hair dye was particularly great, as survivors of the Shoah attest.[233] Shiny blond hair, however, could make a person even more noticeable. Emmanuel Ringelblum (1900–1944), chronicler of the Warsaw ghetto, explains why in his clandestinely written diaries: "because the agents [Polish police workers who collaborated with the National Socialists] examined tufts of hair. In practice the platinum blonds aroused greater suspicion than the brunettes."[234] Even when the pretense was perfect, Jews who had dyed their hair blond were often detected through little things. One eyewitness writes of difficulties the Jewish resistance in Poland faced at the time: "A headscarf could disguise a lot, a cross hung around your neck, dyed hair . . . Jews with an Aryan appearance constantly asked their Aryan friends: 'why are we found out time and time again? Don't we look perfectly Aryan?' The answer was: 'your eyes give you away. Make your expression livelier, happier—then you won't be so noticeable.' "[235]

After the end of the Third Reich, hair color, at least in Germany, was no longer a matter of survival, but in the 1950s and 1960s blond still remained the Germans' favorite hair color.[236] Things looked different in several East Bloc countries, however, where before the fall of the Iron Curtain anti-Semitism was particularly virulent. A Jewish woman who emigrated to Germany from Romania tells in an interview that a friend had left the congregation in Romania and "had her hair dyed blond since she didn't want people to recognize her as a Jew." Even after World War II, she explains, Jews continued to be despised outsiders in Romanian society.[237]

Blond is also a desirable hair color for many women in present-day Israel, as a look at Hebrew fashion magazines shows. Several years ago, the *Jüdische Allgemeine* even ran an article on the topic. There, an Israeli advertising expert is quoted as saying that while he believes plenty of men and women still follow this trend, he also notes a countermovement: "in the end, blond stands for foreign, and for a long time foreign stood for successful. But today there are enough successful natives for the Israelis to identify with. And most of them aren't blond."[238]

One of the ironies of world history is that it was the daughter of Jewish immigrants from Russia, raised in Brooklyn in the 1920s, who turned hair dyeing—and especially going blond—into a mass phenomenon after World War II. Already as a young woman Shirley Polykoff (1908–98) had had her hair dyed blond.[239] In 1956 while working professionally in advertising, she developed a marketing campaign for the American cosmetics company Clairol. The slogan she created—"Does she . . . or doesn't she?"—was such a hit that a growing number of American women began to dye their hair. In the mid-1950s the number of women in the United States who were unhappy with their natural hair color and reached for chemicals was 7 percent. Today, hair coloring is a standard practice for most women—and not just in the United States—that needs no justification, least of all one that includes fear of anti-Semitism.

Smell

Stench is used even today as a metaphor for stigmatizing foreigners and outsiders. The *foetor judaicus*, or evil smell allegedly unique to Jews and supposedly indicating their proximity to the devil, has likewise remained a stereotype well into the twenty-first century.[240] An ostensibly "typical" odor or bad smell had the function of separating and removing foreigners, Jews, prostitutes, and witches; and up to the present day, even social classification categories such as age, gender, and nationality have been linked by association to a specific, usually negative smell,[241] thereby opening the door to stigmatization.

We find assertions already in late antiquity that Jews have a particular smell. Roman author Ammianus Marcellinus (325/330–after 391 CE) described the Jews as "stinky and rebellious" (*Iudaeorum faetentium et tumultuantium*).[242] Doctor of the church Ephraim the Syrian (ca. 306–73 CE) said of the Jews: "the smell of leeks is more agreeable than the breath of their character."[243] Arian bishop Maximus (d. ca. 420 CE) proclaimed that the Jews were marked by the "stench of unbelief."[244] The bishop of Poitiers Venantius Fortunatus (ca. 530/540–ca. 600/ 610 CE) was outraged that the "Jewish stench" slapped Christians in the face.[245] This notion remained powerful in the Middle Ages, as an example from the Cistercian monk Caesarius of Heisterbach (ca. 1180–after 1240) shows. In his dialogue on miracles (*Dialogus miraculorum*) he describes the conversion of a Jewish girl. After learning of her supposedly "voluntary" baptism, the girl's unsuspecting father did everything he could to regain custody over her. "Now when the Jew came to the monastery together with his friends and relatives, his daughter, though completely unaware of their arrival, suddenly noticed a strong nasty odor and stated frankly: 'I do not know where it is coming from. The Jewish odor bothers me.' "[246] The medieval writer Seifried Helbling (b. before 1240, d. soon after 1300) composed a rhyme saying that there was no country on earth so large that it could not be contaminated by thirty Jews with their stench and lack of faith.[247] When the Hungarian city of Ofen imposed a wine tax on the Jews in 1421, it addressed the regulation to "the Jews, the vile, stubborn, stinking betrayers of God." [248] A broadsheet printed in southern Germany in 1472 makes fun of the Jews by, among other things, having them say that because they do not eat pork sandwiches they are yellow and have foul breath.[249] And in *Zedlers Universal-Lexicon* of 1735 we can still read: "To be sure, a Jew has something about him that enables people to quickly recognize him and differentiate him from others. They are disgusting and horrible, and stench and filth make them abhorrent . . . (Deuteronomy 28:37, 46)."[250]

Where does this stereotypical attribute come from? The Jew hater Johann Jacob Schudt tried to find an answer to this question by first citing all the various explanations known at the time. One example: Jews supposedly stink because God wished to mark them forever as the murderers of Christ.[251] Schudt also includes the argument that the evil odor of the Jews is innate, but he finds this theory less than convincing: "if that were true / then all Jews without any differences would have to stink / which is not the case."[252] To support this statement he mentions Italy, "where Jews and Jewesses are clean and neat." In contrast, Jews in Poland and Germany, in his opinion, give off an unpleasant body odor that he attributes to their way of life: the Jews in these countries do not pay attention to cleanliness and wear filthy clothes; they are also known to be garlic eaters. A short discussion follows about the reasons that Jews ostensibly consume more garlic than Christians.[253] This comment, too, is quite revealing for what it tells us about the origins of the prejudice against foreigners. That this is in fact a prejudice was recognized and exposed early on by the English physician and philosopher Thomas Browne (1605–82). However, neither his contemporaries nor later readers paid much attention to his rationally argued refutation of the idea that Jews stink by nature: "it being a dangerous point to annex a constant property unto any Nation, and much more this unto the Jew; since this quality is not verifiable by observation; since the grounds are feeble that should establish it; and lastly: since if all were true, yet are the reasons alleged for it, of no sufficiency to maintain it."[254]

Since anti-Jewish pamphlets from the late Middle Ages and early modern period often compare the *foetor judaicus* with the smell of a billy goat, a different interpretation is also possible. The Jew appears as a demonic creature that gives off a stench typical of goats or rams.[255] In contrast to the devil, saints give off a pleasant smell. This also explains why Jews can allegedly rid themselves of this physical flaw through baptism. Not a few Christian legends deal with the topic, including one spread by Caesarius of Heisterbach.[256] Further evidence is found in the fictional *Letters of Obscure Men* (*Epistolae obscurorum virorum*) from the early

sixteenth century, written to comment on a dispute between the Cologne Domin-
icans and the Hebraist Johannes Reuchlin (1455–1522) over whether Jewish
writings, and the Talmud in particular, should be burned. In this satirical text,
written partially in dog Latin, we read: "the other day a fellow who had resided at
Cologne ten years ago, told me that he believed not that Pfefferkorn was yet a
good Christian: for he declared that he met him a year back and that he still stank
like any other Jew—and yet it is common proof that when Jews are baptized they
smell rank no longer. He believes, therefore, that *Pfefferkorn* is still a knave at the
back of his head, and when the Theologians think him the best of Christians he
will turn Jew again: 'We should put no trust in him,' quoth he, 'for all men have
misgivings concerning baptized Jews.' "[257] The bad opinion of converted Jews at
that time was also shared by Martin Luther, whose later writings express certainty
that the Jewish character could not be permanently changed by baptism. Whoever
as a Jew wished to be rid of the smell without being baptized was even suspected
of obtaining Christ's blood shed from a host. This charge played a role in more
than a few trials for host desecration.[258]

Other converts also helped to reinforce this prejudice. Giulio Morosini
(1612–87), who converted to Christianity in 1649 and was a student of the
prominent Venetian rabbi Leon Modena (1571–1648), claimed, for example,
that the Jewish handwashing ritual had to do with a stench from having touched
unclean body parts.[259] The fact that halakhic rules alone required Jews to be
extremely careful to avoid bad smells is suppressed—either willfully or out of
ignorance—in anti-Jewish polemics of the early modern period.

Just how serious a problem other people's body odor really is for religious
Jews emerges from a recent case in which a rabbi was asked to decide if is allowable to pray near a fellow Jew who smells of sweat.[260] The answer is "no," with
reference made to the Talmud (BT Berakhot 25), which states that a person may
not pray anywhere there is an evil smell. In the Jewish legal codex *Shulchan Arukh*
(first printed in 1565) we also find a rule to the effect that during the recitation of
the *Amidah*, anyone suffering from flatulence must stand four cubits away from
others who are praying if he is unable to keep from passing gas (נפיחה) (Orach
Chayim 80.1). Even though these fundamental texts of Judaism do not explicitly
mention body odor (but instead passing gas and so on), the American rabbi asked
to decide the special case was able to do so by making use of analogies.

As we have seen, in Germany long before Hitler we already find the belief that
Jews are dirty and exude a repulsive smell. American historian John Efron writes:
"The evil smell is apparently an extension of the filth attribute, and a wealth of
evidence from folk culture allows us to conclude that the evil-smelling Jew is
mainly a product of the . . . 'Christian olfactory imagination.' "[261] Ample proof of
this can be found in popular literature. An anti-Semitically tinged Franconian
proverb, probably of nineteenth-century origin, goes: "decent Jews and Jews who

don't stink / you can seek but you won't find" (Anständige Juden und Juden, die nicht stinken / Kannst du wohl suchen, aber nicht finden). Before World War I in Vienna people sang the popular tune, "All Jews stink! All Jews stink! Only Laser Jacob doesn't" (Alle Juden stinken! Alle Juden stinken! Nur der Laser Jakob nicht). Even children's rhymes passed on these negative stereotypes until well into the twentieth century: during the Third Reich children sang, "The Jew Isaac Meyer / He stinks like rotten eggs" (Der Jude Isaak Meyer / Der stinkt wie faule Eier). Günther's standard work on racial biology, reprinted in numerous editions from 1925 until 1944, describes the smell of Jewish skin as "sweetish" and classifies it as a racial characteristic.[262] Another comparably anti-Semitic book with the pseudoscientific title *Der Jude im Sprichwort der Völker* (The Jew in Proverbs of Nations) offers an explanation from racial biology for why a non-Jew has bad breath: "he has kissed a Jew."[263] The popularity of this "racial smell of the Jews" notion is proven by the twenty-six additional pertinent proverbs and idioms included by the author of this sorry piece of work.

It was at that same time (1942) that this overtly racialized prejudice gained a new and murderous power after Hitler used it to help substantiate his anti-Semitism. In *Mein Kampf* the future dictator claims that already during his years in Vienna, the typical smell of a caftaned Jew had turned his stomach:

> This fictitious conflict between the Zionists and the Liberal Jews soon disgusted me; for it was false through and through and in direct contradiction to the moral dignity and immaculate character on which that race had always prided itself.
>
> Cleanliness, whether moral or of another kind, had its own peculiar meaning for these people. That they were water-shy was obvious on looking at them and, unfortunately, very often also when not looking at them at all. The odour of those people in caftans often used to make me feel ill. Beyond that there were the unkempt clothes and the ignoble exterior.
>
> All these details were certainly not attractive; but the revolting feature was that beneath their unclean exterior one suddenly perceived the moral mildew of the chosen race.[264]

The consequences of this "olfactory imagination" are well known. Millions of Jews were killed in gas chambers made to look like disinfection rooms.

Chapter 2

The (Un)covered and Altered Body

Corporeality

In internet forums we occasionally come across expressions like "body-hostile desert religions," which refer for the most part to Judaism. This chapter therefore addresses the relationship of Judaism to the individual physical body, but at the same time also its corporeality. By this I mean how people experience the body both individually and when interacting with others, and also the semiotic character of the body. In *Leibsein als Aufgabe* (Physical Being as Task), the philosopher Gernot Böhme defines the human body, or *Leib*, as "the nature that we ourselves are."[1] In contrast, the body understood as *Körper*, though it too is "my own nature," is constituted through interaction with others: the *Leib* becomes a *Körper* when it is experienced in relation to other *Körper*. In the words of sociologist Roland Hitzler, "whether I want it to be or not, my physical corporeality [*leibhaftige Körperlichkeit*] is to some extent an array of signs over which I have only limited control, a field of evidence for the public 'gaze' focused in my counterpart."[2] Human beings nevertheless try to control the physical impression they make by "masking" it, which means that this technique should be seen as part of social semiotics. As Hitlzer notes, the technique can apply to more than just the most exposed body part, the face: "such 'maskings' are by no means restricted to our faces; instead, they involve the entire body in a fairly sustained way. 'Masking' thus means nothing more than the (cultural) adjustment or the conventionalization of the (natural) body."[3] Possibilities for controlling one's external appearance include concealing it (with clothing or a head covering, for example) and emphasizing it (for example, with tattoos, piercings, or muscle play), thus allowing the *Leib* to shine through the *Körper*.

Muscle Jews

The physical ideal of Eastern Judaism that developed in the *shtetl*, the small largely Jewish towns in Galicia and elsewhere that were strongly influenced by Hasidism, was shaped by the Kabbalah. The teaching about primal man (*Adam Kadmon*) together with the concept of the *sefirot* (the ten divine emanations or channels of divine creative life force) led to the identification of specific body parts with individual *sefirot*. The anthropomorphic concept of the *sefirot* is based on the Kabbalist text *Shiur Komah* (literally, height measurement), in which the beloved's body is described with secret names and measurements in the Song of Songs.[4] The three topmost *sefirot* stand for the divine head, the next two for the arms, the sixth for body and heart, the next two for the legs, and the ninth for the phallus. The tenth *sefira* symbolizes an independent female body, the Shechinah. Above all in the Lurian Kabbalah, this projection of God is found in the mystical figure of *Adam Kadmon*. Herein lie the origins of the Eastern Jewish physical ideal, which begins with the head ("vessel of the intellect")[5] and sees all other body parts as less important. The *schejne Jid* is the scholarly Jew who may be physically weak. In the eyes of the Jewish Orthodoxy, his usually pale face with its full beard reflects the image of a superior intellect.[6] Admired for his keen mind, he enjoys great social prestige in Hasidic circles.

As the nineteenth century came to a close, Zionism countered this physical ideal with its image of the "muscle Jew."[7] The term *Muskeljude* was first used in a speech by Max Nordau (1849–1923) at the Second Zionist Congress in Basel in 1898. Nordau called for Judaism to awaken to a "new life"[8] and held that a "physical education" of the Jews would help reestablish a "Jewry of muscle" that had been lost.[9] Unlike Nordau, Sigmund Freud still held that Judaism had laid the groundwork early on for privileging mental activity. In *Moses and Monotheism* (1939), he writes: "The preference which through two thousand years the Jews have given to spiritual endeavor has, of course, had its effect; it has helped to build a dike against brutality and the inclination to violence which are usually found where athletic development becomes the ideal of the people. The harmonious development of spiritual and bodily activity, as achieved by the Greeks, as denied to the Jews. In this conflict their decision was at least made in favour of what is culturally the more important."[10]

Historian Daniel Wildmann persuasively argues that Nordau may well have been influenced by the idea of "muscular Christianity" in mid-nineteenth-century England, which was propagated mainly by Anglican circles at the universities of Cambridge and Oxford.[11] Advocates of muscular Christianity called for a physical strengthening of the English population not as an end in itself but instead with the aim of securing the empire.

In his highly regarded work *Degeneration* (*Entartung*, 1892), Nordau treated it as a given that people had become weaker not just mentally but also physically.[12] However, his notion of "muscular Judaism" draws only indirectly on this critique of civilization, which was widespread at the time in non-Jewish society as well and was the impetus for the "life reform movement."[13] When promoting a "Jewry of muscle," Nordau was thinking primarily of the oppressive economic and social situation of Eastern Jews coping with poor hygiene and health conditions, yet he doubted that gymnastics was the appropriate way to significantly improve their physical constitution, since Eastern Jews lacked both the necessary time and means. In Western Europe, however, Nordau became the spiritual father of the national Jewish gymnastics movement that began organizing in clubs around 1900.

The term *Muskeljudentum*, at first casually tossed into debates at the early Zionist Congresses, was one Nordau later explained in greater detail in several articles for the Berlin-based *Jüdische Turnzeitung* (Jewish Gymnastics Newspaper). He discovered role models in antiquity, when Jewish athletes had still taken part in competitions and displayed their well-trained bodies naked. He nevertheless saw differences between them and the Jewish national gymnastics movement of his time: "for the ancient Jewish circus fighters were ashamed of their Judaism and tried to conceal the sign of the Covenant by means of a surgical operation."[14] Here Nordau is referring to the early athletes' attempts to have their foreskins restored in order to conform to a notion of ideal beauty that deemed an exposed glans "barbarian." As one of political Zionism's key representatives, he recommended drawing on this "proud past" and stated his firm conviction that "for no other people will gymnastics fulfill a more educational purpose than for us Jews."[15] Just ten years later, when the Jewish national gymnastics movement had many followers throughout Europe and even in Palestine, Nordau was a guest at the 1909 Zionist Congress in Hamburg, where he joined delegates in watching an impressive exhibition by Jewish male and female gymnasts. The demonstration was so inspiring that he declared: "This performance has shown the world what it has not seen for 1800 years."[16] For Nordau, the "muscle Jewry" displayed in Hamburg was an expression of an unconditional will to give Judaism renewed physical strength. Referring to the notion of the *schejne Jid* that placed mind above body, he states: "I have been accused of saying that the Jew cannot easily engage in muscular activity since for him the mental dominates. I have said something like that, but the opposite. I have said that according to all laws of modern physiology, the Jew should be able to become an excellent gymnast if he so chooses, since muscles obey the mind."[17] In his view, then, it was only a matter of willpower if Jews wished to continue the tradition of those earlier times when Hellenized Jews had taken part in competitions.[18] Almost every issue of the *Jüdische Turnzeitung*, which in 1910 reprinted excerpts from Nordau's speech in Hamburg, included reports from individual cities such as Cologne, where in 1909 it was reported that more than a thousand men and women "had become acquainted with the requirements of contemporary body culture" in the local Jewish gymnastics club.[19] That same year readers learned that even in Petach Tikva, Palestine, a Jewish gymnastics club had been founded whose "gymnastics marches" through

Figure 9. Book advertisement, *Jüdische Turnzeitung* [Jewish Gymnastics Newspaper]
10, no. 8 (1909).

the surrounding area had inspired many onlookers to become more active. Physical fitness through both sports and work in the fields was key to the Zionist project, which involved cultivating the land and rebuilding the Jewish population. On his 1898 trip to Palestine, Theodor Herzl was impressed by a group of strapping Jewish porters he met. After approaching them and feeling their muscles, he later remarked to a companion: "if we bring 300,000 Jews like that here, the entire country of Israel will be ours."[20] The "new Jew," the pioneer putting down roots in Eretz Israel, presupposed the "muscular Jew."[21]

The official program of the Jewish gymnastics movement was published in 1900 in the *Jüdische Turnzeitung*. It adopted Nordau's thinking, including his theory of degeneration, by emphasizing right at the outset: "we combat the one-sided development of the mind that has led to our nervousness and mental tension."[22] The "limp Jewish body" would regain its "lost resilience," and it was hoped that this would also boost Jewish self-confidence and feelings of solidarity, strengthen their sense of national identity, and also help confront anti-Semitism "bravely and energetically." In this context, it was particularly important to those who supported a physical renaissance of Judaism that Jewish men become eligible for military service. Members of the German Jewish gymnastics movement looked with envy to England, where a Jewish Lads' Brigade had existed since 1895. There young Jewish immigrants received paramilitary training and played typical English sports like cricket and soccer.[23] Reports in the *Jüdische Turnzeitung* marveled at the role played by Jewish officers in teaching these body practices and the moral values that accompanied them.[24] In the German Empire, the prejudicial belief that Jews were physically unfit for the military persisted until World War I. If Jews were to enjoy complete equality in terms of civil rights—something they had been striving for since the start of the emancipation movement in the early nineteenth century—then military service, which was also an expression of masculinity, was absolutely essential. Even the fact that Jews had given their lives for their fatherland in the Napoleonic Wars and again in the Franco-Prussian War did not change most people's reservations about their fitness for military service, especially in Prussia, and to a lesser extent in the Habsburg territories. These doubts were in part reinforced by Jews themselves. In 1908 the *Jüdische Turnzeitung* published an article by Dr. Elias Auerbach (1882–1971) on the military fitness of the Jews. At the time, draft boards paid particular attention to chest measurements. Auerbach could not ignore the contemporary statistical studies of recruits showing that more Jews than non-Jews were rejected in the empire because of their small chest size. However, he saw this not as a racial feature but instead as the result of urbanization. A remedy was needed here, one that involved physical training in something like gymnastics. Auerbach offered himself as a good example: as a one-year volunteer he had initially had a smaller chest than the standard recruit, but after one year of military exercises he had succeeded in reaching the size that was the norm. He, like Nordau, believed that the Jewish body can be changed: "Since we cannot undo economic development, artificial practice, sport, must be the motto of the Jews."[25] From the early nineteenth century on, the German gymnastics movement pursued national aims in connection with training for the military, and several decades later the Jewish national gymnastics movement drew on these same images of military fitness, virility, and nation-building. World War I was nevertheless an eye-opening experience for the Jewish gymnastics movement. This was not just a result of the infamous Jewish census of 1916. In view of anti-Semitic suspicions of "shirking," this survey was to list the number of Jewish conscripts who were eligible for combat, serving on the front lines, displaced, registered as essential, rejected, and deceased. A look at the Entente armies also made the German Jews, who had counted so heavily on sports to become fit for military service, painfully aware of "the futility as a Jew in Germany of demonstrating masculinity and earning recognition from such a demonstration."[26]

In Eastern Europe, the problem of physical training for "ghetto Jews" was of a completely different magnitude and arose in an entirely different sociopolitical and economic context.[27] This is clearly reflected in a talk given by Professor Max Mandelstamm (1839–1912) at the Fourth Zionist Congress (1900) and excerpted in the *Jüdische Turnzeitung*. The renowned ophthalmologist and Zionist laments the large concentration of small merchants and simple manual laborers among *shtetl* inhabitants and states: "In factories where physical strength and stamina are required Jews are not used, since they lack the necessary muscular strength."[28] In his view, this misery derives primarily from the lifestyle of Eastern Jews with its heavy emphasis on religious education for children and teenagers (*cheder*, Talmud schools). This, he points out, has consequences for the Jewish body. Jews living in the *shtetl* are smaller in stature (162.7 cm on average) than their Christian counterparts. Their chest measurements are also smaller than those of other recruits in the czarist army. To correct this failing, which also explains their greater susceptibility to tuberculosis, Professor Mandelstamm gives the following advice to the Jewish youth of Eastern Europe: "You are able to stretch and extend your limbs, you are able to frolic about as your ancestors were permitted to do for centuries. So, my brothers, strengthen those limbs with physical work, in the garden and the field, on the sawhorse, and anywhere else where muscles can be steeled: in the gymnasium, on the fencing mat, and in swimming schools. Become agile and flexible, muscular and brave like your ancestors before you."[29] Like Nordau and other representatives of the Jewish national movement before him, he recommends the Hasmoneans and Bar Kochba as historical role models.

Zionist circles were by no means alone in placing a high value on the "physical improvement" of the Jews. Immigration offices also deemed it an important criterion if they were to make a positive recommendation. In 1915, for example, the regional council in Düsseldorf was reluctant to have Jewish workers brought to the Ruhr area since their "deficient physical fitness" made them unsuitable for strenuous work in steel and coal mines.[30] The Bochum chief of police thought that bringing Russian Jews to Germany during the first two war years had been a serious mistake. His reasoning: "Almost all of them were frail individuals who are out of the question for work in the pits." He adds: "It was reported that 13 have sexually transmitted diseases and that many have lice. Several had severe bone fractures and eye ailments."[31] Similar concerns and reservations were voiced by American immigration officials when, in the late nineteenth and early twentieth centuries, a vast multitude of Jewish immigrants from Eastern Europe sought to permanently settle in the United States, the *goldenen medine*. Most immigrants realized even before their arrival that the Ellis Island inspectors demanded not only good mental health but also a sound physical constitution. A 1903 memorandum of the American immigration office stated that the "Hebrews" among the European immigrants were generally diligent and intelligent people but often in poor physical shape.[32] Many Eastern Jews therefore quickly landed in the category "poor physique," which justified deportation. One of the criteria was "poor muscular development."[33] Since inspectors often interpreted the term "poor physique" to mean that the person had tuberculosis, as of 1910, "poor development" was the preferred term, which focused more on their physical appearance and could therefore be determined more quickly. Between 1911 and 1918, between 8 and 27 percent of all assessments issued from Ellis Island included this determination.[34] The existing documentation unfortunately gives no further breakdown of immigrant groups, but in all likelihood Jews from Eastern Europe often received this classification. Those who did still had the possibility of applying for help from the Hebrew Immigrant Aid Society (HIAS), a well-connected organization that later merged with its successor, the Jewish Colonization Association. This was the case for a twenty-year-old Jew from Warsaw named David Ostrowitz, who was threatened with deportation because of his ostensible "lack of physical development." The appeal filed by HIAS noted that "physical improvement" was possible if Ostrowitz's miserable living conditions changed: "under the American conditions [he] will be able to develop himself physically much better than he could at home."[35] While this particular appeal was apparently unsuccessful, in other comparable cases HIAS succeeded in getting the recommendation revised by using a two-pronged strategy. First, they brought counterarguments calling into question the decision made in the individual case; in addition, they focused on the fundamental, basic "physical and mental potential" of Jewish immigrants from Eastern Europe. HIAS took a *Muskeljudentum* line of argument and claimed that with enough willpower and more advantageous conditions, potential for development existed. Officials in immigration offices, however, usually had racial stereotypes in the back of their minds when they automatically connected Jewish immigrants from Eastern Europe with the popular "image of the degenerate Jewish *physis*."[36] The American Jewish Committee likewise battled this type of prejudice by seeking dialogue with the immigration commission.

At this time the idea of a "muscle Jewry" was also widespread among American Jews, as seen in a diary entry by a Reform rabbi in Cincinnati. He writes in 1905 about a member of his congregation, a physical education teacher named Morris Isaacs, who responded to the anti-Semitic tirades of a local Presbyterian minister by sending him a written threat. In his letter, Isaacs said he would be happy to meet the Protestant minister at the place of his choice—"with or without boxing gloves"[37]—if he continued to spew hateful remarks against the Jews. That the propagation of *Muskeljudentum* had also become partially internalized by Jewish immigrants from Eastern Europe by this time is evident in a report by Isidor Wolff, the Berlin gymnastics official who accompanied Russian Jewish emigrants on their voyage to the United States. Wolff was extremely upset by the "drawn and pale" Jewish faces that confronted him in steerage, but he then seized the initiative and, acting as their leader, convinced eighty young Jews to do gymnastics on the deck. He proudly reported that even the ship's officer was astonished at the physical change that took place within fourteen days. Even more important to him was the increased sense of self-esteem he could thereby instill in persecuted young Jews from the poorest circumstances: "each one of my young men who at first could do only one or two chin-ups, and in two weeks got up to six or eight, is proud of his strong arm—even without expressly imagining that such arms will be able to fight back."[38] The *Jüdische Turnzeitung* reported another success story in 1908 when a Russian Jew who had emigrated to the United States two years earlier won a sporting event sponsored by the navy. The commentary shows just how widespread the notion of "muscle Jewry" had become at the time: "We find it [this event] only symptomatic that when their economic and political standing enables them to test their physical abilities against others in open competition, Jews do not fare badly at all."[39]

In Eastern Europe there was a time lag in the formation of gymnastics and athletic clubs. In Congress Poland up until the outbreak of World War I there were eight such clubs; by 1918 there were over forty.[40] There were also organizations other than national Jewish athletic and gymnastics clubs. Soccer, table tennis, weightlifting, and boxing were especially popular since, for many, other types of sports were unaffordable.[41] In 1936 the largest contingent of the Maccabi World Union, the international Jewish athletic association, consisted of Polish athletes, who accounted for more than forty thousand members. The group had been founded in 1921 at the Twelfth Zionist Congress in Karlsbad (Karlovy Vary), and its president was the German Jew Dr. Heinrich Kuhn.[42] The first Maccabiah Games notably took place in Palestine. The country's very first sports stadium was built for the games in Tel Aviv, and some 390 people from fourteen countries participated in this first international competition for Jewish athletes.

In Galicia it is not until 1908 that we can speak of a Jewish gymnastics movement. It was in that year that the first Jewish Gymnastics Day was held in Lemberg

Figure 10. Members of the Jewish boxing club Maccabi with the Goldstein Cup. Berlin, January 1932. Gift of John Gendal, Jewish Museum Berlin, inv. no. 2006/22/2.

(Lviv). German Zionist circles viewed Galician Jewry as particularly in need of improvement since large segments of this population were in poor health. In 1909 at the Fourth Jewish Gymnastics Day in Berlin, Josef Katz of Brody explained why in his view it was difficult to implement the idea of "muscular Jewry" in this Eastern European region: "Orthodox youth . . . in a sense pays homage to a type of ascetic view, with as much education and development of the mind as possible while completely ignoring the body. And the effects of this viewpoint are fatal physical ailments and mental disorders. . . . Naturally it is not easy to counter this view; it takes tremendous stamina, time, and energy."[43] Here he is of course criticizing the familiar ideal of the "cerebral" pious Jew, the *schejne Jid*. His suggestion to form an umbrella organization like the one in the German Empire was implemented only in 1912. The physical fitness program also had to be adapted to the health conditions prevalent in Galicia. There they opted for the Swedish system that was designed to train all muscle groups rather than the German model with its narrower focus on developing arm and shoulder muscles.[44] Gymnastics advocates succeeded in convincing even some Orthodox Jews to become members of gymnastics clubs. The *Jüdische Turnzeitung* report on the 1908

gymnastics exhibition in Lemberg (Lviv) noted: "There was particularly enthusiastic applause for one gymnast who stood out because of his appearance. This was
a young man from the Orthodox circles in the city. His deep black sidelocks
(*pejes*) curled in ringlets, he marched proudly and self-confidently, strapping and
full of energy, in the ranks of the gymnasts."[45] This segment of the population
nonetheless remained a minority in Jewish gymnastics clubs in heavily Orthodox
Galicia, despite all the efforts of Jewish sports officials. As Daniel Wildmann
shows with the example of Stanislaus Czyganiewicz (1879–1967), a professional
boxer from Galicia who was apparently quite the muscleman, not all "muscle
Jews" were created equal. Contemporaries thought his Herculean build was more
of an Eastern Jewish ideal body type, while German Jews looked instead to Greek
youths like the *Apoxyomenos* by Lysippos as role models.[46] Another Jewish strongman from Eastern Europe (Stryków, near Łódź, then Congress Poland) was Siegmund "Zishe" Breitbart (1893–1925), who was often compared to the biblical
Samson.[47] Known as the "Iron King" because he could bend horseshoes with his
bare hands, Breitbart had already shown remarkable strength as a child. This
strictly observant Jew trained as a boxer in the United States, then after the end of
World War I returned to Europe, where he amazed thousands of audience members with his feats of strength. He is memorialized in Werner Herzog's 2001 film
Invincible.

"Muscle Jewry," which according to Nordau was supposed to make the Jewish
body visible and improve the morale of the Jewish people, had—as we have
seen—connotations like "virility" and "masculinity."[48] Though in 1909 Nordau
himself had seen Jewish women perform vigorous gymnastics routines in Hamburg, for him *Muskeljuden* were primarily male Jews who embodied the collective.
Non-Zionist circles in particular took offense at women's gymnastics, as we learn
from reactions to the joint exhibition by male and female gymnasts at the Hamburg Zionist Congress. The *Deutsch-Israelitische Zeitung* in Regensburg condemned such behavior in no uncertain terms, stating that "this public display of
Jewish ladies is not in keeping with Jewish customs," which in turn provoked a
response from the *Jüdische Turnzeitung*: "The Jewish girl and Jewish woman have
no less need than Jewish men of thorough education and upbringing, so that the
coming generation will stand more erect and more powerful, and so the sense of
being physically inferior human beings, which saps all will to act, disappears."[49]
Several years earlier, Richard Blum (1878–1963), gymnastics squad leader for the
Berlin Jewish athletic club Bar Kochba, had published a series of articles in the
Jüdische Turnzeitung explaining the logic behind exercise for women and citing
examples from antiquity. He made no direct reference to Jewish women and girls,
but male and female readers of the club journal knew that Jewish women lagged
far behind their Christian counterparts in this area. In this context Blum also
mentioned the role of women in the modern working world with its growing

physical demands. Well-trained women were therefore a necessary part of the Zionist collective that was supported by the Jewish national movement. There was, however, still some debate over which gymnastic exercises should be reserved for women and which for men. We read in a commentary on Viennese female gymnasts' appearance in a 1907 exhibition: "It's difficult to know if you should be more impressed by the manly dash of the female gymnasts or the difficulty of their male exercises."[50] Apparently, though, not all Jewish women felt comfortable in a male gymnastics society. In 1910 the Jewish Women's League for Gymnastics and Athletics split from Bar Kochba Berlin.[51] By 1913 the female group had 181 members and was known throughout the empire for its fencing team. Several representatives of the Jewish national athletics movement were critical of this division, claiming that it represented "the spread of female body practices into areas that were understood to be male,"[52] but after 1918 this trend grew even stronger. Supporters of women's gymnastics all agreed that the physical strengthening of women would benefit their children and thereby Jewry as a whole, which dreamed of having its own homeland again someday.

Long before the "muscle Jew" could develop into the embodiment of Jewish masculinity in the early twentieth century, there were individual Jews whose impressive muscles and punching ability countered the prevailing stereotype of the Jewish body. Worthy of note here are the illustrious careers of Jewish boxers in late eighteenth-century England.[53] Daniel Mendoza (1764–1836) undoubtedly cut a remarkable figure: of Sephardic ancestry, he eventually became the English boxing champion, which at the time was the equivalent of winning the world championship. At the start of his career Mendoza beat two of his toughest non-Jewish competitors, the colorfully named "Harry the Coalheaver" and "The Bath Butcher" Sam Martin. In 1788 he won two out of three bouts against his mentor Richard Humphries, and as champion went on a boxing tour of England, Scotland, and Ireland. Despite his success, though, Mendoza remained an outsider in the world of British boxing, then still done without gloves. His triumphs and losses remained by and large a Jewish affair. Even at the pinnacle of his career he was never considered an "English boxer."[54] On the contrary, he had to confront anti-Jewish stereotypes his entire life. His wins were allegedly due not to power but cleverness, including his footwork technique in the ring, which had decidedly negative connotations. At the same time, his masculinity was never questioned (unlike that of his fellow Jews, who were said to have a "feminine" character), even by the anti-Jewish press. Photographs show that while he was not a strongman type, he was still decidedly muscular. What he lacked in muscular strength he made up for with superior technique. One contemporary admirer wrote that Mendoza, who had also authored a boxing manual, was "one of the most elegant and scientific pugilists in the whole race of boxers."[55] The writer emphasized that his boxing intelligence was what gave him the advantage in bouts against English and Irish opponents. Yet caricatures from the time still show the anti-Jewish stereotype that he repeatedly faced despite his wins. As historian Ruti Ungar puts it, "Jewishness and Englishness" remained mutually exclusive.[56] Though never acknowledged as a national hero, Mendoza did at least manage to become famous.

He was not the only Jew in the boxing ring at the time. Between 1760 and 1820 there were at least thirty Jewish prizefighters in the greater London area, including the well-known Aby Belasco (1797–1853?) and Barney Aaron (1800–1850). Most spectators were Jewish, though the chief rabbinate was not particularly happy about it, since more than once lurid advertisement for the matches had compared the boxing ring with the synagogue. In the nineteenth century, as the integration of the Jews into British society continued to progress, interest in self-promotion through boxing waned. Only in the early twentieth century in the United States did boxing once again become a "Jewish sport."[57] Between 1910 and 1940 there were twenty-seven Jewish world champion boxers; the best known were Benny Leonard (1896–1947) and Barney Ross, born David Beryl Rasofsky (1909–67). American historian Peter Levine has explored boxing's special appeal for Jews who immigrated to the United States via Ellis Island. His explanation: unlike a team sport such as baseball, the American national sport par excellence, a power sport offered Jewish immigrants from Eastern Europe a chance to free themselves of the image of the physically underdeveloped Jew and prove their bravery—a virtue that even today is highly prized in the United States.[58]

Any time a Jewish boxer stepped into the ring after 1933, it was also a fight against anti-Semitic prejudice. When American Max Baer (1909–59), who probably had only a Jewish grandfather but still wore a Star of David on his boxing attire, became world heavyweight champion in 1934, German Jewish Romance scholar Victor Klemperer noted in his diary: "Strange—what pleasure I gain from the report today that the Californian Baer won the world boxing championship against the Italian giant Carnera. Baer, who recently beat Schmeling, is a Jew. Yesterday our newspaper pulled him to pieces and did not give him a chance against the Italian.—So feeling comes to the fore despite myself. Baer = Samson = David and Goliath—bellum judaicum."[59] When the match scheduled for February 18, 1934, in Chicago between Max Schmeling (1905–2005) and King Levinsky (1910–91) was canceled because the Third Reich government refused to let the German fight a "Jew," the exile newspaper *Pariser Tageblatt* smugly commented that actually it was Schmeling who suffered as a result, "since in all likelihood the path to the world championship leads past a Jew, whether Max Baer or Levinsky, for this inferior, feeble race is not badly represented in the sport of boxing."[60]

In the 1940s and 1950s, when Jews had become part of the American myth of the melting pot and universities were gradually doing away with their quotas for Jewish students, economic pressure to use the boxing ring as a path to a higher social status declined. There were still some world-class Jewish boxers in the United States, but they now represented only themselves and no longer the group to which they belonged. Yuri Foreman, who became Israel's first world champion boxer in 2009, contradicts this trend. He was still aware that he had won the title not just for himself and his followers but for the entire Jewish nation. Foreman, who by then was living in the United States, declared: "There should be more Jewish boxers. We need to do much more against anti-Semitic stereotypes: that Jews are frail and so on. I am sure that Jews could player a bigger role in the sport of boxing. They are very inspired and have a rich history."[61] In the meantime Foreman had become a rabbi but had begun working on his comeback as a boxer. In an interview he describes his mission as follows: "Boxing makes me a better Jew, and my Jewishness makes me a better boxer."[62]

In this context it should also not go unmentioned that in concentration camps Jewish athletes secured their survival as boxers, as we see in the fate of Polish Jew Harry (Hertzko) Haft (1925–2007). In 1941 at the age of sixteen Haft was deported to Auschwitz. He survived thanks to his natural talent as a boxer, which he was forced to prove repeatedly in bouts between prisoners organized as entertainment by concentration camp directors. He managed to escape during one of the death marches in April 1945, and in 1946 won the Amateur Jewish Heavyweight Championship in a displaced persons camp near Munich. In 1948 with the help of a relative he finally emigrated to the United States, where he was able to start a new life as a professional boxer.[63]

Already in premodern times when for the most part Jews were still living in assigned quarters, athletic success allowed individual Jews to prove their masculinity when it was otherwise denied them as a group. An Austrian manuscript of the late fifteenth century mentions the "champion Ott the Jew who had been a wrestler at the court of the Dukes of Austria" (Maister ott jud der der hern von osterrich ringer gewessen yst).[64] There are, however, many indications that this fighter was a Jewish convert who got baptized for the sake of his career.[65] In addition, already in late medieval Spain and also the German Empire there were Jews who practiced fencing.[66] Here, muscle power was not absolutely necessary; physical agility and coordination were, in this case, equally important. Even contemporaries like Hans Wilhelm Kirchhof who were not particularly sympathetic to Jews could not deny Jewish fencers a certain masculinity. His story collection *Wendunmuth* (1563) includes the figure of a Jewish fencer "who is described and praised as such a quick, spry and sprightly fencer, and who in manly fashion—whether challenged or being himself the challenger—always won the match."[67] But these remain the spectacular exceptions. Until the late eighteenth century there were very few Jews who sports historians can justifiably call prototypes of the "muscle Jew."

In the last third of the nineteenth century fencing was taken up the by Jewish student fraternities in Germany, though usually not as a conscious effort to invoke a late medieval tradition. What mattered was publicly demonstrating that "the German student of Jewish faith is the same as, and accomplishes like his Christian fellow students."[68] Fencing with a saber was meant to do more than underscore equality with non-Jewish corps students; it also served to train a body that was perceived as weak. Especially after World War I, sports and gymnastics became increasingly important in Jewish student fraternities, not least because of growing anti-Semitism. Some of the groups even offered martial arts like boxing or jujitsu as a means of self-defense.

Nakedness

Human corporeality was central to the phenomenological thinking of Jewish philosopher Emmanuel Levinas (1906–95). He described nakedness as an anthropological phenomenon: "What is the meaning of shameful nakedness? It is this that one seeks to hide from the others, but also from oneself. . . . If shame is present, it means that we cannot hide what we should like to hide. . . . What appears in shame is thus precisely the fact of being riveted to oneself, the radical impossibility of fleeing oneself to hide from oneself, the unalterably binding presence of the I to itself."[69] There are different kinds, or, semiotically speaking, "variants," of nakedness whose forms are determined and influenced by historical, cultural, and psychological factors.[70] For historians, in contrast to ethnologists and cultural sociologists, real "nakedness" remains hidden behind a screen of conceptions about reality in different epochs as well as artistic and literary principles of representation. Unlike clothing, where we have at least isolated examples of actual (pieces of) clothing as far back as the Middle Ages, the "nakedness" of past epochs manifests itself in only two ways: visually and verbally, at least in the arena of European culture.[71]

The notion of shame seems especially pronounced in Judaism as compared with other world religions.[72] This applies first and foremost to attitudes about the naked body, whose biblical foundation is in the story of Adam and Eve. Before falling from grace, they appeared blithely unselfconscious and just as God had created them: "Now they were both naked, the man and his wife, but they had no feeling of shame towards one another" (Genesis 2:25). But after eating the forbidden fruit from the tree of knowledge, they became painfully aware that nakedness is shameful: "Then the eyes of both of them were opened and they discovered that they were naked; so they stitched fig-leaves together and made themselves loincloths" (Genesis 3:7).

Nakedness in the Bible is deemed shameful rather than obscene.[73] Even so, Judaism is not a "shame culture" as understood by Ruth Benedict (1887–1948), who used the case of Japan and the United States to illustrate the idea of shame and/or guilt as a means of social control.[74] Unlike drunkenness, nakedness in public (for example, to relieve oneself) is viewed in Judaism merely as unseemly behavior, not as a vice.[75] This does not change the fact that the behavior is considered shameful. It also explains why according to Jewish law someone can be punished or humiliated by having his body entirely or partially exposed. Behind the metaphorical threat of punishment by the prophet Hosea lies a proven corresponding legal practice:[76] "Plead my cause with your mother; is she not my wife and I her husband? Plead with her to forswear those wanton looks, to banish the lovers from her bosom. Or I will strip her and expose her naked as the day she was born" (Hosea 2:2–3). In ancient Israel as in other advanced civilizations in antiquity, slaves and prisoners of war were humiliated by being forced to appear naked in public.[77] The rabbinical interpretation of the story of Esther mentions this demeaning experience for a Jewish woman: "So too, at the feast of that wicked man, Ahasuerus, when the men began to converse, some said: The Persian women are the most beautiful. Ahasuerus said to them: The vessel that I use, i.e., my wife, is neither Median nor Persian, but rather Chaldean. Do you wish to see her? They said to him: Yes, provided that she be naked. . . . This teaches that the wicked Vashti would take the daughters of Israel, and strip them naked, and make them work on Shabbat" (BT Megillah 12b).

Even inside his own four walls a Jew should feel shame when he sees himself naked, as the Tannaitic commentary on the book of Deuteronomy (chapter 6, verse 9) shows. It says of King David: "He entered the bathhouse and saw himself naked—whereupon he said: 'Woe unto me that I am "naked" of mitzvoth,' but looking upon his circumcision, he uttered praise, viz." (*Sifrei Devarim* 36:9). Only the sight of his circumcised penis, which reminds him of the covenant with God, enables him to tolerate a situation that initially he himself found embarrassing—notably, no spectators are mentioned. Similar passages occur in the Talmud, where the devout Jew is advised: "Rabbi Abbahu said . . . : Three matters bring a person to a state of poverty as a divine punishment from Heaven: One who urinates before his bed while naked, and one who demeans the ritual washing of the hands, and one whose wife curses him in his presence" (BT Shabbat 62b).[78] The nakedness of a stranger also produces shame in Judaism and makes it impossible for someone to fulfill his religious duty, in this case reciting the Shema: "Rav Yehuda said: Opposite a naked gentile, it is forbidden to recite *Shema*. The Gemara asks: Why did the Gemara discuss particularly the case of a gentile? Even with regard to a Jew it is also prohibited. The Gemara replies: Opposite the nakedness of a Jew, it is obvious that it is prohibited; however, opposite the nakedness of a gentile, it was necessary for him to say. Lest you say that it is written about

gentiles: 'Their flesh is the flesh of donkeys' (Ezekiel 23:20), say that his nakedness is like that of a mere donkey and does not constitute nakedness" (BT Berakhot 25b). Here, corporeality begins in relation to the body of a stranger. One of
the ironies of German history is that neo-Nazi and anti-Semite Horst Mahler,
who first gained prominence as the defense attorney for the Baader-Meinhof
Group (the West German far-left militant organization founded in 1970), cited
this very Talmud passage in the criminal proceedings against him and others for
alleged incitement to hatred (District Court Berlin Case 522–1/03). In his view
this passage proves how Jews see themselves as "the Chosen People."[79]

Especially in the Hellenistic period, Judaism was forced to consider the corporeality of fellow human beings more than in the past since it deviated from their
own. Naked Greek athletes were barbarians in Jewish eyes. The Jewish writer
Philo (15/10 BCE–40 CE) did eventually accept this custom, but he still deemed
the regulation barring female spectators a wise one; in *Special Laws III* he writes:
"And it is fitting to praise those who have been the judges and managers of the
gymnastic games, who have kept women from the spectacle, in order that they
might not be thrown among naked men and so mar the approved coinage of their
modesty, neglecting the ordinances of nature, which she has appointed for each
section of our race; for neither is it right for men to mix with women when they
have laid aside their garments, but each of the sexes ought to avoid the sight of the
other when they are naked, in accordance with the promptings of nature."[80] In
synagogues from the Hellenistic period such as Dura Europos in Syria we even
find images of naked youths, women, and children, though the men are notably
depicted without sex organs. As with all visual representations, nakedness here
should be understood in the more precise sense of "nudity," which, according to
Kenneth Clark, is not a real object but an artistic form of expression.[81]

The public sphere is different from the private,[82] which under certain circumstances might also include the woman's workplace, namely, the house. The Mishnah allows a woman to sit naked on the floor when preparing bread dough since it
is possible for her to squat in a way that does not expose her genitals (Challah
2:3). Men cannot do the same in this position, so they must accordingly cover
their genitals with clothing. Given the climate in the Near East, it is easy to
imagine that men working in the field wore almost no clothing. But for prayer, a
devout Jew had to cover himself at the very least with straw or stubble, which in
turn applied primarily to the genitals (Tosefta Berakhot 2:14). As the seat of the
heart, the chest was also supposed to be covered. A man was allowed to squat
wearing almost nothing, but he did have to wear a loincloth or similar covering.
While the learned rabbis offered a compromise solution here, it did not change
anything in their fundamentally negative attitude toward nakedness. The justification that follows comes from a passage in Job, which admittedly had to be
reinterpreted as a metaphorical reference to the creation of the first human: "Or

who shut in the sea with doors, when it burst forth from the womb; when I made clouds its garment, and thick darkness its swaddling band" (Job 38:8–9). Thus, according to rabbinical interpretation, even the fetus is already clothed, since it is enclosed in the covering of the amniotic sac (Tosefta Berakhot 2:14). When a person stands before God in prayer, the appropriate decency and respect must therefore be shown by wearing at least a minimum of clothing.

In the past it was common—and not just among Jews—for people to sleep naked. However, a devout Jew had to observe several things when sharing sleeping quarters with someone other than his wife (Tosefta Berakhot 2:16). If two people were lying naked in the same bed, which at the time was not at all unusual, it was forbidden to recite Shema unless each of them had a separate blanket. If the bed was shared with underage children, however, reciting the prayer naked was allowed, with a cutoff age of twelve for boys and eleven for girls, according to the *Shulchan Arukh* (Orach Chayim 73.3).

Among the special situations in which nakedness is generally acceptable even today is a visit to a steam bath or sauna. In the changing rooms or other common areas some people may still be dressed while others have already removed their clothes. In this case, Jews may not pray, but they are at least allowed to use a greeting that commonly includes God's blessing (Tosefta Berakhot 2:21). In the Middle Ages, it seems, people were more prudish, at least in Orthodox Jewish circles, as a passage from the late medieval *Book of the Pious* suggests: "Even if no one else is present, you should not stand about naked, nor in the presence of others should you appear naked (above the hips) like workers who wear only trousers."[83] Simply closing his eyes to avoid looking at another person's nakedness does not help the devout Jew. Even the blind are bound by the prohibition against saying the required prayers if a naked person is present.[84]

If pedagogical guides like the *Brantspiegel* written in Judeo-German are to be believed, even children were not allowed to scamper about naked.[85] Parents were not to carry around or lay down an undressed infant if other people were present. It was important to instill the attitude of shame in children early on that would later be expected of them as adult Jews.[86] Yet in reality things often looked quite different in the *shtetl* because of the grinding poverty in many Jewish families. In the stories of Sholem Aleichem (1859–1916), for instance, children run around shoeless because their father has no money. As the famous dairyman Tevye laments: "God help me! The little house would be pitch-dark. My naked, barefoot kids would peek out to see if their schlemiel of a father hadn't brought them some bread, maybe even a freshly baked roll."[87]

According to Jewish law, anyone who offends someone's sense of shame must pay that person to make amends. Here, too, the Talmud goes into great detail and gives us a look at Jewish daily life in late antiquity:

The sages taught . . . : If one humiliated another who is naked, he is liable, but the magnitude of the humiliation felt when he humiliated him while naked is not comparable to the magnitude of humiliation he felt had he humiliated him while clothed, since one who chooses to be naked is less sensitive to humiliation. Similarly, if one humiliated another in a bathhouse, he is liable, but the magnitude of humiliation felt when he humiliated him in a bathhouse is not comparable to the magnitude of humiliation felt had he humiliated him in the marketplace. . . . The Master says: If one humiliated another who is naked, he is liable. The Gemara asks: Is a naked person subject to humiliation? . . . Rav Pappa said: . . . Naked? It means where a gust of wind came and lifted his clothes, and then this one came and raised them higher and humiliated him. . . . If one humiliated another in a bathhouse, he is liable. The Gemara asks: is one in a bathhouse subject to humiliation? . . . Rav Pappa said: This is a case where he humiliated him not in an actual bathhouse, but on the bank of a river, which is a place where people behave more discreetly when they undress. (BT Bava Kamma 86b)[88]

The Talmud authorities here differentiate between a place where nakedness is normal (a bathhouse, for instance) and a riverbank, where a bather removes at most his pants and can thus be undressed further, which is what constitutes the shame.

In Judaism it also matters whether it is a man or a woman who is naked. The nakedness of a man is an abomination in holy places, but in other places such as an open field it is merely unseemly and undesirable. In the case of female nakedness, God is not offended, but sexual morals are threatened, since the sight of an unclothed woman (which includes not only the female genitals but also unbound hair) awakens male desire and is therefore sinful.[89] If, however, a person should chance upon a naked woman about to drown in a river, he may set aside his moral scruples, but to the extent that it is possible he should still keep his eyes shut, as we read in *Sefer Hajira,* an ethical (Musar) text by Rabbi Jonah Gerondi (1200–1263) that was also translated into Yiddish in 1546.[90]

Men are warned repeatedly in the Talmud and the Hekhalot literature not to stare at naked or partially naked women's bodies lest they become sexually aroused.[91] This is also the reason for the rule against stoning naked women: "The Rabbis say: A man is stoned naked, but a woman is not stoned naked. The Gemara asks: What is the reasoning behind the opinion of the Rabbis . . . ? . . . The young priests in the Temple who saw her partially naked will become provoked by the sight of her" (BT Sanhedrin 45a). If a woman went out on the street bareheaded, or bathed with other people (that is, in the presence of men), her husband had to divorce her (see BT Gittin, 90b). A naked man, in contrast, was

welcome to use the services of a female aide in medieval and early modern bathhouses, at least according to Ashkenazi rabbis familiar with European bathing
customs of the time. Their Sephardic colleagues, however, had moral reservations.[92] The title woodcut of an anti-Jewish text entitled *The Jews' Bathhouse*
(1535) notably shows only half-naked male figures in loincloth-like "bathing
aprons" who could also have been Christians, since the typical Jewish body stereotypes are absent.[93] In Hebrew, "to have intercourse with a woman" is sometimes paraphrased as "to discover [her] nakedness" (לגלות ערוה).[94] Therefore, a
Jewish man may only see his own wife naked when fulfilling God's commandment. The sight of other women in a state of nakedness is forbidden, which is
explained by the following passage in the Babylonian Talmud (among others):
"There was an incident involving a certain man who set his eyes upon a certain
woman and passion arose in his heart, to the point that he became deathly ill. And
they came and asked doctors what was to be done with him. And the doctors said:
he will have no cure until she engages in sexual intercourse with him. The sages
said: Let him die, and she may not engage in sexual intercourse with him. The
doctors said: She should at least stand naked before him. The sages said: Let him
die, and she may not stand naked before him" (BT Sanhedrin 75a). This rabbinical prohibition was most certainly not heeded by the man in an illustration from a
fifteenth-century Haggadah who hid behind a pillar and watched naked women
romping in a fountain of youth.[95]

In the *Midrash Tehillim* 103:3 the Creator is praised for having given women,
unlike female animals, breasts at the same level as the heart so that a nursing
infant cannot see its mother's genitals.[96] If someone caught sight of a woman's
genitals, she was considered "shamed," if the metaphorical language of the Lamentations accurately reflects the reality of daily life in ancient Judaism: "Jerusalem
has sinned greatly, and so she was treated like a filthy rag; all those who had
honoured her held her cheap, for they had seen her nakedness. What could she do
but sigh and turn away?" (Lamentations 1:8). A Jewish woman may allow her
own husband to see her naked, but even in this case it must occur discreetly.[97]
According to the Talmud, children are born blind if their father has seen their
mother's genitals: "Rabbi Yohanan ben Dehavai said: the ministering angels told
me four matters: For what reason do lame people come into existence? It is
because their fathers overturn their tables, i.e., they engage in sexual intercourse
in an atypical way. For what reason do mute people come into existence? It is
because their fathers kiss that place of nakedness. For what reason do deaf people
come into existence? It is because their parents converse while engaging in sexual
intercourse. For what reason do blind people come into existence? It is because
their fathers stare at that place" (BT Nedarim 20a). In this same passage, the
wife of Rabbi Eliezer ben Hurcanus, a renowned Talmud scholar of the second
generation, explained that she had produced beautiful children because they had

had intercourse only at midnight, that is, in deepest darkness, and that her husband "reveals a handbreadth" of her body and covers himself up, so that he would not think about another woman during intercourse with his wife and thereby give his children "*mamzer* status" (BT Nedarim 20a).[98] In another passage of the Talmud couples are advised to have intercourse in darkness. A Torah scholar might darken the room with the help of his cloak (BT Shabbat 86a). The next generation of rabbis was less prudish and even insisted that marital duties be performed unclothed: "Rav Yosef taught the . . . closeness of flesh during intercourse, which teaches that he [the husband] should not treat her [his wife] in the manner of Persians, who have conjugal relations in their clothes" (BT Ketubot 48a).

In contrast, in the *mikveh*, or immersion bath used for ritual purification, women as a general rule must be completely naked; not even a ring or any other "barrier" may come between body and water.[99] In order to hide her nakedness from other women, however, the woman, standing immersed up to her neck in the water, should swirl it with her feet so that no one can see her body (*Shulchan Arukh*, Yoreh Deah 210.1). This was apparently a practice among Oriental Jews, since in his in-line commentary on this body of laws Moses Isserles (1525–72) adds the Ashkenazi custom: after entering the water, the woman must cover her body with both outer garments and undergarments so that her nakedness remains concealed.

Jewish visual sources confirm how, in this situation, nakedness is discreetly hidden from the viewer.[100] An early fifteenth-century Hebrew manuscript depicts a naked woman with arms extended at her sides and breasts bared as she immerses herself in the *mikveh* (Figure 11). Her genitals are concealed by waves in the water and can only be surmised.[101]

Christian scholars of Judaism such as Johannes Buxtorf the Elder (1564–1629) found it noteworthy that Jewish women entered the cold water completely naked to purify themselves after menstruation:

> When any woman of the Jews hath reckoned up the seven dayes of her uncleannesse, she holds on and addes seven dayes more of her purification unto them, after which time she finding her self thoroughly purified, she clothes her self in white robes, takes another woman with her, and goes to wash her self in cold water, and that so nakedly, that she not have her smock to cover her. . . . They are bound to dive so deep, that not an hair of their head be seen without the water: and in the mean time it is not permitted that they should altogether close either their eyes or their mouth, that the water may enter into both. They ought also to stretch their fingers, bend their body, that their Paps do not touch it, to dishevel their hair by combing of it, to have no rings upon their fingers, lest there

Figure 11. Naked woman in a *mikveh*. Illuminated medieval manuscript. Cod. Hebr. 37, fol. 79v. State and University Library, Hamburg.

should be any place in the body which might not be drencht in the water.[102]

Orthodox circles today use a variety of different practices for modestly dealing with the nakedness required in the *mikveh*.[103]

If a woman must appear naked or half naked in public, it is an intentional humiliation; of this Halakhah leaves no doubt. According to Mishnaic regulations a priest may tear the blouse of a woman suspected of adultery, revealing her breasts, but only if she is unattractive, since it might otherwise arouse the men present and thus have the opposite effect of what was intended (see Sotah 1:5). Late medieval Hebrew illustrated manuscripts were allowed to show Jewish female martyrs with bare breasts, since in this case the point was to emphasize the brutality of the persecutors.[104] As in Christian art of the time, no voyeuristic aims were intended.

Even as trial witnesses in cases involving sex crimes, Jewish women in the past found it hard to overcome their shame and admit that they had seen someone unclothed during the sex act. Only under considerable pressure from the rabbi did a Jewish woman named Freutel testify in a 1790 Gittlingen courtroom that she "had come upon Löser lying on top of Itzel behind the willow trees. The woman had had her dress pulled up and her petticoat undone; and the man had buttoned up his fly when she approached."[105]

If a woman wore her hair uncovered it was also considered a form of nakedness, and hence obscene. In the Talmud, Kimchit, the mother of seven high priests, is praised and asked why she had so many successful sons; her response: "In all my days, the beams of my house never saw the braids of my hair" (BT Yoma 47a). But even Jewish women were not always immune to the strong influence of feminine fashion during the modern period in the Diaspora. Wandsbek and Hamburg Jewish community statutes from the year 1687 required women and girls to cover their arms completely in the name of modesty and never allow them to be seen.[106] A late seventeenth-century ordinance of the Corfu Jewish congregation declared that women should be dressed in a way that showed no skin (לא יראה בשר). This applied primarily to those body parts that might awaken male desires.[107] Several decades later the Altona rabbi Jonathan Eybeschütz strongly criticized the fashion of low-cut necklines that also had its followers among female members of his community.[108] The sharpest critique came from the 1730 takkanot, or legislative enactments, of the Eisenstadt congregation, directed at what an Orthodox perspective deemed shameless behavior on the part of some women: "To heal the breaks of the time and begin to lead a holy life, the wearing of dresses with low necklines and bared shoulders in the manner of boisterous and bawdy women (he-minhag ha-prizot weha-sonot, actually strumpets and whores) should also be forbidden."[109] We get some sense of how popular these revealing garments were among Jewish women of the time from early modern Jewish ethical writings.[110] Tzvi Hirsch Kaidanover (d. 1712), the son of a Frankfurt rabbi, warned all female Jews in 1705 to dress modestly and not appear "naked from the neck down to the breasts" in public lest they invoke the wrath of God.[111] At around the same time, Jewish circles in England also took offense at female members in décolleté.[112] For the same reason a Frankfurt am Main clothing ordinance of 1715 forbade women to expose their arms.[113]

Even in the early twentieth century a revealing neckline was still frowned upon in Jewish circles, as we read in the following description of a visit to the Yiddish theater by Kafka's friend Yitzak Löwy (1887–1942?): "That completely transformed me. Even before the play began, I felt quite different from the way I felt among 'them.' Above all, there were no gentlemen in evening dress, no ladies in low-cut gowns, no Polish, no Russian, only Jews of every kind, in caftans, in suits, women and girls dressed in the Western way. And everyone talked loudly and carelessly in our mother tongue, nobody particularly noticed my long caftan, and I did not need to be ashamed at all."[114]

In the nineteenth century, a Jewish woman who feels no shame and appears naked is still a psychiatric case. The famed French psychiatrist Jean Étienne Dominique Esquirol (1772–1840) describes the case of a nineteen-year-old Jewish girl who crouched naked in the corner of her sickroom even in the winter.[115] It's interesting to note that already in the late Middle Ages, fools were depicted in Hebrew manuscripts as half naked.[116] In traditional Judaism, but to some degree in other cultures, too, removing one's shoes and walking in one's stocking feet in public is considered scandalous: in a nineteenth-century Yiddish comedy, for example, this course of action is punishment for inappropriate female behavior.[117]

Not even Jewish men were generally allowed to be barefoot on the street. The foot had to be shod. Orthodox Jews still today wear socks even in bed. If someone was too poor to afford shoes for attending synagogue, he received a donation of a "decent" foot covering, especially before the High Holy Days. On only one day a year should people go without shoes: the day of communal mourning Tisha B'Av, which commemorates the destruction of the first and second temples.[118] In the eighteenth century, however, exceptions were allowed in Frankfurt am Main, since for one, people did not want to anger or offend non-Jews with their bare feet, and for another, there was so much filth and garbage on the streets that, according to Joseph Juspa Kossmann (d. 1758), no one could be expected to navigate them without shoes on the walk to the cemetery.[119] It was not just the lower extremities that had to be covered; even the sight of a Jewish man with bare arms was considered an abomination in eighteenth-century Orthodox circles, as we read, for example, in the travel diary of Rabbi Chaim Joseph David Azulai (1724–1806).[120]

What applies to the (dirty) lower part of the body, namely, covering it up, applies all the more to the body as a whole. Men are even forbidden by Jewish law to be seen naked by close blood relatives. Here we recall the familiar passage in Genesis about the patriarch Noah's unintentional nakedness, a frequent motif in visual representations such as the corner capital at the doge's palace in Venice (Figure 12): "Noah, a man of the soil, began the planting of vineyards. He drank some of the wine, became drunk and lay naked inside his tent. When Ham, father of Canaan, saw his father naked, he told his two brothers outside. So Shem and Japheth took a cloak, put it on their shoulders and walked backwards, and so covered their father's naked body; their faces were turned the other way, so that they did not see their father naked. When Noah woke from his drunken sleep, he learnt what his youngest son had done to him, and said: 'Cursed be Canaan, slave of slaves shall he be to his brothers'" (Genesis 9:20–25). In the Talmud there is no consensus among rabbinical authorities on whether Ham's curse was solely the result of seeing his father's nakedness, or whether some type of sexual encounter had perhaps taken place between the drunken father and his shameless son. Either way, this Bible passage is of central importance for the Jewish sense of shame (see BT Sanhedrin 70a).[121]

Figure 12. Noah's drunkenness: relief on the doge's palace in Venice. Photo by Robert Jütte, 2015.

Another passage in the Talmud takes up this issue when it addresses the prohibition against bathing with one's father or any other male relative: "A person may bathe with anyone except for his father, and his father-in-law, and his mother's husband, and his sister's husband" (BT Pesachim 51a). Rabbi Yehuda, however, was of a different opinion, and permitted father and son to bathe together so that the son might honor his elder by aiding or waiting on him. The situation of a male teacher and his male students was similar. If the teacher needed help in the bath, this was expressly allowed. Ashkenazi Judaism took a more casual view of the situation in a bathhouse, where nakedness in and of itself was nothing unusual, since loincloths were commonly worn in the late Middle Ages and early modern period. This was noted by Hans Peter Duerr in his critique of Norbert Elias's views on shame behavior of medieval people.[122] The Jewish scholar Alexander Suslin ha-Kohen (d. before 1349) commented that the strict regulations of the Talmud (BT Pesachim 51a) were no longer followed at this time, since men wore an apron or breechcloth in the bath.[123] Roughly one and a half years later Moses Isserles took a similar view, declaring that the prohibition against communal bathing among male relatives or teachers and students was obsolete, since in the meantime it had become normal to cover the genitals with a cloth (Isserles on *Shulchan Arukh*, Yoreh Deah 242.16).[124]

Even so, issues can still arise today when a rabbi visits a sauna together with his students, at least in the United States. In May of 2015, the *New York Times* revealed a scandal involving the modern Orthodox rabbi Jonathan Rosenblatt.[125] For years, the popular religious leader had insisted that, after playing sports together, the young men in his congregation join him in the sauna—a place often linked with sexual temptation, and not only in the United States! There they ostensibly engaged in deep philosophical discussions about existential issues. Several congregation members found it unseemly that the married Rosenblatt and the young men sat together naked in the sauna. Some of the rabbi's former conversation partners, now adults, told the *New York Times* that these sauna discussions had made them extremely uncomfortable and that they had been pressured into them by Rosenblatt; at the same time, there had never been any kind of physical contact between them. After a heated discussion among congregation board members, a statement of support for the rabbi was ultimately issued, since he had not been accused of sexual harassment.

Same-sex sin also lurked in the bathhouse, as a permissive scene described in the medieval Jewish text *Alphabet of Ben Sira* reveals: "Once the prophet Jeremiah went to the bathhouse and saw that all who were in the bathhouse were using their hands to ejaculate. He wanted to leave immediately, but they did not let him. . . . They immediately took hold of him and said to him: 'Why did you watch us? Now you! You do it too!'"[126] The prophet was thus forced by the other bathers, who were presumably naked, to masturbate.

In death, too, nakedness proves to be a problem that requires a gender-specific solution. A woman may wash the naked body of a man, but a man is only allowed to perform this mitzvah on another man.[127] Just how unusual nakedness is in the context of burial rites can be seen in the 1724 will of court Jew and donor Lemle Moses Reinganum (1666–1724), an observant Jew who gives the "funeral brotherhood" the following instructions: they are to "lower me from my bed to the floor, remove my cloak and let me lie on the floor naked, without any boards and not on any straw. And I shall lie on the floor for at least one hour, naked on the floor, as I have commanded."[128] In no case, however, should an observant Jew be buried naked. Even during medieval pogroms following the Crusades when dozens of Jewish men and women were killed, the few survivors used donated clothing to make sure that those who had been murdered had a "decent" burial.[129] The charitable deeds that are part of the canon of ethical duties in Judaism already in antiquity, that is, predating early Christendom, include the commandment to not only bury the dead, but also clothe the naked: "Just as He clothes the naked . . . , so, too, should you clothe the naked. . . . Just as the Holy One, Blessed be He, buried the dead . . . , so, too, should you bury the dead." (BT Sotah 14a). When a brutal persecution of Jews took place in Strasbourg in 1349, however, no one was left who could have performed these duties and mitigated the desecration of the corpses. Sources indicate that before they were burned, the Jews were stripped naked by a mob apparently looking for hidden money and valuables. Only those who consented to be baptized escaped death.[130]

Male nakedness in the presence of women is scandalous in traditional Judaism, as shown in a 1756 case from the small Podolian town of Lanckorona. People on the street could hear noises coming from the house of Leibush and Liba Shabbetai, apparently followers of the Jewish sectarian Jacob Frank (1726–91), that suggested a lively party was underway. A curious passerby peeked in the window and saw "nude men and women frolicking and singing aloud . . . crying the praises of Sabbatei Zevi [whom many at the time still considered the Jewish Messiah]."[131] For both the Christian authorities and the rabbinical court, this was further proof that the followers of this Messianic movement led dissolute lives. Because of these alleged orgies, female Frankists were seen as prostitutes by their adversaries, and their children were considered bastards who should be avoided at all costs.[132]

It therefore sounds absurd when, almost two hundred years later, National Socialist propaganda paints shocking scenarios of a sexual threat to Aryans from the Jewish people's reputed tendency toward nakedness and shamelessness.[133] In the film *Theresienstadt* from late 1944, for example, a scene showing naked men in the shower is introduced with the cynical comment, "a steam room is available for the population." In contrast, historian Peter Gay (1923–2005), who emigrated with his family to the United States and thereby escaped the Shoah, describes how prudish even middle-class Jewish families still were in the early 1930s. He remembers exactly how he felt when a classmate told him that he had seen his mother naked in the bathtub: "a bit of wickedness that struck me as bold beyond imagining, let alone wonderfully, terribly obscene."[134]

To humiliate Jews by forcing them to be naked is not something first invented by the National Socialists. Late medieval and early modern Shrovetide plays include this form of punishment, if only as a fiction. To punish Jews for having claimed that one of their own was the Messiah, the knight in a Shrovetide play by Hans Folz (ca. 1437–1513), suggests:

> I judge, that every year
> we undress them completely bare and naked
> put each one under an outhouse
> let them get smaller for a day
> and then completely freeze over.[135]

In 1486 in Toledo, the Inquisition made female converts suspected of reverting to Judaism form a procession and, carrying candles in their hands, walk naked to the cathedral during an icy storm. The men in contrast were allowed to keep on their outer garments. They did, however, have to walk through the streets bareheaded and barefoot as the Christian population looked on in amusement.[136] At the beginning of the sixteenth century in Jaén, a fifteen-year-old girl was stripped by an inquisitor and then whipped naked in an effort to get her to testify against her mother, who was suspected of secretly being a Jew.[137] During the Chmielnicki pogrom in the Kingdom of Poland (1648/49), Jews in the area near the city of Uman were driven into open fields and made to wait there stark naked, according to an eyewitness account.[138] And in 1820 in Fez, Muslims stormed the Jewish quarter, plundered houses, tore the clothes off of women and girls, and raped them.[139] During the Jewish pogroms of the czarist empire, persecutors likewise made a brutal sport of stripping Jewish women and forcing them to walk naked in front of them.[140] In Argentinian brothels, where Jewish girls were brought after being abducted from Eastern Europe in the late nineteenth and early twentieth centuries, the women were made to strip naked and allow potential buyers to examine and probe them.[141] Nazi henchmen above all were known for shame-lessly humiliating Jewish men, women, and children by forcing their victims to publicly strip before being sent to the gas chambers or machine-gunned as they stood at the edge of mass graves. One eyewitness account that is representative of many others tells of a thirteen-year-old who survived the massacre of thousands on October 29, 1941, near the city of Kaunas:

> A young German officer spoke to us. "You are being taken to work camps in the east. First you will take a shower, and then you will get your work clothes. Get undressed and place your clothes here." He spoke in a civil tone of voice, and despite everything we knew about this terrible place, we let ourselves believe him. But every glimmer of hope was dashed when we heard the long machine-gun salvo and the screams. The Germans had also heard it, and aimed their weapons at us. "Hurry it up, you Jews! Undress

and off to the shower!" an officer shouted. "What you're hearing are just the trucks backfiring." But no one budged; no one seemed able to move a muscle. The officer calmly went up to an elderly man standing near him, raised his pistol, and shot him in the face. His head exploded, his brains splattering in the mud as he fell to the ground. Suddenly everyone was getting undressed. When you are that close to death every minute is precious, as if the next second might bring salvation. Finally we were all standing there naked, covering our shame with our hands and shivering with cold.[142]

Most people simply let this public shaming happen, since resistance was futile and was tantamount to a death sentence. Yet isolated reports do show that a handful of women resisted. When a group of women in Auschwitz was forced to undress, two SS members tried to chat up a particularly attractive woman. She took one of her high-heeled shoes and hit one of them in the face with it, took away his pistol and shot down the other one, whereupon the guards opened fire on all the women who were undressing in the barracks.[143]

Many survivors of the mass murder likewise experienced this forced disrobing as a trauma, as numerous Shoah memoirs attest.[144] Boris Lurie (1924–2008), who came to New York as a young man following the liberation of the camps, tried to process his traumas and obsessions in an unusual way by creating works that juxtapose pin-up and concentration camp motifs. In *Railroad Collage* (1963), for instance, a pin-up model bares her backside in the midst of gassed bodies on a freight car.[145] Media historian Sven Kramer has shown how shocking the naked body is in photo and film documentations of the Shoah, since it makes visible both the complete usability of a human being and the deceptive maneuvers preceding the act of murder. Recent feature films often visualize the killing machinery of the National Socialists by showing naked female bodies and thereby sexualize the Shoah.[146] This representation of naked victims is not unproblematic, as Israeli ultra-Orthodox circles showed in the mid-1990s when they protested against explicit—and, to them, offensive—images at the Shoah commemorative site Yad Vashem in Jerusalem.[147]

Orthodox Jewish prudery stands in sharp contrast to the casual attitude toward nakedness of the Zionist movement. An etching by Lesser Ury (1861–1931), created as a gift from the artist to the Twelfth Zionist Congress in Karls-bad (1921), shows the biblical Joseph among the Ishmaelites as a naked young man standing before a tent in the desert, hands folded in front of his genitals. Two men in capes and head coverings observe him.[148] Kibbutz settlements and their Zionist residents were known for their rather permissive attitudes toward sex, which broke with Jewish tradition.[149] Girls and boys showered together in

Figure 13. Boris Lurie, *Railroad to America*. Collage on canvas, 1963. © Boris Lurie Art Foundation, New York.

daycare centers; nakedness was part of an educational program. In his 2008 novel *Die Krankheit der Dichter oder Hoffmanns Erzählungen* (The Poets' Illness or Tales of Hoffmann), Israeli literary scholar and author Reuven Kritz describes how a Jewish boy named Joy falls in love with a girl his age whom he first saw naked in the communal shower of the kibbutz. For survivors of the Shoah, this casualness was often a problem, as autobiographical comments like the following attest: "In the kibbutz it was common for boys and girls to shower together naked," recalls Polish-born Moshe Schwarz. "For me that was an unbearable situation. For as long as I could remember, my mother had warned me against being seen naked."[150] When Viennese Jew Sonia Wachstein visited Palestine in 1938 and there lived for a short time in a kibbutz, she joined an excursion where the men bathed naked in a desert watering hole while the women still wore bathing suits.[151]

Though public nakedness is not officially allowed in Israel even today, it is now possible to find nude beaches throughout the country. Nonetheless, the enduring effect of the traditional Jewish taboo against nakedness can still be felt in post-Zionist society.

Head Coverings

Wearing a head covering is yet another way to express corporeality. This is especially true with regard to Judaism.

Observant Jews today are recognizable primarily by the *kippah* (skullcap) and/or dark hats they wear in public. Even so, only insiders are able to differentiate between all the different subgroups (of ultra-Orthodox groups in particular) based on such accessories. It depends not least on the proper combination of hat, stockings, style of beard, and sidelocks.

As for hats, nuanced differences in such things as the brim, hatband, height, and material give information about which particular Hasidic movement the wearer belongs to.[152] For instance, followers of the Belz and the Vizhnitz rabbis wear the same hat, but one group wears the hatband bow on the left, the other on the right. The raw material is usually felt, and the felted material is usually hare or rabbit fur from Spain or Eastern Europe. In several ultra-Orthodox circles, boys may wear a hat immediately following their bar mitzvahs at the age of thirteen, while other Haredi groups allow a Jewish man to wear a hat only once he is married as a sign of his new social status. The most elegant shape is the homburg, which is reserved for elite scholars and highly respected rabbis.

Under the hat, men usually wear a less conspicuous head covering, the *kippah*. This doubling is of fairly recent provenance. It is a nineteenth-century reaction of the Jewish Orthodoxy to the liberalization of the commandment that an observant Jew must cover his head. Among the first to come out in support of this combination was the esteemed Belz rabbi Joshua ben Shalom Rokeach (1825–94). When asked why he did this, he allegedly replied that there are two kinds of fear of God (יראה), a lower and an upper.[153] In contrast, numerous sources show that the practice of wearing only the smaller type of Jewish head covering, a circular cloth or leather cap, especially instead of a hat, existed already in the eighteenth century.[154]

The National Socialist image of the Jew was shaped by the appearance of Orthodox Jews, who in addition to wearing caftans, beards, and sidelocks also wore black hats. Since many German Jews were members of the Reform movement and therefore wore no traditional head covering in public, on the *Reichspogromnacht* of November 9, 1938, the National Socialists made a brutal joke of forcibly placing the hats of rabbis and cantors found in one of the many plundered synagogues on the heads of the imprisoned Jews and thereby making them figures of public ridicule. This happened, for instance, in Augsburg.[155] Jews accused of being "racial defilers," who were driven through the public streets, were also subjected to additional bullying by being made to wear a hat with a banderole stating their alleged crime.[156] This public humiliation with a stigmatizing symbol recalls medieval legal customs, where non-Jewish criminals (userers and wizards) were made to wear a Jewish-looking head covering. In the municipal law of Ofen in the fifteenth century, we read for example: "and he [the person accused of wizardry] shall have a pointed Jewish hat on his head" (vnd eynen gespizten judenhút sol er haben auf dem haúpt).[157]

Jewish clothing is a particularly good example of the need to clearly distinguish between traditional clothing worn by a specific group on the one hand and clothing-related stigmatizing symbols on the other. The wearing of different Jewish badges such as the yellow ring, required by secular law under the influence of church synods and council edicts from the thirteenth century on, was most definitely perceived by those it affected as stigmatizing, as proven by documents including petitions to the authorities requesting dispensation from the obligation.[158] This was not true for other articles of clothing that were part of traditional Jewish garb.

Probably the most noticeable characteristic of a medieval Jew in terms of outward appearance was his hat. Initially this was, for the most part, a freely chosen mark of distinction with links to tradition (the question of its obligatory nature within Judaism will be discussed below). We can assume that at first, the wearers of such a commonplace item of clothing did not necessarily perceive it as negative. Only once people began to move away from traditional head coverings (even if only by changing their shape)[159] did the Jewish hat become a kind of stigmatizing symbol, since the decision to wear it became increasingly determined by others. In 1267, for example, the provincial synod of Breslau (Wrocław) required Jews to wear a pointed hat: "we likewise order Jews to once again wear the horned hat that they used to wear in this region, then boldly dared to set aside, so that they can be clearly distinguished from the Christians, as formerly specified by the general council. Should a Jew be encountered moving about without such a sign, he shall pay a monetary fine in accordance with the custom of the country."[160] Secular legal sources from the late Middle Ages likewise make the wearing of a Jewish hat obligatory. The *Schwabenspiegel* (Art. 214) states, for example, that "the Jews should wear hats in all places they are" (die juden sullen juden hüete tragen in allen steten dâ si sint). At the end of the fourteenth century, the Saxon Municipal Area law specifies that "the Jew shall not leave the synagogue without a Jewish hat" (der jude sal nicht uz der synagogen ghen ane judenhut),[161] that is, Jews should not appear in public without the typical head covering.

At a time when in many European countries Jews were required by law to wear a head covering, it was not yet a given that Jews covered their heads of their own accord as an expression of fear of God, as we learn from late medieval Jewish legal sources. In his manuscript *Or Zaru'a*, David ben Judah he-Hasid (end of thirteenth, beginning of fourteenth century), a follower of Kabbalah, commented that in France and Germany it was not customary for Jews to walk even four *amot* or cubits (about two meters) in public without a head covering.[162] Anyone who did otherwise was warned not to appear before the congregation because of his sin. At the same time, the devout rabbi admitted that a few Jews did attend synagogue bareheaded, just as Christians did when attending church.

The question therefore arises: how binding was (and is) the requirement that male Jews wear a head covering, and what differences in terms of time and place do we need to consider? The five books of Moses contain no clearly stated requirements, and debate continues even today in rabbinical circles as to whether this custom derives from a divine commandment (*Dat Moshe*) or merely religious tradition (*Dat Yehudit*).

In the Babylonian Talmud the custom of covering the head is mentioned numerous times, though usually only in connection with scholars or the performance of a religious act. A passage about how to define the term "dark-headed" indicates that not all men followed the custom: "only men are called: Those with dark heads. . . . What is the reason for this? Men sometimes cover their heads and sometimes uncover their heads. They can be called dark heads since, for the most part, they have dark hair which is often uncovered. But women's heads are always covered, and children's heads are always uncovered" (BT Nedarim 30b). The Jerusalem Talmud in contrast makes no mention whatsoever of the topic, since in its sphere of influence, ancient Palestine, apparently even scholars said their prayers bareheaded. This difference is underscored in a Hebrew text from the eighth century that talks about the various religious schools. It mentions, for example, that in Babylon the priest may give a blessing only with his head covered, whereas in Palestine he may also do so with a bare head.[163] Other sources do indicate, however, that in the Jerusalem Talmud's sphere of influence it definitely became an accepted practice over time to wear a head covering as a sign of fear of God.

Among those who represented the Babylonian tradition was the renowned physician and philosopher Maimonides, who writes in the *Mishneh Torah*: "One should not pray wearing [only] his undershirt, bareheaded, or barefoot—if it is the custom of the people of that place to stand before their most respected people with shoes" (Tefila and Birkat Kohanim 5:5).[164] Even so, in fourteenth- and fifteenth-century Spain, for example, wearing a head covering does not appear to have been required during prayer or Torah studies, as we learn from complaints and warnings of individual rabbis from this time in Toledo and other Spanish Jewish congregations.[165]

While the Sephardic tradition became firmly established in southern France, the situation in Jewish congregations in northern and western France as well as in the Holy Roman Empire of the German Nation looked different. Here, too, some considered the head covering obligatory, but we also find references by influential rabbis like Meir of Rothenburg (ca. 1220–93) to the custom as an act of piety (*midat chassidut*) only, not a binding norm.[166] Not until a good century and a half later did Israel Isserlein (1390–1460) declare that as a matter of principle a Jew may never appear in public bareheaded, and any who did could therefore be punished with exile. After noting that this practice is in accordance with religious tradition (*Dat Yehudit*), he also argues that a Jew who does not comply is guilty of imitating forbidden Christian customs. Isserlein did allow that, if necessary, a Jew might swear an oath without covering his head, and sleeping without a head covering was also permissible for a devout Jew.

Considerably more binding and influential than one such individual authority was the *Shulchan Arukh*. It acknowledges that Jewish scholars are divided on the issue of wearing head coverings: "There are those that say that it is forbidden to bring remembrance from one's mouth [that is, say God's name] with an uncovered head. And there are those that say that one should protest against entering a synagogue with an uncovered head" (Orach Chayim 91.3). But in a different passage, the legal text leaves no doubt that covering the head is a halakhic norm rather than a voluntary act expressing piety.[167] Yet Moses Isserles, whose commentary on the *Shulchan Arukh* was extremely influential especially among Eastern Jews, did not view it as an absolute requirement (notes to the *Shulchan Arukh*, Orach Chayim 282.3). His younger contemporary Solomon Luria (ca. 1510–73), known as Maharshal, drew a similar conclusion. In addition, he criticized Polish Jews for strictly adhering to the rules concerning head coverings, yet at the same time being lax about following sumptuary laws (*kashrut*).[168] That Polish Jews in particular clung so closely to tradition is partially explained by the fact that they did not live in ghettos and therefore came into contact with Christians more readily—hence the necessity of attentiveness to external marks of distinction. There was also a rabbinical justification: the above-mentioned prohibition against imitating non-Jewish customs.

In countries where it was customary for Jews to wear head coverings in the early modern period, a problem arose when princes and other dignitaries paid the occasional visit to Jewish congregations and houses of worship. In this case, ceremony dictated that those present remove their hats to pay homage. Some rabbis saw this as a clear exception, making reference to the specific Jewish prayer for the well-being of the sovereign.[169] In the early seventeenth century Leon Modena argued in a similar vein, noting that Ashkenazi Jews in Venice bared their heads in the presence of high-ranking city dignitaries as a sign of respect, especially since they, unlike their coreligionists from the Orient, had a normal hairstyle and did not need to conceal a shaved head under a turban.[170] The well-known Venetian rabbi seems to have followed this practice himself: the portrait accompanying the 1638 print version of his book on Jewish rites shows him with uncovered hair—at least in part out of obvious respect for the royal readership; the text had been written at the suggestion of Sir Henry Wotton (1568–1639), the emissary of King James I in Venice.[171]

Figure 14. Jewish traditional clothing in Nuremberg. Engraving, circa 1750. From
Andreas Würfel, *Historische Nachrichten von der Juden-Gemeinde* ... (Nuremberg: Georg
Peter Monath, 1755).

Aside from such exceptional situations, in the early modern period it became the established rule almost everywhere that observant Jews cover their heads for prayer and in public places. At first even followers of the Reform movement strictly adhered to this custom, but over time an increasing number of voices called the practice into question by pointing to its Oriental origins.[172] In the course of the nineteenth century, regulations began to slightly relax even in neo-Orthodox circles. Jewish schoolboys, for example, were allowed to forgo the traditional head covering during classes on secular topics.[173] After 1870, American Reform Judaism started allowing men to enter the synagogue bareheaded.[174] The situation in czarist Russia had a different look again: there, an edict of 1848 forced Jews to abandon all head coverings in public, including the *kippah*, which led to protests and resistance.[175]

Oriental Jews, who, as noted earlier, had a long tradition of wearing a head covering, faced no such problems or harassment. In Muslim society, where they lived as a minority, wearing a turban or a fez was simply part of daily life. It was only the influence of European Jews emigrating to Palestine that brought change to this practice that had long been a given.

In the second half of the twentieth century among Ashkenazi Jews—with the exception of ultra-Orthodox circles—the view of Rabbi Moshe Feinstein (1895–1986), originally from Belarus, gained influence.[176] Feinstein held that in certain everyday situations it was allowable to remove the head covering, though not for prayer or in the synagogue. He also commented on the issue of how much of the head needed to be covered in order to fulfill the commandment when the crocheted *kippah* came into fashion and also began to shrink in diameter. Up until today, wearing a head covering, no matter what shape (yarmulke, *shtreimel*, and so on), is a sign that a Jew feels himself bound by tradition. But as we have seen, this external sign of belonging to Judaism has never been obligatory and universally applicable.

Shortly after the German invasion of Poland in 1939, Jewish women were forbidden to wear wigs of either natural or artificial hair.[177] Even today the *sheitel*, as this hairpiece is called in Yiddish, together with the headscarf, or *tichel*, is the external sign of strict Orthodox Jewish women, as seen, for example, in Mea Shearim in Jerusalem or the Jewish quarter of Antwerp.[178] There are even nuanced differences between individual Hasidic groups, which can be seen in the type of *sheitel* as well as the wearing of additional headscarves and hats. What is this physical feature of a Jewish woman all about?

The religious custom for women to wear a wig instead of their own hair is of fairly recent origin.[179] Rabbinical texts from early Judaism do occasionally mention this type of hairpiece, but only as an adornment to a woman's hair, and as such regulated only insofar as morality is concerned. Hence we read in the Mishnah tractate on celebrations: "A woman may go out with ribbons made of hair, whether they are of her own hair or her friend's, or an animal's; And with frontlets or head-bangles if they are sewn, And with a hair-net and with a wig into a court-yard" (Shabbat 6.5a). How great the fear was (and not only in Judaism) that a woman's unbraided hair could have an erotic effect can be seen in a Talmud passage that lists possible grounds for divorce. According to this passage, a man may divorce his wife if she goes out in public with her hair showing. Debate among Jewish scholars continues to this day as to whether the issue is a biblical (*Dat Moshe*) or rabbinical (*Dat Yehudit*) commandment.[180] Arguments for both positions can be found in the Talmud passage in question:

> Pentateuchally it is quite satisfactory [if her head is covered by] her work-basket; according to traditional Jewish practice, however, she is forbidden [to go out uncovered] even with her basket [on her head]. R. Assi stated in the name of R. Johanan: With a basket [on her head a woman] is not guilty of [going about with] an uncovered head. R. Zera pointed out this difficulty: Where [is the woman assumed to be]? If it be suggested, "In the street" [it may be objected that this is already forbidden by] Jewish prac-tice; but [if she is] in a court-yard [the objection may be made that] if that were so you will not leave our father Abraham a [single] daughter who could remain with her husband! (BT Ketubot 72a–b)

Whether they were following a biblical commandment or a rabbinical regula-tion, Jewish women already in antiquity appeared in public only with their hair covered, as the Latin church father Tertullian noted approvingly: "Among the Jews the veil upon the head of their women is so sacred a custom, that by it they may be distinguished."[181] Since he, too, was unable to find a biblical command-ment as justification for the practice, he praised the judicial function of custom and tradition for this practice. Devout Jewish women covered their hair even at home, as seen in the aforementioned example of Kimchit, the mother of seven high priests, who asserts: "In all my days, the beams of my house never saw the braids of my hair" (BT Yoma 47a). Until the sixteenth century, married women (unmarried girls were the only exceptions) in both Ashkenazi and Sephardic regions wore a head covering of some style or another. It was not until the early modern period, when non-Jewish female fashion discovered the wig as a hair accessory, that Jewish women—especially in more well-heeled circles—had to go along with the trend. From then on, they too wore wigs made from animal or human hair. The halakhic question that arose was whether such a head covering met the conditions of Jewish modesty. Some women were sure it did; others, to be on the safe side, also wore a scarf or kerchief tied around their heads so as not to attract attention. For complete acceptance, though, a rabbinical decision was needed. Joshua Boaz ben Simon Baruch (d. 1557), a prominent Talmudist and author of a work entitled *Schiltei Giborim,* declared that a wig did fulfill the Jewish commandment for a woman to cover her head.[182] A short time later the authoritative Rabbi Moses Isserles followed suit, acknowledging in his comments on the *Shulchan Arukh* that this new fashion was consistent with Jewish law.[183] Even critics like Rabbi Samuel Judah Katzenellenbogen (1521–97) of Venice and Rabbi Jacob Emden (1697–1776) of Altona were unable to challenge his authority, especially in Eastern Europe.[184] When Lea Cohen, a Jewish woman living in Hannover circa 1790, got her husband's consent to wear a wig but met with disapproval from her father-in-law, she self-confidently declared: "My husband has nothing against it, so no one else can take offense."[185] Tradition-bound court Jew Isaac Gans (ca. 1723–98) stated in his will that his children should continue to wear time-honored traditional clothing, and his daughters should cover their hair with a veil, not a newfangled wig.[186] Even the younger generation had a hard time with this new development, as an example from the province of Posen from the early nineteenth century shows. Young Jewish men made fun of the new fashion by tying a wig to the tail of a dog and chasing it down the street "to the amusement of the men and the deep consternation of the women."[187]

When women's wigs in general went out of style in the late eighteenth and early nineteenth centuries, strictly observant Jewish women faced a decision: they could either wear a headscarf or veil—like Christian nuns—or keep the *sheitel* as a covering for their natural hair. Most of them opted for the wig, especially since in the meantime it had become a widespread custom in Eastern Jewish circles to shear a woman's hair before her wedding. In the time of the Talmud this was not yet the case. When the wife of Rabbi Akiva cut off her curly hair and sold it in order to finance her husband's Torah studies, her gesture was met with astonishment (JT Shabbat 7d). Maimonides even expressly forbade women to cut their hair so that they could not pretend to be men. Only in the sixteenth century do we find evidence that in certain Jewish congregations in Eastern Europe, women cut their hair.[188] The rise of the wig at that time may have been a contributing factor. In addition, a shorn head made complete immersion easier in the Jewish ritual bath, which for anyone with long hair otherwise required special preparation. At the beginning of the nineteenth century women were even pressured to cut their hair, which in turn led scholars advocating a *Wissenschaft des Judentums* (science of Judaism) to weigh in: they deemed it an expression of "false piety" rather than a divine commandment.[189] But such critical voices were unable to stop the *sheitel* from becoming—and remaining to this day—the deliberately worn sign of a traditional Orthodox lifestyle. At the same time, when Jewish women in Eastern Europe dared to put aside the wig completely or secretly wear their natural hair underneath it, some of them wondered when they became ill if God wasn't trying to punish them in this way for disregarding the customs of their forefathers.[190]

The first Jewish women to show their hair in public and demonstratively eschew the wig were for the most part married to representatives of the Jewish Enlightenment. Amalie Beer (1767–1854) was the daughter of Prussian court Jew Liepmann Meyer Wulff (1745–1812). In 1788 she married Jewish sugar magnate Jacob Herz Beer (1769–1825) and, like Henriette Herz (1764–1847), hosted a literary salon. The painting of Beer by Carl Kretschmar (1769–1847) from around 1802 shows a self-confidant woman with her hair uncovered.[191] Henriette Herz had likewise replaced her traditional bonnet with a wig at first, but eventually she eliminated that as well and instead appeared in public showing her natural hair.[192]

For the mid-nineteenth century even more evidence exists that even Eastern Jewish women abandoned the custom when they moved to the city.[193] When Pauline Wengeroff (1833–1916) moved to Kovno after her wedding in 1859, she noticed that she stood out because of her hairpiece: "I still always wore my *sheitel*. All the other women, including the older ones in our circle, had long since given it up. I felt uneasy but the thought never occurred to me to follow the example of other women, though I knew that my own hair could only set me off well. But it was not long before my husband demanded the removal of the *sheitel*. I must accommodate to the manners of the society, he said, and not make myself a laughing stock. I did not comply with his wish, however, and wore the wig for many years yet."[194]

Women long felt considerable social and religious pressure to cover the hair, with or without a wig, but a strong countercurrent also existed, and not just within Judaism. The czarist government forbade Jewish women to continue wearing their traditional head coverings. They were either to wear large bonnets or wear their hair uncovered. In 1871 the newspaper *Der Israelit* reported on a decree then still in effect in the Kingdom of Poland that any "well-to-do Jewish women" who shaved their heads would face a fine of five rubles. In addition, Jewish women were strictly forbidden to "use braids, imitation wigs of wool, etc., that match their hair color and serve to cover the hair, just as some women in Holland cover their hair with sheet gold."[195] Dispensations were allowed, but only if a fee was paid, which only the wealthy could afford.[196] Another solution, and one that was ultimately accepted by many Hasidic scholars, was to wear a wig that looked as realistic or natural as possible. More affluent women even had their wigs made in foreign countries, which enabled them to keep up with the latest styles.[197] During a series of visits to the Marienbad spa starting in 1907, Yiddish writer Sholem Aleichem recorded his impressions and turned them into a satirical epistolary novel, which included a description of how the "pious young women" removed their wigs upon arriving at the secular health spa.[198]

Given the popularity of artificial hairpieces in the female Jewish population, it is no surprise that Jewish merchants dominated the hair trade. That in turn incited anti-Jewish prejudice, as we read in sources from the time. A merchants' manual from the year 1708 says that Jews managed to get girls—primarily in the country, but also in the city—to sell them their hair "for a negligible amount of money,"[199] then resold it to wigmakers at highly inflated prices. The going price at the time for a blond wig is listed as sixteen to twenty *Reichstaler*, a considerable sum that only the wealthy could afford. Almost a century later the same criticism is repeated in the *Patriotisches Tageblatt*, where the author gives a detailed account of the suppliers' doings: "I found that the Jews are the actual agents and suppliers of the hair. They travel to cities with prisons and workhouses, and deal in the hair of prisoners; they travel in regions where war is being waged, wandering the battlefields after encounters and skirmishes. Cutting the hair off of corpses, which they collect in sacks and schlep to the cities of Germany to sell."[200] Here the writer not only accuses Jewish hair merchants of desecrating corpses, but also claims that those who purchase the hair earn more than the wigmakers. Yet even early on there were also Jewish wigmakers. In 1747 the Christian *perruquers* of Prague complained about increasing competition from Jews.[201] In 1931 in Birzai, Lithuania, where over 57 percent of the population was Jewish, there were still eighty manual laborers, sixty-three of whom were Jews (79 percent). These included eight tailors, eight butchers, six wool handlers, six shoemakers, four bakers, four wigmakers, two saddlers, a tanner, a coppersmith, and twenty-three others. All were organized in the "federation of Jewish artisans."[202] Wigmakers today are found primarily in Israel, where they specialize in the production of the traditional *sheitel*.[203] Generally speaking, this hairpiece is worn primarily by women of Ashkenazi descent. The wigs must be kosher, which means that they may not be made of hair obtained in connection with Hindu ceremonies, for instance, since Halakhah forbids the use of anything and everything "in the service of Baal" that could be seen as an offering to a false idol. When it was revealed in 2004 that a large portion of the hair used for Jewish women's wigs came from India, it sparked protest in Orthodox rabbinical circles; since then, the hair has been sourced from China and elsewhere. Among observant women who wear a *sheitel* as their hair covering in public, hair from Eastern Europe is especially popular since it tends to be fine and light-colored. An inexpensive wig lasts up to four years; a more expensive one, up to ten. In Israel, such wigs cost the equivalent of about one thousand euros. A shop also recently opened in Vienna that again produces kosher wigs.[204]

Not only Jewish women but also their husbands wore wigs for over two hundred years since they were à la mode. Trendsetters were the court Jews who early on adopted aristocratic fashions, as documented in the memoirs of Glückel of Hameln (1646/47–1724). Writing of her time in Metz after 1700, she reports: "when I first came here, Metz was a very beautiful and pious community, and the *parnassim* were all worthy men who verily adorned the council-room. In those days not a man who sat in the council-room wore a *perruque*."[205] It was 1715 when she wrote these lines. Thus, in only a few years French court fashion had caught on among leading members of Jewish congregations. In 1715 the Frankfurt Jewish community saw itself compelled to impose a clothing and luxury ordinance in order to regulate the wearing of wigs by men. Anyone wearing a white or colored wig would be banished. At bar mitzvahs, boys were strictly forbidden to appear in the synagogue wearing a wig when called to read the Torah for the first time.[206] Moses Mendelssohn (1729–86) faced completely different problems because of his wig. It apparently offended his fiancée Fromet (1737–1812)—this is at least what the enamored philosopher's letter to his future bride suggests:

> Nature meant man's hair to straggle every which way down his neck, yet we want it to be stiffly arranged. If, then, our time seems too precious to us to be wasted on daily visits to a hairdresser, we simply must invent some means to send our hair to the wigmaker and occupy our head with more important matters at home. This is the advice, and also the personal example, I gave to our friend. One feels virtually bald with only one's own hair on the Sabbath and other holy days, and barely dares to appear in decent company.
>
> You will, I hope, approve of my oral defense of the wig's honor once I'm fortunate enough to see you in person.[207]

Most contemporary portraits of the court Jew Joseph Süß Oppenheimer (1698–1738) show him in a wig (Figure 15). He even wore one at his execution in Stuttgart, though the condemned man had expressly asked for simple mourning clothes.[208] Around 1750 some Jewish physicians had also come to look like Christian colleagues who were their social equals: they not only shaved off their Jewish beards, but they also sported daggers and wigs.[209] Already several decades earlier, the Prague Jewish congregation doctor Salomon Gumpert (1662–1728) had worn a wig befitting his social standing ("Quarée-Peruquen"); he did so in a parade to celebrate the birth of Prince Leopold on May 18, 1716.[210]

In the comedy *Henoch*, Jewish Enlightenment thinker Isaak Euchel (1756–1804) satirizes the wearing of wigs by Jewish men who blindly go along with this fashion: the deceived husband of a no longer strictly observant Jewish woman splutters: "to make her happy, I even put on a powdered wig" (Ihr zu gefallen, hob ich mir a gepuderte peruk ufgesetzt).[211] When the Austrian emperor appointed him chief overseer of Jewish schools in Galicia in 1787, Jewish *maskil* Herz Homberg (1749–1841) sent a clear signal of his assimilation by wearing modern dress and a powdered wig. He also no longer spoke Yiddish, only High German.[212] At the height of the Jewish Enlightenment in the early nineteenth century, the aristocracy had stopped wearing wigs almost altogether. Unlike Jewish women, who for the religious reasons cited did not respond to this shift in fashion, Jewish

Figure 15. Portait of Joseph Süß Oppenheimer (1698–1738) with a wig. Broadsheet with multiple images. Engraving, 1738. Wikimedia Commons.

men abandoned their wigs at that time and adapted their beard styles to those of their Christian surroundings.

Branding and Tattoos

Although *simmern*, the term for branding in underworld slang, derives from Hebrew (*siman* = sign),[213] up until the modern period the only Jews who were marked in this brutal way were those who were to be identifiable as criminals. This, however, made them dishonest only in the eyes of Christian society, not in the eyes of their fellow Jews, as we learn from trials involving Jewish robber bands.[214]

As long as it does not involve members of its own religion, Judaism did and does not take issue with the practice of branding the skin. Researchers have long known that in Aramaic times the slaves of Jews were branded with the names of their owners.[215] In the early modern period this was still the case in the colonies. In Surinam, for example, Jewish plantation owners used the abbreviation of their local congregation (Beracha we-Schalom) to permanently brand their slaves.[216]

Nor did Jews take offense at the tattoos of Jesus's followers, as sources about early Christianity show. Early Christians had Christ's initials "X" or "I. N.," a fish, a cross, or a lamb inked onto their foreheads or wrists, and for most these tattooed religious motifs served as an expression of their membership in the Christian faith. In the Babylonian Talmud it states that Jesus Christ himself had used sorcery by having magic symbols tattooed onto his skin: "Didn't the infamous ben Stada take magic spells out of Egypt in a scratch on his flesh?" (BT Shabbat 104b). This enigmatic Talmud passage has been the subject of controversy among scholars,[217] but according to Peter Schäfer, one of the foremost scholars of Judaism in late antiquity, comparisons with other sources from antiquity leave no room for doubt that the words "ben Stada" (son of Stada) refer to Jesus Christ.[218]

For an observant Jew, however, etching signs on the skin is expressly forbidden even today. "Jews Don't Get Tattoos" is the title of a poem by David B. Axelrod, but here the reference is not to the Old Testament. As the poem explains, American Jewish families in the first decades following World War II associate tattoos with "tough guys, anti-Semites." They also awaken memories of

> my grandparents' friends with
> numbers on their wrists—long
> numbers so you knew how many
> others died.

The poem ends on a resigned note:

> Others
> see art, a personal statement.
> I think it will be the death of me.[219]

Even long before the Shoah, Jews had problems when they saw tattoos, since already in the Torah there is a clear prohibition against making permanent marks or signs (*ketowet ka'aka*) on the body: "You shall not gash yourselves in mourning for the dead; you shall not tattoo yourselves. I am the LORD" (Leviticus 19:28). Another passage is similar (Deuteronomy 14:1); and an additional one specifically forbids priests from engaging in the practice: "Priests shall not make bald patches on their heads as a sign of mourning, nor cut the edges of their beards, nor gash their bodies" (Leviticus 21:5). They were to distinguish themselves from the people in a different way: "Make a rosette of pure gold and engrave on it as on a seal, 'Holy to the LORD.' Fasten it on a violet braid and set it on the very front of the turban. It shall be on Aaron's forehead; he has to bear the blame for shortcomings in the rites with which the Israelites offer their sacred gifts, and the rosette shall always be on his forehead so that they may be acceptable to the LORD" (Exodus 28:36–38).

In the Mishnah, tattooing is a punishable offense, and the punishment is forty lashes. Rabbis differentiate between permanent and temporary markings, however. Scratching the skin's surface (without adding coloration) or writing with (non-permanent) ink is allowed: "One who tattoos: if he writes without engraving, or engraves without writing, he is not liable for lashes, until he writes and engraves with ink or pigment or anything that leaves an impression" (Makkot 3:6). Rabbi Shimon ben Jehuda (fourth century) voices a minority opinion when he describes this as strictly a prohibition against engraving the name of God into the skin and one that differentiates Judaism from other ancient religions, whose believers had themselves tattooed with divine symbols.[220] A prohibition often refers to an existing practice. The following passage from the prophet Isaiah might refer to such a custom: "This man shall say, 'I am the LORD's man,' that one shall call himself a son of Jacob, another shall write the LORD's name on his hand and shall add the name of Israel to his own" (Isaiah 44:5–6). The Babylonian Talmud discusses the question of which "brutal deeds" of Jehoiakim, king of Judah (634–598 BCE), were meant in the Bible passage 2 Chronicles 36:8, and the conclusion is that it must have been a tattoo on his body: "Rabbi Yohanan and Rabbi Elazar disagree; one says that he etched the name of idols on his penis due to his devotion to them, and one says he etched the name of Heaven on his penis in a display of contempt" (BT Sanhedrin 103b). Moreover, Jewish scholars also believe that in ancient Israel tattoos to ward off evil spirits also definitely existed but were later prohibited by Mosaic law. The tefillin straps used even today by a devout Jew to bind the phylacteries to his arm and head have supposedly replaced this type of marking, which too clearly recalled the belief in false idols of neighboring peoples.[221] The Babylonian Talmud specifies the prohibition even further by including not only the purpose the tattoo (gesture of mourning, idolatry) but the way it is executed: "One who cuts an incision over a dead person, whether he did so by hand or with a utensil, is liable. Concerning one who cuts an incision for idolatry, if he does so by hand, he is liable, but if he does so with a utensil, he is exempt" (BT Makkot 21a) The passage is also noteworthy in that it indicates people were already using specialized tattooing instruments and not merely cutting their skin with their fingernails or something similar and then adding color. It was incidentally even forbidden to rub ash into wounds, since that might look like a tattoo (Tosafot, Gittin 20b).

As seen in the Talmud passage above, writing on the skin "without engraving" was allowed, and evidence of this practice is found in early modern amulets that show hands decorated with symbols and texts from the Kabbalah.[222] One Talmud commentary even says that a man may write the official document to divorce his wife (Hebrew *get*) on his hand, provided it is not done with permanent ink (Tosafot, Gittin 20b).

In the Middle Ages Maimonides justified the tattoo prohibition by noting that "this was the custom of the idolaters, who would make marks on their bodies for the sake of their idols, as if to say that they are like servants sold to the idol and designated for its service" (*Mishneh Torah*, Avodat Kochavim 12:11).[223] Rashi's commentary on the tattoo prohibition emphasizes the permanence of the marking (כתיבה בעולם). This passage (Rashi on BT Makkot 21a) has been invoked repeatedly up to the present to explain the rabbinical decision to allow cosmetic (that is, nonpermanent) tattoos such as those done with henna.[224] The influential sixteenth-century codex of laws, the *Shulchan Arukh*, confirms the prohibition on tattoos and makes exceptions only insofar as it makes free will the criterion for a punishable offense: if a person was forced to get a tattoo, he is absolved of liability (Yoreh Deah 190.2).

Because of this tattoo prohibition grounded in the Bible, tattoos are fairly uncommon among members of the Jewish faith, though the recent trend among American and Israeli Jews, both male and female, is to copy their peers.[225] The first Israel Tattoo Convention in 2013 had over one thousand attendees. The second such convention, which took place one year later, attracted four times as many participants.

Public discourse contains repeated warnings in this context that a tattooed Jew supposedly cannot be buried in a Jewish cemetery. This is clearly a black legend, long since debunked even by rabbis who comply with the regulation, since, as the relevant responsa indicate, far more serious sins than getting a tattoo are forgiven by God.[226] The fact that British singer Amy Winehouse (1983–2011), whose body was covered in tattoos, still received a Jewish burial, albeit a regular one, is further evidence that the warning is for the most part an empty threat issued by well-meaning parents. An entirely different question is whether or not an existing tattoo should be removed. This applies primarily to three groups of people: Shoah survivors, secular Jews who now wish to live traditionally, and non-Jews who wish to convert.

Figure 16.   Tattoo parlor on Shenkin Street in Tel Aviv. Photo by Robert Jütte, 2014.

The decision of Rabbi Ephraim Oshry (1914–2003) concerning survivors of Auschwitz was that they should not have their tattooed prison numbers removed but should instead consider them a "badge of honor."[227] The generation of Shoah survivors' grandchildren draws on this decision, even if unintentionally, by having numbers tattooed on their forearms as a sign of identification with grandparents persecuted and murdered by the Nazis and as a way to keep the memory of that brutality alive.[228]

For the survivors themselves, being reduced to a number was a degrading and traumatic experience. Most recalled the actual procedure carried out on Auschwitz prisoners after their arrival in the camp as not especially painful. Even so, as Primo Levi (1919–87) recounts in *If This Is a Man*, it had long-term psychological consequences:

> Häftling: I have learned that I am a Häftling. My name is 174517; we have been baptized, we will carry the mark tattooed on our left arm until we die.
>
> The operation was slightly painful and extraordinarily rapid: they placed us all in a row, and, one by one, according to the alphabetical order of our names, we filed past a skilled official, armed with a sort of pointed tool with a very short needle. It seems that this is the true initiation: only by "showing one's number" can one get bread and soup. It took several days, and not a few slaps and punches, for us to become used to showing our number promptly enough not to hold up the daily operation of food distribution; weeks and months were needed to learn its sound in the German language. And for many days, when the habits of freedom still led me to look for the time on my wristwatch, my new name, ironically, appeared instead, a number tattooed in bluish characters under the skin.[229]

In *The Drowned and the Saved*, also about his experiences in the Auschwitz concentration camp, Levi explains why despite such terrible memories he has not had the tattoo removed. Frequently asked why not, his response is: "why should I? There are not many of us in the world who bear this testimony."[230] Jean Améry, who suffered the traumatizing aftereffects of Auschwitz his entire life and ultimately committed suicide, likewise chose not to have the tattoo removed: "On my left forearm I bear the Auschwitz number; it reads more briefly than the Pentateuch or the Talmud and yet provides more thorough information. It is also more binding than basic formulas of Jewish existence. If to myself and the world, including the religious and nationally minded Jews, who do not regard me as one of their own, I say: I am a Jew, then I mean by that those realities and possibilities that are summed up in the Auschwitz number."[231] The writer and essayist, who had been born as Hans Mayer in Vienna, even insisted that the six-digit Auschwitz identification number 172364 be engraved on his headstone next to his birth and death dates. Elie Wiesel (1928–2016), an equally well-known Shoah survivor, also decided to keep his Auschwitz number. He explained to students at the University of Dayton in 2010: "I don't need that to remember, I think about my past every day, but I still have it on my arm—A7713. At that time, we were numbers. No names, no identity."[232] Ever since, Holocaust deniers and anti-Semitic groups have tried to prove that the Nobel Peace Prize winner was lying and that when he appeared in public in short sleeves, no number could be seen on his forearm. Prominent literary scholar Ruth Klüger, also a survivor of Auschwitz, decided otherwise and had the prisoner identification number removed, as she recounts in her memoir.[233]

As noted above, young people in Israel and the United States are now having numbers tattooed on their forearms as a way to keep the memory of the Shoah alive. This trend may have been prompted in part by performance artist Marina Vainshtein, who at the end of the 1990s had her entire body tattooed with numbers symbolizing the history of the Shoah. After a *Los Angeles Times* article brought her wider attention, Orthodox circles were quick to deliver a sharp rebuke, claiming that her body art was an insult to victims of the Shoah and a mockery of Jewish tradition.[234]

Even with a tattoo—according to the majority opinion of Orthodox rabbis—*teshuva*, or the return to religious Judaism, is possible, since the attendant risk of laser removal and/or surgical procedures is felt to outweigh the "sin" that was committed.[235] As so often in Judaism, maintaining good health and thereby human life clearly takes precedence. Even so, this liberal attitude has apparently not stopped Ethiopian Jews who have emigrated to Israel from having their tattoos removed with the aid of cutting-edge medical technology.[236]

Non-Jews who wish to convert to Judaism do need to clear several hurdles first, but they are not required to have existing tattoos removed unless they are offensive or obscene.[237]

Piercing

Piercing the skin so that rings, posts, or similar items may be attached to different parts of the human body is a type of body modification also familiar to Judaism. Two basic types should be distinguished: one for labeling a dependent person such as a slave as property and the other for aesthetic appeal.

According to Mosaic law, it was permissible to own another Jew as a slave, but only for a maximum of six years. The slave was then to be freed unless he wished to remain in the service of his master. In this case a special procedure was required: "then his master shall bring him to God: he shall bring him to the door or the door-post, and his master shall pierce his ear with an awl, and the man shall be his slave for life" (Exodus 21:6; see also Deuteronomy 15:17). The Babylonian Talmud gives detailed instructions on how this type of piercing should be performed and mentions instruments, including the spike, thorn, needle, auger, and stylus, which should be all made of metal. Even the place on the body is precisely named: "When they pierce, they pierce only the earlobe" (BT Kiddushin 21b). The only point of disagreement among rabbis was whether a Hebrew slave who wanted to become a priest could also be pierced. "No" answers were based on the argument that the practice made a person "prone to infirmity" and hence unsuited for the priesthood. Biblical exegetes have pondered the question of whether the ear piercing could have been a symbolic act intended to express obedience rather than the physical marking of a person as a slave. We do know that ear piercing as a sign of enslavement was also done by other Oriental peoples[238] such as the Mesopotamians (Juvenal, *Satires* 1.5.104) and the Carthaginians (Plautus, *Poenulus*, 5.2.21). In the cited Bible passage, the regulation about the way in which this person relinquishes his freedom likewise invites interpretation, since the ear (presumably the right one) is to be pierced against a door or doorpost. According to Christian exegesis, this is a symbolic indication that the slave belongs to the house and, by extension, the head of the household.[239] The Talmud, however, refers to the story of Passover and arrives at a different interpretation:

And Rabbi Shimon bar Rabbi Yehuda HaNasi would likewise expound this verse as a type of decorative wreath [that is, metaphorically]: Why are the door and a doorpost different from all other objects in the house, that the piercing is performed with them? The Holy One, Blessed be He, said: The door and the doorpost were witnesses in Egypt when I passed over the lintel and when I passed over the two doorposts of houses in which there were Jews (Exodus, chapter 12), and I said: "For to Me the children of Israel are slaves," and they should not be slaves to slaves. And I delivered them at that time from slavery to freedom, and yet this man went and acquired a master for himself. Therefore, let him be pierced before them, as they are witnesses that he violated God's will. (BT Kiddushin 22b)

Pierced ears were also a sign of membership in a specific professional group. In this case the piercing was voluntary, though a certain amount of social pressure may well have played a role. As we read in the Talmud, those who practiced certain occupations wore a sign of their trade in their ear:

As it was taught in a *baraita*: The tailor may not go out with his needle that is stuck in his clothing, and a carpenter may not go out with the wood chip that is behind his ear for use as a measuring stick, and a comber of wool may not go out with a cord with which he ties bundles of wool and which is usually placed that is on his ear, and a weaver [*gardi*] may not go out with a bit of wool [*ira*] that is on his ear which he uses for the purpose of his work, and the painter may not go out with the sample of dyed wool that is on his neck, and a money changer may not go out with the dinar that is in his ear. (BT Shabbat 11b)

While the preposition in Hebrew is clearly "in" (בְ) and not "on" (עַל), Rashi has interpreted this passage to mean that these professional signs were a clip-on type of earring worn in public places in order to attract attention (Rashi on BT Shabbat 11b). However, more recent responsa assume that these could instead have been piercings in the sense that we use the term today.[240]

We know from multiple passages in the Torah that women in ancient Israel wore earrings and nose rings as jewelry. In Genesis we read that at the well, Abraham's servant gives Rebekah a ring (נֶזֶם) for her nose as well as a bracelet. In Hebrew it is clear that the reference is to the nose (וָאָשִׂם הַנֶּזֶם עַל אַפָּהּ) and not the forehead (Genesis 24:47), which means that Luther's German translation of the passage is inaccurate. In another passage the prophet Ezekiel is clearly speaking about nose rings (also in Luther's German translation) when he compares the city of Jerusalem with a beautiful woman: "For jewellery I put bracelets on your arms and a chain around your neck; I gave you a nose-ring, I put pendants in your ears and a beautiful coronet on your head" (Ezekiel 16:11–12). While in Protestant exegesis it was well established already in the nineteenth century that rings worn through the nose really were meant,[241] Jewish historian Heinrich Graetz (1817–91) seems to have found it a terrifying thought that Israelite women might have worn nose rings like those of American Indians: "it is an indestructible mistake of archaeologists to hold that Israelite women from the Bible right up until the recent past wore *nose rings* in the pierced septum just as the American savages. That is how they explain נֶזֶם. Admittedly, it can also mean a piece of jewelry for the ears, but whether this was ring-shaped is not known. The jewelry נֶזֶם which is mentioned in connection with the nose was most decidedly not a ring, but a *small elongated round post* used to fasten the half-veil."[242]

In all of these Bible passages the references are to (semi)permanent piercings. The pieces of jewelry could be removed at any time, as we read in the story of the golden calf: "Aaron answered them, 'Strip the gold rings from the ears of your wives and daughters, and bring them to me.' So all the people stripped themselves of their gold earrings and brought them to Aaron" (Exodus 32:2–4). When Voltaire, who was known for his skepticism, expressed doubts about the truthfulness of this account, he quickly heard back from Jewish authorities that the amount of gold indicated could very well have been collected if the average weight of an earring was multiplied by the number of Israelites at the time. Other Old Testament passages also clearly indicated that such jewelry was worn in biblical times.[243] A side note: the quantity of gold and silver in earrings taken from Shoah victims may well have approached this biblical amount, as the careful notations of Nazi henchmen prove.[244]

A woman who committed adultery was punished and publicly shamed by, among other things, being stripped of her jewels and made to wear different clothing: "If she was clothed in white, they clothe her in black. If there were golden jewels on her, necklaces, nose-rings and finger-rings, they remove them from her so as to disgrace her" (Mishnah Sotah 1:6). An earring or nose ring leaves no lasting trace on the body; if it is removed, the opening in the skin will heal shut, though it could possibly leave behind a scar. To prevent that from happening, young Jewish girls often wore pieces of wood in their ears to keep open the holes that had been pierced, as we read in the Mishnah (Shabbat 6:6).

In the Middle Ages, a number of northern Italian towns had regulations requiring Jewish women to wear earrings as a Jewish badge instead of the yellow ring or piece of cloth that was obligatory for Jewish men. In Ferrara, a 1476 provision stated that Jewish women must wear rings on both ears, which were not to be concealed, but instead remain visible to all in public. This was intended to guarantee that the provisions of the Fourth Lateran Council of 1215 were being upheld. In fifteenth-century Perugia, Jewish women were required to wear either round earrings or two blue stripes on their veils.[245] In 1416 a Jewish woman named Allegra was sentenced to pay a sizable fine for walking on the street without earrings.[246] Prostitutes were also identified in this way in Italy during the early modern period.[247] It became a problem only once Christian women also began to wear jewelry in their ears, and even the sermons of Franciscan monks had little effect in pointing out that Jewish women, being uncircumcised, wore earrings so they could be distinguished from Christian women.[248] In the early sixteenth century at the latest, we find increasing evidence that upstanding Christian women now dared to appear in public wearing what had formerly been a stigmatizing symbol. Trendsetters included Bona of Savoy (1449–1503), wife of the Duke of Milan, and Caterina Cornaro (1454–1510), queen of Cyprus, who returned as a widow to her former home of Venice. What had once been a Jewish marker now became jewelry for affluent women with a taste for luxury. Regulations concerning luxury items and clothing in northern Italian cities had to be adjusted accordingly. As of 1585 in the Duchy of Milan, for instance, Christian women were allowed to wear earrings if they were not too elaborate.[249] In early modern Jewish communities in Germany, in contrast, earrings were never a government-prescribed mark of distinction between Jewish and Christian women, though a rogues' gallery did regard earrings as typically Jewish. There a baptized Jewish woman is described as "still going about Jewish-ly with ear-hangings."[250] Wanted posters from the late eighteenth and early nineteenth centuries occasionally even mention Jewish men from the criminal milieu who wear earrings.[251] Admittedly, these may well have been the exception, but it nonetheless shows that piercings for men have apparently had a long tradition, including in Europe.

It was not just in Renaissance Italy that Jewish women proudly wore valuable earrings, and the practice occasionally came under scrutiny from the Jewish authorities. On the one hand, they did not wish to provoke envy on the part of Christians, and, on the other, they had to be mindful of the commandment of *zniyut*, or propriety. Surviving documents from a 1662 trial in the Jewish Community Archives for the city of Prague show that earrings also served as valuable collateral in loans arranged between Jews.[252]

The custom of wearing earrings ostensibly found its way into Eastern Jewry only in the eighteenth century and was linked to a change in head covering.[253] The rings, worn on both sides, were worn in the pierced earlobes and/or fastened to the *sterntichel*, the traditional headdress of pearls and silver or gold that was sewn to a woman's bonnet (*kupkale*). Even young girls wore earrings, since it was believed that after death, worms would make holes in the earlobes of women who in life had never worn earrings.[254] Earrings also functioned as amulets intended to protect children (including boys) against premature death. Russian-born Hebrew poet Shaul Tchernichovsky (1875–1943) writes that his parents had him wear an earring after both of his sisters had died.[255] Since the nineteenth century, earrings (often with diamonds) have been a popular wedding gift in well-to-do Eastern Jewish families, as Pauline Wengeroff tells in her memoir: "Wealthy families sent the bride diamonds, earrings in particular; strings of pearls; and a golden chain— without the clock, however—which came into fashion only in the 1840s."[256]

Wearing earrings has a long tradition in Oriental Judaism as well. Manuscript fragments in the Cairo Geniza indicate how widespread this fashion was among Mediterranean Jews during the Middle Ages.[257] In Jerusalem at the end of the nineteenth century, it was customary among Jewish women to pierce the ears of even young girls.[258]

In contrast to its stance on tattoos, Judaism thus has no general objection to piercing, albeit on two conditions: neither the piercing of the skin nor the placement of a piece of jewelry in the opening may pose any health risks.[259] Already in the Talmud the issue of whether a person may injure himself is explored (BT Bava Kamma 91b). One group responds "no," the other says "yes." In the *Shulchan Arukh* (Choshen Mishpat 420.31), the later legal text, which for many rabbis even today is decisive in interpreting biblical regulations, prohibition is favored, but with one exception: "He who injures himself is free [from punishment] although it is not permitted to do so." At the same time, observant Jews who want to obtain piercings are warned not to treat this step too casually, since the self-harm is taking place not for medical but aesthetic reasons.[260]An additional reservation stems from the Jewish conception of man as the image of God (*bezelem elohim*, Genesis 1:27). This means that there are certain limits when it comes to body

modification. In view of today's various forms of piercings (gauges, nipple piercing, and so on) we really do need to ask to what extent this traditional biblical
notion of the body is still tenable. In this context, Orthodox circles invoke the
commandment of *zniyut*, or chastity and modesty, which continues to be applied
beyond specific questions of sexual mores. For the erotic connotation of women's
earrings is not to be lightly dismissed. It is for this reason that portraits of the *belle
juive*, or beautiful Jewess, include not only dark, flowing hair but often also large
earrings as a pictorial element, thereby giving the figure erotically charged "Oriental" traits.[261]

Chapter 3

The Sex of the Body

(Un)Equal Treatment of the Sexes

In *Jüdische Merckwürdigkeiten* (Jewish Peculiarities) by Frankfurt high school professor and Jew hater Johann Jacob Schudt, the morning prayer required by Halakhah of observant Jews is cited as an example of Judaism's low regard for women: "it is easy to see how little respect the Jews have for women, for upon entering the synagogue, men immediately thank God in their daily prayer for creating them men and not women."[1] The prayer Schudt refers to and even cites correctly in the original Hebrew is the blessing still recited today by Jewish men in Orthodox congregations. In English translation it reads: "Men—Blessed are you, Hashem, our G-d and king of the world, who did not make me a woman." The misogynist impression seems to be confirmed when we look at the corresponding words of praise recited by women: "Women—Blessed are you, Hashem, our G-d and king of the world, who made me according to his will."[2] Like men, women also thank the Creator, but in this case it is for making them according to his will and not otherwise. The different wording in the respective expressions of praise reflects an underlying division between the religious duties of men and women in Judaism. The positive commandments (*mitzvot asse*) in Halakhah distinguish between men's and women's obligations to keep those commandments. Women are fundamentally exempt from all commandments that must be carried out at a specific time of the day or year. The strict division between time-specific commandments and those that are not time specific, together with the fact that Jewish woman are not required to keep the temporal ones, thus provides the justification for excluding the female sex from public religious duties.[3] This privilege is also implied in the wording used by women to praise God in the morning prayer. Ideally speaking, a man interprets the additional obligations as a distinction rather than a burden, but this is only one of many possible explanations. We find many different interpretations of the way in which God made men and women different and gave them different abilities when he created them, both in rabbinical literature and in Jewish folklore.[4]

Special prayer books in Yiddish for women (*tkhines*), published in many different places beginning in the seventeenth century, provide insight into how the gender-specific variants of the traditional text were interpreted and organized.[5] An early edition of one such *tkhine* from mid-seventeenth-century Amsterdam explains the difference by noting that male and female bodies are not built the same:

Strengthen my bones,
So I may stand before You
In awe of Your Name,
To worship You
With all my heart
And with all the limbs of my body,
That You alone created.

You gave 252 Commandments
To Your children Israel to carry out,
And 248, that must be observed and kept,
As many as men have parts of their body.
And you have given to women,
To correspond with our four [additional] limbs,
Four Commandments of our own:
To kindle lights for the holy Sabbath,
To purify ourselves from impurity,
To divide the *khale* dough,
And fourth, to serve our husbands.[6]

Here, the difference between the sexes that finds expression in religious rituals is traced back to God-given anatomical differences. This means that the commandments for men and women alike are written, as it were, on their very bodies.[7]

As described in Chapter 1, the Talmud teaches that women have four more "limbs" than men. Judaism interprets this deviation from the masculine norm positively insofar as it grants the female sex particularly honorable and important religious tasks such as lighting candles at the start of the Sabbath—a duty that to this day may only be performed by women.

The *Midrash Tanhuma-Yelammedenu* offers a different interpretation of the additional commandments imposed by God on the female sex.[8] According to this text, the *niddah*, or monthly purification commandment, is penance for Eve's having robbed Adam of eternal life in the fall from grace. In doing so she committed a crime that must be atoned for; accordingly, the lighting of the Sabbath candles is a form of reparation for Eve's having, as it were, snuffed out the light of

Adam's life. In contrast, the production of bread for the Sabbath is explained with the help of a dough metaphor that draws on the story of creation (Genesis 2:6–7), and Eve thereby enters the picture once again, if only indirectly.

The fine distinction between the sexes is visible not only in the body, but, according to rabbinical interpretation in the Book of Books, the Torah, also in a single letter.[9] About the impurity of man we read: "Speak to the Israelites and say to them: When any man has a discharge from his body, the discharge is ritually unclean" (Leviticus 15:2). For women, the corresponding verse reads: "When a woman has a discharge of blood, her impurity shall last for seven days; anyone who touches her shall be unclean till evening" (Leviticus 15:19). The decisive difference lies in the preposition: מ ("out") (מבשרו [literally, "out of his body"]) is used for men; for women, in contrast, we find the preposition ב ("in") (בבשרה [literally, "in her body"]). Such nuanced distinctions are difficult to translate adequately, as passages like these from the New English Bible show.

Not surprisingly, anti-Jewish polemics of the early modern period often use the above-cited Hebrew praise in the morning Shema as evidence of Christianity's superiority over Judaism. Johann Christoph Wagenseil writes, for example: "even if we are hardly of a different opinion about the inferiority [*minime*] of the female sex, we Christians do not praise the male sex to the degree that he alone is granted the honor of being the image of God."[10]

The Jewish Enlightenment was also a contributing factor when hegemonic masculinity, which for centuries had also dominated Judaism, was first called into question.[11] With the development of the religious reform movement in Judaism in the nineteenth century, the different morning Shema versions for men and women became a bone of contention for progressive rabbis who felt this text was no longer in step with the times. Abraham Geiger (1810–74), for instance, held that the men's morning prayer gives women praise that is "unworthy" of them, and he asked the rhetorical question: "how can a woman with feelings have love of her faith when even the prayer expresses her inferiority?"[12] He rejected the traditional justification involving the different religious duties of men and women: "from now on let there be no division between duties for men and women unless they flow from the natural laws of both sexes."[13] In his view, "the social standing of the woman in Judaism [is] unnatural, since it is encircled by legal barriers that nature has not imposed on her."[14] Geiger was nonetheless a child of his time, since his thinking was still firmly anchored in traditional stereotypes concerning the sexes; he, too, presupposed the existence of biological differences between men and women that justify their different roles in society. At the third conference of German rabbis in 1846 in Breslau (Wrocław), David Einhorn (1809–79) ultimately proposed that the discriminatory wording in the prayer for men be removed altogether.[15] This was a radical departure, since early representatives of the Haskalah tended to have more moderate views in this regard, supporting only a different religious interpretation. In the early nineteenth century, for example, David Fränkel (1779–1865) explained the Jewish morning prayer for women with a reference to Isaak Euchel, who had stated that men thank God only that they "are not afflicted with the multifarious natural pains and discomforts" of women.[16] By midcentury such answers were no longer sufficient. In 1855 in Karlsruhe when a Reform rabbi was about to lose his job for eliminating the morning prayer that he found discriminatory, female members of the congregation protested. They had been happy that the "offending" wording of the blessing was no longer part of the religious service, since they saw it as an affront to "women's dignity and women's worth."[17]

Circumcision as Sexual Difference

Why it is that women are not circumcised, but only men, was a question posed already by Philo of Alexandria in *Questions and Answers on Genesis, III*. Philo cites two different reasons in his explanation. First, through circumcision God keeps the sexual impetuosity of men in check. And second—in keeping with teaching about procreation in antiquity—he claims that male semen is more essential to procreation than the menstrual blood of women. But to put a check on man's pride in his indispensability for the production of offspring, the superfluous "drive" must be cut off.[18] Notably, the question why Jewish men are circumcised while this sign of God's covenant does not apply to women attracted little attention in the rabbinical literature of late antiquity. It was only under the influence of Christian polemics that Jews began to take positions on the issue. In the mid-twelfth century, for instance, Rabbi Joseph Bekhor Shor wrote in a commentary on Genesis 17:11 that women also bear an external sign of the covenant: granted, not in the form of circumcision, but in their menstrual blood, which reminds their husbands as their period begins that during the days of the woman's "impurity," sexual abstinence is required by their religion.[19] The same explanation is given in an anonymous medieval text entitled *Sefer Nizzahon Vetus*, a manual about how to respond to anti-Jewish polemics. If asked why Jews only circumcise men, unlike Christians who baptize members of both sexes, the reader is advised to answer that women's specific way of handling menstrual blood is what makes them into Jews.[20] Incidentally, a different version of this argument can be found many centuries later in the work of Bruno Bettelheim (1903–90), who compares circumcision with menstruation from a psychoanalytic perspective.[21] In his view, circumcision is a "symbolic wound" that men inflict on themselves ostensibly because they are envious of women's ability to bear children. Thirteenth-century physician Jacob ben Abba Mari ben Simson Anatoli (ca. 1194–1256) felt that female circumcision was superfluous, since God had created women solely as "helpmates" for men and not as independent beings.[22] A polemical text by a

Jewish author known only by his first name Menachem argues along the same lines: in a dispute with a convert named Pablo Christiani, Menachem, too, defends the noncircumcision of women by saying that woman was created from Adam's rib and hence was actually part of the male body. Just as women were taxed in accordance with their husbands, male circumcision alone sufficed for the two of them.[23] In the early fifteenth century, Rabbi Yom Tov Lipman of Mühlhausen declares that although women are exempt from the commandment of circumcision, they are required instead to bring gift offerings after giving birth.[24]

In contrast, in Christian theology the issue of female noncircumcision was addressed already in late antiquity and continued to be a topic of discussion on into modernity. In his *Dialogue with Trypho*, church father Justin, known as the Martyr (ca. 100–165), points out to the Jews that circumcision is nothing more than a relatively unimportant sign:

> Indeed, *while Abraham himself was still uncircumcised, he was justified and blessed by God because of his faith in him,* as the Scriptures tell us. Furthermore, the Scriptures and the facts of the case force us to admit that Abraham received circumcision for a sign, not for justification itself. ...
>
> Moreover, the fact that females cannot receive circumcision of the flesh shows that circumcision was given as a sign, not as an act of justification. For God also bestowed on women the capability of performing every good and virtuous act. We see that the physical formation of male and female is different, but it is equally evident that the bodily form is not what makes either of them good or evil. Their righteousness is determined by their acts of piety and justice.[25]

An anti-Judaic dialogue between church and synagogue from late antiquity likewise focuses the question of why Jewish women are not circumcised, a condition that the author holds against the Jews. The church, personified as Ecclesia, gives the following critique:

> For if you say that your people is going to be saved by the sign of circumcision, what will your young women do, what will your widows do, what also the mothers of the synagogue, if you testify that circumcision has resulted in eternal life in the sign of the people? Therefore it is not becoming of Jewish men to have wives. For the men are circumcised, the women do not receive a foreskin; therefore, if you are saved by circumcision, they cannot be saved. Therefore you see that you can consider the men, that is, the circumcised ones, to be Jews; I profess, however, that the women, who cannot be circumcised, are neither Jews nor Christians, but pagans.[26]

The synagogue notably does not respond to this point; its answer focuses instead on a side issue, which may well be because, as noted earlier, rabbinical literature up until the Middle Ages took no explicit stand on the issue.

Hildegard of Bingen (1098–1179) approaches the question of why God does not expect women to be circumcised from a Christian and female perspective. She links it to a woman's role as wife and mother: "For a woman is not to be circumcised, since the maternal tabernacle is hidden within her body and cannot be touched except as flesh embraces flesh; and she is also under the power of a husband like a servant under his master."[27] Through her marriage, a woman becomes part of the covenant sealed between God and the people of Israel. Noticeably absent in this passage from her work *Scivias* is even the slightest hint of anti-Jewish polemic.

In the early modern period the question of why Jews do not circumcise their girls faded from view in Christian literature and did not reappear until the nineteenth century, when it resurfaced in anti-Semitic discourse. Already in the early 1820s the notorious Jew hater Hartwig von Hundt-Radowsky (1780–1835) polemicized against the Jews by ridiculing the practice of circumcision: "Circumcision itself takes place on the big toe of the right foot, and what is circumcised is called the foreskin (Latin *praeputium*), since it is located at the extreme tip of the human body. Only boys are circumcised; why not girls, too, I have no idea! Maybe for the same reason that Jews clip ducats but not pfennigs."[28] The poet Jean Paul (Johann Paul Friedrich Richter, 1763–1825), known for his humoresques, also draws an ironic comparison between coin clipping and the noncircumcision of Jewish girls,[29] but he does so without including a clearly anti-Semitic undertone.

In the nineteenth century, word spread of a curious incident that took place in the town of Forchheim in 1833. There, a Jewish mother had given birth in 1816 to a child who was presumed by parents and relatives to be female. Upon entering puberty, however, the child assumed to be a girl began to have semen discharges (pollutions). The parents were shocked, but allowed the child to decide whether to be baptized or circumcised. "Circumcision was the option chosen. In the presence of the municipal physician, the city surgeon and the rabbi, the operation was performed by a Jewish circumciser, and the former Johanna was given the Jewish man's name Baruch (or Benedict). This circumcision was easily done—since only a small piece of foreskin that hung to the side was cut away, hence allowing the newly named Baruch to survive the operation quite happily."[30] If a child who at birth was classified as female turned out later to actually be male, then the child was circumcised, even if it was at a later point in time. Conversely, as we see in the Forchheim case of sexual developmental disorder, even girls whose female sex was perhaps not entirely clear at first by no means underwent the procedure.

Since girls are not circumcised in Judaism, the name of a female newborn is announced on the Sabbath when she is brought to the synagogue by her mother for the first time after the birth.[31] This custom continues even today.

The "Effeminate" Jew

Social psychology teaches that identity formation rests in large part on autostereotypes, or self-concepts. Recall, for example, the debate—primarily in anti-Semitic circles—over the essay "Höre, Israel!" (Hear, O Israel!) by Walther Rathenau (1867–1922), published under a pseudonym in 1897.[32] With regard to the Jewish body, however, we need to begin by looking at clichés that non-Jews connected with Judaism. The terms "Jew" and "man" constitute powerful categories in that they emphasize and generalize specific characteristics and traits. The resulting stereotypes are by no means confined to utterances by old and neo-Nazis who openly admit to being anti-Semitic. The fact that in the mid-1980s someone who counts himself a member of the peace movement could still lament that modern-day Jews no longer revere the "beauty of defenselessness," then go on to interpret the Shoah as a "traumatic offense to Jewish masculinity,"[33] shows how enduring such sexual and racial stereotypes are. They are concepts that find their fullest expression not only in National Socialist propaganda but also in the works of Jewish writers known for their self-hatred, first and foremost Otto Weininger (1880–1903). The impact of Weininger's renowned work *Sex and Character* (*Geschlecht und Charakter*, 1903) (Figure 17) cannot be overestimated, for it seemed to confirm the prejudices against Jewish men that had been held by Christians for hundreds of years.[34]

According to Weininger, "the Jew is as persistent as the woman, but his persistence is not that of the individual but of the race."[35] In social psychology, the process of drawing a connection between a general category (together with all of the cognitive, affective, and connotative expectations it includes) and an individual person is known as hypothesizing. Perceptions about a group or an individual begin with the interpretation of a social situation. Out of this social situation, expectations and attribution processes arise, both of which are based on implicit hypotheses about the character and actions of the person in question. In this context it is important to realize that the term "Jew" understood as a general category actually refers to two such categories: it is just as much a category of sex—namely, male—as it is a category of race.[36] In Sander L. Gilman's view this represents an essential characteristic of Jewish identity formation, which was shaped decisively by the "relationship between the stereotype of the Jew and that of the woman (as parallel categories of the Christian and the male)."[37]

In Wagner's *Ring of the Nibelungen* the powerful, blond, battle-tested warrior Siegfried embodies the ideal image of the Aryan man. For Weininger, this legendary figure from German antiquity is, so to speak, the physiognomic antithesis of

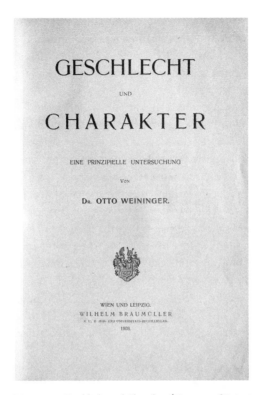

Figure 17. Otto Weininger, *Geschlecht und Charakter* (Vienna and Leipzig: Wilhelm Braumüller, 1903), title page.

the Jewish man, who tends to have "feminine" traits.[38] Weininger, a Viennese Jew tormented by self-loathing and misogyny, no doubt had an intuitive sense of Christianity's repeated efforts from the Middle Ages onward to cast doubt on the masculinity of the Jew. At the same time, Gilman is certainly correct in claiming that it was not until the late nineteenth century that the "antithetical figures of the Jew and the woman" determined the discourse on sex and race, a time when both groups began to "make substantial claims in the political world on the power held by the Aryan male."[39] At that time, women and Jews increasingly pressed to be admitted to areas dominated by men, such as the university, and to certain professions that had previously been largely off limits to them.

To understand what "being Jewish" meant for Weininger, but also for Sigmund Freud and other Jewish intellectuals in the early twentieth century, we need to trace the stereotype of the Jewish man's alleged deficient masculinity back to its historical roots. In the heavily Christian Occident, these reach all the way back to late antiquity. In his *Eight Homilies Against the Jews* (386/87 CE), John Chrysostom describes them as weaklings and uses the Greek word *malikoi* to do so: "For, as a rule, it is the harlots, the effeminates, and the whole chorus from the theater who rush to that festival."[40] With this slanderous comment the church father was trying to hit a nerve with the Jews by questioning their masculinity. Anyone who is a Jew or who converts to Judaism is thus no real man, and is placed on the same level as women, the "weaker sex."[41]

Also of interest in this context is when Jews themselves began to make use of this concept, which was long before it was thematized and popularized by Otto Weininger. In 1839, the German rabbi and Bible translator Gotthold Salomon (1784–1862) characterized the Jews as "effeminate."[42] Even earlier, Baruch de Spinoza (1632–77) felt he could detect a tendency toward effeminacy in his Jewish contemporaries. However, when the Jewish philosopher used the Latin verb *effeminare* he was referring not to a physiognomic appearance but instead to a lax religious attitude.[43] The "discovery" of the purportedly feminine character of Judaism was primarily the work of Jewish reformers of the first half of the nineteenth century.[44] In 1858 Rabbi Samson Raphael Hirsch (1808–88) declared: "the entire history of the Jews since the Fall of Jerusalem is nothing more than the triumph of the 'feminine' over the 'masculine.' "[45] Jewish philosopher of religion Adolf Jellinek (1820/21–93) followed the same line of thinking. In his view, the Jews clearly belonged to a group of races or tribes with feminine traits:

> According to an ancient Jewish legend, the progenitor of all humanity was created as a man-woman (androgynes); in other words, the first human being from whom woman was drawn, according to the Bible, at first contained the basic calling of both male and female creatures, which were divided at the time woman was created. In fact, the study of different tribes shows that some have more innate male elements, others more innate female elements. The Jewish tribe belongs to the latter, namely the series of tribes containing more female traits and at the same time representing femininity among different peoples.[46]

Jellinek attempted to prove the ostensible femininity of the Jewish people with the help of ethnomusicology. He claimed for instance that among Jews the bass vocal range was far less common than the baritone.[47] Only several decades later, such statements became grist for the mill of anti-Semites who profited from these early forms of Jewish self-hatred.

At the same time, the groundwork for this discourse—as suggested above—had been laid long before.

For Christians, from the late Middle Ages onward this stereotype of the effeminate Jew was closely linked with one particular image: the menstruating Jewish man. Though in the Middle Ages and early modern period it was widely believed that even a Christian man could become pregnant, the phenomenon of a man having regular monthly bleeding like a woman was—with very few exceptions—allegedly unique to Jewish men.[48] The connection between a physiological process that was largely a taboo subject and the "wrong" biological sex is a historical paradox. It shows that a deeply Christian society clearly had serious difficulty in trying to reconcile both the social and biological components of the expression "male sex" with the category "Jew." The Jewish man apparently had to be different from his Christian male counterparts already in a purely physical sense. No characteristic was better suited to express this distinction than a physiological phenomenon that not only combined taboos with purifying and exclusionary rituals, but was also inseparably linked to the female sex, namely, menstruation.

Thanks in large part to American philosopher of religion Daniel Boyarin, the discourse of masculinity has been broadened to include a consideration of Judaism.[49] Boyarin notes that "the feminine," which in non-Jewish eyes was for centuries seen primarily from the perspective of hegemonic masculinity, has no negative connotations per se. Feminine characteristics need not automatically be interpreted as a lack of masculinity. We should not equate a refusal to identify as masculine with castration and thereby a loss of the strength and superiority that are defined by a man's reproductive ability.[50] To support his thesis Boyarin invokes Jacques Lacan's (1901–81) distinction between the phallus and the penis and claims that despite its close link to Hellenistic-Roman culture, rabbinical Judaism or the Judaism of late antiquity was not a phallocentric culture.[51] Therefore, Jewish sources suggesting "feminization" need to be interpreted differently: in this context the term should be understood not as an indication of weakness but as an expression of the refusal to adopt the prevailing concepts of hegemonic masculinity in "pagan" cultures such as the Roman world. One example of this alternate way of thinking is in a passage from the Babylonian Talmud that equates masculinity with erudition and spirituality rather than fighting ability: "The verse states: 'To you men [ishim] do I call, and my voice is to the sons of men' (Proverbs 8:4). Rabbi Berekhya said: the word ishim, although it means men, is similar to the term isha, woman. It may therefore be taken to refer to these Torah scholars, who are similar to women in that they are physically weak . . . , but nevertheless, they act mightily like men when engaged in Torah study" (BT Yoma 71a).[52]

What is ostensibly true of rabbis and can still be seen today in Hasidic circles[53] even applies to Moses, according to Howard Eilberg-Schwarz, another scholar who has done extensive work on the history of the Jewish body. As proof, Eilberg-Schwarz cites two Bible passages in which the prophet adopts feminine traits, even if they are merely tropes or stylistic features. The first reads: "Am I their mother? Have I brought them into the world, and am I called upon to carry them in my bosom, like a nurse with her babies, to the land promised by thee on oath to their fathers?" (Numbers 11:12). The second passage involves the veil worn by women, which in antiquity was not limited to Judaism. In this case the feminine article of clothing serves to conceal God's splendors: when Moses descends from Mount Sinai, his face is so radiant from the glory he has seen that the Israelites cannot bear to look at it, so he covers his face with a veil (Exodus 34:33–35). Eilberg-Schwarz admits that the Hebrew term used here for concealment (מסוה, *masveh*) is not normally used for the veil of a woman; he nonetheless maintains that the very fact that a man is concealing his face with an article of clothing has feminine connotations.[54]

What began as a consciously constructed antithesis to the hegemonic masculinity of the environment in which Jews lived in the Diaspora was transformed into its very opposite by Zionism.[55] This at least is the standard view in gender research within the field of Jewish studies.[56] The "new Jew" was proud of his masculinity and proved it in daily life, but above all in battle. With time, this mythical valorization of the sabra, the Jew born in Israel and tested in battle, came under critique. The Israeli army (despite equal rights for women, who were nonetheless long forbidden to serve in combat) still continues to project an image that promotes this type of masculinity—the image of the strong man.[57] Meanwhile, the *rosh katan* (Hebrew for "small head"), in army slang the person not always in the first row on the battlefield, has entered Israeli society and no longer has negative connotations.[58] Whether this behavior is deemed feminine is a question that receives different answers at different times in Jewish history.

Homosexuality

Homosexuality—or, more specifically, men having sex with men—is described in the Bible with the expression *mishkav zachar* (משכב זכר), or, literally, "to lie with a man like a woman" (that is, to have intercourse).[59] Today Orthodox rabbis speak of *netja hafucha* (נטיה הפוכה), or a "reversed orientation" when describing a nonordinary behavior. In colloquial modern Hebrew, homosexuals are characterized as *hafuchim*, or men who are "the other way round."

The Torah leaves no doubt that homosexual relationships are strictly forbidden: "You shall not lie with a male as with a woman: that is an abomination" (Leviticus 18:22). Two chapters later, the penalty for doing so makes the gravity of the offense clear: "If a man has intercourse with a man as with a woman, they both commit an abomination. They shall be put to death; their blood shall be on their own heads" (Leviticus 20:13). Neither passage occurs in isolation; instead, each is part of a whole series of prohibitions against a wide variety of sexual practices such as incest. In such cases the Talmud threatens severe punishment (BT Sanhedrin 54a), but makes the following distinction: if two adult partners are involved and the action is consensual, both must die; otherwise only the adult partner or the rapist is punished.

As so often in the Torah, we learn nothing of the reasons for the prohibition. Both of the cited Bible passages that strictly forbid homosexuality simply brand it as an abomination (תועבה, *toeba*). The Talmud interprets it as sacrilegious behavior that leads a person astray since he prefers unnatural to natural sexual intercourse (BT Nedarim 51a). In Jewish exegesis, however, we do find justifications for the prohibition, including a reference to human nature, which God created otherwise (Genesis 2:24). The procreation commandment so central to Judaism is also repeatedly cited by rabbis in this context.

Feminine homosexuality is not mentioned in the Torah,[60] though a rabbinical commentary from the Mishnaic period (*Sifra*, Acharei Mot 8:8) does cite the biblical prohibition (Leviticus 18; Leviticus 20) with an eye toward lesbian practices.[61] The Talmud also speaks about sexual relationships between women, and while it does describe them as an "abomination," they are still considered a type of reprehensible "licentiousness" (*prizut*): "an unmarried man who has intercourse with an unmarried woman not for the sake of marriage renders her a *zona*, a woman who has had sexual relations with a man forbidden to her by the Torah, this applies only to intercourse with a man, but lewd behavior with another woman is mere licentiousness" (BT Yevamot 76a). Lesbian love is characterized by the rabbis as *mesolelut* (for example, BT Shabbat 65a); what this means in concrete terms we learn from later commentators such as Rashi, namely, the rubbing of the sex organs against each other.[62] Maimonides recommends that husbands take care not to let their wives come in contact with women having same-sex preferences. Otherwise he sees no need to punish lesbian behavior, since it does not entail sexual intercourse in the traditional sense (*Mishneh Torah*, Issurei Biah 21:8).[63]

The characterization of homosexual intercourse as sodomy well into the early modern period goes back to the following relevant Bible passage:

> Before they lay down to sleep, the men of Sodom, both young and old, surrounded the house—everyone without exception. They called to Lot and asked him where the men were who had entered his house that night. "Bring them out," they shouted, "so that we can have intercourse with them."
>
> Lot went out into the doorway to them, closed the door behind him and said, "No, my friends, do not be so wicked. Look, I have two daughters, both virgins; let me bring them out to you, and you can do what you like with them; but do not touch these men, because they have come under the shelter of my roof." (Genesis 19:4–8)

How God punished the residents of Sodom for this offense is well known. This is also referenced in a midrash that characterizes homosexuality as human misconduct before the Flood:

R. Huna said in R. Joseph's name: The generation of the Flood were not blotted out from the world until they composed nuptial songs in honour of pederasty and bestiality. R. Simlai said: Wherever you find lust, an epidemic visits the world which slays both good and bad. R. Azariah and R. Judah b. R. Simon in R. Joshua's name said: The Holy One, blessed be He, is long suffering for everything save immorality. What is the proof? THE SONS OF MEN SAW, etc., which is followed by, *And the Lord said: I will blot out man* (Gen. VI, 7). R. Joshua b. Levi said in Bar Padiah's name: The whole of that night Lot prayed for mercy for the Sodomites. They [the angels] would have heeded him, but as soon as they [the Sodomites] demanded, *Bring them out unto us, that we may know them* (*ib.* XIX, 5)— for intercourse—they [the angels] said, *Hast thou here any besides"* (*ib.* 12). (*Midrash Rabbah Genesis* 26.5)

A story similar to that of Lot occurs in Judges 19:22, which describes the rape of men by the Benjamites. At the time of King Rehoboam there were even male temple prostitutes in Juda: "all over the country there were male prostitutes attached to the shrines, and the people adopted all the abominable practices of the nations whom the LORD had dispossessed in favour of Israel" (1 Kings 14:24). In the Talmud, King Nebuchadnezzar is reprimanded for indulging in this vice (BT Shabbat 149b).

All of these passages from the Bible and Talmud suggest that homosexual behavior was either significant to the Jewish people only in prehistoric times or practiced only by neighboring peoples of the Israelites. The intensity of Judaism's aversion to same-sex relationships between men is expressed in a reference from a Talmud tractate. There, such actions are described as so heinous that even tribes that have only halfheartedly adopted the seven Noahide commandments at least keep one, namely: "they do not write a marriage contract for a wedding between two males" (BT Chullin 92a–b). Such marriage contracts were possible for example in the early Roman Empire,[64] but, as we see here, according to Jewish law they were strictly taboo.

Judaism's efforts to quasi-categorically exclude homosexual behavior from its own ranks can be seen in a passage from the *Shulchan Arukh*, one of Judaism's most significant legal texts, where we read: "We do not suspect Jewish men of lying with another man or with beasts. Therefore, we do not prohibit them from being alone with them, and if one wants to distance themselves from men or beasts, it is a praiseworthy thing. For the great sages (of old) used to keep beasts at a distance in order that they would not be alone with them. But in these generations because such corrupt people exist one should (therefore) try not to be alone with a man" (Even HaEzer 24).

At the same time, it is not inconceivable that in the Diaspora there were also isolated cases in which Jewish men had sex with men (*mishkav zachar*), but surviving legal sources, including non-Jewish ones, are noticeably silent about such extreme misconduct. Jewish moral teachings from the early modern period likewise mention the topic of same-sex love only rarely, and when they do, it does not include the threat of draconian punishment. Anyone who had committed such a sexual offense merely had to do penance by fasting and self-flagellation.[65] Here Judaism was at odds with its environment at the time, where homosexuals had to reckon with being burned at the stake. In the modern Jewish state, the same sodomy laws from the time of the British Mandate still applied at first, but following a court decision in 1963 they were no longer in effect, and in 1988 they were revoked entirely. As of 1993, the Israeli army has also accepted applicants regardless of their sexual orientation.[66]

Though sex researchers who studied homosexuality around the turn of the twentieth century had different opinions about its causes, they all agreed that penal law was an inappropriate way to solve the problem. Perhaps no one campaigned more vigorously to have Paragraph 175 (a provision that made homosexual acts between males a crime) stricken from the German penal code than the Jewish physician and sexologist Magnus Hirschfeld (1868–1935), who had openly acknowledged his homosexuality early on. He sent countless letters to politicians and testified as an expert in court, arguing that homosexuals should not be labeled and condemned as posing a "general threat." Already in 1898 he drew up a petition to abolish Paragraph 175 and included all the arguments advanced again later by numerous scientists and public figures against punishing same-sex love. To add weight to the petition Hirschfeld gathered over six thousand signatures. His political efforts were ultimately in vain, but he did accomplish one thing: from then on he was considered the leader of the homosexual movement. True to his motto, "liberation for homosexuals can only be the work of homosexuals," in 1897 together with publisher and writer Franz Josef von Bülow (1861–1915) he founded the Wissenschaftlich-Humanitäres Komitee (Scientific-Humanitarian Committee), whose goal was the repeal of Paragraph 175. To ground his political struggle in science, Hirschfeld published the *Jahrbuch für sexuelle Zwischenstufen unter besonderer Berücksichtigung der Homosexualität* (Yearbook for Sexual Intermediate Stages with Particular Consideration of Homosexuality) beginning in 1899. Also worth noting in this context is that fin de siècle caricatures of homosexuals frequently made use of motifs from anti-Semitic sexual satire.[67]

In the course of the twentieth century, religious attitudes toward homosexuality relaxed somewhat as a result of sociopolitical changes and insights gained from the scientific field of sexology. Within Judaism, however, this is true only of liberal branches.[68] In Israel, as well as in the United States and Western Europe, there are now Jewish gay and lesbian organizations. Their representatives contend that the Torah's strict prohibition is not entirely clear-cut and needs to be seen in connection with neighboring peoples' practice of male temple prostitution: this alone was what the men of Israel had to avoid in order to preserve the "sanctity" of the Jewish people. Homosexuality in the modern sense is, in their view, not the topic of these Bible verses, since same-sex relationships as we understand them today involve more than just a sexual practice; moreover, such relationships should not be labeled "unnatural," since, as they point out, God created each and every person in his own image (Genesis 1:27).

In recent years, Tel Aviv and Jerusalem have hosted gay pride parades that have attracted tens of thousands of participants from Israel and the entire world.[69] The highlight of each event is a wedding ceremony for gay and lesbian couples. In Jerusalem these parades have not always been peaceful. In 2015, for example, a female participant was fatally stabbed by an ultra-Orthodox Jew. Many same-sex couples also wish to have children, and in Israel there is already talk of a "gayby boom" that enlists the services of surrogate mothers from other countries. In Germany, Jewish gays and lesbians do not yet have their own congregations as they do, for instance, in the United States, but a transregional party does exist (Yachad, Hebrew for "together") that aims to promote tolerance and recognition within Jewish circles. These men and women who openly acknowledge their same-sex partnerships are increasingly visible beyond Christopher Street Day (the annual LGBTQ celebration). In recent years they were included in two separate exhibitions in Berlin: one in the Jewish Museum called "The Whole Truth: What You Always Wanted to Know About Jews" (2013); the other, a biographically organized special exhibit of the Gay Museum, "Lesbian, Jewish, Gay" (also 2013) that has since been shown in other German cities as well.

Knowledge About Sexuality

A look at the Talmud reveals a surprising candor among the legal scholars when it comes to discussing the body and sexuality: "Three matters do not enter the body yet the body benefits from them, and they are: Washing, anointing, and usage [*tashmish*], commonly used as a euphemism for conjugal relations" (BT Berakhot 57b). There is almost no aspect of sexuality that is not addressed already in Halakhah. That said, what matters most is always an ethical or moral issue relating to sex, not knowledge per se. An exception is the sex manual *Fi-'l-jima*, written by Maimonides toward the end of the twelfth century for the sultan of Hamat in Syria, a nephew of Saladin the Great.[70] In it, the renowned Jewish doctor and legal scholar gives a detailed description of how to increase male potency—the ruler's, in this particular case. The fact that this tractate, originally written in Arabic, also exists in Latin (*De coitu*) and Hebrew (*Ma'amar Hamishgal*) translation shows that its advice for a better, more fulfilling sex life was of interest to a Jewish readership as well. Maimonides's booklet might be described as a precursor to a contemporary best seller entitled *Kosher Sex*, whose title may raise more expectations in the reader than the content can actually meet.[71] Additional works of Maimonides—both medical and theological—also contain detailed passages on human sexuality.[72] Other Jewish legal scholars and rabbis followed him in writing marriage advice manuals that were equally frank, though on some points their opinions and recommendations differed from those of Maimonides. Among them was Abraham ben David of Posquières (ca. 1122–98), also known as Rabad.[73] Another well-known book of this type was the *Iggeret Hakodesh* (The Holy Letter) from the thirteenth century,[74] whose anonymous author refers to Maimonides when discussing human sexuality but is even more strongly influenced by the Kabbalah. Later, parts of what David Biale has termed the "erotic theology" of Hasidism were also added to this body of work.[75]

As in Christian literature, in Judaism "we are dealing less with *a* discourse on sex than with a multiplicity of discourses," as Michel Foucault puts it in his *History of Sexuality*.[76] Each of these discourses originates in a particular attitude toward the body. In the first phase, which lasted into the eighteenth century, the prevailing discourse on sex was what Foucault describes in broad terms as *ars erotica*. In the nineteenth century, this gave way to what he terms *scientia sexualia* as society "pursued the task of producing true discourses concerning sex,"[77] a task in which Jewish physicians played a decisive role.

Prior to 1907 no comprehensive, generally applicable term existed for research on sexuality, a field that initially focused mainly on anomalous and/or abnormal phenomena, which at the time meant, above all, masturbation and same-sex desire.[78] This changed with the publication of *Das Sexualleben unserer Zeit* (The Sexual Life of Our Time) by Iwan Bloch (1872–1922). It's in this text that the term "science of sexuality," so familiar to us today, was first introduced. Bloch, a Berlin dermatologist from a Jewish family, attended the Kaiser Wilhelm high school in Hannover, and later studied medicine in Bonn, Heidelberg, Berlin, and Würzburg, where he earned his doctorate in 1896. Together with Magnus Hirschfeld, also of Jewish descent, Bloch is considered Germany's best-known sexologist. From the very start he emphasized the interdisciplinarity of the field he had helped to found. In the preface to the first edition of this now standard work of modern sexology he writes: "To do justice to the whole importance of love in the life of the individual and in that of society, and in relation to the evolution of human civilization, this particular branch of inquiry must be treated in its proper subordination as a part of the general science of mankind, which is constituted by a union of all other sciences—of general biology, anthropology and ethnology, philosophy and psychology, the history of literature, and the entire history of civilization."[79]

Bloch's theoretical and methodological considerations served as reference points for Magnus Hirschfeld, who was occasionally referred to as the "Einstein of sexuality."[80] The journal he founded in 1908, *Zeitschrift für Sexualität* (Journal of Sexuality), also underscored the interdisciplinary nature of the field, and in its first year of publication it included two programmatic essays on the organization and methods of the science of sex. Hirschfeld included research in fields ranging from anatomy to psychology and ethics, and in addition to the descriptive method preferred in earlier scientific work on sex, he added the scientific method (measurements, lab experiments, and so on). Hirschfeld also acknowledged the value of statistics and surveys and realized how useful historical and ethnographic studies might also be in contributing to greater knowledge about sexuality. He was somewhat skeptical, or at least reticent, on the topic of Freudian psychoanalysis.

As early as 1896 Hirschfeld wrote in his diary that he someday hoped to found an "institute for the scientific exploration of the entirety of human love life from biological, medical, ethnological, cultural, and forensic perspectives."[81] The wish did not become a reality until 1919. On July 6, the institute was officially opened in a Tiergarten villa that Hirschfeld had recently acquired for this purpose. Located in one of Berlin's most desirable residential neighborhoods, the institute conducted research in areas including biological, pathological, sociological, and ethnological aspects of human sexuality. A wide variety of activities were undertaken already in its first year of existence; among those noted in the institute's annual report for that year were counseling services for engaged couples, public discussion forums and lectures on topics in sexology, and providing expert opinions in legal cases.

In short, it would be impossible to overstate the achievements of the Institute for Sexual Science, which long served as the sole research institute of its kind in the entire world. In under a decade it grew into the leading center for research, working in cooperation with almost all leading sex researchers and providing help and support to a tremendous number of people with the widest variety of sexual problems imaginable. When the National Socialists came to power, however, the fate of the internationally renowned institute was sealed.

Among the things needed for a new or fledgling scientific field to become established and institutionalized is the staunch support of the scientific community, a community in which Jewish scientists and physicians long enjoyed a strong presence. The first professional organization in this field was the Ärztliche Gesellschaft für Sexualwissenschaft und Eugenik (Medical Society for Sexology and Eugenics), founded on February 21, 1913. Led by the above-mentioned pioneers in the field Iwan Bloch and Magnus Hirschfeld, its members included the psychiatrist Wilhelm Fließ (1858–1928), which in turn prompted Sigmund Freud not to join the group, since he had quarreled with him.

In 1926 the second, considerably expanded edition of Marcuse's standard work on sexual science was published. Today this groundbreaking work, subtitled a "complete encyclopedia of the sexual sciences," is considered a classic text in the field of sexology. Entries include pioneering contributions by sex researchers, psychiatrists, sociologists, and scholars of cultural studies.[82] Its editor was the now largely forgotten German Jewish sexologist Max Marcuse (1877–1963), who was forced to emigrate to Palestine in 1933. In the early 1920s Marcuse had successfully recruited eminent researchers to contribute to the work, including Sigmund Freud, whose entries include those on libido theory and psychoanalysis. The spectrum of topics in the encyclopedia ranges from abortion to zoophilia. Its value, which is still recognized today, lies in its combination of broad thematic scope and precise descriptions by competent writers. Published when the still fairly new science of sex was experiencing its first heyday during the Weimar Republic, the standard reference work was able to provide only a strong initial spark, however; its long-term effect was blunted since, when the National Socialists came to power, the scientific field of sex research fell into disrepute, and its most prominent active researchers—including many German Jews—were forced into exile.

In contrast to many other specialized disciplines, sexology was long excluded from academic offerings, and not only because its leading figures were Jews or of Jewish ancestry. Despite a widespread lack of university recognition, after 1918 it did at least become an established field also outside of Germany. When the Weimar Republic came to an end in Germany, so too did the discipline, which in *völkisch*-conservative circles had always remained suspect and was decried as both "Jewish" and an example of "cultural Bolshevism."[83] Once Hitler was in power, the promising young field of sexual science was completely eradicated. In the view of the National Socialists, sexual research per se was superfluous, since the investigation of human sexuality had now become a part of the biology of race.

As we know, sexology found a new home in the United States, though in the second half of the twentieth century among American sexologists only a small number of researchers of Jewish ancestry remained. The best-known American sex therapist today is Dr. Ruth, Ruth Karola Westheimer (née Siegel). Born to Jewish Orthodox parents in a small Franconian town, her life was saved by a *Kindertransport* in 1938; her parents died in Auschwitz. She is the author of more than thirty-one books on the topic of sexuality.

Prostitution

While a virgin is the epitome of the chaste woman who is allowed to have sexual relations only once she is married, a prostitute represents the unchaste woman par excellence. The Hebrew Bible uses two different words for this type of woman: *zona* and *kedesha*. The first term is used for a woman who sells her body, while the second (derived from the Semitic root *q-d-sh*, meaning "holy") refers to the temple prostitute, a special figure in cultures of antiquity, including ancient Israel, as we see in the following Bible passage: "Eli, now a very old man, had heard how his sons were treating all the Israelites, and how they lay with the women who were serving at the entrance to the Tent of the Presence. So he said to them, 'Why do you do such things? I hear from all the people how wickedly you behave'" (1 Samuel 2:22–23). This did not deter later rulers from introducing this form of temple service in Jerusalem as well. But under the rule of King Josiah at the latest, it came to be viewed as a form of idolatry. The verdict of the Torah therefore reads: "You shall not allow a common prostitute's fee, or the pay of a male prostitute, to be brought into the house of the LORD your God in fulfillment of any vow, for both of them are abominable to the LORD your God" (Deuteronomy 23:18). Temple prostitution thus made only a temporary appearance in Judaism that resulted from the influence of neighboring cults.[84]

Ordinary prostitution, a problem found in almost every society, is a completely separate issue. An attempt is made already in the Mishnah to demonize this form of sexuality as well and make it an abomination for devout Jews. There we read: "licentiousness and sorcery destroyed everything" (Sotah 9:13). In an apocryphal Jewish text called the *Book of Jubilees*, prostitution is even said to be responsible for the Flood: "For owing to these three things came the flood upon the earth, namely, owing to the fornication wherein the Watchers against the law of their ordinances went a whoring after the daughters of men, and took themselves wives of all which they chose: and they made the beginning of uncleanness" (*Book of Jubilees* 7:25–26). Rabbinical authorities likewise condemned all forms of prostitution. According to Maimonides, prostitution leads to disputes among men that can even end in death.[85] However, the only women threatened with severe penalties like those predicted in Leviticus were daughters of priestly ancestry or those who had deceived their fathers about their unchaste behavior. Otherwise it would be hard to explain why priests were not allowed to wed prostitutes. Conversely, this also means that doing so was an option for all other Jewish men.[86] The Talmud even reports on rabbis' sons who hired prostitutes (BT Bava Metzia 85a). Moreover, sometimes law-abiding Jewish men lived in districts inhabited primarily by prostitutes plying their trade: "Rav Hanina and Rav Oshaya, who were cobblers, lived in Eretz Yisrael, and they would sit in the marketplace of prostitutes and fashion shoes for prostitutes. And the prostitutes would enter their shops and look at them. However, due to their piety, these Sages did not raise their eyes to look at the women" (BT Pesachim 113b). The passage underscores that while the two men did not succumb to temptation, they at the same time did not avoid social contact with this much-maligned group of women. Other Jewish men seem to have been more inclined to give in to the feminine charms of such women, otherwise the Talmud would not include the parable of the careless father who leaves his son in front of a brothel with a money pouch around his neck (BT Berakhot 32a). Reminding potential clients of the sinfulness of their behavior was one strategy; the other was to protect women and girls against sinking into this milieu.

As might be imagined, not all young women were so convinced of the great value of a chaste life that if threatened with a life of forced prostitution they would throw themselves into the sea (BT Gittin 57b). Hence the warning issued to all fathers: "Do not prostitute your daughter and so make her a whore; thus the land shall not play the prostitute and be full of lewdness" (Leviticus 19:29). In ancient Israel it was often foreign women who were prostitutes, as verses like the following indicate: "For why shouldest thou, my son, be ravished with a strange woman, And embrace the bosom of a foreigner?" (Proverbs 5:20).[87] In antiquity, Babylon in particular was seen as a playground for prostitutes.[88]

From late antiquity until Jewish emancipation in the early nineteenth century, source materials barely mention Jewish prostitutes. In addition, the history of lower-class Jews for this period has still not been adequately researched, which in turn is partially due to the dearth of surviving sources. Another contributing factor might be notions about ethics that became ingrained over the course of generations. In the Middle Ages and the early modern period, if Jews and brothels are mentioned together, it usually refers to Christian prostitutes receiving illicit visits from Jewish men. We do find occasional evidence that a Jew was caught in the act of visiting a brothel.[89] In all likelihood, this was an exception, however, since otherwise the many early modern ordinances for these establishments would contain specific language denying access to Jews.[90] Such a regulation was not absolutely necessary, since Jewish men were not allowed to have sexual relations with Christian women. It was precisely to avoid this situation that clothing regulations for Jews (and, incidentally, also Muslims) were put in place already in the Middle Ages. It was, hence, superfluous to specifically regulate brothel visits for this group. Anyone still unable to resist temptation faced more than just strict punishment from the Christian authorities, usually in the form of a steep fine. He was also subject to the strict social controls of the Jewish community. They responded to such offenses (which also violated their own sexual ethics) with sanctions and the occasional mocking song. The latter happened mainly when it was felt that the offending party had been let off too easily,[91] as evidenced in a Yiddish song from the early seventeenth century that mentions many such "sinners" by name, chiding them as follows:

> I want to name one more:
> he calls himself Lima Schnabach
> he rewards the whores handsomely.
> He has already squandered four hundred crowns.[92]

Only toward the end of the nineteenth century does the anti-Semitic trope of the Jewish pimp develop, a figure who ruthlessly exploits the poverty and desperation of young women (especially in Eastern Europe) and plunges them into the moral abyss.[93] There certainly were Jewish men, and even a small number of women, who engaged in human trafficking,[94] and whose victims themselves were often Jewish. Most of these girls came from the czarist empire and the Habsburg monarchy, and they shared the dream of a life without pogroms and social misery.[95] Instead, they often fell prey to sex traffickers who used false promises, but also threats, to lure them into brothels (mainly in South America). They were the topic of a 2012 exhibit in Berlin's Centrum Judaicum.[96] Toward the end of the nineteenth century in Buenos Aires alone, supposedly more than four thousand female Jews were registered as prostitutes, almost one-fourth of all the women practicing this "trade." In the social trouble spot of Berlin during the Weimar Republic, the Jewish Women's League offered "train station aid" (*Bahnhofshilfe*) to Eastern European girls at risk by meeting these young female immigrants on arrival right on the train platform and accompanying them to safe places of residence.[97]

In Russia toward the end of the nineteenth century there were also so-called "pseudo-prostitutes." Young women from middle-class Jewish families who were eager to get an education officially registered as prostitutes and received a "yellow slip" that allowed them to live outside the perimeters of the Jewish settlements in St. Petersburg and Moscow. In most cases they did not work as prostitutes, but instead attended secondary school. In 1897 in St. Petersburg only seventeen Jewish women were registered as prostitutes,[98] so this phenomenon is largely an urban legend.

During the Shoah, Jewish women were among the long-overlooked victims of forced prostitution.[99] NS henchmen occasionally found loopholes in the racial defilement regulations and circumvented them by declaring Jewish women "objects."[100] In addition, Jewish women among the partisans who could deny their identity if put in prison were often forced into prostitution. They were tattooed with the words "whore for Hitler's troops." When one of these women who survived was reunited after the war with her Jewish husband who had also managed to survive, he was shocked by the tattoo on her arm. This in his eyes branded her as a whore, and as such represented a serious halakhic problem for him as a pious man. The couple therefore asked Lithuanian-born Rabbi Ephraim Oshry, himself a Shoah survivor, for an interpretation of the law (*tschuwa*). Drawing on Maimonides and other rabbinical authorities, he determined that in this case it had been sexual intercourse with a stranger under duress and required no testimony from individual witnesses since the National Socialists' sexual transgressions against women in the camps could be presumed as proven, generally known facts.[101]

The women placed in camp brothels were primarily German women categorized as "asocial," but also Poles. Despite the prohibition against racial defilement, however, it is not entirely inconceivable that—for the reasons given above—individual Jewish and Roma women may also have been forced into prostitution in the concentration camps.

Procreation and Childlessness

Judaism's relatively uninhibited attitude toward sexuality is expressed in the following Jewish joke: A young Jewish woman from a good home becomes pregnant. Her outraged parents want to know the name of the guilty party, and the young lady accuses a rabbi known for his piety and wisdom. The rabbi immediately calls the girl in and asks her to explain her slanderous statement. She innocently explains: "I speak the truth, rabbi. Some time ago my aunt [*muhme*] came to you since she had been unable to have children. You gave her a flask of water from the Holy Land and said that if she drank from it, she would become pregnant. I took a nip from the flask, just out of curiosity. . . ." "But child," asks the obviously perplexed rabbi, "do you not know that a man must also be present?" The girl replies with a question of her own: "So, rabbi, you think we don't have *bochern* [young men] in the *shtetl*?"

The joke also refers to one of the most important commandments in Judaism, namely, the production of offspring.[102] Numerous passages of the Torah call on the people of Israel to bring children into the world. This commandment is first issued on the fifth day of creation: *p'ru ur'vu*, "Be fruitful and increase" (Genesis 1:28). When, by the grace of God, Noah becomes the father of a new human race after the Flood, God repeats this exhortation: "Be fruitful and increase, and fill the earth" (Genesis 9:1). And speaking to biblical patriarch Jacob, God addresses him with the words: "I am God Almighty. Be fruitful and increase as a nation" (Genesis 35:11). Other passages in the Torah include similar words lauding the ability to reproduce that God has granted mankind.

We can see how seriously Judaism took and still does take this commandment in many commentaries and interpretations in the Talmud. There Rabbi Eliezer states: "Anyone who does not engage in the mitzva to be fruitful and multiply is considered as though he sheds blood, as it is stated: 'Whoever sheds the blood of man, by man shall his blood be shed' (Genesis 9:6), and it is written immediately afterwards: 'And you, be fruitful and multiply' (Genesis 9:7)" (BT Yevamot 63b). The Hebrew *Sefer Chasidim* (Book of the Pious), one of the most significant medieval texts of German Judaism and an outstanding source of information on religious developments among Ashkenazi Jews in the late twelfth and early thirteenth centuries, contains the following story: The in-laws of an unfaithful husband ask a rabbi to cure the man of his skirt-chasing ways. The rabbi actually does know of an herb that could help control the man's sex drive, but he refuses to provide it, saying that it would also make the man unable to have lawful sex with his wife. He adds that giving such a remedy to an unmarried man or a man who already has children would also be forbidden, since even this goes against Jewish law.[103] A different passage in this same well-known scholarly work is also of interest here. It shows that medieval Judaism not only had medical knowledge about how to decrease a person's sex drive and prevent fertilization, but also possessed the proven means to do the opposite, namely, increase male potency. Roasted garlic is recommended as an aphrodisiac, and men looking to increase their sperm count are advised to eat large amounts of cooked lentils.[104]

In the Hebrew Bible, the high value given to the production of offspring is expressed in another way as well, namely, as a critique of the choice to remain unmarried.[105] Only one case is known: the prophet Jeremiah, supposedly in accordance with God's will, should renounce marriage and children, thereby demonstrating with his own body the criminal punishment that threatens Israel (Jeremiah 16:2). His unmarried, childless state is intended as a sign for Israel to change course. On this point the Old Testament is diametrically opposed to the New Testament, where we find not only praise of virginity but also a relative indifference toward procreation and a rather ambivalent attitude toward marriage. Orthodox Judaism in stark contrast goes so far as to suspect the unmarried person of not being fully human: "Rabbi Elazar said: Any man who does not have a wife is not a man" (BT Yevamot 63a).

A person must marry primarily in order to fulfill the commandment of procreation, and the earlier the better. In the Babylonian Talmud Rabbi Huna gives his opinion: "If one is twenty years old and has not yet married a woman, all of his days will be in a state of sin [concerning sexual matters]" (BT Kiddushin 29b). Marriage thus helps a person not to sin: "Whoever finds a wife finds good, and obtains [veyafek] favor of the Lord" (BT Yevamot 63b). A Bible reference (Proverbs 18:22) is included here to reinforce the idea that marriage is advantageous. Even a widower who had children should remarry according to the author of the Sefer Chasidim, who cites Ecclesiastes 11:6: "In the morning sow your seed betimes, and do not stop work until evening, for you do not know whether this or that sowing will be successful, or whether both alike will do well."[106]

According to Jewish belief, children should issue from marriage, but the institution does not exist solely for this purpose, as important as this commandment is in Judaism. In marriage, people also find true partnership and fulfillment (including the sexual kind), as the marriage blessing testifies. Its earliest form is found in the Talmud: "Blessed are You, Lord our God, King of the universe, Who has created joy and gladness, groom and bride, delight, exultation, happiness, jubilation, love and brotherhood, and peace and friendship" (BT Ketubot 8a). Even with regard to sexual positions, Judaism—similar to Islam, incidentally[107]—is quite open-minded: "Whatever a man wishes to do with his wife he may do. He may engage in sexual intercourse with her in any manner that he wishes. . . . As an allegory, it is like meat that comes from the butcher. If he wants to eat it with salt, he may eat it that way. If he wants to eat it roasted, he may eat it roasted. If he wants to eat it cooked, he may eat it cooked. If he wants to eat it boiled, he may eat it boiled. And likewise with regard to fish that come from the fisherman" (BT Nedarim 20b). The only exception was anal sex, since it did not serve the purpose of procreation. At the same time, it was believed (and not by Jews alone) that certain sexual positions could result in fetal abnormalities. In 1575 when Siamese twins joined at the tailbone were born in the ghetto of Venice, Jewish natural philosopher Abraham ben Hananiah Yagel interpreted this "monstrous" birth by citing a Talmud passage: "For what reason do lame people come into existence? It is because their fathers overturn their tables, i.e., they engage in sexual intercourse in an atypical way" (BT Nedarim 20a).[108] The scholar then lists other examples from the Talmud that say certain sexual practices can cause physical abnormalities (deafness, muteness, blindness).

In Jewish legal texts we even find explicit recommendations concerning how often married couples should engage in sexual intercourse, guidelines that were later adopted in part by Christianity. When asked how often conjugal duties should be performed, Martin Luther supposedly answered:

That is the obligation for women
twice a week
[It] harms not you nor her
that makes one hundred four a year

(Das ist der Frau'n Gebühr
In der Woche zwier
Schadet weder Dir noch ihr
Macht im Jahre hundertvier)[109]

In the Mishnah we find a much more differentiated answer: "[The law of provid-ing sexual] pleasure [to one's wife] that is stated in the Torah [is as follows]: one at leisure, daily; laborers, twice a week; donkey drivers, once a week; camel driv-ers, once every thirty days; navigators every six months; these are the words of Rabbi Eliezer" (Ketubot 5:6). Here once more we see how pragmatic and life-centered Judaism is, since the conjugal duties of a man are directly linked to his profession.[110] His health is also a factor: anyone who is ill should only exchange caresses with his wife and resume sexual intercourse only after a complete recov-ery.[111] Torah scholars are advised to have sex with their wives only once a week so that they may better focus on their study of sacred texts,[112] and the Babylonian Talmud indicates the best time for doing so by referring to a psalm: "When is the ideal time for Torah scholars to fulfill their conjugal obligations? Rav Yehuda said that Shmuel said: The appropriate time for them is from Shabbat eve to Shabbat eve" (BT Ketubot 62b). In case a member of this group has not yet fulfilled his duty to produce children, he is allowed to have sex also on other days of the week. The wife's situation must also be considered. It is strictly forbidden to have sexual relations with a woman during her period and on the days of impurity that follow.[113] Josel of Rosheim (1476–1554) records in his chronicle that a Jew named Raphael, who died a Christian convert in Colmar, had slept with his wife during her period while he was still a Jew. Afterward she had had a crying fit and reported the disgraceful behavior to her aunt.[114] Rabbinical authorities therefore explicitly recommended intercourse only on the night *after* a woman returned from the *mikveh*. If a wife desires sex and there are no forbidden times to consider, her husband may not refuse to have intercourse with her. Before a man begins a journey, his wife may also demand that he perform his marital duty. Only on specific Jewish holy days involving fasting (Yom Kippur, Tisha B'Av) is intercourse forbidden.

Aside from these exceptions, a Jewish woman may not refuse her husband. If she does, the Talmud deems her behavior "rebellious" and defines the term as follows: "What are the circumstances in which the *halakha* of a rebellious woman applies? Ameimar said: The case is where she says: I want to be married to him, but I am currently refusing him because I want to cause him anguish due to a dispute between us. However, if she said: I am disgusted with him, we do not compel her to remain with him" (BT Ketubot 63b). On this last point some scholars admittedly did not agree.[115] Unlike Judaism, Christianity remained somewhat vague on this issue, even if the apostle Paul did emphasize the duty of both partners in the marriage to have sexual relations:

> It is a good thing for a man to have nothing to do with women; but because there is so much immorality, let each man have his own wife and each woman her own husband. The husband must give the wife what is due to her, and the wife equally must give the husband his due. The wife cannot claim her body as her own; it is her husband's. Equally, the husband cannot claim his body as his own; it is his wife's. Do not deny yourselves to one another, except when you agree on a temporary abstinence in order to devote yourselves to prayer; afterwards you may come together again; otherwise, for lack of self-control, you may be tempted by Satan. (1 Corinthians 7:1–5)

Jewish tradition teaches that a woman, too, should be able to satisfy her sexual desires. Unlike a man, however, she may not show it openly, as the Talmud states: "the woman demands her husband in her heart but is too shy to voice her desire, but the man demands his wife verbally" (BT Eruvim 100b). In contrast to church fathers, rabbinical scholars admit that a woman also feels pleasure when fulfilling her marital obligation. The Babylonian Talmud cites Rabbi Bar: "didn't Rava say that a man is obligated to please his wife through a mitzva?" (BT Pesachim 72b). An explanation found in a different passage echoes the teaching about conception from antiquity, namely, that a woman's pleasure during sex promotes fertility (BT Bava Batra 10b). The Greek physician Soranos of Ephesus (ca. 100 CE), for instance, taught that female orgasm was the prerequisite for conception to occur.[116]

Even the time of day when coitus should take place is regulated by Halakhah. Intercourse was forbidden during broad daylight, and the Babylonian Talmud explains why: "Rav Hisda says: It is prohibited for a person to engage in intercourse by day, as it is stated: 'And you shall love your fellow as yourself' (Leviticus 19:18). The Gemara asks: From where is this inferred? Abaye says: If one engages in intercourse by day, perhaps the husband will see some repulsive matter in his wife and she will become repugnant to him" (BT Niddah 17a). People should therefore wait until dark. If necessary, a scholar who was overcome by sexual desire could use his cloak to create the required darkness.[117]

For the same reason (shamefulness), no one else may be privy to a married couple's sexual relations. Rabbis therefore recommended that intercourse not take place late in the night but instead around midnight, since at that time sleeping neighbors would be unaware it was taking place. Children are also not allowed to know what was happening, unless they are so young that they have not yet begun to speak. To avoid the risk of having others see or hear them in the act, a Jewish couple is advised to house guests only in separate rooms or outside of their home. Also, for the sake of the children, it is recommended that the parents' sleeping area be separated from the rest of the living space at least by dividing walls. Moreover, no Torah scrolls should be nearby in the room where intercourse occurs. Tefillin and holy writings must also be stored in a locked container. In view of such conditions, it is unsurprising that even today it is absolutely forbidden for observant Jews to have sexual intercourse in public (streets, public squares)— even if they are not creating a public disturbance.[118]

In view of the procreation commandment, childlessness represents a serious problem in Judaism, as we have already read in the Bible.[119] Hannah, one of Elkanah's two wives, was childless; in contrast, his second wife, Peninnah, had borne him numerous sons and daughters. Peninnah tormented and humiliated Hannah because of her barrenness, but "her husband Elkanah said to her, 'Hannah, why are you crying and eating nothing? Why are you so miserable? Am I not more to you than ten sons?'" (1 Samuel 1:8). In other words, he tried to comfort her and distract her from her sorrow—but in vain. When the couple once again attended the annual prayer in Shiloh, Hannah prayed silently for a son and vowed to dedicate him to the Lord. She later did have a child with Elkanah and called him Samuel; as soon as she had weaned him, she presented him to the priest Eli, who blessed Elkanah and Hannah during a later visit to the temple. Through God's grace they had three more sons and two daughters, we are told. The Old Testament contains a number of other such miraculous stories of motherhood, including those of Abraham's wife Sarah (Genesis 16:1), Rebekkah, the wife of Isaac (Genesis 25:21), and Rachel (Genesis 29:31), mother of Joseph and Benjamin. All three matriarchs are linked by their temporary infertility.[120] The Talmud makes it clear how heavy a burden this lot is in Judaism: "Any person who does not have children is considered like a dead person. . . . Four are considered as if they were dead: A pauper, and a leper, and a blind person, and one who has no children" (BT Nedarim 64b). This also explains levirate marriage, which serves to guarantee descendants by requiring a man to marry his deceased brother's widow, even if he is already married. A son born to this couple is considered the rightful heir of the deceased man (Deuteronomy 25:6).

In the opinion of Jewish legal scholars, there can be many natural causes of childlessness. Male infertility received and still receives particular attention. For instance, a man should not hold in his urine too long, lest he become "sterile" (BT Bekhorot 44b). A blockage in the male genitals ("he does not shoot like an arrow, i.e., his semen is not emitted forcefully," BT Nedarim 90b), is also mentioned in the Talmud as a possible cause of male impotence. After ten childless years, a Jewish woman may demand a divorce if she can convincingly show that her husband is impotent. The reverse is also true: a man is advised to divorce his wife if she is the one responsible for not producing children in the same ten-year period. And if a woman has suffered three miscarriages, her ability to bear children is called into question, which can also result in separation via a declaration of divorce (*get*).

It is therefore unsurprising that in addition to prayer, both the Bible and rabbinical writings mention many natural remedies that supposedly cure infertility ranging from mandrake to wine and the enjoyment of certain foods. Maimonides expanded the toolkit by adding several types of medical and psychological therapy,[121] and his dietetic recommendations, based on Greek and Arabic texts, were highly prized both in and outside of Jewish circles in the Middle Ages and long thereafter.

Since in Judaism the fear of being childless is so great, even advanced reproductive technologies (including stem cell research) have now been accepted, though not all of them. Artificial insemination, which was introduced in modern medicine almost forty years ago, usually poses no problem in actual practice, as long as the parents and egg and sperm donors are all of the Jewish faith. The unconditional commandment to produce offspring makes many things possible, unlike in the Catholic Church, for example, which has both moral and dogmatic reservations about such intervention.

Contraception

The Jewish faith allows birth control in certain cases, since marriage is not restricted solely to the duty of procreation. A Talmud commentary from the early fifth century summarizes the prevailing opinion as follows: "It follows from here and from all discussions elsewhere that *intercourse* with a woman incapable at all of child-bearing is permissible, and the prohibition of hash-hatat zera is not involved so long as the intercourse is in the manner of procreation; for the Rabbis have in every case permitted *marriage* with women too young or too old for childbearing."[122] But where do things stand with women who are fully capable of having children yet for various reasons do not wish to become pregnant? The rules about exceptions that are provided in the Talmud are very narrowly focused. Most of the authorities allow birth control if the woman's health is at risk or if postponing the pregnancy appears crucial to protecting the religious or social status of the future child.[123]

A medical indication is without a doubt the most important reason. Rabbi Isaiah di Trani, for example, who lived in Italy in the first half of the thirteenth century, stressed in his Talmud commentary: "If one's intent is to avoid pregnancy so as not to mar his wife's beauty or so as to avoid [always] the fulfillment of the mitzvah of procreation, then [the contracepted coitus mentioned there] is forbidden. But if his intent is to spare her physical hazard or to pursue his own pleasure, then this is permitted."[124] In other words, there must be serious grounds for making an exception to Jewish law. Accordingly, a man must consider his wife's health when claiming his conjugal rights, rights that the Talmud also regulates down to the smallest detail. Abstinence is not expected of him; but he is expected to accept his wife's use of contraception, provided that it does not violate the commandment against squandering semen.

In Judaism there is thus no general prohibition against contraception. Instead, what we find is a highly differentiated casuistry derived from the example of three women mentioned in the Talmud in this context:

> Rav Beivei taught a *baraita* before Rav Nahman: Three women may engage in relations with a contraceptive resorbent, a soft fabric placed at the entrance to their wombs to prevent conception, despite the fact that this practice is generally prohibited. They are as follows: a minor, a woman who is already pregnant, and a nursing woman. . . . A minor may do so lest she become pregnant and perhaps die; a pregnant woman, lest she become impregnated a second time and her previous fetus becomes deformed into the shape of a sandal fish by being squashed by the pressure of the second fetus. As for a nursing woman, she does so lest she become pregnant and her milk dry up, in which case she will wean her son too early, thereby endangering him, and he will die. (BT Yevamot 12b)

Some schools of thought do not even allow these exceptions. Jewish scholar Hayyim ben Joseph Vital (1543–1620), for example, cites his teacher's view that a man must fulfill his marital duty even when his wife is pregnant or nursing, since this union of man and woman is what maintains the world.[125]

It is unclear whether the absorbent used as a contraceptive device was inserted before or after coitus, but this same method is mentioned in three additional Talmud passages.[126] They, too, deal with exceptions to religious law. For instance, rabbinical scholars find it acceptable for women with certain types of legal status (proselytes, prisoners, and freed slaves) to use "cotton wool" to avoid pregnancy (see BT Yevamot 35a).

In contrast, a different type of prevention was frowned upon despite the fact that it was occasionally recommended by medical authorities of antiquity such as Hippocrates. A man who made his wife jump up and down after sex in order to shake the semen from her vagina was giving her grounds for divorce: "If he said to her: . . . 'that you will fill and pour out in the garbage,' he must divorce her and give her the ketubah" (Mishnah Ketubot 7:5).

Notably, it is women who are allowed by Jewish law to use contraception in exceptional cases. This is because men are obligated to reproduce, but women are not, as the Talmud clearly states. Rabbi Joseph, for example, explains this sex-specific difference by giving the following interpretation of a familiar Bible passage: "Rav Yosef said: The proof is from here: 'And God said to him: I am God Almighty, be fruitful and multiply' [*perei urvei*] (Genesis 35:11), which is in singular, and it does not state: Be fruitful and multiply [*peru urvu*] in the plural" (BT Yevamot 65b). In Rabbi Joseph's view, this unmistakable command to the patriarch Jacob, issued in the second personal singular, extends to the entire male sex.

The male duty to be fruitful is not without limits, however. In the Gemara, the second part of the Talmud, we read that a man who already has children need not produce more, but he must continue to live with a wife (BT Yevamot 61b). Should we therefore assume that men were allowed to use contraceptive methods or even coitus interruptus? The Jewish scholars provide a clear answer to this question: "No, it means that if he does not have children he must marry a woman capable of bearing children, whereas if he has children he may marry a woman who is not capable of bearing children" (BT Yevamot 61b). Only in the case of a second marriage is it permissible for a man to limit the number of his offspring, unless any of the above-mentioned medical indications apply to his wife.

Contraception in ancient Judaism thus lay largely in the hands of the woman, as we see in the story of Yehudit, the wife of Rabbi Hiyya, who experienced great pain during the birth of twins. After recovering from the delivery, Yehudit went to her husband in disguise and asked him if a woman was required to be fruitful and multiply. He said no, and afterwards she drank an infertility potion. When he discovered what she had done, Hiyya rebuked her: "If only you had given birth to one more belly for me, i.e., another set of twins" (BT Yevamot 65b).

As noted above, Jewish teaching explicitly forbids men to take precautions of their own against unwanted pregnancy, in other words, to do what God punished Onan for doing. The Bible story is well known: after Er, Judah's firstborn, had to die because he displeased God, the father directed his second son, Onan, to marry Er's wife and enter into a levirate marriage. But as the Torah says, Onan "spilled the seed on the ground, so as not to raise up issue for his brother" (Genesis 38:9). God punished him with death. While in Christian Bible exegesis Onan's sin is generally seen as a cautionary example of coitus interruptus in marriage, not all Jewish scholars agree whether Onan's sin actually consists in the method he chose, still known today by its Latin name. Support for such an interpretation can be found in a Talmud passage about the husband of a woman who has just given birth: "he penetrates inside and spills his semen outside for the entire twenty-four months while the baby is breastfeeding" (BT Yevamot 34b). This recommendation by Rabbi Eliezer caused a great deal of speculation among later commentators, who pondered whether this behavior was comparable to Onan's. A number of them felt that there was definitely a difference, arguing that in the one case it was still a matter of normal intercourse, while in the other it was "unnatural."

Even today Jewish Orthodox circles continue to uphold the strict interpretation of the Bible and Talmud commentaries and allow contraception only in cases where the life of the woman is in danger.[127] In 1988 Rabbi Moshe Tendler still maintained: "In general, only the health requirements of the wife, both physically and psychologically, can modify the halakhic disapproval of all contraceptive."[128] In (Israeli) reality, though, even self-described ultra-Orthodox women who regularly visit the ritual immersion bath, or *mikveh*, take a pragmatic view. A survey conducted in the late 1990s found that 48 percent of these women admitted to using contraception. The majority favored the "coil" (21 percent), but even coitus interruptus, which is strictly taboo in these circles, was nonetheless mentioned by 5 percent of those surveyed.[129]

Generally speaking, Conservative and Reform Judaism support family planning as long as there is no danger that the Jewish people will die out. The Central Conference of American Rabbis, which represents the Reform movement in the United States, even went so far as to state that in certain family situations birth control is mandatory. Liberal rabbis no longer have reservations about also accepting condoms as contraception. Among them is the Boston Reform rabbi Herman Blumberg: "When young people ask me if Judaism says it's okay to use condoms, I reply, Judaism says that if you are having sex, you should use condoms. Judaism says: 'take care.'"[130]

In the Jewish state, where the religious concerns of Orthodox Jews are respected in many regards, contraceptives are nonetheless readily available. Israel has recently even become one of the few countries in which the so-called "morning-after pill" is available without a prescription. Even so, the health insurance required by law in Israel will cover the cost of contraceptives only in certain cases. According to a now somewhat dated study, 87.2 percent of female Israelis use some form of birth control,[131] a statistic confirmed by demographic data: at the time of the study, the fifteen- to seventeen-year-old age group showed a larger drop in birthrate than in the previous decades. Nevertheless, the average Jewish family in Israel has 2.7 children, far surpassing the birthrate in most European countries. And if sociologists and demographers can be believed, a second trend is also emerging. In ethical matters relating to sex, young Jewish women look less and less to religious norms for orientation, and instead behave pragmatically. This also—or, rather, especially—applies to the decision for or against the use of contraceptives. More and more religious women in Israel now take measures against unwanted pregnancy. Overall, roughly two-thirds of all Israeli women use contraception; however, the rate fluctuates between 69 and 48 percent depending on the denomination (traditional, Orthodox, ultra-Orthodox).[132] The numbers behind these statistics refer to the years 1987–88; more recent data are unfortunately not available.

Virginity

While in present-day Israel marriageable women see virginity as more of a state of mind, in the past it was inseparable from the physical characteristic of an intact hymen. The Torah leaves no doubt about the importance of this sign: "When a man takes a wife and after having intercourse with her turns against her and brings trumped-up charges against her, giving her a bad name and saying, 'I took this woman and slept with her and did not find proof of virginity in her,' then the girl's father and mother shall take the proof of her virginity to the elders of the town, at the town gate" (Deuteronomy 22:13–15). The Talmud even states exactly how the check for a woman's virginity should proceed in case of dispute. In addition to looking at the bedsheet after the wedding night, other measures can also be taken, including the following:

> A certain man who came before Rabban Gamliel bar Rabbi Yehuda HaNasi said to him: My teacher, I engaged in intercourse and did not find blood. The bride said to him: My teacher, I am still a virgin. Rabban Gamliel bar Rabbi Yehuda HaNasi said to them: Bring me two maidservants, one a virgin and one a non-virgin, to conduct a trial. They brought him the two maidservants, and he seated them on the opening of a barrel of wine. From the non-virgin, he discovered that the scent of the wine in the barrel diffuses from her mouth; from the virgin he discovered that the

scent does not diffuse from her mouth. Then, he also seated that bride on the barrel, and the scent did not diffuse from her mouth. (BT Ketubot 10b)

This method was later abandoned, since people realized that a sniff test might well be deceptive.[133] According to biblical regulations, women who had lost their virginity because of loose behavior were to be stoned. The Babylonian Talmud stipulates further that witnesses are required who can swear that the woman in question actually had committed adultery and had not, for instance, been the victim of rape (BT Ketubot 11b). Since in reality things were often more complicated, this draconian measure was probably imposed only rarely, not to mention the fact that since the time of exile the Jewish people no longer had the judicial power over life and death.[134]

Unlike other religions that place an equally high value on virginity at the time of marriage, Judaism developed a complex casuistry early on. This allows for individualized decisions that may also consider a woman's anatomical features.[135] For example, the stage of her sexual development (from small child to woman capable of childbearing) is taken into account. Unlike the church fathers who tended to be prudish, rabbinical authorities could be quite explicit and detailed when discussing such delicate matters. Take the case of the man who claimed that on his wedding night when he penetrated his bride's vagina he felt virtually no resistance (Hebrew *dochak*) and suspected that perhaps his wife had been deflowered already:

> A certain man who came before Rabban Gamliel said to him: I encountered an unobstructed orifice. Rabban Gamliel said to him: Perhaps you diverted your approach and therefore, encountered no obstruction? I will tell you a parable to which this is similar. It is similar to a man who was walking in the blackness of night and darkness and he arrived at the entrance to the house; if he diverts the object preventing the door from opening, he finds it open; if he does not divert it, he finds it locked. Perhaps you too diverted your approach and entered from a different angle and that is why you did not encounter an obstruction. (BT Ketubot 10a)[136]

To limit the potential abuse of such a defense, Maimonides, who we recall was not only a rabbinical scholar but also a doctor, placed a condition on it: a tight vagina and traces of blood were required as proof of the woman's virginity. However, this only applied in the case of a small child (Hebrew *ketana*) or prepubescent girl (Hebrew *na'ara*).[137] The legal custom involving *mukat ez* (literally, "injured by a piece of wood"), a tradition unique to Judaism, should be mentioned in this context. It refers to accidental loss of virginity due to a physical activity such as jumping or climbing. On this topic the Mishnah states: "She says, 'After you betrothed me I was raped and your 'field has been flooded' [i.e., it is your loss]. And the other one says, 'Not so, rather, before I betrothed you [you lost your virginity], and [consequently], 'my purchase was made in error.' Rabban Gamliel and Rabbi Eliezer say, 'She is believed'; Rabbi Yehoshua says, 'We do not live by [the words of] her mouth. Rather, she is presumed to have had relations before she became betrothed and that she deceived him, until she brings proof for her words'" (Ketubot 1:6). A woman was not always believed, so proof had to be furnished as soon as possible after the incident (usually in childhood) that had caused the unintentional rupturing of the hymen. For this purpose, some Jewish communities had formularies in place as early as the Middle Ages that could be put into action if need be.[138] Witnesses were usually adult women who had either seen the actual accident or done a vaginal examination of the girl immediately afterward. For a child under the age of three, the loss of the intact hymen did not have to be documented since it was assumed that with time, the injury would heal completely and return to its original condition (BT Kiddushin 45a). The Talmud also mentions cases in which women had deflowered themselves, such as Tamar, the daughter-in-law of Judas ("who broke her hymen with her finger," BT Yevamot 34b), and thereby became pregnant more quickly.[139] As we read in one midrash, Lot's daughter supposedly also tore her own hymen so that she could conceive without difficulty (*Rabbah Genesis* 51.9). In both cases it is suggested that the women were nonetheless still virgins in the halakhic sense, since they had acted in good faith and also had not yet had intercourse with a man.[140]

Some rabbis also wondered if it was possible to tell the difference between the blood that resulted from a ruptured hymen and that of a menstrual period: "As Rabbi Meir would say: The appearances of impure and pure blood differ from one another. How so? The blood of a menstruating woman is red, whereas the blood that comes from a torn hymen, indicating that she was a virgin, is not red. The blood of a menstruating woman is cloudy; blood that indicates that she was a virgin is not cloudy. Finally, the blood of a menstruating woman comes from the uterus; blood that indicates that she was a virgin comes from the sides of the virginal wall" (BT Niddah 65b). However, the majority opinion was that differentiating between the two was impossible. In one regard, however, these two types of blood are not identical. Menstrual blood makes a woman ritually impure, whereas the bleeding caused by the tearing of the hymen does not. Still, Orthodox couples are nevertheless encouraged to wait several days after the woman has lost her virginity before resuming sex; some rabbis even require seven clean days and immersion in a ritual bath in order to avoid mixing of the bleeding of defloration with the menstrual blood.[141]

Given the importance of an intact hymen in (matrimonial) law and sexual morality in Judaism, an importance it still has today in Orthodox circles, it stands to reason that sometimes even white magic was employed to re-create virginity. Italian recipes and incantation formulas from the early modern period have survived that were intended to serve this purpose.[142] Today it is usually not Jewish but primarily Muslim girls who undergo the medically risky procedure of so-called hymenorrhaphy.[143]

An external sign of how highly virginity is prized in Judaism is the special blessing given after the consummation of the marriage; however, it has only been preserved from the post-Talmudic period onward.[144] Be that as it may, every now and again it did happen that a bride was no longer a virgin, but also not a widow. In such cases in the eighteenth century, when there was already greater tolerance, the legal custom developed in the Jewish community in Altona, for instance, of not writing the word "virgin" (Hebrew *betula*) on the marriage certificate, but simply "that woman." The bride's dowry was also reduced to the amount expected for a widow.[145]

In the meantime, Israel has become one of the countries where girls lose their virginity fairly early, on average at 16.7 years of age,[146] which puts the country in eleventh place in the world.

Chapter 4

The Intact Body

Different Views of Health

"A little sun, a little rain, a quiet place to rest; the main thing is to be happy. A pair of shoes, a pair of socks, a smock without patches, a pouch with three or four coins. The main thing is to be healthy, then a man can be happy. Air doesn't cost a thing."[1] So goes the English translation of a well-known Yiddish song claiming that good health is more important than worldly goods. A Yiddish lullaby that was sung to Jewish children contains the same wish: "the main thing is: be healthy."[2] Yiddish private letters from the eighteenth century often begin with a salutation saying that the writer is in good health and hopes the same is true of the recipient.[3] Even today, when someone sneezes, one says in Yiddish "Zay gesunt" or "Gesundheit," a custom rooted in the Jewish legend that originally there was no illness in the world and that human mortality began with the first sneeze, which allowed the soul to escape.[4]

Almost no other religion pays so much attention to physical health as Judaism. Think, for example, of the famous verses from the book of Ecclesiasticus: "Better a poor man who is healthy and fit than a rich man racked by disease. Health and fitness are better than any gold, and bodily vigour than boundless prosperity. There is no wealth to compare with health of body, no festivity to equal a joyful heart" (Ecclesiasticus 30:14–16). The opposition between "healthy" and "sick" occurs already in the Torah, where it is linked to the will of God and the divine plan of creation. A similar notion is found in the traditional prayer of a Jewish doctor, long attributed (incorrectly) to the renowned Jewish philosopher and physician Maimonides:

> Almighty God, Thou has created the human body with infinite wisdom. Ten thousand times ten thousand organs has Thou combined in it that act unceasingly and harmoniously to preserve the whole in all its beauty the body which is the envelope of the immortal soul. They are ever acting

in perfect order, agreement and accord. Yet, when the frailty of matter or the unbridling of passions deranges this order or interrupts this accord, then forces clash and the body crumbles into the primal dust from which it came. Thou sendest to man diseases as beneficent messengers to foretell approaching danger and to urge him to avert it.[5]

The human body is a divine miracle, as we read at the start of the prayer, but even so it is not immune to illness.

The concept of health found in Judaism of antiquity, which is fundamentally metaphysical, was shared by other advanced civilizations of the Levant.[6] The only difference is that in Judaism there are not multiple gods but only a single God who may punish the disobedient by taking away their health. Sickness is thus viewed as the result of God's profound anger or as punishment from Yahweh, as expressed in Psalms 6 and 88. Whoever wants to stay healthy would therefore do well to keep God's commandments (Exodus 15:26, 23:25). The Mishnah also imparts this wisdom: "Great is Torah for it gives life to those who practice it, in this world, and in the world to come, As it is said: 'For they are life unto those that find them, and health to all their flesh' (Proverbs 4:22). And it says: 'It will be a cure for your navel and marrow for your bones' (Proverbs 3:8)" (Pirkei Avot 6:7).

In the post-exile period the notion developed that God uses particular "instruments" in this context. Here we think first and foremost of Satan and/or demons of sickness. To restore health, in contrast, God relies on angels (see Tobias 12:5–20). Doctors, who are occasionally mentioned already in the Bible, do not compete with divine healing but are instead the colleagues or helpmates of God, as Old Testament commentator Otto Kaiser puts it,[7] citing the verses from Ecclesiasticus: "Honour the doctor for his services, for the Lord created them. His skill comes from the Most High, and he is rewarded by kings" (Ecclesiasticus 38:1–2).

Along with the common stereotype of Jews as more prone to illness than their fellow men, we also find the opposite idea early on, namely, that their health is better than that of other tribes.[8] Tacitus (ca. 58–ca. 120 CE), no great friend of the Jews, emphasized the robust health of those Jews living in Palestine at the time: "The inhabitants are healthy and hardy."[9] In *The Jewish Synagogue*, Protestant theologian Johannes Buxtorf the Elder claimed—though admittedly without specific evidence or further explanation—that Jews live longer than Christians and that unlike the latter they are also immune to all kinds of disease.[10]

In the nineteenth century this topic was addressed by both Jewish and Christian doctors, who viewed the hygiene regulations connected to Jewish rites as beneficial to health. Ritual washing linked with a number of different situations (before the morning prayer and synagogue visit, after a bowel movement, and so on), purification baths after menstruation, and other long-standing traditional religious regulations that could be interpreted in medical terms were now cast—or in some cases recast—as part of modern and progressive hygiene: at the Dresden Hygiene Exhibition of 1911, for instance, and at the GeSoLei trade fair in the 1920s (the name based on abbreviations for *Gesundheitspflege* [health] + *soziale Fürsorge* [social welfare] + *Leibesübungen* [physical exercise]).[11] The same is true for sexual ethics and dietary laws. Of the many contemporaries who shortly before and after the turn of the twentieth century praised the specific dietetics of Judaism as a form of prophylaxis, it was no less than Rudolf Virchow who posed the following question at the Fifty-Eighth Convention of Natural Scientists and Physicians in 1885: "to what extent is the remarkable immunity shown by the Jews in the most varied circumstances . . . based on their particular way of life: the stricter hygiene of their housekeeping, the greater care dictated by dietary laws, the greater domesticity of their lifestyle and similar things."[12] Virchow left the question open, but a later comment makes it clear that unlike many of his contemporaries, he had little regard for explanations based on racial biology, even if he did not wish to exclude them altogether. In contrast, his American colleague Ephraim M. Epstein (1829–1913), who had practiced in Vienna and Russia before settling in Cincinnati, Ohio, rejected the notion that religious dietary laws were responsible for the lower morbidity rate of the Jews. Instead, he credited other factors (strong family ties, solidarity, and a highly developed social welfare system) with the generally better physical condition of the Jewish population.[13] At around the same time, an American Reform rabbi suggested alternatively that the relatively low morbidity rate among Jews was primarily due to their strict adherence to their religious purity laws.[14] In more recent medical literature we find echoes of this discussion of Judaism and hygiene, when, for example, lower rates of cancer (in this case penile and cervical carcinomas) among Jews are attributed to the religious commandment about circumcision.[15]

Discussion about the health advantages of being a Jew contradicts the anti-Semitic equation of sickness and Judaism, both literally and figuratively. Jewish doctors and rabbis participated in this discussion, but so did non-Jews who realized that Jewish preventive health measures not only confirmed new scientific information but also had a certain exemplary character. This meant reducing Mosaic law to practices relevant to daily life that could be scientifically interpreted and justified. A larger goal was also reached in the process: liberating Judaism from the interpretive monopoly of the rabbinate and thereby modernizing it. In this context, the biblical Moses came to be viewed as the archetype of the healthy Jew.[16] The laws named after him were interpreted as guidelines for good physical hygiene and health care. Jewish social hygienist Alfred Nossig (1864–1943) thus declared toward the end of the nineteenth century that "Moses placed the commandment of work at the head of his laws, and it is to their credit that modern doctors studying Mosaic hygiene have examined the importance of this commandment."[17] Nossig emphasizes one advantage of Mosaic hygiene in particular:

Die Hygiene der Juden

Im Anschluß an die Internationale
Hygiene-Ausstellung Dresden 1911

herausgegeben

von

Dr. MAX GRUNWALD.

Verlag der Historischen Abteilung der
Internationalen Hygiene - Ausstellung
:::   Dresden 1911   :::
DRESDEN N., Großenhainerstraße 9

Figure 18. Max Grunwald, ed., *Die Hygiene der Juden* (Dresden: Verlag der Historischen
Abteilung der Internationalen Hygiene-Ausstellung, 1911), title page.

"that it includes and consciously implements the strong influence of a moral element on physical health."[18] Here Moses is depicted as a role model since his health regulations reflect a type of holistic thinking that views body and soul as one. In the nineteenth century there were also Christians who suggested that Judaism had something to teach in this regard. American doctor Edward T. Williams (1824–99), for example, wrote in 1882: "However degenerate, morally speaking, some of their modern descendants may be, they [the Jews] certainly have not degenerated physically, a sufficient answer to the often repeated assertion that civilization tends to physical weakness, for the Jews have been longer civilized than any other highly civilized people. May we not then venture the inference that the rite of Abraham, or Moses, has had its share, in the production of these wonderful results, and that it might perhaps be profitably imitated by other nations?"[19] Many health-conscious non-Jews continue to follow this advice—though sometimes unknowingly—when they avoid even natural food stores in the wake of grocery scandals and instead buy kosher grocery items, since the latter are required to give a detailed list of all artificial additives.

The Obligation to Maintain Good Health

The Bible tells us: "before you fall sick, consult a doctor" (Ecclesiasticus 18:19). According to rabbinical interpretation the duty to maintain good health derives not only from this apocryphal text but also from the Torah itself: "take good care: be on the watch not to forget the things that you have seen with your own eyes" (Deuteronomy 4:9). The Bible even includes warnings about avoiding certain very specific threats to life and limb: "When you build a new house, put a parapet along the roof, or you will bring the guilt of bloodshed on your house if anyone should fall from it" (Deuteronomy 22:8). In the content of this verse we find an early example of an accident prevention regulation.

Concern about having a sufficient food supply is also voiced in the Torah: "When you are at war, and lay siege to a city for a long time in order to take it, do not destroy its trees by taking the axe to them, for they provide you with food; you shall not cut them down" (Deuteronomy 20:19).

Since the body is a work of God, Jewish thinking requires that it be given particular attention and care. Everything the body needs (food, drink, movement, rest, and so on) thus helps to serve the Eternal One, as the *Shulchan Arukh* spells out with specific everyday examples.[20] These in turn refer for the most part to Maimonides's teachings on health in the *Mishneh Torah*, where we read: "A person should direct his heart and the totality of his behavior to one goal, becoming aware of God, blessed be He. The [way] he rests, rises, and speaks should all be directed to this end" (De'ot 3:2). The renowned doctor and philosopher then adds: "Since maintaining a healthy and sound body is among the ways of God—

for one cannot understand or have any knowledge of the Creator, if he is ill—therefore, he must avoid that which harms the body and accustom himself to that which is healthful and helps the body become stronger" (De'ot 4:1).

Not health maintenance per se, in other words, but serving God and sanctifying his work are behind these words of advice, which for the most part follow the dietetics of antiquity. Maimonides makes this clear with everyday examples:

> A person who accustoms himself to live by [the rules of] medicine does not follow a proper path if his sole intention is that his entire body and limbs be healthy and that he have children who will do his work and toil for him. Rather, he should have the intent that his body be whole and strong, in order for his inner soul to be upright so that [it will be able] to know God. For it is impossible to understand and become knowledgeable in the wisdoms when one is starving or sick, or when one of his limbs pains him. [Similarly,] one should intend to have a son [with the hope that] perhaps he will be a wise and great man in Israel.
>
> Thus, whoever walks in such a path all his days will be serving God constantly; even in the midst of his business dealings, even during intercourse for his intent in all matters is to fulfill his needs so that his body be whole to serve God.
>
> Even when he sleeps, if he retires with the intention that his mind and body rest, lest he take ill and be unable to serve God because he is sick, then his sleep is service to the Omnipresent, blessed be He.
>
> On this matter, our Sages have directed and said: "And all your deeds should be for the sake of Heaven." This is what Solomon declared in his wisdom: "Know Him in all your ways and He will straighten your paths" (Proverbs 3:6). (Mishneh Torah, De'ot 3:3)

Another particularly striking formulation of this duty to maintain good health is found in a midrash. One day, when the pupils of renowned Jewish scholar Hillel the Elder (d. ca. 10 CE) accompanied him after a lesson and asked where he was going, he replied that he was off to fulfill an obligation. They asked which one and were astonished by his reply that he was on his way to the bathhouse. When they asked how this could be considered a mitzvah, or good work, he explained: "Just like regarding the statues (lit. icons) of kings, that are set up in the theaters and the circuses, the one who is appointed over them bathes them and scrubs them, . . . I, who was created in the [Divine] Image and Form, . . . even more so!" (Vayikra Rabbah 34.3). Similarly, the Talmud emphasizes that even such things as guidelines for defecation should by no means be considered profane but are instead so important for maintaining good physical health that they are handed down by knowledgeable rabbis. One time, for instance, Rabbi Huna chided his son Rabba for not attending class with Rabbi Hisda. The son defended his decision by saying that the rabbi was teaching about only "mundane matters" like how to avoid hemorrhoids. His father answered in no uncertain terms: "He is dealing with matters crucial to human life, and you say that he is dealing with mundane matters? Now that I know what you meant, all the more so go before him" (BT Shabbat 82a). No church father would have dared to describe human digestion so explicitly and follow up with specific advice.

In the Torah and above all in the Talmud, numerous rules show just how extensively Judaism internalized Greco-Roman teachings on dietetics, expanded on them, and aligned them with religious regulations. Among these are the *sex res non naturales* (six nonnatural things) that according to Hippocrates and Galen need to be attended to: light and air (*aer*), food and drink (*cibus et potus*), work and rest (*motus et quies*), sleep and waking (*somnus et vigilia*), secretions and excretions (*secreta et excreta*), and the stimulation of the soul or spirit (*affectus animi*). Correspondingly, the dietetic spectrum found in the Talmud and other rabbinical texts ranges from the practice of bloodletting, which remained common up into the nineteenth century, to detailed advice on digestion.[21] In a wide variety of contexts relating to religious practice we find valuable tips about exercise, fasting, handwashing, bathing, sleep, and sexual activity. Many recommendations in these texts about ways to promote good health are still valid today. Take, for instance, the advice to avoid gluttony ("More have been killed due to the chamber pot, because they were not careful about relieving themselves in a timely manner, than those swollen due to starvation," BT Shabbat 33a) or about walking after a meal ("One who ate and did not walk four cubits after eating, what he ate rots," BT Shabbat 41a). In contrast, the recommendations for bloodletting are now obsolete, since the practice is no longer part of conventional medicine; teaching about illness is no longer based on the humoral pathology of antiquity. Similarly, Maimonides's advice about wearing clothes made of sheepskin rather than fox or weasel is no longer relevant today. In recent halakhic literature there is therefore general consensus that health care as described in the Talmud, above all, was specific to its time and that contemporary standards and information should be used today when following religious laws.[22]

The Particular Hygiene of the Jews

In discussions about the health advantages religious Jews supposedly enjoy by because of their adherence to ritual laws, three types of prophylaxis are key: (1) the "monthly purification" of women in the Jewish ritual bath, or *mikveh*, (2) circumcision, and (3) dietary laws. These three will therefore be treated in greater detail, bearing in mind that we are dealing first and foremost with God-given regulations that are not meant to be rationally analyzed but simply followed. That said, it is entirely possible to also interpret them as more or less sensible measures to promote good health, even if they were originally codified for entirely different reasons. Thus, already in 1912 Jewish folklorist Max Grunwald (1871–1953) stated in an anthology of essays about Jewish hygiene: "it does not matter if something is taught and expressly labeled as hygiene; instead, what matters is that a hygienic effect is intended, that a recommendation proves to be hygienically effective."[23] As a medical historian, I do need to interject here that our modern concepts of hygiene, believed to be scientifically proven, have also undergone change over time. Consider for instance the famous dispute over the causes of epidemics between Robert Koch (1843–1910) and Max von Pettenkofer (1818–1901). The latter, a highly respected professor of hygiene in Munich, disagreed with the famous bacteriologist in Berlin (home to a research institute that still bears his name today) and held that secondary environmental conditions were considerably more important in the development of an illness than the presence of pathogens alone.

The "Monthly Purification" of Women

It was not until the early nineteenth century that doctors more or less favorably inclined to Judaism began to investigate why it is that Jews, despite many social and economic disadvantages, often have not only a lower mortality rate but also better health. One of the first to explore this phenomenon using empirical observation was the Laupheim chief medical officer Dr. zum Tobel (1769–1848), who was forced to admit that "the Jews are very concerned about maintaining good health, which is partially required by their religion. They enjoy a number of regulations that would be worthy of imitation by other confessions if they were applied in a practical way with more of an eye toward salubrity."[24] In his view, two of these hygienic achievements of Judaism were especially noteworthy: the *mikveh* and the dietary laws. He explained why in fact Jews are not as healthy as one might expect, given their exemplary health care, by noting their "lives spent fighting poverty and various burdens."[25] The cited example of the Jewish ritual bath reveals how much the discourse on health had shifted in the nineteenth century.[26]

One of the most contentious aspects of the Jewish Enlightenment is the questioning of religious customs in light of desired social changes (keyword: "emancipation"), political demands, and recent scientific advances. Two customs were particularly controversial: early burial (to which we will return in Chapter 7) and the ritual bathhouse, or *mikveh*, which was scrutinized from the perspective of hygiene.[27] This debate peaked in the 1820s and 1830s. Jewish and Christian doctors alike critiqued the poor hygienic conditions in most "cellar spring baths" (*Kellerquellenbäder*), as they were then known in the Jewish community, which fit right in with the efforts of the *maskilim* promoting a "more timely" Judaism. One of the movement's leading figures was Moritz Mombert (1799–1859), a Kassel doctor who saw the dirty, musty bathhouses he had encountered as an inspector as dangerous places of contagion. He blamed these conditions in part on "fanatical rabbis" and/or "rabbinism,"[28] and as medical historian Thomas Schlich has shown, by mentioning opponents of reform in the same breath as gonorrhea, scabies, and tuberculosis, Mombert implied that illness, filth, and immorality were linked to Jewish Orthodoxy.[29] The reformers were successful. Between 1810 and 1850, official ordinances were passed concerning the ritual baths, which were either closed or remodeled to meet contemporary hygiene standards, all in keeping with Mombert's motto: "the means for the universal reformation [of the Jews] lies within the power of doctor alone, allowing him to act faster and more successfully."[30] The authority of the rabbi was challenged and was to be replaced by that of the doctor—a transitional process that in the nineteenth century was also visible in the shifting attitudes toward science and medical questions in Christian denominations (keywords here: "miracle cures," "pastoral medicine").

The second half of the nineteenth century saw a major change in the discourse about the *mikveh*. Jewish authors were not alone in their efforts to prove the progressiveness of Judaism by citing its early appreciation of such laudable establishments as the ritual bathhouse. For example, the *Encyclopädisches Wörterbuch der Staatsarzneikunde* (Encyclopedic Dictionary of Public Pharmacology) of 1872 states that while these bathhouses had admittedly had certain deficiencies in the past, from a physician's standpoint the contemporary ones were to be commended.[31] The unqualified positive evaluation of the *mikveh* is expressed most clearly in the catalog that accompanied the 1911 Dresden Hygiene Exhibit, where the Jewish ritual bath is cited as an admirable example of the high standard of hygiene in Judaism and one that dates back to biblical-Talmudic times.[32] The *Jüdisches Lexikon* (1927) echoed this positive verdict, claiming that the *mikveh* had "hygienic importance that cannot be praised highly enough."[33] For all these accolades, however, it should be noted that in 1906 only 55 percent of Jewish congregations in Germany still had a *mikveh*, and its use had declined considerably. At the turn of the twentieth century only about 15 percent of Jewish women made visits to the ritual bathhouse.[34]

Circumcision from a Hygienic Perspective

In 1882, medical advisers to the Grand Ducal Ministry in Baden furnished an expert opinion on circumcision. In it we read: "Circumcision, a Jewish religious act of the highest value, is incidentally . . . of not insignificant sanitary importance: it apparently prevents uncleanliness and disease of the glans caused by decayed smegma, reduces the transmission of sexual diseases, is considered an impediment to and therefore a reduction in the vice of masturbation, and serves as an

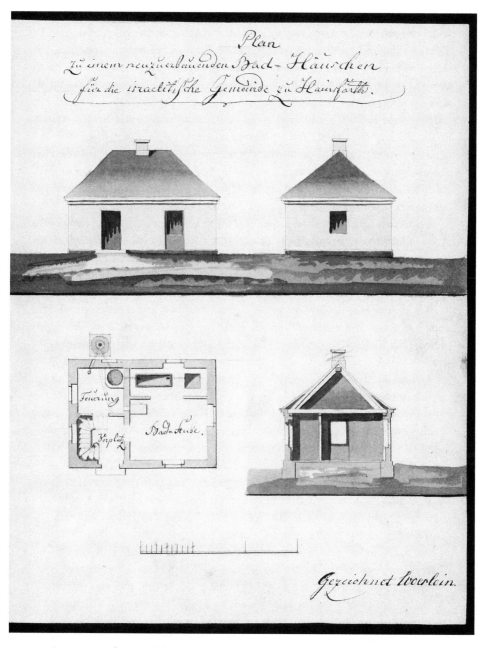

Figure 19. Architectural plans for a *mikveh* at Hainsfarth. Drawing by Wörlein, circa 1829. State Archive, Augsburg, file no. 168.

early corrective to a frequently occurring malformation (overly tight foreskin) which for other boys requires a surgical intervention similar to circumcision."[35] Today we still find a similar line of argument in the medical discourse on circumcision. For example, it is believed to even protect against infection with the AIDS virus.[36] In contrast, the belief that circumcision can act as a deterrent to masturbation is now obsolete.[37] Masturbation is no longer an issue for doctors; instead, it is only in conservative Christian groups and Orthodox Judaism that it is still considered a problem and stigmatized as sinful behavior.[38]

Since the early nineteenth century, when the Jewish Enlightenment attracted a growing number of followers, two distinct discourses on circumcision have existed—at times even simultaneously. One argued that removing the foreskin has medical advantages, while the other took the exact opposite stance.

Let us first consider the argument that while circumcision is religiously motivated in Judaism, it can also be understood as a form of medical prophylaxis. In this context, recent—though not uncontroversial—studies are often mentioned, claiming that male circumcision apparently not only reduces the risk of HIV infection but may also possibly inhibit the growth of prostate carcinomas.[39]

The first known positive assessment of circumcision as a measure promoting good health is found in late antiquity in book 1 of *On the Special Laws, I* by Jewish philosopher Philo of Alexandria.[40] Philo outlines the following advantages:

> First of all, that it is a preventive of a painful disease, and of an affliction difficult to be cured, which they call a carbuncle; because, I imagine, when it becomes inflamed it burns; from which fact it has derived that appellation. And this disease is very apt to be engendered among those who have not undergone the rite of circumcision. Secondly, it secures the cleanliness of the whole body in a way that is suited to the people consecrated to God; with which object the Egyptian priests, being extravagant in their case, shave the whole of their bodies; for some of these evils which ought to be got rid of are collected in and lodge under the hair and the prepuce. Thirdly, there is the resemblance of the part that is circumcised to the heart; for both parts are prepared for the sake of generation; for the breath contained within the heart is generative of thoughts, and the generative organ itself is productive of living beings. Therefore, the men of old thought it right to make the evident and visible organ, by which the objects of the outward senses are generated, resemble that invisible and superior part, by means of which ideas are formed. The fourth, and most important, is that which relates to the provision thus made for prolificness; for it is said that the seminal fluid proceeds in its path easily, neither being at all scattered, nor flowing on its passage into what may be called the bags of the prepuce. On which account those nations which practice

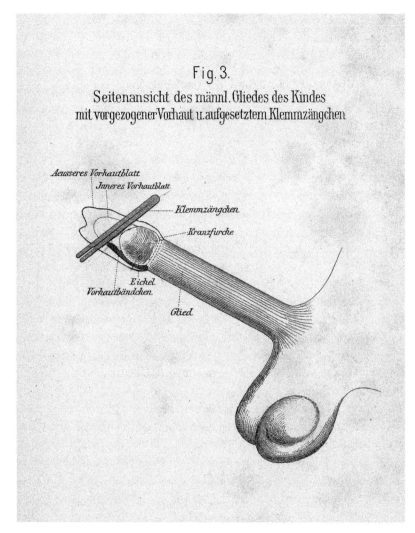

Figure 20. "Sideview of a child's phallus." Official instructions for mohels. From *Dienstvorschriften für Mohelim* (Karlsruhe: Malsch & Vogel, 1897).

circumcision are the most prolific and the most populous. These considerations have come to our ears, having been discussed of old among men of divine spirit and wisdom, who have interpreted the writings of Moses in no superficial or careless manner.[41]

One of the many medical arguments cited here by Philo is taken up in the Middle Ages by Maimonides among others, who held that circumcision had been introduced not least as a way to "counteract excessive lust; for there is no doubt that circumcision weakens the power of sexual excitement."[42]

In the mid-nineteenth century, the health benefits of circumcision were supported by numbers for the first time in studies conducted by doctors, even if from today's perspective the methodology behind the statistics looks somewhat problematic. The most influential study was done by British doctor Jonathan Hutchinson (1828–1913). Using patients from the Metropolitan Free Hospital in London, in 1845 he attempted to prove that circumcision successfully prevented infection with syphilis.[43] At the International Hygiene Exhibition of 1911 in Dresden, the medical advantages of circumcision were once again showcased and backed up by numbers.[44]

At almost the same time a debate began that continues to this day, in which (primarily) doctors focus on the risks posed by circumcision, in particular the transmission of disease.[45] It was argued already in the nineteenth century, for example, that instead of preventing syphilis, circumcision actually had just the opposite effect. In this context, the ritual of *metsitsah*, or sucking blood from the wound, was deemed especially dangerous. There were admittedly isolated voices of dissent: in an expert opinion of 1847, for instance, four professors of medicine at the university in Würzburg stated that *metsitsah* was a medically safe procedure and that it even helped the wound to heal.[46] But criticism of the practice did not fall on deaf ears. In France this part of the ritual was eliminated already in 1844, and by the end of nineteenth century most German states had followed suit.[47] In places where the custom had not been discontinued, a small glass tube with a filter was placed over the penis, and the circumciser sucked on the tube's mouthpiece instead of directly on the wound. Writing in 1911 about the *brit milah* of his nephew in Prague, Franz Kafka (1883–1924) describes the traditional circumcision including the *metsitsah* as a relic of Eastern Judaism:

> When I arrived at W.'s yesterday noon I heard the voice of his sister greeting me, but I did not see her herself until her fragile figure detached itself from the rocking-chair standing in front of me.
>
> This morning my nephew's circumcision. A short, bow-legged man, Austerlitz, who already has 2,800 circumcisions behind him, carried the thing out very skillfully. It is an operation made more difficult by the fact that the boy, instead of lying on a table, lies on his grandfather's lap, and by the fact that the person performing the operation, instead of paying close attention, must whisper prayers. First the boy is prevented from moving by wrappings which leave only his member free, then the surface to be operated on is defined precisely by putting on a perforated metal disc, then the operation is performed with what is almost an ordinary

knife, a sort of fish knife. One sees blood and raw flesh, the *moule* [circumciser] bustles about briefly with his long-nailed, trembling fingers and pulls skin from some place or other over the wound like the finger of a glove. At once everything is all right, the child has scarcely cried. Now there remains only a short prayer during which the *moule* drinks some wine and with his fingers, not yet entirely unbloody, carries some wine to the child's lips. Those present pray: "As he has now achieved the covenant, so may he achieve knowledge of the Torah, a happy marriage, and the performance of good deeds."

Today when I heard the *moule*'s assistant say the grace after meals and those present, aside from the two grandfathers, spent the time in dreams or boredom with a complete lack of understanding of the prayer, I saw Western European Judaism before me in a transition whose end is clearly unpredictable and about which those most closely affected are not concerned, but, like all people truly in transition, bear what is imposed on them. It is so indisputable that these religious forms which have reached their final end have merely a historical character, even as they are practiced today, that only a short time was needed this very morning to interest the people present in the obsolete custom of circumcision and its half-sung prayers by describing it to them as something out of history.[48]

For Sigmund Freud, in contrast, circumcision posed a threat completely different from infection and the spread of germs. His interpretation of the *brit milah* as an act of castration still carries weight today with those opponents of the practice who invoke the welfare of the child and view circumcision as an early childhood trauma.[49] In 1893 Freud writes in the "preliminary communication" to *Studies of Hysteria*: "Circumcision is, no doubt a trauma, releasing a tendency in the ego to repeat it in one way or another and to form reactions to it."[50] At the same time, Freud stresses the meaning of circumcision for the non-Jewish man: "the castration complex is the deepest unconscious root of antisemitism; for even in the nursery little boys hear that a Jew has something cut off his penis—a piece of his penis, they think—and this gives them a right to despise Jews."[51] Thus, the ostensible concern for a child's welfare and the prevention of child abuse used by non-Jews today as arguments against circumcising underage boys may well be concealing other motives. Some opponents of circumcision even see it as a violation of the Nuremberg Code of 1947. As we know, this set of internationally recognized ethical principles for conducting medical research was formulated as part of the judgment delivered in the Nuremberg "Doctors' Trial."[52] But in this case the opposite is claimed: the crimes against humanity are now allegedly committed by the Jews themselves, in that they circumcise innocent children unasked.

Within Judaism itself, voices critical of circumcision were heard for the first time—not surprisingly—during the Haskalah. Lawyer and pioneer of emancipation Gabriel Riesser (1806–63) thought circumcision could be dispensed with, and in 1824 Philipp Wolfers (1796–1832), a Jewish general practitioner and obstetrician, argued that circumcision was a dangerous procedure and should be overseen by the "medical police."[53] Incidentally, this was already the case in 1819 in the Berlin Jewish community, where a doctor's presence was required at a *brit milah*. Reform rabbi Samuel Holdheim (1806–60) contended that circumcision was an "unhealthy" practice that should be abolished.[54] Several years later, an incident in the Bavarian town of Hürben made headlines. There, a Jewish doctor named Ignatz Landauer (d. 1868) blocked the circumcision of his son, yet at the same time insisted that the boy's name be added to the communal registry. The presiding rabbi, Joachim (Hayum) Schwarz (1800–1875), refused. Landauer could not prevail, and moved to Speyer.[55] At the time he was the sole Jewish father who rejected the traditional ritual of circumcision for his male offspring. Many doctors and rabbis at the time saw no contradiction between Enlightenment and maintaining religious traditions like the *brit milah*. Among them was Ludwig Philippson (1811–89), editor of the *Allgemeine Zeitung des Judentums*, the most important organ of liberal Judaism in the nineteenth century.[56]

Around the middle of the nineteenth century, the authorities finally entered the debate on whether to retain the ritual of circumcision, which was not confined to within Judaism. In many places, the mohels, or ritual circumcisers, were placed under the supervision of medical officials, or a regulation was passed requiring a doctor to be present at a circumcision. At the same time, some communities were reluctant to interfere in Jewish religious affairs. The city of Dresden, for example, continued to allow mohels to perform their duties despite their limited medical knowledge, invoking the principle of freedom of religion.[57]

When in 2012 a high-ranking representative of the medical profession called on lawmakers to issue clear regulations allowing doctors to continue performing circumcisions without fear of prosecution, so that "these children do fall into the hands of some barbers or other semi-skilled assistants,"[58] it was no coincidence that the wording echoed the mid-nineteenth-century discourse on circumcision, when doctors were eager to demonstrate their increasing power as experts in areas including matters relating to circumcision. They insisted not only that they be allowed to speak on such "vital issues," but that they alone were competent to do so. In the meantime, in most Western countries—Israel being the exception—they have achieved the very thing an anonymous member of the Orthodoxy feared in 1847: "they [the Reform movement] want to surround the circumcision chair, this consecrated altar of Juda . . . with drawbridges, medical guards, police and sanitation departments; they want to take the noble, green branch of a deed fraternally performed for God and weave it into a common bread basket for doctors."[59]

Dietary Laws

Responding to a comment that Jewish dietary laws promote good health, a member of the strictly observant Chabad movement once said: "if these commandments were about health, then all rabbis would look like [Arnold] Schwarzenegger! And anyone who does not live kosher would look sick. But it seems to be the opposite: most religious people look rather thin (or overweight), while those who do not eat kosher have bulging biceps."[60]

Before turning to the question—still discussed today—of whether eating kosher has health benefits or is strictly the fulfillment of a religious commandment, let us briefly summarize the most important Jewish dietary regulations themselves, as presented already in the Bible.[61]

It is permissible to eat mammals with cloven hooves if they are also ruminants. These include cows and goats. However, if an animal has only one of the two characteristics, such as a pig, which has cloven hooves but only one stomach, then it is not kosher. Insects and reptiles are also not kosher. As for animals that live in water, the ones deemed edible are those with both fins and scales. While this applies to most types of fish and ocean-dwellers, it is not true of eels, mussels, snails, shrimp and prawn, or crabs. Fowl that eat carrion and birds of prey are not kosher, but "domesticated" birds such as geese, ducks, and chickens may be eaten by observant Jews.

The consumption of blood is strictly forbidden, so when animals are slaughtered, as much of their blood must be removed as possible. The kosher slaughtering of an animal involves slitting its throat without anesthetizing it first, since anesthesia inhibits bleeding out. A special knife with an extremely sharp blade is used, and meat bought from a kosher butcher, or *shochet*, is usually cleansed of any remaining blood in the house kitchen with water and salt. Only then is it considered kosher and fit for consumption.

In addition, meat from animals whose consumption is normally allowed may not to be eaten under certain circumstances. This restriction derives from, among other things, the following passage in the Torah: "you shall not eat the flesh of anything in the open country killed by beasts, but you shall throw it to the dogs" (Exodus 22:31). The term for this meat that is ritually unfit for consumption is *treifa* (Hebrew *trefa*). Maimonides explained the term, which derives from "torn (by beasts)," by saying that such an animal has a *mum* (Hebrew for "injury," "deformity," or "mutilation"). Even if the animal appears to be healthy, if its projected lifespan is a year or less because of such an impairment, it is *treifa* and may not be eaten. These defects include a perforated lung. Halakhah determines that an animal like a steer with this type of injury, no matter how small, will not survive a full year. It is for this reason that after an animal is slaughtered its lungs are also examined. If they are undamaged, or *glatt*, the animal is kosher. If a lung is damaged, however, the entire animal is deemed unfit for consumption. According to

Rashi (1040–1105), the suspicion alone of some flaw made an animal unfit for Jews to eat. Rashi's grandson Jacob ben Meir Tam (ca. 1100–1171) disagreed. In his opinion, suspicion alone was not sufficient; it was the examination of the animal that was decisive.

In keeping with the biblical rule that a kid may not be cooked in its mother's milk (Exodus 23:19), Judaism strictly forbids the consumption of meat and dairy products together. There are meaty food items and dairy food items, and if a person has eaten meat, up to six hours must elapse before dairy can be consumed. Strictly kosher households even use two separate sets of dishes to prevent all contact between these two categories of food.

Some food groups belong to neither the "meat" nor the "dairy" category, such as fish, eggs, vegetables, and fruits. These are characterized as *pareve*, or neutral with regard to dietary laws, and may therefore be eaten together with meat or milk products.

Up until the nineteenth century, Jewish traditional regulations concerning food were not questioned but merely interpreted. This remained unchanged until the Haskalah. Suddenly Jews admitted to also eating pork, as Heinrich Heine writes in the frequently cited lines from *Deutschland: A Winter's Tale*:

> The Jews can be subdivided again—
> the distinction's really quite simple:
> the old-style lot go to Synagogue,
> and the new-fangled ones to the Temple.
>
> New Jewry eats pork—when it comes to the Law,
> they're great rebellion-backers;
> they're democrats where the old-style Jews
> are mostly aristocrackers.[62]

The situation ironically depicted here by the sharp-tongued writer, himself a convert to Christianity, sparked heated debates in Jewish congregations, which led numerous rabbinical conferences in the 1840s to consider revising the dietary laws.[63] In the memorandum to the second such conference in Frankfurt am Main (1845), we read, for example: "our profession is not to examine whether the grounds for these prohibitions still exist today, much less draw a dividing line between the simple biblical rules and the towering list of Talmudic requirements; but we feel compelled to say that this area, so broad in scope, is a cancer on the state of our religion."[64] The document further states that the Jewish kitchen is a "place of religious refuge" no longer in keeping with the times. At the third meeting of German rabbis in 1846, which took place from July 13 to July 24 in Breslau (Wrocław), Rabbi David Einhorn declared: "In support of the claim that the

Mosaic dietary laws in Leviticus 11 are no longer binding today . . . thus far only two main points have been advanced: they were seen either as sanitary laws whose relevance rested on local and temporally specific conditions that no longer exist; or, because of their ceremonial nature, they together with the entire ritual law were declared no longer obligatory for the current developmental stage of Judaism (and Jewishness, or rather, humanity)."[65] Another member of the commission, Samuel Holdheim, chief rabbi of Schwerin, took it even a step further. He questioned the validity of all the purity commandments by underscoring their rootedness in a particular point in time:

> For us, the connection between external symbolic holiness and purity on the one hand and moral holiness and purity, for all its importance in biblical antiquity, has been severed and dissolved. Priests, temples, and sacrificial offerings no longer have meaning for us, nor does the uncleanliness of animals or human corpses. We have moved away from the entire way of thinking of antiquity, and no power can magically return us to it. What was once sacred and pure has ceased to be so, and the same is true for what was once deemed unholy and impure. We recognize no sanctity except the moral one, and have no concept of impurity except that which is morally impure.[66]

Radical ideas like these provoked correspondingly strong reactions from Orthodox Jews. The intense debate was marked by irony and mockery, and not just from Heinrich Heine. Israel Deutsch (1800–1853) wrote the following sarcastic lines about those who favored reforms:

> See how on the Sabbath the highly educated Herr Doctor hurries from the shaving basin to the pulpit, carefully arranging his face in accordance with the strict rules of mimicry so that his artificially pious expression may make a good impression. Now listen to how knowledgably this man speaks, waxing eloquent on outdated forms and reforms, on Zeitgeist, on statutes and regulations, the sanctity of good works, and faith based solely on belief.—We see him hasten from the pulpit to the nearest Christian restaurant to dine and enjoy a cigar. We are surprised. An acquaintance notices and assures us that the Herr Doctor has just published—or will shortly publish—a pamphlet in which it will be philosophically, historically, and critically demonstrated that the dietary laws are local and temporary. In the Arabian desert, says the pamphlet, where neither Leipzig larks nor Braunschweig sausages were to be had and manna fell from heaven, there such dietary laws could be observed, but not during our

time, in refined Europe, where [such] teachings and life would constantly collide.[67]

Deutsch was a rabbi in Beuthen, Upper Silesia. Together with his brother David (1810–73), he belonged to a group that sought to block the appointment of the liberal rabbi Abraham Geiger, who openly supported the move to abolish the dietary laws.

Samuel Hirsch (1815–89), though basically a supporter of reform,[68] nonetheless defended Jewish tradition in the matter of the dietary laws, but not tradition for its own sake. He saw the turn away from Jewish purity commandments as primarily an effort to adapt to non-Jewish surroundings, to assimilate. His critique also explicitly includes the first generation of *maskilim*:

> Our fathers professed that the dietary laws had been passed solely to promote good health under open skies; but as seriously as they meant it, they only deceived themselves, and we should no longer let ourselves be deceived, since that which excused them cannot excuse us. They confused appearance with truth, and believed they had to be ashamed of their Jewishness, whereas actually they needed to be ashamed only of their awkward behavior and their non-German language, for which Judaism was truly not responsible. And because they were ashamed to face life as Jews, they dismissed the dietary laws and all the commandments of the sacred Torah that would have distinguished them as Jews. And because they did not dare turn against Holy Scripture, they invented the next best reason, ignored its flimsiness and let it stand in the absence of anything better, limping along and wanting to have it both ways: wanting to have a life, but also not eager to be on bad terms with Holy Scripture—that is the reason for this nonsense about the dietary laws having lost their validity or relevance today and in our climate. But can we be excused if we wish to continue this madness? May we still claim to be Jews today?[69]

His answer was a resounding "no."

Reforming the dietary laws continued to be a controversial topic at German rabbinical gatherings up into the 1860s, but in the decades that followed, discussion tapered off. A contemporary who himself had actively participated in the disputes gave the following reason: "Due to the death of several eminent progressive rabbis, but even more importantly, the anti-Semitic movement that followed, things have come to a standstill in the area in question."[70] And indeed, in the last third of the nineteenth century the efforts of animal rights proponents and anti-Semites to bar the kosher slaughter of animals led Jewish communities to sweep their internal disagreements over dietary laws under the rug and close ranks. The political thrust of the discussion about kosher slaughtering is easy to see, especially given its resemblance to the debate on banning circumcision.[71]

In the first half of the nineteenth century, however, those rabbis who still adhered to the traditional purity commandments found support among Christians, and Protestants in particular. Admittedly, in addition to religious grounds they also had some pragmatic considerations, including medical ones. These included "attention to the health of the body, and thus for what is beneficial and unbeneficial," "attention to the health of the soul, in that unhealthy foods are disadvantageous and impair understanding of the truth," but also the promotion of "other religious and ethical goals."[72] The medical field, and Christian doctors in particular, also sang the praises of Jewish tradition for the many hygienic benefits it provided. Prussian medical adviser Johann Anton Heinrich Nicolai (1797–1882) noted approvingly: "For their own use and enjoyment Jews are careful to use only good, healthy meat; therefore, we may certainly assume that whatever the Jew himself eats is healthy."[73]

Toward the end of the nineteenth century, the science of Judaism took up this set of issues. The most detailed treatise was written by the liberal rabbi Adolf Wiener (1812–95), the predecessor of Leo Baeck (1873–1956) in Oppeln (today Opole, Poland). Wiener deliberately wrote in German, and in his introduction he laid out the broad scope of the project. It was to be an examination of the dietary laws from a number of different perspectives: historical, religious, "antiquarian," and interconfessional. His simultaneously historicizing and comparative approach was also used by others working in the science of Judaism. First Wiener traces the "development of the dietary laws" from biblical times up through the Talmudic period. He then gives a detailed account of Jewish exegetes' various opinions on the religious foundations of the laws. This is followed by a comparison of Jewish dietary laws with those of other groups in antiquity. Though not a physician himself, Wiener also discusses the question of whether adherence to the dietary laws, or *kashrut*, promotes good health. Finally, he addresses the effect of Jewish dietary laws on relations between Jews and non-Jews.

At the end of the book, which includes detailed accounts of each individual dietary regulation and numerous references in Hebrew that show his familiarity with the language of rabbinical writings, Wiener draws the following conclusion: "The reform of Jewish dietary laws is an urgent need for our time and fully justified, insofar as and to the extent that they have been proven to be biblically unfounded and erroneous. . . . By 'Jewish dietary laws' we mean only the Talmudic-rabbinical ones; the Mosaic or biblical ones should be left intact."[74] In his view, the prohibition against consuming meat and milk together has no basis in the Bible. Here he is explicitly *not* trying to defend Judaism against anti-Semitic attacks: "No! For the sake of truth and of a purified [Reformed] piety, for our own sake and that of our honorable, worthy fellow citizens . . . we call for reform of the burdensome, socially limiting, non-biblical, fictitious rabbinical dietary restrictions."[75] The liberal rabbi explains this discarding of outdated religious ballast by saying that the Jews no longer live in the Middle Ages, when social isolation was the norm; now a new era has begun in which "all dividing walls and boundary posts" must fall.[76] Wiener here not only writes in support of reform within Judaism but shows decided assimilationist tendencies.

At the 1911 Hygiene Exhibition in Dresden, where Judaism was assigned its own section, the full extent of this adaptation to non-Jewish surroundings was plain to see. In the catalog of essays that accompanied the exhibition, Jewish dietary laws are treated almost exclusively in terms of hygiene: "whatever concerns human nutrition is controlled by a strict and, though unusual, nonetheless basically hygienic regimen."[77] Only when it comes to the debate still swirling around the possible ban on ritual slaughter is religion still in the picture: "The slaughterer, called a *shochet*, is following a religious commandment in plying his trade, which is why he bears no trace of coarseness: he is more priest than butcher. As such, he is part of the spiritual hygiene that Jewish slaughterhouses instill in the Jewish people."[78]

Though Jewish regulations on meat were repeatedly described as exemplary, it became a moot point after Hitler's rise to power. On April 21, 1933, ritual slaughter was declared a punishable offense, and the law concerning the slaughter of animals required all warm-blooded animals to be anesthetized before being bled. This law was an expression of the widespread anti-Semitic hostility of the time, and restricted the religious freedom of the Jews considerably. One exception was made, though only in the final phase of World War II and only for Muslims sympathetic to the NS regime, which underscored the decidedly anti-Semitic thrust of the law.[79]

Today we again find much that is reminiscent of the discourse on hygiene at the turn of the twentieth century. Kosher products are now considered "super-organic" products and therefore healthy, since additives often provoke allergic reactions or are hard to digest. A non-Jew who buys groceries with a kosher certificate wants one thing above all: products that are virtually free of additives. As we now know, the "organic" designation still allows for some things that the *mashgiach*, or supervisors of *kashrut*, do not permit since they are considered unclean (*treifa*). Most preservatives, for example, some of which can trigger allergic reactions, are not allowed in kosher items. The same is true of the antioxidants used to keep meat and sausage fresh longer. This is not to say that everything labeled "kosher" is necessarily healthy. An American study revealed, for instance, that kosher poultry is often teeming with bacteria. The meat examined in the study was shown to contain almost twice the amount of E. coli bacteria as ordinary poultry. According to the authors, this finding contradicts the commonly held view that kosher foods are generally healthier and safer.[80] Since to date this remains the only scientific study of its kind, and one that has not gone unchallenged, its findings will probably not stop health-conscious Jews and non-Jews alike from continuing to buy meat and other products with the kosher stamp. For example, one Jewish website advertises a particular *kashrut* certificate with the statement: "The reason most consumers value the kosher stamp so highly is that it guarantees the careful and seamless supervision of the products and their contents. Its consistency thus makes it similar to the German law concerning groceries—but by no means identical to it, for it goes far beyond that law. . . . Kosher is not just good for Jews."[81] In contrast, for Orthodox Jews who today still adhere to the commandments of the Torah (dietary as well as other regulations), religion is the sole motivation. Even so, a number of them emphasize that their pious lifestyle, including the sense of solidarity and community it produces, has a positive effect on their health.[82]

Health Spas and Wellness

While Jews were not trailblazers in the development of health spas, they were nonetheless early and enthusiastic devotees of these baths and resorts, which in Europe date back to antiquity and had become fashionable destinations as early as the sixteenth century.[83] A stay at a health resort has thus long been about more than taking care of one's health; social status and class distinctions have also played a central role.

Long before the nineteenth century and the development of "spa anti-Semitism," Jews could be found as guests (and also musical performers) at health resorts. In Johann Jacob Schudt's *Jüdische Merckwürdigkeiten*, for instance, we read the following foolishness: "The arrogant performance of a number of wealthy Jews when availing themselves of the Ems baths or the Schwalbach mineral water treatment never ceases to astonish. Some twenty years ago no Jew could show himself at the Schwalbach fountain until the Christians had drunk each morning; but nowadays one sees Jews there in carriages with one or more Jewish lackeys riding in front and back, dressed in magnificent clothes and, like grand lords, having a servant present them with their glass of water on a silver tray."[84]

If Schudt's time frame is accurate, the "reprehensible" social behavior he describes could be found in Langenschwalbach in the early eighteenth century at the latest. Like later writers who commented on the presence of Jews at health resorts, the Frankfurt high school professor did not wish to have them banned completely, but he did think that a certain distance should be maintained between social classes, especially in cases when a Jew dared to narrow this gap or close it altogether, as the following passage shows: "In Schwalbach an argument developed between Christians and Jews at the acidulous water fountain. The Christians do not wish to hinder or interfere with the Jews who wish to take the waters for their health (which would be neither fair nor Christian), if only they adhered to the tried and true orders prescribed by the princely authorities and arrived somewhat later, when the Christians were completely finished drinking, or at least remained on one side of the fountain when partaking of the water."[85] In short, Jews were welcome to enjoy the water's healing powers, just not side by side with Christians.

In 1716, the Frankfurt Jewish community itself felt compelled to pass some regulations about visits to neighboring Bad Schwalbach. They did so for religious reasons. Future visits to the health resort were not to take place between the first and ninth day of the Jewish month of Av.[86] On these days, which commemorate the destruction of the temple, all forms of entertainment are forbidden. Even the argument that a spa visit was actually taking care of one's health (something of great importance in Judaism) did not help, since, as Schudt reports, the days in question were "important days of suffering and sorrow . . . when people are to abstain from all meat and wine. However, those who take the water at Schwalbach abstain from neither meat nor wine, claiming that it is for their health."[87] Apparently the Jewish upper class did not wish to look inferior in any way to the well-heeled Frankfurt middle class, whose wedding contracts since 1734 had promised the wife an annual visit to the Langenschwalbach health resort; they did not want to miss out on this important social event, which had to occur during the brief six- to eight-week summer season. This was true even in those years when the Jewish calendar threatened to upset travel plans and the traditional period of mourning in the Jewish month of Av coincided with the height of the spa season. Just how many Frankfurt Jews followed the example of the city's patrician families and had jugs of mineral water delivered to their homes from Langenschwalbach we do not know, but the practice itself has been documented for as early as the seventeenth century.[88]

Langenschwalbach was one of the few German health resort locales that after the Thirty Years' War attracted a growing number of Jewish guests each year up until the early nineteenth century. In 1668, seven Jewish families were already permanent residents of Langenschwalbach. The existence of a prayer house in the town has been documented as far back as 1683, and in 1715 a new synagogue was built. A description of the area from 1807 already shows traces of "spa anti-Semitism," but nonetheless offers a realistic picture of how resort guests passed their days, doing more than just thinking about their health.

> From 6 to 7 in the morning, the entire swarm of resort guests gathers at the spring water fountains. . . . The larger and more glittering circle is first. The entire society is scantily clad in negligées. . . . This morning assembly

offers the observer a bountiful harvest in terms of craniometry, physiognomy, and facial expression, especially among the sons and daughters of Israel. Around nine o'clock the society disperses, either returning home for breakfast or gathering in the Jewish saloon, where good quality chocolate, coffee, tea, liqueurs, etc. are available at very low prices. Here the gaming tables are already set up, and the surging crowd divides up among the various tables. For the most part it is Jews who carry on their business in this large room, which incidentally deserves a more attractive location and better setting. They have turned their small fortune into a bank, and lure and torture and pester every passerby, making the grandest promises, trying to get them to play at their bank.[89]

In 1863 the German-American writer and privateer Charles Sealsfield (Karl Postl, 1793–1864) traveled to the Schwalbach spa. There, it was not only the presence of Jews he found intolerable. He took offense particularly at the vain behavior of "Frankfurt Jews," "Englishmen and women," and "Russians and Poles," all of whom he called "shaven and refined barbarians."[90] Jews were also unwelcome guests in municipal bathhouses built around the turn of the nineteenth century in a number of German cities, and in some places they were even forbidden outright to enter.[91]

Since the nineteenth century the annual trip to a health resort has been a ritual for the German as well as the Jewish middle class. However, attending to and restoring one's "health" were often secondary, even if the daily schedule did include much drinking of mineral water and curative bathing. From the 1850s on, Jews—including well-to-do Eastern Jews—accounted for such a large segment of the resort guests that historian Michael Brenner is justified in referring to the health spa in this context as a "Jewish space."[92] Until 1939, the Bohemian towns of Carlsbad, Marienbad, and Franzenbad were particularly popular destinations for Jews and Christians alike. Not only assimilated middle-class Jews from Germany and Western Europe flocked to these places, but also middle-class Jews from Eastern Europe, and even the Chassidim.[93] Here we are dealing with something more than the imitation of a bourgeois tourist practice; the phenomenon also has definite intra-Jewish aspects, including Jewish doctors' early interest in balneology, the study of baths and bathing's therapeutic effects.[94] At some health resorts they comprised the majority of "spa doctors," thereby contributing to the formation of a "Jewish" infrastructure.

Traditional health spas offering a wide array of hydropathic treatments were not the only places that attracted many Central and Eastern European Jews in the nineteenth and early twentieth centuries. Nature sanatoriums, whose visitor numbers grew as a result of the life reform movement,[95] were also popular with Jews and non-Jews alike. Franz Kafka has provided us with impressive account of

Figure 21. Grüngard family during their stay in Marienbad. Photo, 1938. Private collection.

his time at one such institution.[96] In all likelihood, other Jewish guests had similar experiences during their stays at therapeutic baths and health spas that preached a natural way of life, but unfortunately no written records remain.

Kafka's probably most intensive exposure to natural medicine was in July 1912 when he spent three weeks at Jungborn, a nature therapy establishment in the Harz. He traveled there together with Max Brod, stopping along the way in Weimar and other places, and when Brod returned to Prague, Kafka entered the nature sanatorium near Stapelburg. According to the medical report he had given his employer, his visit was prompted by "troubles with digestion, low body weight and a series of nervous complaints."[97] As might be expected, Kafka used the time at the facility to not only try a variety of natural remedies but also take advantage of the peace and quiet to do some concentrated reading. This included Plato's *Republic*; Flaubert's *Sentimental Education*; a biography of Schiller by Eugen Kühnmann; *Aus Traum und Wirklichkeit der Seele: Stille Gedanken aus einsamen Stunden* (1907, From the Dreams and Reality of the Soul: Quiet Thoughts from Lonely Hours) by Walter Kinkel; and the Bible, which was provided in all guest rooms. He also attended open-air religious services, thereby possibly coming into closer contact with Christianity than ever before. This presumably first serious engagement with New Testament texts did not fail to influence his literary works, as evidenced in his unfinished novel *Amerika* (or *The Man Who Disappeared*).

Kafka's descriptions give a striking picture of the daily routine in Jungborn. Morning activities included "washing, setting-up exercises, group gymnastics . . . , some hymn singing, ball playing in a big circle."[98] Afternoons were spent outdoors lying in the grass (usually naked), taking walks in the area, picking cherries, or helping turn hay (tedding). In the evening, guests attended social events such as lectures or occasionally went to a local dance.

At the very outset of his stay, Kafka was lectured by the (unnamed) medical director of the sanatorium on how to lead a healthy life, and his diary lists all the things he should do or should not do in the future:

> [The doctor] forbade me to eat fruit, with the proviso that I needn't obey him. I'm an educated man, I should listen to his lectures, they have even been published, should study the question, draw my own conclusions, and then act accordingly. From his lecture yesterday: "Though your toes may be completely crippled, if you tug at one of them and breathe deeply at the same time, after a while it will straighten out." A certain exercise will make the sexual organs grow. One of his health rules: "Atmospheric baths at night are highly recommended"—(whenever it suits me, I simply slip out of bed and go out into the meadow in front of my cabin)—"but you shouldn't expose yourself too much to the moonlight, it has an injurious effect." It is impossible to clean the kind of clothes we wear today![99]

We also learn from the travel diary what the accommodations were like at Jungborn. Kafka stayed in one of the many individually named cabins: "My house is called 'Ruth.' Practically arranged. Four dormers, four windows, one door."[100] The furnishings were spartan but practical: in addition to a bed and table there was a mirror on the wall and a chamber pot, in case at night a guest felt it was too far or too inconvenient to visit the toilet. Kafka praises the stillness of his airy, light-filled living quarters, and enjoyed the smell of the fresh grass growing in front of his cabin.

He disliked a number of the sanatorium guests for various reasons, including their inability to carry on an intellectual conversation. Far more disturbing, however, was that most of the guests at Jungborn spent the day in a state of undress. Here this was actually the norm: people lay in the grass naked and strolled through the meadows and woods completely undressed. Kafka was horrified more than once when a naked stranger appeared at his cabin door or when he saw nudists "prowling about among the haystacks on the meadow." In one passage he even speaks of getting "light, superficial attacks of nausea" on seeing these "stark-naked" people.[101] His only concession to the nudist culture of Jungborn, which was also common at other health resorts promoting fresh air and bathing, was to wear a swimsuit. This earned him the nickname "the man in the swimming trunks."[102] Yet in his childhood and youth the author had been anything but prudish. The family governess writes in her memoirs that on vacations the Kafkas swam in the Elbe River "always separate and without swimsuits."[103] And in a letter from August 1907 to his friend Max Brod, Kafka describes spending an enjoyable summer in Triesch with his favorite uncle, Siegfried, a country doctor, riding a motorcycle and often lying "naked in the grass by the pond."[104] In other words, Kafka did not reject nudism altogether, but he did have something against "organized" nakedness. He did not want to be forced to—quite literally—expose himself to strangers or people who were merely acquaintances.

Around the turn of the twentieth century, it was especially younger Jewish men and women who eagerly adopted both the ideas and practices of the German youth movement and the life reform movement (the healing power of nature, skepticism about large cities, "back to nature," the primacy of "soul" and "spirit," and so on), and, for the most part, they did not seem perturbed by its racial components and/or the anti-Semitic tone adopted by many members of this revival movement.[105] The National Socialist rise to power in 1933 brought a change of heart; after that, only the Zionist youth movement continued under different auspices to uphold some of the ideals of the life reform movement. Their quest for a "genuine" Jewishness outside the conventions of their parents' generation now made emigration to Palestine an essential prerequisite.

National Socialist persecution of the Jews also brought an end to Jewish health spa tourism. As of mid-June 1939, Jews in the German Reich were forbidden to visit therapeutic baths and other health resorts. Exemptions were granted only for places where it was possible to maintain a strict physical separation between non-Aryans and Germans. In addition, they needed a letter of referral from a Jewish doctor, or *Krankenbehandler* ("tender of the sick," since Jewish physicians were no longer allowed to call themselves doctors after 1938), and were required to register with the police upon arrival.[106]

After 1945, areas that once again attracted the occasional guest who valued kosher meals and Jewish religious services included Bad Sobernheim and Bad Kissingen. Immediately after the end of World War II, Shoah survivors used former sanatoriums to restore their health. In August 1946, for example, Jewish children from the Fürth displaced persons (DPs) camp spent their summer vacation in Bad Kissingen at the Hotel Reichshof sanatorium. At the end of April 1945, the French military government confiscated the parklike grounds and buildings of Jordanbad near Biberach and made it a camp for Jewish DPs.[107] And from 1947 to 1951 following seizure by the Allies, Schloss Elmau, formerly the home of *völkisch*-nationalist ideas and today one of the leading hotels of the world, served as a place to recuperate for Jews who had survived Nazi atrocities and were initially stateless.[108] Today, victims of National Socialism are still eligible for government-paid stays at therapeutic health spas under the Federal Compensation Act.

A separate category of places for rest and recuperation should also be mentioned here: seaside resorts. In the early nineteenth century, as a growing number of Jews began to visit these increasingly popular resorts, they—like Christians of the haute bourgeoisie and aristocracy—were not thinking only of their health. Instead, they too were looking for a pleasant summer retreat in a place where perhaps they might do something for their health in the bargain. Here, as in the traditional health spa locales, social tensions were palpable. Members of the petty bourgeoisie felt particularly threatened by so-called Jewish parvenus.[109] Starting in the 1880s, the Central Organization for German Citizens of the Jewish Faith issued regular warnings in its journal that listed names of vacations spots, hotels, and bed and breakfasts known for their anti-Semitic leanings. Seaside resorts repeatedly mentioned in this context included Borkum, Juist, Wangerooge, Langeoog, Spiekeroog, Scharbeutz, Müritz, and Heiligenhafen. In contrast, the traditional bathing spots of Norderney, Helgoland, Westerland, Wyk auf Föhr, and Heringdorf were considered welcoming to Jews.

While Germans preferred vacations that included swimming, Austrians— who were a long way from the North Sea or the Baltic—relaxed in so-called summer retreats. From the late nineteenth century on, an increasing number of Austrian Jews temporarily left the big city far behind in search of "something like a place of refuge or a home during hiking trips."[110] In contrast to the German "spa anti-Semitism," here the traditional, often religiously motivated animosity toward Jews was barely visible during the tourist season. Only toward the end of World War I, as ever more Eastern Jewish refugees began to settle in the Salzburg area's popular "climactic health resorts" and the rural supply situation became precarious, were there numerous outbursts of anti-Semitic hatred among the locals. It is no coincidence that the novella *Badenheim 1939* by Israeli author Aharon Appelfeld (1932–2018) takes place in a fictional Austrian health spa. When longtime Jewish patrons return in the spring of 1939, few take any notice of the omnipresent health ministry that advertises a trip to "the Promised Land of Poland" and requires all Jewish spa guests and residents to register with the ministry. Soon the health spa is transformed into a ghetto, and early one morning an order comes for all Jews to depart. A train with four filthy freight cars awaits them at the station, prompting one of the characters to remark: "If the coaches are so dirty it must mean that we have not far to go."[111]

Yet soon enough, after the end of World War II as tourism began to flourish once again in the Alpine republic and the economic crisis was past, people focused on business and tried not to annoy the Jewish summer guests. But in contrast to the Federal Republic of Germany, Jews in postwar Austria still had to contend with being unwelcome tourists or spa guests, as proven by more than one incident that took place in connection with the Waldheim affair of 1986. In 2011, a Viennese family trying to book a hotel in Serfaus (Tyrolia) was told that while a vacation rental apartment was available for the desired dates, because of "a bad experience in August 2008, [the hotel] no longer wishes to accommodate Jewish guests."[112]

Conceptions of Beauty

According to traditional Jewish thinking, a healthy body does not necessarily have to be beautiful. This idea admittedly contradicts in a way the modern notion we find already in Johann Gottfried Herder (1744–1803) that physical beauty is merely an expression of health and strength.[113] Writing from the perspective of an assimilated Jew, Arnold Zweig paints the following picture in *The Face of Eastern European Jewry*:

> For this kind of Jew, his body is not present merely as representative of his health—by which it is often ridiculously pampered—nor as a measurement of self-worth. Here the sexual ethos takes revenge on the individual man, just as at the beginning of marriage, as seen earlier, it did on the woman. The vital worth of man experiences a crisis: strength, dexterity, the joy of strolling, physical exercise, elasticity, physical youth, healthy physical beauty. The clear, soulful, and noble beauty of the mature man, and of the old, has as a youthful preliminary stage a cerebral beauty that sparkles from intellectuality. But the simple precious beauty that befits the youth so enthrallingly—often seen in girls, and with children all over—is missing among these young men (perhaps only during such an epoch devoid of young men as that of our current occupation) more frequently than among the Russians or Europeans. Taking pleasure in one's body, the happiness of nudity, bathing for its own sake: all this is not possible in the ghetto. And since erotic culture makes body culture mandatory, one might understand why, in accordance with the laws of nature, in every generation aesthetically sensitive Jewish girls resort to non-Jewish or Western Jewish young men.[114]

Before turning to the Eastern Jewish ideal of beauty sketched here by Zweig, let us first recall what the Torah has to say on this topic. Here we read that the ideal woman's attributes include not only obedience, reticence, efficiency, and a good education, but also beauty. In addition to all other virtues, beauty occupies the highest and presumably most important spot. The reader cannot help but notice how often the Hebrew Bible mentions and praises the flawless appearance of women. Abraham's wife Sarah is so beautiful that the patriarch advises her to tell people she is his sister; that way the Egyptians will not kill him for her sake (Genesis 12:1–14). Judith uses her beauty to creep into Holofernes's quarters and kill him: "Her sandal entranced his eye, her beauty took his heart captive" (Judith 16:9). Rachel's radiance famously surpasses that of her older sister Leah: "Leah was dull-eyed, but Rachel was graceful and beautiful" (Genesis 29:17) The Song of Songs offers the most comprehensive description of female beauty, and the attributes named there shape our image of the beautiful Jewess, or *belle juive*, still today:[115]

> How beautiful you are, my dearest, how beautiful! Your eyes behind your veil are like doves, your hair like a flock of goats streaming down Mount Gilead.
> Your teeth are like a flock of ewes just shorn which have come up fresh from the dipping; each ewe has twins and none has cast a lamb.
> Your lips are like a scarlet thread, and your words are delightful; your parted lips behind your veil are like a pomegranate cut open.
> Your neck is like David's tower, which is built with winding courses; a thousand bucklers hang upon it, and all are warriors' shields.
> Your two breasts are like two fawns, twin fawns of a gazelle.
> While the day is cool and the shadows are dispersing, I will go to the mountains of myrrh and to the hills of frankincense.
> You are beautiful, my dearest, beautiful without a flaw.
>
> (Song of Songs 4:1–7)

As research has shown, this biblical ideal of beauty is not entirely free of Hellenistic influences.[116]

In later times, too, Jews were among those who continued to place a high value on the beauty of the bride, as we see in the advice of Rabbi Eliezer Papo (1785–1828): If a choice must be made between a beautiful woman and a pious one, parents should choose the God-fearing woman for their son. But if a pious one is available who is also beautiful, then they "should definitely choose the beauty"[117] to keep the groom from desiring other women in the future.

The Bible tells of not only beautiful women but also beautiful men. The future King Saul is described as "a young man in his prime; there was no better man among the Israelites than he. He was a head taller than any of his fellows" (1 Samuel 9:2). Of young David we read: "He was handsome, with ruddy cheeks and bright eyes" (1 Samuel 16:12). David's son in turn inherits his father's good looks: "No one in all Israel was so greatly admired for his beauty as Absalom; he was without flaw from the crown of his head to the sole of his foot" (2 Samuel 14:25). His brother Solomon receives the following compliment from his beloved Sulamith: "How beautiful you are, O my love, and how pleasant!" (Song of Songs 1:16). For men, even age was apparently not necessarily a detriment: "There was Eleazar, one of the leading teachers of the law, a man of great age and distinguished bearing" (2 Maccabees 6:18).

At the same time the Bible warns that external beauty can also fade if a person lacks inner values and has sinned: "When thou dost rebuke a man to punish his sin, all his charm festers and drains away; indeed man is only a puff of wind" (Psalm 39:11). Grief can also destroy beauty. After Antiochus had plundered the temple and killed many people, "great was the lamentation throughout Israel; rulers and elders groaned in bitter grief. Girls and young men languished; the beauty of our women was disfigured" (1 Maccabees 1:25–26).

Women's beauty is of course not everything. As we learn already in the Bible, other things such as a bountiful harvest may be more important to men: "A man likes to see grace and beauty, but better still the green shoots in a cornfield" (Ecclesiasticus 40:22). Ultimately, a wife's efficiency and piety can be more valuable than her beauty: "Charm is a delusion and beauty fleeting; it is the God-fearing woman who is honoured" (Proverbs 31:30).

The Diaspora sees a change in the ideal of male beauty. A man's external appearance no longer indicates vigor and wisdom as it had for King Saul and King David. Inner beauty becomes more important, as represented in the above-mentioned ideal image of the *schejne Jid*. However, the Eastern Jew as depicted in a seventeenth-century engraving that was included in the Breslau Jewish oath looks nothing like this ideal type.[118] The unclothed right side of the body looks more like the "muscle Jew" that Zionism hoped to produce.

The *schejne Jid* in contrast is characterized by the superiority of the spirit or mind over the body. This inner radiance is achieved through engagement with the Torah and spiritual or religious matters. An Eastern Jew, according to one self-assessment, should "not be big, not small, not fat, and also not delicate, but refined. . . . And the harmony between exterior and interior should find expression above all in the face."[119] Pale and fine-boned hands are proof that the Jew spends his days doing intellectual things rather than manual labor. This outward appearance also includes neatly trimmed fingernails, which no field hand or manual laborer would have.[120] The paler and gaunter he is, the more spiritual a Jewish man appears. The most important feature of a man's beauty is his intellect. In contrast, physical strength and a robust body are considered "goyish," or non-Jewish, in the Diaspora. One can't help being reminded here of the photos taken by Ephraim Moses Lilien (1874–1925) of young Jewish men in Romania in the early twentieth century.[121]

In contrast, the so-called "new Jew," or sabra, that the Zionists hoped to produce in Eretz Israel following Nordau's ideas embodies the ancient biblical bodily ideal: tall, muscular, of imposing stature, and tanned by the sun. He also has the features of the "muscle Jew" just discussed. Women likewise tried to achieve the visual appearance of pioneers, or *chalutzim*, though in reality their role in agriculture was smaller than most had expected to have in view of gender equality.[122]

The Eastern Jewish ideal woman, in contrast to the man, is not defined by spiritual traits. The image is instead closer to the biblical ideal. It includes black hair, black eyes, white teeth, fair skin, ruddy cheeks, and rosy lips, as described in a Yiddish song lyric:

> Your figure like a beautiful wax figurine
> and your lips as sweet as sugar
> your little eyes like black cherries
> Oh where can I still get your kiss.
>
> Your cheeks like rose-colored flowers
> and your hair as black as coal
> your delicate white hands like fallen snow
> Oh how my heart is drawn to you.[123]

Songs in which Eastern Jewish women themselves do the talking also contain this ideal of beauty, though much of the time it is accompanied by sorrow and woe. Precisely because women can be beautiful, they pose a threat in the view of Jewish Orthodoxy. The erotic charms that go with beauty must therefore be subdued, at least in public, in order to protect the precious asset of modesty for women and men alike. The Eastern Jewish ideal of female beauty is also linked to a woman's role as mother. Aside from beauty, physical characteristics including a healthy complexion and a build that is not too delicate improve a woman's chances on the marriage market. According to a Yiddish proverb, "a pretty girl is half a dowry" (*a schoijn mejdel is a halber nadán*).[124] This everyday experience is also reflected in Jewish jokes, which often involve the troubles that a *shadchan*, or professional matchmaker, has in finding a husband for an ugly bride.[125]

While even an older Jewish man can be "beautiful" in that he is dignified and learned, no corresponding image exists for the older woman. The external advantages she enjoys during childbearing years are replaced by internal values (the loyal, pious woman), as many headstone inscriptions in old Jewish cemeteries eloquently testify.

In closing, let us also take a brief look at the physical ideal of the Sephardic Jews. Jewish anthropologists of the late nineteenth and early twentieth centuries saw them as representatives of archetypal Judaism and believed that they could detect Israelite features in their faces.[126] Maurice Fishberg, one of the most influential Jewish researchers of race, was not alone in lavishly praising the special beauty of this type:

> The traditional Semitic beauty, which in women often assumes an exquisite nobility, is generally found among these Jews, and when encountered among Jews in Eastern or Central Europe is always of this type. Indeed, it is hard to imagine a Jewess, who looks like a Jewess, presenting any other physical type. It appears that in addition to the delicacy and the striking symmetry of the features which are often met with, it is also the brilliant, radiant eyes which give these Sephardim their reputation for bewitching elegance and charm. The Spanish and Andalusian women are said by some to owe their charms to these beautiful eyes, which are alleged to have their origin in the small quantities of Semitic blood which flows in their veins.[127]

The familiar stereotype of the *belle juive* thus has clearly Oriental features. Sephardic and Ashkenazi ideals of beauty often coincided, as shown, for example, by the beauty contest winners who were crowned Queen Esther during the festival of Purim in 1920s Palestine. In 1926 it was a young Ashkenazi woman and the next year a Sephardic woman, both of whom had long dark hair, dark eyes, and an oval face.[128] As for the male ideal of beauty, literary and religious texts alike show that there are no differences between the two branches of Judaism: for Sephardic as for Ashkenazi Jews, a man's beauty lies primarily in his intelligence and a woman's in her outward appearance.[129]

Chapter 5

The Ailing Body

"Jewish Diseases"

The persistent belief that Jews contract certain diseases more often and are therefore partially to blame for the spread of some infectious diseases is still alive today. When a dangerous intestinal pathogen (EHEC) caused an outbreak of stomachaches, nausea, diarrhea, and permanent liver damage in Germany in 2011, even resulting in fifty-three deaths, fear of infection was widespread. One place it surfaced was an anti-Semitic blog containing the absurd claim this was a "Jewish ailment" that had been brought into the country by the Jews.[1]

The topos of Jews' alleged susceptibility to certain diseases dates all the way back to antiquity. In *Against Apion*, Flavius Josephus (ca. 37–100 CE) quotes the Thracian ruler Lysimachos (361/360–281 BCE), who described the Jews as a people "afflicted with leprosy, scurvy, and other maladies."[2]

In later times, when Jews continued to be linked with diseases such as leprosy,[3] this was probably not because of the often-cited Bible rules for dealing with people who had contracted the disease (Hebrew *zara'at*). It was more likely due to Roman historian Tacitus's statement that the Jews had originally been leprous Egyptians,[4] a generalization that became part of anti-Jewish polemics influenced by Christianity. For example, church father Ambrosius of Milan (339–397 CE) criticized the Jews for being "avaricious, leprous, and lewd."[5] An anti-Jewish tract by convert Francesco da Piacenza,[6] published in German as part of a seventeenth-century text on the legend of the Wandering Jew (Ahasverus), includes numerous diseases and ailments supposedly inflicted on the twelve tribes of Israel as punishment for their shameful treatment of Christ.[7]

But not all Christian theologians shared this negative view of the Jewish body as afflicted with certain stigmatizing diseases. Lutheran theologian Johannes Buxtorf wrote: "Many are of the opinion, that the Jews are more lively then the Christians, and not obnoxious to so many diseases. But experience speaks to the contrary; and their often funerals, even incident unto them in their younger years, confirmes it for a tale. Yea, every man daily sees how they are lyable to the Mezels,

Botches, to the frail disease, Plague, and other Maladies, no less then other people."[8] While no great friend of the Jews, Buxtorf is nonetheless certain that they
die of the same dreaded diseases as Christians (smallpox, measles, epilepsy,
plague). Convert Antonius Margaritha had also written something similar already
a century and a half earlier in his treatise on the Jewish faith.[9]

Hemorrhoids

In the Middle Ages, what had been a fairly commonplace ailment now became a
"typically Jewish" one, namely, hemorrhoids. French monk and physician Bernard
de Gordon (ca. 1258–1318) was the first to claim that Jews suffer more often
from hemorrhoids than Christians for reasons including an imbalance in the four
humors (an excess of black bile). In his early fourteenth-century medical compendium *Lilium medicinae* he writes that "the Jews suffer greatly from hemorrhoids for three reasons: first, because they are generally sedentary and therefore
the excessive melancholy humors collect; secondly, because they are usually in
fear and anxiety and therefore the melancholy blood becomes increased, besides
(according to Hippocrates), fear and faint-heartedness, should they last a long
time, produce the melancholy humor; and thirdly, it is the divine vengeance
against them (as written in Ps. 78:66), and 'he smote his enemies in the *hinder
parts*, he put them to a perpetual reproach.'"[10] Since Bernard de Gordon was an
influential medical author, it is not surprising that this statement found widespread acceptance. It went unchallenged except for a single instance when he
was contradicted, notably by a Jew. In 1387 *Lilium medicinae* was translated into
Hebrew by Jekuthiel ben Solomon of Narbonne, who "translates the first and
second reasons but when he reaches the third, he states with indignation, '*sheker
shekosaf veamaminim sheker*,' i.e., what is written is a lie and they, who believe it,
lie."[11]

   This mistaken belief nonetheless still persisted for many centuries, and it
fostered an additional anti-Jewish stereotype: that of male menstruation, usually
from the anus.[12] One of the earliest known mentions is in a work by Thomas de
Cantimpré (1201–70/72), a prominent Dominican monk and author of *De
natura rerum*, a twenty-volume comprehensive encyclopedia of natural history
that earned him the reputation of a scholar with wide-ranging interests. It is in a
different work, *Miraculorum et examplorum memorabilium sui temporis libri duo*,
that Thomas discusses Jewish men's supposed menstruation.[13] Though he
invokes Saint Augustine here as a theological authority, a search of Augustine's
comprehensive work finds nothing to support the claim.[14] Thomas de Cantimpré
also contends that Jewish men menstruate because God has condemned the Jews
for murdering Christ. The image of the Jew as the weaker sex is well-suited to
conceptions about the corrupt nature of woman, personified by Eve after the Fall.

The stereotype only became inflammatory when the eloquent Thomas de Cantimpré, a member of an order that gained tragic fame in the Middle Ages for its incitement of hatred against the Jews, linked this Christian male fantasy with the legend of ritual murder. The contemporary background for his comments was apparently such an alleged case in Pforzheim in the year 1267, which even before the large waves of pogroms in the late thirteenth and early fourteenth centuries sparked discussion of occult practices in Judaism ostensibly involving blood.[15] To support his claim that male Jews bled from the only anatomically possible orifice of the lower body, namely, the anus, Thomas de Cantimpré cited the New Testament passage where Pontius Pilate, responding to the Jews' cries of "crucify him," speaks the famous words: "My hands are clean of this man's blood; see to that yourselves" (Matthew 27:25). In light of this splendid biblical proof, it seemed unnecessary to look for any convincing explanation of why it should be hemorrhoidal bleeding—as opposed to nosebleeds, for example—that God used to punish Jews forever for their alleged crime and unbelief. But what did this have to do with the idea that Jews murder Christian children in order to get to their blood? According to Thomas de Cantimpré, Jewish men were trying to make up for the loss of blood they experienced through this hemorrhaging. In his view, this "blood sacrifice" also had a symbolic meaning. The Jews would reputedly take the blood of a Christian as a replacement for the blood shed by Christ to redeem the world.

The notion that Jewish men menstruate survived well into the eighteenth century.[16] The most avid discussion of the phenomenon took place in Spain, where "purity of blood" had become an absolute ideal in the estate-based society, and the hunt for crypto-Jews had been the main business of the Inquisition since 1492.[17] The specific occasion was the arrest of a converted Jew named Francisco de Andrada, described in an account by the Spanish physician Juan de Quiñones de Benavente (1600–1650). Andrada was said to have a menstruation-like discharge each month. Since at the time many people apparently no longer believed in such a phenomenon, or at least had some doubts, the doctor was determined to get to the truth. Quiñones was utterly convinced that God had punished the Jews by making some, though not all, Jewish men menstruate. As proof he cites passages from both the Old and New Testaments (Psalm 78:66, Samuel 5:6, and Matthew 27:25). Accordingly, he sees the Jews' "flux of blood in the posterior parts" that was now a matter of doubt as a "perpetual sign of ignominy and opprobrium,"[18] a mark of Cain deservedly worn by the people who had put Christ on the cross.

The Spanish doctor is not content to leave it at this religious explanation, however, since he does not seem completely sure about it. So he also offers a different explanation, this one a medical variant. Quiñones invokes the above-mentioned Bernard de Gordon, who had claimed that the Jews' way of life could be the cause of anal bleeding. Examples of this are also found in medical case books of the sixteenth and seventeenth centuries, where cases of male hemorrhoidal bleeding were generally interpreted as a surrogate for the humoral balance that menses produces in women.[19]

Though Jews, including Isaac Cardoso (1603/4–1683), quickly countered the fantastical stories about Jewish male menstruation, calling them anti-Jewish fables and Christian mythmaking,[20] such old wives' tales continued to circulate for quite some time, and both in and outside of Spain they were often believed to be true. Their spread was helped in part by the text of a baptized Jew named Francesco da Piacenza that was translated into German in 1643.[21] Among the typical Jewish diseases mentioned in the text is male menstruation. According to Piacenza, Jewish men—unlike Jewish women—menstruate only four days each year. He further asserts that these claims, supposedly proven by holy scripture, have been repeated by numerous other Christian authors.[22] These include Abraham a Sancta Clara (1644–1709), the imperial court preacher at Vienna known for his highly expressive language, who states: "Third / every month our LORD punishes [Jewish] men and women with the disgusting illness of blood flow [hemorrhoids] / if they drink no Christian blood / then they will die of such blood flow."[23]

The few exceptions were Protestant theologians like Andreas Osiander (1498–1552), who believed neither the legend about ritual murder nor the idea that God punished all Jews with "blood flow."[24] It is not until the Age of Enlightenment that this once powerful stereotype finally seems to disappear from the canon of falsely attributed Jewish physical characteristics. Scholarly works on Jewish diseases no longer mention this obvious trait, in any case, though they do still describe hemorrhoids as the result of the Jewish lifestyle. In a lengthy treatise on the condition, for example, country doctor Gottlieb Ludwig Rau (1779–1840) writes that Hungarian Jews' overindulgence in garlic allegedly causes them frequent trouble with hemorrhoids. Rau does immediately qualify this statement, however. "Other harmful things are doubtless also involved: the fiery wine there, [and] the religious restrictions that prohibit these people from taking most food and drink when they are in foreign places and among Christians, which is why they drink almost nothing but coffee."[25] Even this educated, enlightened doctor closes what began as a strictly medical explanation with the familiar prejudice that the Jews must "endure this disease as a judgment from God."

The idea that unhealthy behavior was responsible for the high incidence of hemorrhoids among Jews was emphasized primarily by Jewish doctors. Elcan Isaac Wolf (1735–?) was the first. In his well-known work of 1777, *On the Diseases of Jews* (*Von den Krankheiten der Juden*) (Figure 22), he claimed that excessive coffee and tea drinking in Jewish households was to blame for their being "stricken with and plagued by hemorrhoids."[26] In the late nineteenth and early twentieth centuries a different "bad habit" was declared responsible, namely, Eastern Jews' reputed long hours of sitting on hard benches in school and in the synagogue.[27] It therefore comes as no surprise that hemorrhoids are even part of Yiddish folk wisdom: "wus jarschenen jüden?—zurojss ün meriden" (What do Jews inherit? Trouble and hemorrhoids).[28] A well-known Yiddish story likewise connects this allegedly typical Jewish condition with the circumstances of Eastern Jews, giving it an ironic twist:

> Funny thing, though. I mean about how once a body's got past this awful hankering for nourishment, he gets so eating just don't count for all that much anymore. Well, at least that's so if he's Jewish. Because then, you see, he can get by without tasting any foodstuffs at all, practically. I mean specially nowadays, when there's so many Jews who have got scarcely any trace of a innard nor bowel left in 'em to speak of—except maybe it's that wee nub of a reminder they still keep tucked away inside. Which is by way of being only a token of the real thing, don't you know. And there's some, too, as even entertain great hopes that, given time enough maybe—that is, if the kosher meat tax and the Patrons of Charity, and like Benefactions of the Parish Corporation which we are so fortunate as to enjoy, are allowed to go on working on our behalf undisturbed—well, anyhow: given time enough, they say, Jewish folks may eventually get completely shot of their wicked habits in point of eating. So that, by and by, we'll lose what little gut we've managed to hang on to up until now—apart from the piles, of course.[29]

Scabies

The link between Judaism and a skin ailment that was also familiar to the Christian population, one so strong and so enduring that even Jews could joke about it,[30] is exemplified in so-called *Judenkrätze* (Yiddish *parech*):[31] A Jewish mother hastens to the rabbi after her son's traditional head covering, or *kippah*, has slipped off his head and fallen into a meat dish. She wants to know if the food is still kosher. After a moment's consideration the rabbi says he would first need to know what might have been stuck to the kippah. The woman thinks for a second: "there was probably dirt on it." "Kosher," the rabbi decides. The mother then remembers: "Well, the poor child has a *parech* (Jewish scabies), so a bit of something might have been stuck to the kippah." "*Parech*—skin—kosher!" The woman is relieved, but then remembers something else: "The boy sometimes eats butter bread. It could be that he touched the kippah with his greasy fingers." "Butter?!!" cries the rabbi in horror, "*Treifa!*" (not kosher).[32]

We encounter scabies already in the Bible in the Hebrew term *garaw* (Leviticus 21:20). Anyone with this skin disease was barred from performing temple duties. Early modern period references to Jews as having scabies definitely include this biblical connotation of exclusion from temple service.[33]

Elcan Isaac Wolf
der Weltweisheit und Arzeneiwissenschaft
Doktor in Mannheim,

von den Krankheiten

der Juden.

SeinenBrüdern in Deutschland gewidmet.

Mannheim,
bei C. F. Schwan, kuhrfürstl. Hofbuchhändler
1777.

Figure 22. Elcan Isaac Wolf, *Von den Krankheiten der Juden* (Mannheim: Schwan, 1777), title page. University Library, Frankfurt am Main.

In 1840 it was discovered that a parasitic mite causes the disease in humans. The most typical symptom is intense itching at the site of the mite burrows, and scratching the irritated area causes a rash of small red welts and the formation of scabs. Areas of the body most commonly affected are the wrist, elbow, and knee joints; folds of skin on the hands and feet; armpits, buttocks, and genitals, where the track-like burrows of the mites can become visible. Usually the head hair, back, and face are unaffected.

In the eighteenth century, Christian physicians were the first to take an interest in the predisposition of particular social groups or occupations to certain illnesses. One of these was Bernardino Ramazzini (1633–1714), the founder of occupational medicine. He too believed that scabies was more prevalent among the Jews: "As for the Men, they either sit in their Shops all Day long patching up their old Rags, or stand waiting to catch Customers, and almost all of them are Chachectick, Melancholy, Surly, and generally Scabby, for there are but a few, even of the Richer Jews, that have not some tincture of the Itch; so that this Foulness seems to be a natural Disease, and the remains of the Elephantiasis that was formerly so familiar to their Nation."[34]

Aside from mentioning (biblical) leprosy, Ramazzini does not provide a religious explanation here. Instead, he holds the living conditions of less well-off groups of the Jewish population responsible for the spread of skin diseases like scabies. Other contemporary physicians note that while the ailment is contagious, it is not transmitted through food. As proof, one author tells the story of a Jewish owner of a cookshop covered in scabies "who served food to Christians and Jews alike. The guests inevitably got a good deal of scabies matter mixed in with their food, but I know of not even one who became infected as a result."[35]

Jews themselves do not contest the high frequency of scabies among Jews,[36] but for the most part it is non-Jewish doctors who weigh in on the matter. A county physician writes in 1836 that "the Jews in Poland believe that every Jew, male or female, develops a rash after getting married, and also every young woman after delivering her first baby."[37] This was not just in Poland: even in the German Empire, scabies was apparently rife among Jewish youth. We read, for instance, in a report from Lower Franconia that in 1820 in the town of Unterriedenberg, 90 percent of all school-age children were infested with scabies.[38]

It is therefore not surprising that in the nineteenth century, health officials kept a watchful eye on high-risk groups among the Jews. If they had the skin disease, "lower-class foreign Jews should be treated like immigrating scabies-infested journeymen," according to an ordinance that applied to all Prussian lands.[39]

During the Third Reich scabies literally did become a "Jewish disease," since poor hygiene conditions in the ghettos and concentration camps led to the rapid spread of the scabies pathogens. Survivors relate in their memoirs how much they suffered from the relentless itching caused by this skin condition.[40] Scabies was likewise ubiquitous in the Russian gulag, and Russian expressions like *parchatyj* or *parchac*, meaning "lice-infested" or "having scabies," were anti-Semitic swear words.[41] Jews who had survived the Shoah were deeply offended by such expressions. Israelis of Ashkenazi descent were apparently unaware of this when in the

1950s they disparagingly referred to recent immigrants from Arab regions as *frenk parech*. The designation *parech* also entered Yiddish folklore fairly early on,[42] and as a result has now lost a bit of its original anti-Semitic connotation. It is even the title of a Yiddish song written by Bessarabian Jewish songwriter Moyshe Kupit, which begins with the following lines:

> All the parkhes formed a circle,
> danced from the poorhouse to the bathhouse.
> Hey-hu, parkhenyu,
> Give yourself a scratch in your head.[43]

This can certainly be understood as a self-ironic take on a stigmatizing disease.

Plica Polonica

Though *parech* and *plica polonica* are sometimes confused in the literature, from a medical-historical standpoint they count as two separate diseases that, while not unique to the Jews, were often associated with them and had decidedly negative connotations.[44] Unlike scabies, *plica polonica* affects only the hair on the head, as the word "braid" (*Zopf*) in the second half of its German names suggests (*Wichtel-, Weichsel-* or *Judenzopf*). The hair becomes matted and resembles the ropes of intentionally created dreadlocks. The first known description comes from Herculis Saxonia (1551–1607), a doctor whose lengthy treatise of 1600 about this rare condition was based on reports he had received from an Eastern European correspondent.

Physicians puzzled over the origin of the disease until well into the nineteenth century.[45] In an article for a standard medical reference work at that time, Budapest dermatologist Ernst Ludwig Schwimmer (1837–98) describes where research stood in the 1880s as follows:

> "Plica polonica, cf. *Trichoma* cf. *Lues sarmatica*, Polish braid / leprechaun's braid, is the term for that inextricably tangled and matted head hair that in earlier years was an endemic disease in Poland, on the banks of the Vistula [German Weichsel], and also in Russia. Barely several decades ago the *plica* was still considered a peculiar dycrasic affection [a pathological condition of the blood], sometimes seen as a derivative of syphilis and leprosy, sometimes as a form of gout, and scholars took umbrage if a dispassionate physician dared to presume that the *plica* was perhaps merely a local skin condition. . . . The literature on this form of disease has grown tremendously from the seventeenth century until almost our time. . . . The cultural progress of our century and the enlightened views of unprejudiced

researchers have cleared the thicket. . . . We close these brief remarks with the statement that the *plica* is not a disease; where such matting of the hair occurs, one should look for the general and local causes of this abnormal behavior.[46]

Twenty years earlier, Bromberg doctor Emanuel Hamburger had called repeated claims about the existence of such a disease "erroneous,"[47] but several decades still needed to pass before it was generally accepted in the medical community that this was not a separate, distinct disease. As the German dermatologist Albert Jesionek (1870–1935) determined in the early 1920s, plica was nothing more than a severe infestation of head lice and resultant irritation of the skin. The matting of the hair was caused by fluids seeping from the wounds and pustules.[48]

As the variety of common names indicate, the ailment is not an exclusively Jewish "disease." But because it occurred primarily in Eastern Europe, and because a large segment of the population consisted of poor Jewish social classes, it gradually became known as both "Polish braid" and "Jewish braid." Contemporary statistics for several regions beyond the Vistula show that in fact more Jews than non-Jews (Poles, Germans) did have the condition. In the early 1790s, the Polish king's personal physician estimated that 20 to 30 percent of farmers, beggars, and Jews in the voivodeships (Polish administrative units) of Cracow and Sandomir suffered from plica, while it affected only between 5 and 6 percent of the middle class and nobility.[49] In the Posen district of the Grand Duchy of Poland in the 1830s, it afflicted 1.92 percent of the Jews, 0.86 percent of the Germans, and 1.2 percent of the Slavs in the regional population.[50] The situation was similar in other parts of the country with mixed populations, namely, the districts of Krotoszyn, Samterschen, Chodzież, Gniezno, Schubin, and Wyrzysk. Viewed selectively, this information was able to help create the link between a condition found noticeably often in Poland and the Jewish population above all: "The Polish braids that have been described by some authors with the name Jewish braids are not a different type than the one just described. The name Jewish braid may well come from the fact that many Jews have this disease."[51] As a writer at that time noted, an anti-Semitic intent was often behind such statements. Some medical authors went beyond merely calling the rural Polish population primitive; misguided by the basest passion for revenge, they "have no less untruthfully denigrated the Polish Jews as monsters."[52]

An early example of the term "Jewish braid" is found in a medical dissertation from the year 1682, though it does not appear in the title.[53] This happens only some forty years later, when the German word is included in the Latin title of a Königsberg (Kaliningrad) medical doctoral thesis of 1717.[54] From the mid-eighteenth century on, the term *Judenzopf* appears in sources with about the same frequency as *Weichselzopf*, an expression still commonly used in German today.

Figure 23. Jew with *plica polonica*. Engraving. From F. L. de La Fontaine, *Chirurgisch-medicinische Abhandlungen* (Breslau and Leipzig: Korn, 1792).

The latter refers to the geographical area where the condition was found (the Vistula), and therefore seems semantically more neutral, but many writers treated the two as synonyms. For example, an itemized catalog of the king of Saxony's Dresden cabinet of curiosities lists among many other oddities a "Polish or Jewish braid . . . four cubits long, two inches thick, a handbreadth wide, obtained from a former personal physician to the noble House of Radziwil and permanently preserved."[55]

Diseases of the Eye

A common eye disease among Eastern Jews in the nineteenth century (trachoma) was likewise used by anti-Semites to suit their purposes. In the debate that took place in Romania prior to World War I over whether Jews should serve in the army, opponents claimed that not only were Jews known for their cowardice, they were also susceptible to eye diseases.[56] To support the second argument, they stated that several Romanian soldiers had lost their sight after having come in contact with Jews suffering from an eye disease. In this case, it can only have been the dreaded trachoma, a contagious bacterial infection of the eye caused by the pathogen *Chlamydia trachomatis*. Chronic infection can lead to scarring of the conjunctiva, and eventually to corneal clouding and even blindness. Today, trachoma remains the most frequently occurring eye disease worldwide (five hundred million cases). That it often affected Jews, primarily in Eastern Europe, is noted already fairly early in travel journals and place descriptions. Poor hygiene and living conditions in the *shtetl* are mentioned among the causes: "the Galician Jews likewise suffer frequently from dripping eyes," wrote Lemberg police inspector Joseph Rohrer (1769–1828) in 1804, though he gave no specific numbers. His explanation: "if those suffering from eye inflammations took a different approach to identifying the cause of the illness, they would certainly be sure to find it in their habits and way of life."[57] In addition, Rohrer felt that "irritating foods" such as cold fish and pickled eggs made people more susceptible to illness. To Jewish doctors from Western Europe traveling through the Russian czardom, trachoma appeared to be endemic to the Jewish population. Maximilian Heine (1806–79), brother of the poet and a military doctor in the Polish-Russian war of 1830/31, concluded from his observations that the ritual immersion bath of the Jews might be a possible explanation for the spread of this highly contagious eye disease.[58]

Yet it was not in Russia and Galicia alone that the risk of infection seemed particularly high in areas inhabited by Jews. At the end of the nineteenth century, local pockets of disease existed even in Western European locations such as Amsterdam, where overcrowding in the Jewish quarter led to catastrophic hygiene conditions. This situation prompted Dutch doctors to do statistical follow-up investigations in order to determine the epidemiology of trachoma.

One pioneer in the field was the Amsterdam ophthalmologist Willem Marius Gunning (1834–1912), who conducted surveys in schools and clinics in the 1870s in an effort to prove the high incidence of this contagious eye disease. He found that in two municipal polio clinics, the proportion of trachoma patients among all non-Jewish patients examined was only between 3.5 and 4.5 percent, whereas among Jewish patients it was between 44 and 70 percent.[59] A similar discrepancy emerged between the two populations among school-age children he examined. Notably, the schools with the highest rates of children suffering from trachoma were those that charged no tuition and so were attended by the poorest of the poor. Several later studies showed a similarly catastrophic picture of the health conditions in which Amsterdam's Jewish lower class lived.[60] In 1914, the health administration used this as a reason to appoint a special commission that once again came up with shocking numbers. According to their figures, only 0.6 percent of 66,418 Christian schoolchildren had the illness, while 8.8 percent of the 7,062 Jewish schoolchildren were infected. Various solutions to the problem were proposed, one of which was to place all of the infected children in special schools. This idea was abandoned in favor of providing mandatory treatment for the sick children. However, it was only when the Jewish quarter was renovated in the 1920s that the spread of the disease was effectively halted.

The greatest perceived threat from this "Jewish disease" was in the United States, where if the health inspectors checking Eastern European immigrants suspected trachoma, it spelled the end of their dream of life in the land of opportunity. This fear was disproportionate to the actual health risk these people posed. Between 1897 and 1925, each year roughly 1,500 cases of trachoma were discovered, in other words, in less than 1 percent of those seeking entry.[61] American health authorities focused on particular groups of immigrants where the incidence was allegedly high, first and foremost, the Jews from Eastern Europe, which in turn sparked widespread discussion within this population. The pointed interest in this particular illness had something to do with its visibility: even a layperson could easily diagnose oozing, dripping eyes. As a result, this symptom as an obvious external sign quickly led to the stigmatization of the person who had it. In the control stations of American ports, though, only the acute cases were seen, since on the European side of the Atlantic medical examinations done at transit points already included a check for trachoma, especially among Eastern European emigrants (the majority of whom were Jews). Doctors at the border station of Tilsit, for instance, checked a total of 11,599 people from Russia in 1905, of whom 657 were sent back due to various illnesses. The majority had eye diseases (367 with granulosa, 52 with conjunctivitis, 134 with trachoma). In the same year, the nine Prussian border stations turned back a total of 5,179 Russian prospective emigrants, 5,009 of them because of eye conditions.[62]

The effectiveness of these checks, according to standards at the time, was attested to by the Jewish doctor and anthropologist Maurice Fishberg, who in 1905 traveled on behalf of the U.S. Senate through Jewish settlement areas in Eastern Europe and also visited the points of embarkation Hamburg and Bremen.[63]

Russian officials noted—not without anti-Semitic undertones—that trachoma was a problem primarily in the Jewish population of the so-called Pale of Settlement, the region in imperial Russia where Jews were allowed permanent residency. This finding was vehemently contested by leading eye doctors around the turn of the century, the majority of whom were notably Jews. But even non-Jewish ophthalmologists such as Julius Boldt called the notion that trachoma was a "Jewish disease" pseudoscientific: "Trachoma is not dependent on nationality and race: all nationalities and races acquire it if opportunity presents itself. The Jews, who are so severely affected in Galicia, suffer extremely rarely in Hungary, where civilization is more advanced."[64]

Jewish immigrants had an easier time than other immigrant groups in the United States as they prepared for the thorough medical examination at the border checkpoint and the second one on Ellis Island. Jewish aid organizations circulated information pamphlets and produced posters in Yiddish warning prospective emigrants about this grave health issue and its consequences for immigration.[65] Those desperate Jews who despite their affliction still hoped to reach the *goldene medine*, as America was called in Yiddish, sought help from others than just legitimate, professional eye doctors. Many turned to shady healers known in Yiddish as *trachoma shleppern*,[66] since if even a single family member had the disease, the entire family was often denied permission to emigrate or continue in transit. Whoever was "fortunate" enough not to be sent back upon arrival in the United States had to proceed to a quarantine station on Ellis Island. There the contagious eye ailment was treated with therapeutic measures that (by ophthalmological standards at the time) were sometimes quite drastic.

Trachoma represented a major problem for Jews in another region as well: Palestine. The disease (known in settlement circles as *daleket ha-enajim*) was acknowledged to be endemic in not only the Arab population but also the Jewish colonies.[67] One pioneer in the battle against trachoma in Eretz Israel was Abraham Albert Ticho (1883–1960), an eye doctor from the Moravian town of Boskovice who settled in Jerusalem in 1912. Immediately after arriving,[68] he assumed directorship of the eye clinic there, which was run by the society Lema'an Zion (For the Sake of Zion). With financial support from the American Zionist women's group Hadassah, Ticho organized an information campaign about Egyptian trachoma in schools and other educational institutions. Even today, poor hygiene and poor water supply play a critical role in the spread of the disease, especially in tropical countries. From 1917 until British forces under

Figure 24. Examination for trachoma, Ellis Island. Photo, circa 1910. National Library of Medicine, Bethesda, MD.

General Edmund Allenby (1861–1936) conquered the city, Dr. Ticho served as an eye doctor to the fighting forces of the Central Powers. In 1919 he opened a private hospital for eye ailments near Jaffa Street in central Jerusalem. Ticho Hospital, today a museum displaying many paintings by his wife Anna Ticho, became famous throughout the Levant. Its director enjoyed great renown both among Jewish colonists and the Arab leadership. On March 31, 1914, thanks to the efforts of Dr. Abraham Albert Ticho, the first physicians' conference in Eretz Israel took place in Jerusalem and went down in the annals of Israeli medical history as "the trachoma conference."

Diabetes

A Jewish joke goes like this: "If a goy is thirsty, he goes to the pub and gets hammered. If a Jew is thirsty, he goes to the doctor and gets his blood sugar tested." The basis for the joke is a tried-and-true stereotype that has been around since the late nineteenth century, namely, that Jews suffer more often than other people from diabetes mellitus. For this reason, the condition has often been called a Jewish disease.[69] Even Sigmund Freud notes this association in his *Interpretation of Dreams*, recalling one of his own dreams in which he chanced to meet with a certain Mr. Zucker. The name provides the founder of psychoanalysis with the key to the meaning of the dream: "Moreover, the name Zucker (English, sugar) again points to *Karlsbad*, whither we sent all persons afflicted with the *constitutional* disease, diabetes (*Zuckerkrankheit*, sugar-disease). The occasion for this dream was the proposal of my Berlin friend that we should meet in Prague at Easter. A further allusion to sugar and diabetes was to be found in the matters which I had to talk over with him."[70]

The negative association of Jews with diabetes continues to live on in the present. In 1984 the Dutch filmmaker Theo van Gogh (1957–2004), later murdered by a radical Muslim, caused a scandal with a leaflet directed against the Dutch Jewish filmmaker and writer Leon de Winter with "a cartoon of two copulating yellow stars in a gas chamber and the joke 'Why does it smell like caramel here? Today they're burning only the diabetic Jews.' "[71]

Notably, the first statistics intended to prove that Jews suffer more often from this metabolic disorder come from a medical practice in Carlsbad. Employed there as a spa physician, Viennese professor Josef Seegen (1822–1904) noticed that of the 140 diabetics he treated, 36 were Jews, or 25 percent. "This percentage is immense, even keeping in mind that Israelites visit health resorts in large numbers. . . . We can assume that at best, the contingent of ill Jews is 10%."[72] A Carlsbad colleague, Arnold Pollatschek (1848–1923), estimated that out of every 1,000 Christian patients who consulted him between 1891 and 1900, 124 were diabetic. In the case of Jewish patients, the ratio was 155 to 1,000.[73] In the medical literature, statistics on mortality rates in various cities (Boston, New York, Frankfurt am Main) and regions (Prussia, for instance) were also cited as proof. These numbers supposedly also demonstrated the greater susceptibility of Jews to diabetes. At the time, neither Jews nor non-Jews questioned the validity of these numbers. Debates focused instead on what could be responsible for this concentration. A line of argument taken by some doctors was that it was a racial characteristic. Jewish doctors Felix Theilhaber (1884–1956) and Elias Auerbach, both influenced by the discourse of racial biology at the turn of the twentieth century, speculated that "the missing decisive moment that might explain the tendency toward diabetes among the Jews is perhaps . . . found in a racial disposition."[74] In contrast, other medical professionals such as Martin Engländer, a follower of Theodor Herzl, felt it was due to a way of life that fostered diabetes: "nervous disorders, grueling mental work, physical agitation—we have found all of these predisposing moments among Jews in more than sufficient measure. That said, it comes as no real surprise that Jews are noticeably prone to nerve-based diabetes."[75]

At the time, animal experiments had led to the realization that there was a link between diabetes and the insulin-producing pancreas. However, the actual physiological process that causes diabetes mellitus remained unexplained until the early twentieth century. As a result, the suggested causes—many of which today sound quite far-fetched—usually involve some behavioral difference between Jews and non-Jews. For example, Berlin Jewish doctor H. Ludwig Eisenstadt (1872–1918) proposed this thesis: "for them [the Jews], the natural satisfaction of the sex drive is restricted by the causes explained here. They therefore return to the emotions of child-like autoeroticism and experience pleasure in sweets, which their mother had given them in childhood."[76] This etiology of the disease, reminiscent of Freudian psychoanalysis, failed to gain traction in the medical literature.

If not a racial characteristic, diabetes was at least considered hereditary by a number of Jewish and non-Jewish doctors; in their view, within Judaism it was caused by frequent marriages between close relatives.[77] Still others traced this metabolic disorder back to a combination of factors including those just mentioned. Berlin internist Friedrich Theodor von Frerichs (1819–85) wrote for example: "innate excitability of the nervous system, the usually strenuous type of occupation, but above all marriage within narrow circles and the hereditary nature manifested here in particular might cast light on this fact."[78]

At the time, very few doctors considered the important question of whether these noticeable factors might have to do with a statistical artifact. One of them was the above-mentioned Jewish health resort doctor Arnold Pollatschek: "As in every other science, in medicine it also often happens that when impressions are supported by—not always entirely reliable—statistical data and various other factors, they gradually become hard and fast beliefs, dogmas that from time to time are shattered only by chance."[79]

After more than a century of diabetes research there is little more to say, even though epidemiological studies have now become far more reliable. Current surveys, for instance, show that type 1 diabetes occurs more frequently among Israeli Arabs than in the Jewish population.[80] Among Jews living in Israel, specific emigrant populations (Ethiopian Jews) show a higher risk of infection. The suspected cause is a combination of genetic factors and environmental influences.[81]

Sexually Transmitted Diseases

In several German dialects (Palatine, Hessian), the expression "Jewish disease" is a synonym for syphilis.[82] This attribution is surprising, since the epidemiological literature of the nineteenth and early twentieth centuries repeatedly emphasized the very limited spread of this sexually transmitted disease in the Jewish population.[83] It may be that the association has more to do with the prominence of Jewish physicians (Albert Neisser, 1855–1916; August von Wassermann, 1866–1925; Paul Ehrlich, 1854–1915) involved in the research and treatment of this illness.

Why were the Jews less prone to develop syphilitic infections than the Christian population? In 1842, Dresden surgeon Elias Collin (1788–1851) gave the following suggestion: "Based on my long years of practice, which afforded me ample opportunities to treat both Christians and Jews, I believe that on the whole the latter have a lesser predisposition to infection. What part morality plays in this connection remains to be seen."[84]

Other contemporary writers speculated that the reason was not a difference in sexual mores, but the result of circumcision. The absence of foreskin, it was argued, resulted in a hardening of the testicles that made them less sensitive to germs. This thinking brings to mind the contemporary discussion of whether circumcision can reduce the risk of HIV infection. Here, too, despite advances in research, the statistical evidence is not entirely clear, and as a result, this type of prophylaxis has been questioned repeatedly.

Even early on, many doctors—including Jewish ones—agreed that circumcision alone did not entirely explain the lower rate of infection. Already in 1903 Jewish neurologist Hugo Hoppe (?–1918) attributed the rarity of syphilis among Jews to a variety of different factors: "Syphilis . . . is seldom found among Jews for one because of the untarnished moral family life that most of them lead and that makes contracting the illness—at least among those who are married—a rare exception; also because of certain anatomical peculiarities resulting from circumcision . . . ; and finally, because states of drunkenness, when syphilis is contracted with extraordinary frequency, are so rare among Jews given their proverbial moderation."[85]

The risk of contracting syphilis was lower for Jews than their non-Jewish peers for one additional reason, at least in the nineteenth century: military duty. Doctors both in and outside Germany knew that the soldier's life posed a major risk of infection.[86] While Jews in the German Empire were not barred outright from joining the military, enlisting was often made harder for them since they were deemed unfit for service for a variety of reasons (including physical ones). Another contributing factor was the pride of place enjoyed by Prussian officers, who were recruited almost exclusively from the nobility. This meant that few Jews aspired to a military career, thereby decreasing their risk of infection.

Genetic Disorders

Until well into the eighteenth century we find only passing references to a noticeably high incidence of illness among Jews, but just around the time that the

Enlightenment begins, the first text specifically devoted to this issue is published: the above-mentioned treatise *On the Diseases of Jews* (*Von den Krankheiten der Juden*, 1777) by Jewish doctor Elcan Isaac Wolf. The work is about those illnesses "that are in many respects unique to my co-religionists, since they derive in part from our destiny, but are also the consequences of our abuses."[87] Wolf organizes the text by age groups. For example, he traces the frequency of skin rashes among Jewish children to the fact that boys were required to wear a head covering even as young children. In addition to dietary errors and insufficient health practices, he blames the poor health conditions of the Jewish population on political circumstances: "It would be a fundamentally good thing for the health of the Jews if they were not confined in some cities to one narrow street like herring in a barrel. How fortunate we Jews are in the blessed Palestine of a Palatinate ruled by an affectionate prince! This best of rulers grants us not only the freedom to do business undisturbed, but also multiple streets where we may reside."[88]

In contrast, anti-Jewish stereotypes are used in a treatise by Franz Leopold de La Fontaine (1756–1812), the king of Poland's personal physician. He admittedly makes only general references to frequently occurring diseases among Jews: "no people is more subject to multiple diseases than this one."[89] Reasons for the high incidence of illness include "their religion, their schools, their fasting, their supernatural shrieking and singing, the way they bend their bodies in various ways, their untimely bathing."[90] Several decades later, Ettenheim medical officer Dr. Peter Joseph Schneider (1791–1871) sounded a similar note when he contended that religious practices were responsible for the Jews' greater susceptibility to disease: "This strict fasting that lasts precisely twenty-four hours [e.g., on the Day of Atonement] and the seemingly endless time spent in the . . . often . . . full to bursting synagogue; the heavy and decidedly mephitic air; . . . the protracted standing, praying, and singing . . . is extremely disadvantageous for women, young people, the elderly, convalescents and especially those already carrying the germ of some illness. . . . What I saw the most were pneumonia, persistent abdominal obstructions, inflammatory colics, and in some people also edematous swelling of the lower limbs."[91]

Even so, from these medical-ethnographic treatises in the Age of Enlightenment it is still a long way to the late nineteenth- and early twentieth-century studies in racial anthropology aimed at proving that the Jews contracted certain diseases at higher rates than other races. In these later works the focus also shifts to completely different illnesses such as tuberculosis and sexually transmitted diseases, but, first and foremost, mental disorders.[92]

These debates, which today seem outdated because of genetic research, involved more than a few Jewish researchers.[93] Discussion about the lower and/or higher morbidity of the Jews reached its first peak shortly before World War I. Between 1901 and 1910 alone, over 175 works were published on the topic, almost as many as in the entire time before 1900. And for reasons that are well known, during the Weimar Republic and Third Reich there was no ebb in the discussion about the incidence of illness among the Jews. For equally obvious reasons, after World War II the racial biological orientation of this research lost its ideological breeding ground and, above all, its political legitimacy.[94] Since then, in addition to medical sociologists and cultural anthropologists, it has been primarily geneticists who have studied the respective spread of particular diseases, especially hereditary ones, in Jewish and other populations. Notably, German researchers no longer play any significant role in this discussion. The majority of the scientific studies have been done by American or Israeli researchers.[95]

According to current information, a small number of genetically determined illnesses have been proven to be more prevalent among Jews, primarily those of Ashkenazi descent, than in other populations.[96] One reason is that for many centuries Jews in Eastern and Central Europe lived in relative isolation, so they barely intermingled with the local population. This meant that their risk of suffering from rare genetic diseases was greater than for the rest of the European population. For this reason, in Israel as well as the United States screening programs have long existed for couples of Ashkenazi descent who plan to have children.[97] One of the best-known organizations offering anonymous genetic screening for hereditary diseases, primarily to marriage-age Orthodox Jews, is Dor Yeschorim (Hebrew for "generation of the upright," Psalm 112:2), known in English as the Committee for the Prevention of Genetic Diseases.

Among the most common serious genetic disorders that affect Ashkenazi Jews in particular are the following, together with their carrier frequencies in parentheses: Tay-Sachs disease (1:15), cerebellar ataxia, neuropathy, and vestibular areflexia syndrome, or CANVAS (1:36), Gaucher's disease (1:15), familial dysautonomia (1:30), Niemann-Pick disease type A (1:90), Fanconi anemia (1:89), Bloom syndrome (1:100), mucolipidosis type IV (1:127), and cystic fibrosis (1:29). Of these, Tay-Sachs disease has long been the best known. Research studies long had decidedly racist undertones, and in the first half of the twentieth century even played a significant role in the debate over emigration restrictions for Jews.[98] Tay-Sachs is a hereditary disease that usually appears in three- to seven-month-old infants; it causes an excess of a fatty substance to build up in the brain, which in turn destroys nerve cells in the brain and spinal cord. Tay-Sachs belongs to a group of congenital disorders known as gangliosidoses, sometimes also called lysomal storage disorders. Another of the so-called rare diseases also affecting Ashkenazi Jews is CANVAS, which causes spongelike degeneration of the brain. Almost 2 percent of all Jews are carriers of the disease, making it one of the most frequently occurring genetic disorders in the Jewish population. For this reason, it is often characterized as a "Jewish disease." Unlike in the case of Tay-Sachs, today we still have no way to treat the cause of CANVAS.

A small number of other hereditary diseases also exist that Sephardic Jews are more prone to contract. These include the long-known familial Mediterranean fever. This genetic disorder is characterized by recurring bouts of fever, stomachache, chest or joint pain, and swelling of the joints. As the name suggests, it affects not only Oriental Jews from the Mediterranean region, but also Turks, Arabs, and Armenians, and less frequently also Greeks, Italians, and Spaniards.[99] In 2014, researchers at Ben Gurion University identified a genetic defect (progressive cerebello-cerebral atrophy type 2, or PCCA2) that appears much more often in Jews of Moroccan descent than in the rest of the Jewish population. This type of genetic mutation can trigger epilepsy among other things. Its discovery led the research team to conclude that among Sephardic Jews, additional disorders may also be caused by genetic defects.

Physical Disabilities

Sigmund Freud tells the following Jewish joke about a tricky negotiation with a marriage broker, or *shadchan*: "The suitor objects because the bride has a short leg and therefore limps. The agent contradicts him. 'You are wrong,' he says. 'Suppose you marry a woman whose legs are sound and straight. What do you gain by it? You are not sure from day to day that she will not fall down, break a leg, and then be lame for the rest of her life. Just consider the pain, the excitement, and the doctor's bill. But if you marry this one nothing can happen. Here you have a finished job.'"[100] We laugh about the "faulty reasoning" that, according to Freud, is the underlying basis of the joke.

Limping

Examples of foot dragging are to be found already in the Bible: the patriarch Jacob limped (צלע) after receiving a blow to the hip while wrestling with the angel. As we read in Genesis: "This is why the Israelites to this day do not eat the sinew of the nerve that runs in the hollow of the thigh; for the man had struck Jacob on that nerve in the hollow of the thigh" (Genesis 32:32). There is no consensus among Bible exegetes, however, on whether this means Jacob was actually disabled, since the physical impairment resulting from his encounter with the angel is mentioned only in this one passage. That does not necessarily mean that Jacob's impairment must have been only temporary. But at least for Jacob it had no negative consequences, since it was not an indication of weakness. Just the opposite: the physical defect testifies to his courageous encounter with a divine power.[101] The situation was different in the case of Mephibosheth, son of Jonathan, who is described in the Bible not as limping but lame. Due to a childhood accident he was lame in both feet (ויפסח), so he needed to ride on the back of an ass to get from place to place (2 Samuel 4:4, 19:27). Here it is clearly not a matter of a temporary disability.

Whether a person walked with a permanent or temporary limp, he was unfit to serve in the temple according to Torah regulations: "The Lord spoke to Moses and said, Speak to Aaron in these words: No man among your descendants for all time who has any physical defect shall come and present the food of his God. No man with a defect shall come, whether a blind man, a lame man, a man stunted or overgrown, a man deformed in foot or hand, or with mis-shapen brows or a film over his eyes or a discharge from it" (Leviticus 21:16–20). In Talmudic writings, people with concave, crooked, or sickle-shaped feet are also included among those who limp.[102] Only Rabbi Yehudah takes the minority position in the Mishnah that someone who hobbles may also be considered for temple service (Bekhorot 7:1).

The Torah justifies the restrictions on eligibility for religious duty by referring to limping as a deviation from the physical norm. Impairments are categorized as "deficiency" (מום, mum) and equated with defects (Leviticus 21:18). Though people disabled in this way were barred from presenting food offerings in the temple, at the time they were still allowed to taste such food: "He may eat the bread of God both from the holy-gifts and from the holiest of holy-gifts, but he shall not come up to the Veil nor approach the altar, because he has a defect in his body. Thus he shall not profane my sanctuaries, because I am the LORD who hallows them" (Leviticus 21:22–23). In the Qumran or Dead Sea Scrolls, the exclusion of this group from religious service as described in the Hebrew Bible is extended even further.[103] Those who limp, are blind, or have been lamed are forbidden to enter the army camp at the end of time (1 QM VII, 4–5). In addition, the lame (together with the blind, deaf, and mute) are banned from gatherings in eschatological Israel (1 QWa II, 3–11). Also worth noting is that judging from biblical references, the lame (in addition to others) were deemed unfit for battle (2 Samuel 5:6; Isaiah 33:23).

As noted above, in the Dead Sea Scrolls it says that the lame will not be allowed in the army camp at the end of time, an exclusion that is directly linked to their ineligibility for religious service (1 QM VII, 4–5). This almost sounds like an anticipation of the nineteenth-century debate about the military fitness of Jews, when the widespread stereotype—even in medical circles—of Jewish men as constitutionally suffering from foot ailments cast doubt on their fitness for army service (a key prerequisite for equal rights), since they were allegedly unable to march.[104] Hence the Zionist movement's commitment to refuting this and other similar charges by using gymnastics as a corrective to the Jews' perceived physical deficiencies.[105]

Limping was part of an anti-Jewish stereotype already in the early modern period.[106] It was linked to the notion that Jews are especially prone to deformities of the lower limbs such as clubfoot and flat feet.[107] The equation of Jews with the devil, who was often depicted as limping, also played a role. In the nineteenth century, limping Jews are a popular literary motif in both non-Jewish and Jewish literature. The Christian king in *The Jewess of Toledo*, a drama by Franz Grillparzer (1791–1872), remarks:

> I love them not, these people, but I know
> That what disfigures them, we cause ourselves.
> We lame them, then are angry if they limp.[108]

In Joseph Roth's prose we also find a noticeable number of hobbling Jews. These literary examples are not surprising, since around the fin de siècle doctors, anthropologists, and others debated whether "intermittent limping" (*claudicatio intermittens*) was a disability found predominantly among Jews. The term was introduced by French psychiatrist Jean Martin Charcot (1825–93), teacher of Sigmund Freud and Max Nordau, in one of his earliest publications from the year 1858.[109]

Several decades later this symptom would become incorporated into racial theory. In his 1911 overview of the alleged racial characteristics of the Jews, Maurice Fishberg cited numerous older and more recent studies ostensibly proving that this gait disorder was especially widespread among Russian and Polish Jews.[110] Even a standard neurological work from 1929 did not question the high incidence of intermittent limping in the Jewish population, but merely relativized it somewhat.[111] As to what caused the noticeably high incidence of the ailment among Jews, literature of the time frequently emphasized the "nervous burden of the Jewish race."[112] Another contemporary interpretation was that the condition resulted from nerve damage due to excessive tobacco consumption. This second view, in other words, targeted the unhealthy way of life in the *shtetl*: Eastern Jews were considered heavy smokers, and this was used to explain the striking concentration of intermittent limping in this segment of the Jewish population.

Blindness

Like lameness, blindness is a frequent topic in the Bible.[113] Both forms of impairment are placed on the same level: "That is why they say, 'No blind or lame man shall come into the LORD's house' " (2 Samuel 5:8). Exegetes do not agree on how to interpret this verse. It could well be that it reflects some historically based justification for requiring physical flawlessness in those who serve in the temple,[114] since blindness (עָוֵר) is one of the infirmities named in the Torah that make a person ineligible to perform priestly functions.[115]

Its cause was usually seen as a punishment from God for some human transgression. The Talmud, for instance, tells of a blind man from Gam Zu named Nahum: after failing to give food to a poor man in danger of starving to death, he cursed himself, saying: "May my eyes, which had no compassion on your eyes, be blinded" (BT Taanit 21a).[116] This moral is echoed in the New Testament, where we read: "As he went on his way Jesus saw a man blind from his birth. His disciples put the question, 'Rabbi, who sinned, this man or is parents? Why was he born blind?' 'It is not that this man or his parents sinned,' Jesus answered; 'he was born blind so that God's power might be displayed in curing him' " (John 9:1–3).

In addition to God's will, other, "natural" causes are named in Jewish texts. A Talmud passage warns, for instance, against looking at a woman's vulva during intercourse, since it could cause blindness (BT Nedarim 20a). The same tractate contains a warning that grime on the head can lead to blindness (BT Nedarim 81a). Medieval responsa called blindness the work of demons but also thought it occurred if a patient was bled too often.[117] A person could also become blind if his eyes were gouged out, which had happened to Samson at the hands of the Philistines (Judges 16:21).

Only in the nineteenth century are explanations sought in science. Anthropologists and physicians discussed whether the high incidence of blindness observed in the Jewish population that they found in some contemporary statistics was a racial characteristic or the result of other factors.[118]

In literary sources, blindness is not always to be taken literally. Already in the Bible we find the term used metaphorically. It can refer to lack of moral insight, for example (Isaiah 29:9–10). Gifts can make a judge unable to "see" justice (Exodus 23:8; Deuteronomy 16:19). Blindness is also a metaphor for injustice and oppression (Deuteronomy 28:28–29; Isaiah 59:9–10). In medieval Christian iconography the synagogue is usually depicted with a blindfold, a reference to the blindness of the Jews to the true faith. A stained-glass window in the rear nave of the Freiburg cathedral, for instance, depicts two people riding toward each other with lances as in a medieval joust. The figure on the right is blindfolded and seated backward as he rides toward the other figure. These attributes make it clear that the figure should be read as an allegorical reference to the synagogue. The animal he rides has the horns of a ram, a play on the Jewish scapegoat, but also a reference to the supposedly devilish character of the Jewish people. The backward-facing hunched position and broken standard, but above all the blindfold, signal religious blindness in this allegory: Judaism is unable to recognize the true Messiah, and the Catholic Church will therefore ultimately triumph.

Even today blindness can rarely be cured, though in some cases it can be prevented by medical interventions such as eye surgery. We can therefore hardly expect to find a natural remedy for it in Jewish writings. It is only when the Savior comes that "blind men shall see" (Isaiah 35:5). The sole exception in the Bible is the apocryphal parable Tobit that tells how Tobias, on the advice of the archangel Raphael, anoints his blind father's eyes with fish gall and thereby restores his sight (Tobit 11:7–8). Here, however, we are in the realm of miracle cures. In reality, for a very long time all that could be done was to care for the blind and help make their lives as easy as possible through financial and material support.

The difficult lot of the blind is underscored in many passages in the Bible and the Talmud: "Four are considered as if they were dead: A pauper, and a leper, and a blind person, and one who has no children" (BT Nedarim 64b). A blind person needs help from those around him. A boy leads Samson by the hand, for example, after he has been blinded (Judges 16:26). The blind usually had to beg for a living, as we read in the New Testament (John 9:1–10, 21). Here, Jewish charity, or *tzedakah*—similar to Christian *caritas*—tried to provide relief,[119] but this was still a far cry from services designed specifically for the blind, both in and outside of Judaism. The first Jewish institutions of this type were founded in the first half of the nineteenth century, some at approximately the same time as Christian organizations for the blind and some even earlier. They included the association known as the Jewish Blind (now called the Jewish Blind and Disabled), founded in London in 1819. In Vienna it was Ludwig August Frankl (1810–94), a doctor, journalist, author, philanthropist, and secretary/archivist for the Israelite Religious Community, who took the initiative. With the support of Jonas Freiherr von Königswarter (1807–71), banker and president of the Viennese Israelite Religious Community, Frankl founded the Israelite Institute for the Blind in 1871. In the United States, the New York Guild for the Jewish Blind started its work in 1908. At almost the same time, the Jewish Institution for the Blind was founded in Berlin-Strelitz. In Israel, where a relatively large number of blind emigrants needed care in the first decades after the founding of the state, the Association for the Blind and Prevention of Blindness provided assistance beginning in 1953.

How treatment of the blind looked during biblical times is spelled out in special legal regulations intended to protect people with this disability from arbitrary violence (Leviticus 19:14; Deuteronomy 27:18). Another passage describes help for the blind and the lame as charity (Job 29:15), which suggests that the disabled needed to rely on this help, given on an individual and voluntary basis in the absence of government-provided assistance.[120] Here is where *tzedakah* (literally, "justice"), or Jewish social welfare, began.

The blind were easy targets of violence, as we learn from another Bible verse: "so that you will grope about in broad daylight, just as a blind man gropes in darkness, and you will fail to find your way. You will also be oppressed and robbed, day in, day out, with no one to save you" (Deuteronomy 28:29).

Because of their difficult lot, the blind are granted several privileges in the Jewish community under both criminal and religious law.[121] During the temple period, for instance, they were not required to participate in the large pilgrimage celebrations, so they did not have to travel to Jerusalem. Moreover, a blind Jew who had accidentally killed someone was not banished at that time. But the limited liability also had and still has certain disadvantages. For example, according to Jewish law, a blind person is disqualified from giving testimony in court under certain circumstances (BT Bava Batra 128a). He is also not allowed to be a judge (BT Sanhedrin 34b). An even more severe constraint is that a blind man may not be called to read the Torah, though admittedly, Jewish scholars find this exclusion controversial.[122] Orthodox circles continue to uphold this halakhic rule, but they do allow the blind to recite freely from the *haftara* (reading from the books of the prophets) or read in braille.[123]

These restrictions of a ritual kind differentiate Judaism from Islam, which allows a blind person to become a *hafiz*, for example—the term for a Muslim who has memorized the entire Qur'an. *Hafiz* also recite parts of the text aloud on certain occasions and accordingly enjoy great prestige.

Blind Jews had a particularly difficult time after 1933, when the National Socialist regime singled out this especially vulnerable group for persecution and made their already precarious existence even harder, sometimes to the point of extermination. After July 17, 1942, blind and hard-of-hearing German Jews were still allowed to wear identifying armbands in public, alerting traffic to their presence, but any improper use of this emblematic "disability identity card" was strictly forbidden.[124] Jews who had been blinded in World War I were even forbidden to wear the awards they had earned in that war.

After 1938 in Vienna, the blind were evicted from their apartments and lost their meager source of income, the permission to operate kiosks. While other "non-Aryans" suffered this same fate, the visually impaired had virtually no other occupational alternatives and even greater problems trying to emigrate. In Austria, blind adults whose apartments were seized after the Anschluss (the annexation by Nazi Germany) and who could no longer stay in their familiar surroundings were for the most part taken in by the Viennese Israelite Institute for the Blind. On October 1, 1941, the institute still housed 117 severely visually impaired people between the ages of ten and over eighty years old, together with 27 deaf people ranging in age from twenty-one to eighty-plus, and 5 other disabled people between the ages of twenty-one and seventy.[125] They were later deported, some to the Theresienstadt ghetto. Their life there was captured in a 1943 watercolor painting *The Blind of Theresienstadt* by Leo Haas (1901–83), a German painter and graphic artist who survived not only Theresienstadt but also the concentration camps of Auschwitz, Sachsenhausen, Mauthausen, and Ebensee. Today, a Berlin museum tells the story of the Otto Weidt Workshop for the Blind. During World War II, the non-Jewish small businessman of the same name employed mostly blind and deaf Jews here to make brooms and brushes. But even he was unable to save all of his blind workers from death in the extermination camps.

In hopeless situations, black humor was often the only available escape. One of these jokes, which reflect both the will to live and a sense of enduring pride, goes like this: "Early in 1933 a Jew passes by a beggar who is wearing dark glasses and sitting by the roadside. On the beggar's chest is a placard with the inscription, 'Completely blind. I don't accept any handouts from Jews.' The Jew approaches the beggar nervously, whispering, 'Here are five marks, but please remove your placard.' To which the 'blind' Nazi replies, 'Don't give me any of your *ezes*! Are you trying to teach *me* how to beg from these bandits?' "[126]

Deafness

Disabilities mentioned already in the Bible also include the sensory impairments of deafness and muteness. At the same time, it is not always entirely clear whether both are meant or only deafness, since the Hebrew term *heresh*, which specifically means "deaf," can occasionally also mean both deaf and mute.[127]

From a Jewish perspective, deaf-mutes are more seriously disabled than the blind,[128] since they are considered incapable of reason: "Just as an imbecile and a minor are among those who are not of sound mind, so too the deaf-mute. The *heresh*, whom the Sages discussed everywhere, is one who does not hear, and does not speak" (BT Chagigah 2b). According to Jewish law, deaf-mutes are not required to attend the pilgrimage festivals in Jerusalem; however, this does not extend to someone who can hear but not speak, or a person who is deaf but can speak. In a different Talmud passage the sages again emphasize that the mental faculties of a deaf-mute tend to be poorly developed, and this belief is the basis for a large number of halakhic regulations.[129] A deaf man is not bound by any of the Torah commandments, since he can neither hear nor speak. He is not required to wear the ritual knotted tassels (*tzitzit*), or prayer shawl, though he may not be prevented from doing so. He is also not counted toward the *minjan*, or required quorum for public prayer; he is not even required to have his sons circumcised. Rabbinical authorities do not all agree about whether he may recite the morning prayer silently. The deaf may not perform the ritual slaughter of animals, nor are they allowed to make the unleavened bread for Passover. Further, they are not punished if they disobey religious commandments. Deaf-mutes are allowed by Jewish law to marry and divorce, for as the Mishnah indicates, "A deaf-mute can gesture and be gestured at [and thereby conduct transactions]" (Gittin 5:7), but the regulations about levirate marriage (*chalitzah*) do not apply to men or women who are deaf.

Though the deaf may not serve as witnesses in court, the Talmud does describe court cases in which their gestures provided valuable help in locating fields where the grain for meal offerings could be found (BT Menachot 64b). Their liability is limited in another regard as well: "If one of the parents was without hands, or lame, or mute, or blind, or deaf, their son does not become a stubborn and rebellious son" (BT Sanhedrin 71a). In other words, if a parent has one of these disabilities, no one may bring a legal claim against the "rebellious" son. If a deaf person is insulted or injured, she or he is entitled to compensation. There is some disagreement about whether a purchase and/or a sale made by a deaf person is binding according to Jewish law. Some rabbis hold that this restriction applies only to the sale of property.

Because of their disadvantages in daily life with its strong religious bent, and also because of their lower legal status, the deaf are entitled to special care and attention on the part of the Jewish community.[130] For example, the deaf should not be given any nonkosher food, and they must be paid a fair wage for any work they perform. In addition, it is forbidden to cheat or steal from the deaf. If a deaf man has a child, then his obligation to reproduce is fulfilled. And should a deaf person be in grave danger, it is permissible to break the Sabbath commandment and offer help.

Today we know that there are a number of different medical causes of deafness (genetic, prenatal, and perinatal). But while natural factors such as heredity and injury to the hearing organs are mentioned fairly early in Jewish sources, the dominant explanation still remains the will of God. The Creator could inflict physical punishment for infractions against sexual morality, for instance: "For what reason do deaf people come into existence? It is because their parents converse while engaging in sexual intercourse" (BT Nedarim 20a).

Aside from the miracles performed by Jesus (Mark 7:32), we have no proof of any deaf-mutes being cured in early Judaism. Although not a cure, efforts were nonetheless made beginning in the early modern period to better integrate them into society by teaching them to speak or use sign language. Initially, though, it was not Jews, but French and Spanish Catholics who were pioneers in this field. Until the mid-nineteenth century, Jewish schoolchildren occasionally took part in the general instruction of the deaf. Between 1810 and 1826, six Jewish girls and boys were enrolled at the Royal Institution for the Deaf in Berlin, forming the largest religious minority in this nondenominational but heavily Protestant establishment.[131] Between the years of 1845 and 1868 a rabbi gave Jewish religious instruction there, but that was not the case everywhere. Jewish parents were therefore often reluctant to send their deaf children to such a school. Even if they did grudgingly decide to send their children to a basically Christian establishment, enrollment was often blocked because of anti-Jewish sentiment. The only solution was to open their own facilities; hence the founding of Jewish institutions for deaf-mutes in Vienna (1844) and Berlin (1873). Here, deaf Jewish children received instruction tailored to their specific religious and cultural needs. In the Israelite Institution for the Deaf in Berlin-Weißensee founded by Markus Reich (1844–1911), the father of a deaf child, "the German, the Jewish, and the deaf were combined. The nurturing of Jewish identity went hand in hand with the development of German patriotism, and sign language was on equal footing with spoken language."[132]

The journal *Der Taubstummenfreund* (Friend of the Deaf-Mute), first published in 1872, recognized the special situation of Jewish deaf-mutes early on: with the founding of associations for the deaf in the nineteenth century, the Jewish deaf ran the risk of being doubly stigmatized, since they might be seen only as Jews by the deaf community, and only as deaf by the Jewish community.[133] In 1875/76, for example, the journal published a serial novel called *Jetti, die taubstumme Jüdin* (Jetti, the Deaf-Mute Jewess) about the unhappy marriage of a deaf woman and a hearing man, both of the Jewish faith. The marital conflicts that arise since one partner can hear and the other cannot are notably not depicted as something specifically Jewish. In 1885, Bernhard Brill (1851–?), son of a rabbi and trained in the Viennese Israelite Institution for the Deaf, founded the journal *Taubstummencourier* (Deaf-Mute Courier). His goal was to liberate the deaf movement from the influence of the church, particularly Protestant denominations. At approximately the same time as this attempt to "secularize the deaf movement" (Y. Söderfeldt), Jewish deaf people began to form their own organizations. Behind this movement was the understandable wish to be active in not only general associations for the deaf, but also specifically Jewish ones. This idea of dual membership did not sit well with everyone in the deaf community, however. Deaf Germans were encouraged to organize instead in a spirit of "*national* and *religious* liberalism."[134] Even so, in the course of the early twentieth century a number of associations for the Jewish deaf were founded: in Breslau (Wrocław), Westphalia-Rhineland, in countries neighboring Germany, and also in the United States. We need to distinguish here between Jewish societies for the deaf and Jewish societies for the care of the deaf. The latter were usually charitable initiatives on the part of hearing people, founded in order to take care of their own deaf loved ones. One such association was Jedide Ilmim (Hebrew, meaning "friends of deaf-mutes"). Founded in 1884 in Berlin, its goals, according to its articles of incorporation, were to provide education and occupational training for poor deaf Jewish children.

Starting in 1926, a journal for the Jewish deaf was published called *Das Band* (The Link), edited by Felix Reich (1885–1964), the director of the Israelite Institution for the Deaf in Berlin. Many of the articles dealt with the history and current situation of the Jews and were therefore helpful in the process of identity formation. Readership extended to other countries and even beyond Europe.

Censuses taken in the second half of the nineteenth century sometimes also included information on the number of deaf-mutes in a given area. With few exceptions (Baden, 1871; Saxony, 1880; Hungary, 1881/82; Russia, 1887), there was a higher percentage of deaf among Jews than in the general population.[135]

Figure 25. Advertisement for an Israelite Institute for the Deaf in the journal *Der Israelit*, November 27, 1890.

One commonly held view at the time was that this was due to marriage between close relatives. But toward the end of the nineteenth century a different explanation gained even more credence: the view that deafness was an issue of racial biology. Between 1882 and 1892 in the United States, Alexander Graham Bell (1847–1922) had researched the high incidence of deafness on the island of Martha's Vineyard, and his warning that marriages between deaf people could lead to the development of a "deaf variety of the human race" attracted considerable attention at the time.[136] Jewish physician Alfred Waldenburg (1873–1942) even characterized deaf Jews and their families as "degenerative elements" within Judaism,[137] though in his opinion these unfortunate individual cases posed no threat to the health of Jews in general. American Jewish anthropologist Maurice Fishberg felt that sociocultural factors accounted for the disproportionately high incidence of deafness among Jews. In his view, Jews were more likely to seek medical help for their infants and children, thereby increasing their chances of surviving childhood illnesses caused by deafness.[138]

Racial biology gained even greater influence with the National Socialist rise to power, and from then on, the deaf—like other people with disabilities—ran the risk of being persecuted as "people with hereditary diseases." After 1933 Jewish members were also excluded from the deaf movement since it, like all other clubs and associations, became subject to the regime's bringing into line, or *Gleichschaltung*.[139] Jewish associations for the deaf still remained in existence at first.

For the Jewish deaf, emigration was more difficult than for those without the disability. Many of the countries where they hoped to flee such as the United States and Palestine under British mandate were closed to them, since emigration regulations were influenced by eugenics. Felix Reich, director of the Israelite Institution for the Deaf in Berlin, was able to escape to England in 1939. Though he managed to take ten deaf children from the school with him, his plan to also rescue the remaining schoolchildren and teachers failed. Almost without exception they, like the other deaf Jews in Germany, were murdered.[140] It is estimated that of the approximately one thousand deaf of Jewish descent living in Germany at the time, only about three dozen survived the Shoah.[141] To date, almost no research has been done on the fate of deaf-mutes in other countries affected by National Socialist persecution of the Jews except Hungary. We do know from individual cases that despite this handicap some Jews managed to survive in concentration camps by concealing their disability.

Treatment of the Disabled

According to a Yiddish proverb, "you're more likely to give alms to a cripple than to a destitute scholar."[142] Though the physical ability to fulfill divine commandments is emphasized in Jewish law, what may initially seem like stigmatization of the disabled[143] actually only applies to certain religious actions (such as temple service). In the Israelite society, the disabled were entitled to special protections such as the right to receive alms.[144] These rights were apparently such a given that some people merely pretended to be disabled so that they might take advantage of this charity. However, these swindlers, who, of course, also existed in later Christian society, are warned in the Mishnah about the fate that awaits them: "And anyone who is not lame or blind but pretends to be as one of these, he will not die of old age before he actually becomes one of these" (Peah 8:9).

It seems that the disabled did not always meet with goodwill, so laws were needed. For example, beating the disabled is expressly forbidden in this Mishnah passage about the use of force: "It is a losing proposition to meet up with a deaf-mute, an idiot or a minor: he that injures them is obligated" (Bava Kamma 8:4). The medieval *Book of the Pious* goes even a step further and demands that the feelings of the disabled be taken into account: if someone blind in one eye is present, for instance, the term "one-eyed" should not be used lest it cause offense.[145] And if a blind person is called to read the Torah, he should not be given the Hebrew Bible passage (Leviticus 22:22) about sacrificial animals in the temple: "You shall present to the LORD nothing blind, disabled, mutilated, with running sore, scab, or eruption, nor set any such creature on the altar as a food-offering to the LORD."[146]

As in many other highly secularized Western societies, in present-day Israel little remains of this religiously determined treatment of the disabled outside of ultra-Orthodox circles. Here, the Zionist narrative of the perfect Jew is still in effect, as we see even in the treatment of Shoah survivors and other emigrants in the first years following Israeli independence.[147] In the Jewish state today, approximately 16.9 percent of the population have some type of disability. This percentage is considerably higher than in most other countries, where on average 10 percent of the population self-identify as disabled or are counted as such in statistical rubrics. Comparisons are admittedly difficult to make, however, given the lack of standardization at the international level.

Judging from a 1997 Israeli report on disabilities, this group of people faces widespread discrimination and exclusion.[148] In public buildings—to say nothing of restaurants—accessible entries are still a rarity, and critics note that despite the passage of an antidiscrimination law in 1998, little has actually changed for the disabled.[149] Isolated acts of protest, most of which concerned increased financial support and improved services, were nonetheless more successful in terms of percentages than in many Western countries.[150] In the past two decades, this has been primarily due to the fact that the disabled have joined forces at the national level to form Bizchut, the Israeli Human Rights Center for People with Disabilities.

Old Age

The most common term for old age in Hebrew is *zikna*. This derives from the word normally used for an elderly man (*zakan*) and has the same base form as *zaken*, the Hebrew term for beard. Extreme old age is usually referred to as *sebah*.[151] In Judaism, the age pyramid image that we also find in other cultures has more different bands or stages than in Christianity, for instance, where seven- to ten-year stages are the norm.[152] In the Mishnah we read: "He used to say: At five years of age the study of Scripture; At ten the study of Mishnah; At thirteen subject to the commandments; At fifteen the study of Talmud; At eighteen the bridal canopy; At twenty for pursuit [of livelihood]; At thirty the peak of strength; At forty wisdom; At fifty able to give counsel; At sixty old age; At seventy fullness of years; At eighty the age of 'strength'; At ninety a bent body; At one hundred, as good as dead and gone completely out of the world" (Pirkei Avot 5:21). Some of these stages correspond to religious and educational rites of passage (Bible and Talmud study, bar mitzvah), but they also reflect important social turning points like marriage or the start of a career. In the second half of life, cognitive abilities and achievements (life wisdom and advice-giving function) are foregrounded, before the physical manifestations of old age (bent walk and diminished life force) come to dominate.

According to traditional Jewish belief, the only person who will grow old is someone God rewards with additional years for a life spent studying the Torah.[153] This belief is based on writings including the following Talmud passage:

> When the Sages told Rabbi Yohanan that there are elders in Babylonia, he was confounded and said: It is written: "So that your days will be length-ened and the days of your children upon the land the LORD swore to your forefathers to give to them like the days of heaven on the earth" (Deuteronomy 11:21); lengthened in Eretz Yisrael but not outside of the Land. Why then, do the residents of Babylonia live long lives? When they told him that the people in Babylonia go early in the morning and go late in the evening to the synagogue, he said: That is what was effective for them in extending their lives. (BT Berakhot 8a)

But just how long can a person live according to Jewish tradition? Even today, Jews wish someone celebrating a birthday *ad mea we-esrim* ([may you/he/she live] until 120), a number that refers to the lifespan determined by God prior to the Flood: "But the LORD said, 'My life-giving spirit shall not remain in man for ever; he for his part is mortal flesh: he shall live for a hundred and twenty years'" (Genesis 6:3). Yet a number of the patriarchs reached a more advanced age than this biblical one: Enoch was already sixty-five when he sired his first child. His son

Methuselah surpassed even that, becoming a father for the first time at age 187 and ostensibly siring numerous other sons and daughters in the 782 years that followed. He was an incredible 969 years old when he died, the oldest person in the Bible. And he was not the only biblical patriarch to live for what from our perspective is an inconceivably long time. Adam supposedly lived to be 930, and his son Seth 912. These are, of course, the kind of legendary exaggerations found in many cultures. More realistic is the number mentioned in a different place in the Hebrew Bible: "Seventy years is the span of our life, eighty if our strength holds; the hurrying years are labour and sorry, so quickly they pass and are forgotten" (Psalm 90:10).

According to rabbinical interpretation, the first humans did not experience the phenomenon of aging. A commentary by the translator of a pertinent passage in the Talmud explains: "Until Abraham, there was no aging, i.e., old age was not physically recognizable. Consequently, one who wanted to speak to Abraham would mistakenly speak to Isaac, and vice versa: An individual who wanted to speak to Isaac would speak to Abraham, as they were indistinguishable. Abraham came and prayed for mercy, and aging was at last noticeable, as it is stated: 'And Abraham was old, well stricken in age' (Genesis 24:1), which is the first time that aging is mentioned in the Bible" (BT Bava Metzia 87a; cf. *Midrash Rabbah Genesis* 65.9). Old age also serves the purpose of differentiating between people and determining their social status. This makes sense primarily in a society that, like so many ancient Oriental cultures, grants the elderly a privileged status or at least shows them great respect.

While Jewish writings repeatedly describe old age in positive terms since it is linked with increasing wisdom, there are no illusions about the physical deterioration that goes with it.[154] Solomon gives this physical and sensory decline its most poetic expression:

Remember your Creator in the days of your youth, before the time of trouble comes and the years draw near when you will say, "I see no purpose in them." Remember him before the sun and the light of day give place to darkness, before the moon and stars grow dim, and the clouds return with the rain—when the guardians of the house tremble, and the strong men stoop, when the women grinding the meal cease work because they are few, and those who look through the windows look no longer, when the street-doors are shut, when the noise of the mill is low, when the chirping of the sparrow grows faint and the song-birds fall silent; when men are afraid of a steep place and the street is full of terrors, when the blossom whitens on the almond-tree and the locust's paunch is swollen and caper-buds have no more zest. For man goes to his everlasting home, and the mourners go about the streets. Remember him before the silver cord is snapped and the golden bowl is broken, before the pitcher is shattered at the spring and the wheel broken at the well. (Ecclesiastes 12:1–6)

The Talmud also emphasizes that the senses fade in old age. Wisdom is the only thing that can increase with age, but even this will happen only to those who dedicate themselves completely to the study of spiritual matters. In contrast, "as ignoramuses grow older, foolishness is increased in them" (BT Shabbat 152a), or, as we would say today, they are threatened with dementia.

Barzillai, the Gileadite who was King David's loyal and trusted servant for many years, gives a personal account of the aging process when he explains why he can no longer serve the king: "I am already eighty; and I cannot tell good from bad. I cannot taste what I eat or drink; I cannot hear the voices of men and women singing. Why should I be a burden any longer on your majesty?" (2 Samuel 19:36).

Since energy and the senses diminish in old age, they should not be squandered during youth. Instead, it is important to prepare for the aging process at an early age, to ready the mind and body for the inevitable since it is God's will. This notion of timely preparation (which includes making an individualized life plan) and of making old age meaningful, found for example in the work of Altona rabbi Jonathan Eybeschütz,[155] has a remarkably modern sound to it when compared with key findings of modern gerontology. The idea of lifelong learning is also expressed early on in Judaism: "It is not your duty to finish the work, but neither are you at liberty to neglect it; If you have studied much Torah, you shall be given much reward. Faithful is your employer to pay you the reward of your labor; And know that the grant of reward unto the righteous is in the age to come" (Mishnah Pirkei Avot 2:16). In the same Mishnah tractate, we find the apt image of learning in old age as writing on a palimpsest (4:20).

Respect for one's elders, which is commanded time and time again in the Bible, is one side of the coin; the other is the moral obligation of younger people to care for the elderly when they are in need (see, for example, Ruth 4:15). In his "Hypothetica: Apology for the Jews," Philo praises the Jewish sect of the Essenes in this connection:

If any one of them is sick he is cured from the common resources, being attended to by the general care and anxiety of the whole body. Accordingly the old men, even if they happen to be childless, as if they were not only the fathers of many children but were even also particularly happy in an affectionate offspring, are accustomed to end their lives in a most happy and prosperous and carefully attended old age, being looked upon by such a number of people as worthy of so much honour and provident regard that they think themselves bound to care for them even more from inclination than from any tie of natural affection.[156]

Little is known about what form this eldercare actually took among the Israelites, but the appeal to the duty of children to care for their aged, weak parents shows that this commandment was not something that could be taken for granted; instead, occasional reminders were needed. At the same time, it should be emphasized that in the Bible, the elderly—unlike widows and orphans—are not among the social groups that depend on the larger community for their care.

Unlike in Christianity, where special eldercare institutions, or *gerontocomia*, exist as early as in late antiquity, the Jewish retirement home is a much later development. The first establishments of this kind did not open until the eighteenth century, when they appeared in Cracow and Amsterdam (1749), that is, in both Ashkenazi and Sephardic communities. In the nineteenth and twentieth centuries, institutional care for the elderly had become common throughout the Jewish world. A study from the year 1989 indicates that at this time, a majority of the elderly were now dependent on such forms of Jewish charity.[157] In Israel, the JDC-ESHEL organization (Association for the Planning and Development of Services for the Aged in Israel) has been working to improve eldercare in the country since 1969.

During the Weimar Republic in Germany a large number of different Jewish foundations provided services for the elderly. The Jewish retirement home in the Grindel neighborhood of Hamburg, which had opened in 1886 as the outgrowth of an early foundation established by Isaac Hartvig (1777–1842), cared for people of both sexes.[158] In Berlin, a Jewish rest home that had existed since 1829 was by the 1920s nowhere near large enough to accommodate all those in need. An agency called Jewish Aid for the Aged of Greater Berlin was therefore founded in 1926; its mission was to support needy Jews over the age of sixty. During the Weimar Republic more than 450 people of the Jewish faith regularly took advantage of this aid, 58 of whom were over the age of eighty.[159] In addition, different denominations provided care through their own organizations for the elderly in their religious communities.

Until the end of 1941, the Reich Association of Jews in Germany (Reichsvereinigung der Juden in Deutschland) was able to continue operating Jewish retirement homes. After that, even the residents of such facilities were deported and ultimately murdered. Here we recall that Theresienstadt served as the National Socialist "old age ghetto" and transition camp. As Jewish communities began to rebuild after the Shoah, Jewish retirement homes opened in a number of different German cities, including Berlin, Cologne, and Frankfurt am Main. Demographic shifts now pose great challenges for the Jewish community, and not just in Germany. The segment of the community over the age of sixty rose from 33 percent in 2000 to 45 percent in 2013.[160] As a result, the need for eldercare options in the Jewish community is particularly great and will only continue to grow.

Chapter 6

The Body in Need

Coping with Pain

Are Jews self-pitying? When they get a simple headache do they feel like they are actually ill? The ready answer offered by medical anthropology is that while each individual perceives and manages pain differently, these processes are strongly influenced by culture, and cultures approach pain in widely different ways. The Irish ostensibly withdraw, since expressing pain is considered unseemly. In contrast, North Americans see a doctor as soon as possible, dispassionately explaining what ails them in the hope of receiving prompt treatment. Italians are said to vociferously express pain in order to get sympathy from their families. Jews apparently endure pain because it means God is trying to give them a sign. According to medical anthropologist Norbert Kohnen, "the religious Jew is convinced that only God can really help with the management of life and pain. . . . His approach to pain is that it must be borne and endured in order to understand the message from God. . . . Pain is annoying and may be expressed (sometimes loudly), so lamentation is certainly permitted, but that does not mean that it [pain] may by completely suppressed or relieved with medicines."[1] Kohnen writes in this context about various strategies for handling pain. He identifies the following types: religious (Jews); intentional (Irish); familial (Italians); rationalistic (North Americans and Northern Europeans); fatalistic (Filipinos); Buddhist (Burmese). Setting aside the fact that, like Judaism, Buddhism is also a religion, the question arises as to whether the religious response of observant Jews to illness and pain is actually all that different from the attitude of committed Pietists or other fundamentalist Christians. A glance at the sociological and ethnological literature reveals the existence of the opposite stereotype as well, namely, the self-pitying Jews who allegedly overreact to physical pain and are preoccupied with it.[2] They are also said to fear the consequences of pain and distrust pain medication. This stereotype, it should be noted, has been contradicted by experiments whose results suggest that Jews and North Americans have a higher pain threshold than the Italians and the Irish.[3]

There is no longer any doubt that differences exist in how people manage pain depending on their cultural background. But as Berthold B. Wolff observes, "while there are undoubtedly differences in pain reaction between various ethno-cultural groups, it is not at all clear if these are this due more to ethnic or to other cultural and/or psychosocial factors."[4] In the United States in 1993, for example, a researcher returned to the main population groups used by Jewish anthropologist and onetime Soviet secret agent Mark Zborowski (1908–90) in his landmark study of 1969.[5] In the later study, which asked patients to rate categories of pain following a heart attack, people of different ethnicities showed no significant differences in their behavioral responses to pain. Acculturation had apparently diminished the differences between them.[6] In the first study, which was based on his own field research, Zborowski asserted that Jews complain when in pain because they believe that it helps.[7] According to his findings, Jews always expect the worst, even in the case of fairly minor complaints, since unlike the group called the Old Americans, they have no "anxiety-relieving devices. There is no such thing as attributing a painful symptom to an insignificant cause like an ordinary cold or a simple injury."[8] In addition, when Jews are sick and in pain they think not only about themselves, but instead view everything in the context of family. Zborowski also observed that Jews see a doctor more often and, unlike Old Americans, have no fear of the diagnosis. His impression was that Jews and Italians show similar behavioral responses to pain and also ask for a doctor's advice sooner than the other groups studied. Zborowski's conclusion, cited in many a later interpretation of "typically Jewish" responses to pain, was that "in pain and illness the behavior of the Jewish patient reflects a value system that has developed throughout the ages and has been transmitted from parents to children."[9]

At least concerning the frequency of doctor visits, today it is not Jews—or, more precisely, Israelis—but Germans who are world champions. In no other country do people see a doctor as often as in Germany. According to data from German health insurance companies, the number of doctor visits per insured person rose from 13.7 in 2008 to 14.7 in 2017.[10] Organization for Economic Cooperation and Development (OECD) statistics indicate that the corresponding number for Israel in 2009 was 6.1.[11] Only the Japanese, who averaged 13.1 consultations per year, even came close to the German numbers. In contrast, Swedes go three times a year to the doctor, and Americans four times. As we know, however, this response to illness is not merely a matter of attitude. Disincentives in the health care system itself—specifically, the out-of-pocket costs for the individual—likewise play a role, as any economist will confirm.

Yet we still find the stereotype of the self-pitying Jew who does not bear illness patiently as the Bible and Midrash command but instead quickly seeks medical help. This stereotype incidentally dates as far back as the early modern period. In

1781, an otherwise unknown French doctor by the name of Le Pau wrote with more than a hint of anti-Jewish resentment: "It is relevant to note that the apprehensions and the indecisiveness of sick Jews, [and] of their relatives and assistants, are capable of exhausting the patience of the calmest of people. They are extremely mistrustful, consult so-called practitioners of the art in the neighborhood one after the other, give way to lamentations in urgent circumstances that call for quick action, often preferring the advice of people of questionable origin; in a word, it would be hard to expect success [in the treatment] of a people who are timid, indecisive, coarse, and ignorant."[12]

The persistence of such stereotypes is due at least in part to Jewish humor, which repeatedly and self-ironically pokes fun at the unique take on illness of the Jews, as in the following joke: "A man comes to see a psychiatrist. 'Doctor, I've been talking to myself.' 'Don't worry about that,' says the doctor. 'Many people do the same thing.' 'Yes,' responds the patient, 'but you don't know what a *nudnik* I am!' "[13]

The Doctor Visit

While in early Christianity the recommended doctor was usually the Savior, Judaism acknowledged the legitimacy of the doctor's profession early on. The Talmud requires that any Jewish community with a rabbinate court must also have a certain amount of infrastructure, which includes the presence of a doctor and a public bathroom (BT Sanhedrin 17b). The reason given by renowned Jewish physician and philosopher Maimonides: "Those engaged in speculation have taught that the art of medicine is very necessary for man, and especially for people of the cities, because of the abundance of foods, and that the physician is indispensable at any time, or in any condition."[14] In fact, he even deemed this requirement the top priority in larger Jewish settlements.[15] In his view, the legitimacy of the doctor is derived from the Torah passage about the duty to return to someone anything he has lost (Deuteronomy 22:2). For Maimonides, these possible losses include physical and spiritual health.[16]

Another important medieval Talmud scholar, Nachmanides, had less confidence in the doctor, though he did not rule out medical help altogether when a person fell ill. In his opinion people should not seek medical help immediately; putting trust in God was more important. While Nachmanides realized that the majority of his coreligionists would probably not heed his advice, he felt they should at least be aware of the consequences their actions might have. By consulting a doctor, they were exposing themselves to the vagaries of nature.[17] To justify how he set his priorities Nachmanides was able to cite the Bible: Psalm 38, for example, speaks of pain and suffering that must be borne and of placing hope in God's help. The tale of the death of King Asa likewise shows the limits of the art of medicine: "Asa became gravely affected with gangrene in his feet; he did not seek guidance of the LORD but resorted to physicians. He rested with his fore-fathers, in the forty-first year of his reign" (2 Chronicles 16:12–13).

These Bible passages do not suggest that early Judaism was characterized by a generally hostile attitude toward doctors. But what about the clear verdict in the Mishnah, "The best of doctors are destined for Gehenna (hell)" (Kiddushin 4:14), which has long posed such an interpretive challenge to rabbis? Rashi explained in his commentary that this refers only to those doctors who do not stand humbly before God and who refuse to treat the needy without an honorar-ium (on BT Kiddushin 82a). Other authorities saw it merely as a warning to doctors not to harm their patients or felt the statement should be taken as only the minority opinion.[18] One seventeenth-century rabbi claimed that it referred only to a doctor who considers himself the best and does not seek advice from his colleagues.[19] A similarly critical opinion of doctors was voiced by Rabbi Acha around the time the Talmud was written. He felt that while consulting a doctor was not an actual right, it had become a habit: "One who enters to let blood says: May it be Your will, O Lord my God, that this enterprise be for healing and that You should heal me. As You are a faithful God of healing and Your healing is truth. Because it is not the way of people to heal, but they have become accustomed" (BT Berakhot 60a).

In contrast to these anti-physician sentiments, however, we also find numer-ous places in the Bible and the Talmud indicating that not only were doctor visits an age-old common practice of the Jews, but also that members of this profession enjoyed great social prestige.[20] These include the often-quoted Torah passage in which God grants the physician the authority to heal: "When men quarrel and one strikes the other with a stone or with his fist, not mortally, but enough to put him in bed, the one who struck the blow shall be acquitted, provided the other can get up and walk around with the help of his staff. Still, he must compensate him for his recovery time and make provision for his complete healing" (Exodus 21:18–19).[21] Notably, the final phrase (*werapo jerape* in the original Hebrew) makes no explicit mention of paying a doctor, but it is from this phrase that the obligation to give a doctor an honorarium for his services was later derived.[22]

The most familiar reference is the hymn of praise in Ecclesiasticus:

Honour the doctor for his services, for the Lord created him. His skill comes from the Most High, and he is rewarded by kings. The doctor's knowledge gives him high standing and wins him the admiration of the great. The Lord has created medicines from the earth, and a sensible man will not disparage them. Was it not a tree that sweetened water and so disclosed its properties? The Lord has imparted knowledge to men, that by their use of his marvels he may win praise; by using them the doctor relieves pain and from them the pharmacist makes up his mixture. There is no end to the works of the Lord, who spreads health over the whole world. My son, if you have an illness, do not neglect it, but pray to the Lord, and he will heal you. Renounce your faults, amend your ways, and cleanse your heart from all sin. Bring a savoury offering and bring flour for a token and pour oil on the sacrifice; be as generous as you can. Then call in the doctor, for the Lord created him; do not let him leave you, for you need him. There may come a time when your recovery is in their hands, then they too will pray to the Lord to give them success in relieving pain and finding a cure to save their patient's life. When a man has sinned against his Maker, let him put himself in the doctor's hands. (Ecclesiasticus 38:1–15)

A parable in the *Midrash Shmuel* depicts the doctor as the one who carries out God's will. Once when a farmer was accompanying Rabbi Ishmael and Rabbi Akiva, they were asked for medical advice by a sick man. The rabbinical authorities both responded promptly, but their companion criticized them for helping someone God had punished. The scholarly men answered by citing Psalm 103:15 ("Man's days are like the grass; he blossoms like the flowers of the field"). Similar to a farmer tilling his fields, a doctor cares for his patients and maintains their health with the "fertilizer" of medicine.[23]

A doctor is not competing against the healing power of God; rather, he is "God's assistant," in the words of Old Testament scholar Otto Kaiser (1924–2017).[24] The *Shulchan Arukh* explicitly states that the Torah allows doctors to heal the sick, even calling it a mitzvah, or religious duty. If a doctor were to refuse someone treatment, he could be accused of shedding blood and committing a deadly crime (Yoreh Deah 336:1). An exception to this rule is made for the doctor who finds himself in the position of having to treat his own parents. Only if no other colleague is available must he be the one to provide treatment.[25] This provision is apparently intended to protect the son from a guilty conscience in case he should make any errors.

In this same context, Jewish religious scholars also discussed the matter of consulting a non-Jewish doctor. This option was allowed only under certain circumstances, since it was feared that this type of healer also used magic practices and was thereby guilty of idolatry.[26] In the Talmud, visiting non-Jewish doctors is allowed in cases of so-called "monetary treatment" but not "personal treatment," a difference explored in the following passage:

If we say that monetary treatment is medical attention provided in exchange for payment, whereas personal treatment is medical attention provided for free, then let the mishna teach: One may be treated by gentiles in exchange for payment, but not for free. The Gemara suggests another explanation: Rather, monetary treatment is referring to medical treatment for a matter that poses no life-threatening danger, whereas personal treatment is referring to medical treatment for a matter that does pose life-threatening danger. The Gemara rejects this suggestion as well. But doesn't Rav Yehuda say: Even with regard to the wound from a bloodletting incision [*rivda dekhusilta*] we are not permitted to be treated by gentiles. . . . Rather, monetary treatment is referring to medical treatment provided for one's animal, whereas personal treatment is referring to treatment provided for his own body, and this is in accordance with that which Rav Yehuda says. (BT Avodah Zarah 27a)

In a different passage of this Talmud tractate we also find the opinion that Jews may seek help from gentile doctors only for certain ailments (such as wounds). These include a serious injury that would justify breaking the Sabbath commandment in order to save a patient's life. In isolated cases—though only in true emergencies—even rabbis may seek medical help from gentiles, as we read in the case of Rabbi Yohanan, who was treated for scurvy by a Roman matron (BT Avodah Zarah 28a). Nachmanides nonetheless still had reservations. He felt that exceptions should only be made in cases where a Christian or Muslim doctor enjoyed a sterling reputation among the Jews and would under no circumstances employ magic (especially spells).[27] Two centuries later, the authoritative Jewish legal codex known as the *Shulchan Arukh* likewise permitted the use of a gentile doctor, but only as a last resort (Yoreh Deah 155.1).[28]

Hebrew sources from the twelfth century onward include many references to Jews seeking out Christian healers. The famous rabbi Jacob ben Meir Tam felt it was acceptable for Jews to see Christian barber-surgeons for bloodletting, since they were more experienced in this type of therapy.[29] This sort of consultation was by no means out of the ordinary, as a regulation in the medieval *Book of the Pious* shows, where even the duty to pay a non-Jewish doctor for treatment is mentioned.[30] This was not something to be taken for granted, as proven by an incident in Gerona, where in 1321 a Jewish patient named Cresques de Turri had refused to pay a Christian surgeon.[31]

When they fell sick, Jews were even willing to make use of Christian "remedies" such as reliquaries, as we read in the *Book of the Pious*, where they are also criticized for this behavior.[32] In the late Middle Ages, Jews on occasion even made pilgrimages to Christian pilgrimage sites.[33]

But let us return to the normal case scenario, the visit to a Jewish physician. Proof that it was quite normal for a sick person to seek medical treatment is found in sources including many Talmud references to doctors, some even by name.[34]

The oldest known work on medical ethics written in Hebrew is ascribed to a person named Assaf ha-Yehudi, whose birth and death dates are unknown and whose existence is even somewhat in doubt. Starting in the Middle Ages, we find an increasing number of Jewish doctors in both Jewish and non-Jewish sources.[35] Many references document the presence of doctors even early on in Jewish communities in the Diaspora, or *galut*. In 1631, for instance, the Frankfurt Jewish community council, or *kahal*, requested permission from municipal authorities to appoint a Jewish communal physician.[36] The petition was granted, despite opposition from local Christian physicians. The person they chose was renowned Jewish doctor Joseph Salomo Delmedigo (1591–1655), and even his contract, written in Hebrew, has been preserved. That same year, a Jewish doctor named Isaac Bacharach (d. before 1666) was also appointed communal physician in the Posen Jewish community.[37] In the eighteenth century, these doctors were often employed by the local society for visiting the sick (*chevrat bikur cholim*)—in the Hague, for example, where the appointed doctor earned fifty guilders for his services in 1768.[38] With emancipation and the transformation of Jewish congregations into a denominational community in the second half of the nineteenth century, the institution of the communal doctor disappeared. Today, Jewish communities in Germany with particularly large numbers of Russian Jews provide medical advice from Russian-speaking Jewish doctors, usually free of charge.

Because of their success at healing and their empirical knowledge, Jewish doctors had a good reputation already in premodern times both among their coreligionists and at all levels of society. Their social prestige was correspondingly great, and was further reinforced by the fact that many also held privileged positions as personal and court physicians.[39] Not until German universities also opened their doors to Jewish students in the eighteenth century did the number of Jewish doctors in Germany rapidly increase.[40] One key factor was that in the age of emancipation, secular education (and the study of medicine in particular) was seen as the entrance ticket to middle-class society. The modern Jewish doctor is thus a product of the Enlightenment. Think for example of Marcus Herz (1747–1803) in Berlin, whose patients included Moses Mendelssohn.

As Jewish doctors became pioneers in the late nineteenth and early twentieth centuries in many different fields of scientific medicine, made radical discoveries, and achieved unprecedented treatment results, it was hard to demonize them as charlatans and dispute their medical capabilities in anti-Semitic propaganda. The National Socialists therefore accused them instead of rationalism, coldheartedness, and interest in financial success alone. With the National Socialist rise to power began the displacement of Jewish doctors from the medical profession. Beginning in 1933, Jewish doctors were fired, excluded from insurance providers, and ultimately forbidden to practice medicine altogether, slowly but surely being deprived of their livelihood. During the Third Reich, between 8,000 and 9,000 doctors were persecuted as "non-Aryans." The majority emigrated, but approximately 1,500 died in the Shoah.[41]

Visiting the Sick

In addition to treatment from a competent doctor who was committed to Jewish ethics, the patient's surroundings also played an important part in the healing process. Christianity also lists visiting the sick among the seven charitable deeds (Matthew 25:39), but Judaism takes it even a step further and makes this good deed a duty. The biblical role model is Joseph, who brought along his two sons on a visit to his sick father, Jacob, and received his father's blessing on this occasion (Genesis 48:1). In the Talmud an example is set by Rabbi Akiva (50/55–135 CE), who visited one of his sick pupils. Later, when the student recovered, he "said to Rabbi Akiva: My teacher, you revived me. Rabbi Akiva went out and taught: With regard to anyone who does not visit the ill, it is as though he is spilling blood" (BT Nedarim 40a). The passage also indicates that those who follow this commandment will be spared the judgment of hell. And what about earthly rewards? The Talmud gives an answer in the form of a psalm (Psalm 41:3): "The Lord will preserve him and keep him alive, let him be called happy in the land" (BT Nedarim 40a). The tale of Rabbi Akiva's good example is also told in the *Ma'aseh Book*, a popular Ashkenazi book written in Yiddish in the early modern period: "R. Akiba visited one of his students, who was very ill. The lady greatly impressed thereby took special care of him and he got well."[42]

We find evidence that visiting the sick is a special mitzvah in the fact that a devout Jew recites a blessing before fulfilling the commandment about putting on tefillin, but does not do so before visiting a sick person. Thirteenth-century Jewish legal scholar Isaac ben Moses (ca. 1180–ca. 1260) gives this explanation in *Or Zarua* (Hebrew for "Light Is Sown"): a blessing is recited only for a mitzvah that is fulfilled from time to time—even if it is as often as once a day. No blessing is required, however, for those mitzvoth that are required at all times, and *bikur cholim*, or visiting the sick, is one such religious commandment.[43]

The Talmud does not limit the number of times someone may visit ("even a hundred times a day"), but the well-being of the sick person should always have top priority: "Let one not visit a sick person, neither in the first three hours of the day, nor in the last three hours of the day. . . . During the first three hours the person is relieved, as after a night's sleep his suffering is somewhat alleviated. . . . In the last three hours of the day his weakness is exacerbated" (BT Nedarim 40a). These guidelines also reflect good practical wisdom based on experience.

Visiting someone with a contagious disease like dysentery or anyone suffering from a headache, eye ache, or stomach pains is discouraged. In contrast, a person

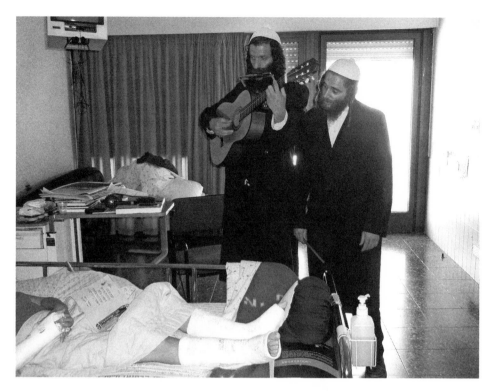

Figure 26. Sickbed visit in Sheba Medical Center, Tel Hashomer, Israel. Photo, n.d. David Shay, Wikimedia Commons.

with a fever should definitely be visited, since according to Rabbi Yehuda, speaking is harmful to someone with eye pain but is bearable for someone with a fever. And though it is highly unlikely that anyone actually practiced what Hasidic rabbi Moshe Leib of Sassov (1745–1897) preached—"He who is not willing to suck the pus from the sore of a child sick with the plague has not climbed even halfway up the mountain to the love of his fellow men"[44]—his challenge powerfully expresses the highest form of charity toward someone who is ill.

Over time rabbinical authorities specified the *bikur cholim* commandment further, with Maimonides as the most authoritative voice. In his *Mishneh Torah*,[45] the religious commandment to visit the sick is described as rabbinical in origin, but also based on the Torah's general commandment to love one's neighbor (Leviticus 19:18). He specifies that people of higher social standing have a duty to visit those of lower rank. Visiting a sick person several times a day is not only allowed but also highly recommended, unless of course it is too taxing for the sick person. It is customary to wait three days before visiting a sick person, unless the illness is sudden and severe. The visitor should not sit on the bed or on a chair or a bench higher than the bed, nor should he stand at the head of the bed. Instead, wearing a prayer shawl, he should be seated so that he is looking up to the head of the sick person. Comforting those in mourning always takes precedence over visiting the sick (Avel 14:4–6). In the *Book of the Pious*, the topic of neediness is also addressed: if both a poor and a rich person are ill, the poor one should always be visited before the wealthy one, even if the latter is a Torah scholar. Only if a scholarly Jew is also impoverished does he take precedence. An additional criterion is the godliness of the sick person in question.[46]

The *Shulchan Arukh* provides the most detailed rules concerning sickbed visits, drawing on those familiar from the Talmud and the authoritative work by Maimonides. Additional regulations concern the form of the prayer for the sick and proper behavior in the event that the sick person is indisposed (for example, if he has a particular disease). Finally, it is even decreed that in the name of peace (דרכי שלום), a non-Jew should be visited when he is ill (Yoreh Deah 335.1–10).

Like his famous namesake Rabbi Akiva, Rabbi Akiva Eger (1762–1837), one of the greatest Talmudic scholars of the late eighteenth to early nineteenth century, served as an exemplary role model in the duty of visiting the sick. While serving as rabbi in Friedland, he made daily visits to all sick members of the community. After moving to the larger community of Posen, however, he lacked the necessary time, so at his own expense he hired two people to visit the sick regularly and report back to him.[47] Jewish autobiographical texts of the early modern period also give us a picture of how widespread the practice of visiting the sick was in Jewish society. When Rabbi Leon Modena of Venice heard that his sister-in-law was ill, he did not hesitate to make a dangerous stormy voyage from Venice to Ancona. Upon arriving he found her already recovered, but his half brother's reaction signaled how much the visit meant: "He was very happy and was a bit comforted. He respected me very much, and I was also esteemed in the eyes of the people of the city."[48] Something similar happened in 1635 when the chronic gambler Modena, suffering from shortness of breath and stomach pains, was bedridden for about twenty days; during this he was visited by his daughter Diana and her husband, Moses of Padua.[49] Glückel of Hameln notes in her memoirs that once while she was ill her son-in-law Moses Krumbach came to visit: "It was in Tebet, 5475 [January 1715]—my son-in-law Moses visited me and said to me, I must dwell with him. He wanted to give me a room on the ground floor of his house, to save me climbing stairs."[50] In these autobiographical accounts it is noteworthy that the visits are usually from the sick person's closest relatives. Usually no details are included about what specific kind of help is offered (such as nursing care); what apparently matters most to the sick person is that a family member has stopped by to support the family and the patient however they could, even if it is only to offer moral support.

We also learn about the spiritual aid and moral support offered in times of illness from certain religious texts that include detailed guidelines for sickbed

visits and handling the dead. One such work was published in 1714 in Wilherms-
dorf near Fürth. Entitled *Refuat Neschama*, or "Medicine for the Soul," it describes
the ritual used by various *chevrat bikur cholim*, or societies for visiting the sick, in
the Fürth Jewish community as follows:

> As the visitor dispatched by the Holy Brotherhood came to the bed-
> side of the sick man, he recited a petition for his recovery. Then he spoke
> encouragingly to him in order to dispel his fear. . . . He was also careful to
> enquire if the sick man needed any money to maintain his health. . . .
>
> Then the visitor told the sick man that although he was not seriously
> ill he ought to order his business affairs and even to make a will. . . . If he
> had taken advantage of someone or insulted someone, he was told he
> must send for him and seek his forgiveness. If one hesitated to send for
> him or if he was afar off, he was instructed to ask forgiveness publicly, in
> the presence of three men. . . .
>
> Then, if the sick man was prepared—this might happen at a later
> day—he recited the *Shema* and the Ten Commandments. The Decalogue
> is important for it contains 620 letters to include the 613 biblical and
> the seven rabbinical injunctions and by *gematria* 620 is *keter* or "crown."
> Through the observance of the commandments, man "crowns" with glory
> the God of glory.[51]

As Rabbi Shimon explains in the "Sayings of the Fathers" (Pirkei Avot 4.13):
"There are three crowns: the crown of torah, the crown of priesthood, and the
crown of royalty, but the crown of a good name supersedes them all." Even if his
life was not in danger, the sick person was also to be advised to practice charity
(*zedakah*) and start charitable foundations—though without reducing his wealth
too drastically, since he would need it if he recovered. The pragmatism repeatedly
seen in Judaism's approach to daily life is also apparent in the advice to the visitor
not to utter only pious sayings and prayers, but also to make conversation with
the sick person and thereby improve his mood. News from near and far and also
jokes were allowed, but not gossip. When saying farewell, the visitor once again
requested that God the Almighty grant a speedy recovery to the patient, whose
religious and moral edification had been the reason for the sickbed visit.

As early as the seventeenth century, these societies for visiting the sick existed
in all sizable Ashkenazi communities. In Amsterdam, for example, a group of Jews
who had fled to the city from Eastern Europe in the 1670s formed a society whose
primary function was to care for the poor who fell ill. This job was performed by
two officers in charge of visiting the sick (*gabbaei bikur cholim*) who made home
visits once a week. They also had the power to make small payments to those in

need, using funds raised in part through collections taken at religious feasts.[52] Later (1737) these officers became members of the communal council, and as such seem to have had a role in the supervision of the special society for visiting the sick. In Hamburg, the Sephardic congregation also had a charitable organization dating back to at least 1609 that cared for its sick and provided home visits.[53] Already in the early eighteenth century a sick-care society called Chevra Kadisha Bikur Cholim existed in Altona. Its statutes of 1701 contain regulations concerning "how *zedakah* for the sick should be done, what mitzvah instruments are necessary, and other things that are needed for the sick."[54] The society was led by three chief officers (*gabbaim*) and three deputies.[55] New members could join only after receiving a majority of votes from the governing body. Membership dues were fifty-two shillings per year, but most of the society's funds came from donations and fines. They were used to pay for, among other things, two messengers, or beadles (*shammashim*), who regularly visited the seriously ill to find out what they needed. These messengers could assign society members to hold vigil, but first they were required to consult the communal doctor about the condition of the patient. If the sick person needed medicine, the chief officer, or *gabbai*, had to be informed; it was he who procured and dispensed the prescribed medications. A sickbed vigil usually consisted of six Chevra Kadisha Bikur Cholim members, who were allowed to leave their post only once their relief had arrived. As is fairly obvious, these regulations probably applied primarily to those who were gravely ill; we read in one passage, for instance, that the "watcher" should inform one of the officers when a sick person was dying. The society even had a certain number of bedsheets in reserve for the impoverished sick (1701, six; and as of 1760, twelve).

While the Altona Chevra Kadisha Bikur Cholim statutes required visits and spiritual as well as material aid to all adult male (!) community members, in practice, well-to-do patients most likely received support only in the form of encouraging words and spiritual guidance. The transition to caring for the dying was presumably somewhat fluid, as suggested by the double name of the brotherhood itself, referring to the care for the dead as well as for the sick.

Not everyone was eligible to receive these official visitors. If a man had offended the community or been disloyal, by disregarding Jewish community council decisions, for example, he would not be visited by members of the brotherhood. And as we learn from the statutes of the Berlin Society for Visiting the Sick, any adult who had "dared to have recourse to the Gentile courts" was also denied visitation.[56] In Königsberg (Kaliningrad), the patient was explicitly asked who should be allowed to visit his bedside and who should not, since upsetting the bedridden person could cause him further harm and was to be avoided. In Breslau (Wrocław) it was common to ask the sick person on the third day of his

illness if he wished to see any visitors at all outside of family members. Some
statutes also limited the number of official visitors to between two and a maximum of four.

More affluent community members could usually afford to hire their own
caregivers, as we read in the memoirs of Glückel of Hameln. She writes the following about her son Loeb's illness: "Then my son fell grievously ill, and I had to send
two doctors daily [from Hamburg] to Altona, besides attendants and other needs.
Again this cost me much money."[57] But in times of sickness sometimes even well-
to-do Jewish families had to rely on the help of volunteers, as we read in another
passage from Glückel's memoirs. When her husband became seriously ill while
attending the Leipzig trade fair, her brother-in-law Jost Liepmann (ca. 1640–
1702), "who was likewise at the fair, tended my husband and nursed him with
great care."[58]

According to Jewish marriage law, a husband is also required to get medical
treatment for his wife if she falls ill, as Moses Mendelssohn emphasized already in
the late eighteenth century in his seminal work on marriage and inheritance law
in Judaism. He writes:

> The duty to provide medical care for one's wife extends to all illnesses,
> regardless of whether the cost is determinate or indeterminate. (The cost
> of treatment for acute illnesses is considered "determinate," whereas the
> cost of treating chronic illnesses is considered indeterminate.) But after
> the death of the husband, a man's heirs are only required to pay his wid-
> ow's indeterminate expenses, since such expenses are to be calculated as
> part of her board. However, determinate expenses for medical care must
> be borne by the widow's relatives, since heirs are not obligated to cover
> her treatment. . . . Should the expense prove too burdensome for a hus-
> band, he is legally allowed (though it may be considered unfair and
> unkind) to give his wife a choice: she may have the amount of money
> included in her dowry plus any interest it had earned returned to her, and
> use it to pay for her medical care, or if she prefers, she may ask for a
> divorce.[59]

The cost of treatment mentioned here by Mendelssohn presumably also included
payments to one or more caregivers, in case no relatives were available to provide
such care. Conversely, a woman could divorce a sick man if his illness was his own
fault and the cost of care exorbitant, as shown by a case in late eighteenth-century
Italy.[60]

In 1873 the Altona Jewish community revised its statutes, and three years later
also changed the bylaws of its Chevra Kadisha Bikur Cholim. As stated in section
1, the society's purpose is to "attend to the sick male . . . during his illness, insofar

as it is allowed or wished, through visits and nursing care; particularly, to fulfill the *bikur cholim* commandment [the commandment to visit the sick] in urgent and life-threatening periods in accordance with religious rules."[61] Only in second place is there any mention of material support for the impoverished sick. As Gabriele Zürn notes, a comparison of the old and the new statutes shows that beginning in the second half of the eighteenth century, "members' sense of obligation to perform these tasks decreases noticeably."[62] Whether this was due in part to the Jewish Enlightenment with its questioning of religious traditions we can only speculate. More important was a development taking place at the time in mainstream Christian society as well, namely, the increasing importance of professional medical care for the sick. Though initially still committed to the ideas of *caritas* and social welfare work, over time this model took on an increasingly worldly look. This meant that it was now primarily spiritual aid that community members provided to the sick, aid that was no longer necessarily organized by a brotherhood, but instead recommended to the individual as a religious duty— insofar as he still felt some connection to the Jewish faith. In 1931, for instance, the Chevra Kadisha of Greater Berlin explained its decision to charge annual dues by saying that every Jew was connected to this charitable organization at least in his soul.[63] This claim has remained essentially unchanged up to the present. Even today, *bikur cholim* societies like the one in Frankfurt am Main are by and large subdivisions of the traditional *chevra kadisha*. In smaller communities, visits to the sick are not institutionalized or organized, but instead are made by individual members on a voluntary basis, with the full support of the supervisor and the rabbinate. Outside of Germany, the names of Jewish hospitals, such as the Bikur Cholim Hospital in Jerusalem, still recall the long period when caring for the sick was the task of fraternal organizations.

Most such societies did not get the special name of *chevrat bikur cholim* until the eighteenth century. Before that time these brotherhoods, whose complete history has yet to be written, were usually integrated into either the burial society (*chevra kadisha*) or a charitable organization (*gemilut chasadim*). The 1750s saw the start of another trend as well: dissatisfaction with the kind of care for the sick provided by these communally run societies led to the establishment of separate societies—some communal, but the majority semiprivate and organized by the young, unmarried men in the community.[64] One such society was the Agudda Jeschara (literally, "Upright Society"), founded in Hamburg in 1780. In 1844 this group changed its name to the Sick-Care Society of Consoling Brothers (Krankenverein tröstender Brüder), which gave a clearer sense of their actual function.[65] A social institution in the Fürth Jewish community looked more like the communal type. According to its new statutes of 1786 (*hanhagat bikur cholim*), the presiding officials were to task an administrator with visiting the impoverished sick either in the hospital or at home and attending to their needs.[66] As in mainstream Christian society, there was a growing tendency in Jewish communities to make caring for the sick a communal responsibility, particularly if they were poor, even as existing religious societies continued to do this work.

Societies dedicated to the business of visiting the sick—regardless of specific type or orientation—were distinct from organizations known as *Krankenunterstützungsvereine*, whose purpose was to provide financial support to the sick. These precursors of health insurance companies and relief funds existed in the non-Jewish world as early as the sixteenth century and were sometimes organized by guilds. In Jewish communities this type of sick fund was a later development. In 1761, for instance, five women in Frankfurt am Main established the Israelite Women's Health Insurance Company (Israelitische Frauenkrankenkasse).[67] Other women's associations have likewise been documented for cities including Dresden and Mannheim in the eighteenth century.[68]

Even so, for the most part, entities like these were—and still are—in the hands of men, in accordance with tradition. In Frankfurt am Main, Elias Maas founded a relief fund in 1738.[69] During the first year of its existence, the fund attracted between twenty and twenty-five men; each member contributed three Kreuzer (a small coin worth 4.2 cents) per week and in return was promised aid if he should become ill. Another male health insurance company was later founded in the same city, and it merged with the older relief fund in 1829. In the Altona Jewish community, one of these funds named Chevra Chemed (literally, "Association of Joy"), which had apparently existed for some time, drew up new statutes in 1833.[70] These stated that membership dues would be used to provide support in cases of illness or death only to those who had paid into the fund. When a member did become sick or die, the head of the association had to be notified. A doctor's certificate was also required stating that the person needed to remain in bed because of his illness. Sick benefits were paid only after seven days of unemployment, in the amount of two Reichsthaler and eight shillings a week. Certain illnesses and conditions such as "external injuries" were not eligible for compensation. Another prerequisite was that the member had made regular contributions. As historian Gabriele Zürn describes it, "while the health insurance principle of later epochs already existed in part, it could not fully meet the needs of members, who were frequently unemployed because of illness."[71] With the enactment of Bismarck's social security legislation, the exclusively Jewish relief funds lost a considerable amount of their earlier importance by the late 1880s, especially since fund members were not exempt from mandatory contributions to the statutory health insurance.

Prayer for the Sick

The Societies for Visiting the Sick sometimes published special prayer books. These contained texts that could be recited either communally or at the patient's bedside to bring him the healing power of God. One of the earliest examples was prepared by Venetian rabbi Leon Modena in 1619, *Balm for the Soul and Cure for the Bone* (*Tzori la-nefesh u-marpeh la-etsem*).[72] An even better-known work of this type was an abridged edition of the massive *Maabar Yabbok* (1626) first published in 1682 and reprinted at least eighteen times, the *Kizzur Maabar Yabbok*. Its influence was surpassed only by an ethical work by Kabbalist Isaiah ben Abraham Horowitz (ca. 1565–1630) entitled *Shinei Luchot HaBrit* (Two Tablets of the Covenant), first published in 1648–49 and even larger than the unabridged *Maabar Yabbok*.[73] Like other works of its kind, it contained invocations for the sick together with prayers for the dead and texts of consolation for mourners.

The best-known prayer for the sick is the *Mi Sheberach*, which takes its name from the opening verse, "who blessed." It was originally a prayer for the entire congregation and therefore contained various blessings for different groups of people (donors, benefactors, the poor, guests, and so on). Over time, a prayer containing blessings was added at the point in the liturgy when someone is called to read from the Torah. The community member who has been given this honor now has the chance to ask for God's blessings on family members and especially those who are ill.[74] In return, a donation for charitable purposes (*zedakah*) is usually expected. In medieval Mainz, the famous rabbi Yaakov ben Moshe Levi Moelin, called Maharil (1375–1427), is said to have gone to each person in attendance with a small Torah scroll and spoken a *Mi Sheberach* with him that was specifically tailored to that person's situation. This custom almost certainly improved the chance of receiving donations. At the end of the service he gave an additional blessing to all present before handing the Torah scroll back to the cantor (*chazzan*) and returning to his place.

Even today in Jewish congregations worldwide, after the Torah reading this special prayer for the sick may be recited.[75] A congregation member says the name of the sick person together with the Hebrew name of that person's mother. Unlike when someone is called to read the Torah, here the mother's name is required instead of the father's, since according to traditional Jewish belief it is "the maternal" that stands for life and soul. For a long time, this prayer was not usually recited on the Sabbath: on this day of joy, attention was not supposed to focus on suffering and need. Rabbi Judah ben Barzilai (1070–1130) thus contended that while the mitzvah to visit the sick applied even on the Sabbath, it was an altogether different matter to in effect bring illness into the synagogue by mentioning it. Other scholars disagreed, claiming that a prayer for the sick was permitted on this day if the person was mortally ill. Still others felt that even if it was not a matter of *pikuach nefesh*, or saving someone's life, it was not a problem. In that case, however, the person reciting it should add that while an intercession was not allowed on the Sabbath, recovery was near at hand. The sick person was in any case not supposed to be present. If he was, it was preferable to say only the general prayer for healing. Several rabbis were unsure that it should be recited if it was unclear whether the sick person was still in the same place, since he might not even still be alive. In contrast, the severity of his illness was immaterial: even someone with an incurable disease could be included in the intercession, since there was always hope for a miracle cure.

Here is the traditional prayer for the sick male in one of the many variations that exist in English translation:

> May He who blessed our fathers, Abraham, Isaac and Jacob, Moses and Aaron, David and Solomon, heal [sick person's Hebrew name and that of his mother], because [Hebrew name of the person who pledged charity for the sake of the sick person and that of his/her father] pledged charity, without a vow, for his sake. In this merit may the Holy One, blessed be He, be filled with mercy for him, to restore him to health and to cure him, to strengthen him and to invigorate him. And may He hasten to send him from heaven a complete recovery to his 248 bodily parts and 365 veins, among the other sick people of Israel, a healing of spirit and a healing of body; and let us say, Amen.[76]

On the Sabbath and on holy days, as noted above, the prayer is followed by the qualifying phrase: "It is Shabbat when it is forbidden to plead; healing will come soon; and let us say, Amen."

In addition to reciting this special prayer for the sick, it is also possible at one point in the *Amidah* (*Shemone Esreh*) at the center of the Jewish liturgy to invoke the Lord's help in the case of illness. The corresponding excerpt goes as follows: "Heal us, O Lord, and we shall be healed, save us and we shall be saved, for You are our praise. Bring complete healing to all our wounds, for You are God and King, the faithful and merciful healer. Blessed are You, O Lord, Who heals the sick of his people Israel" (*Siddur Ashkenaz*).

Why this is the eighth blessing is explained in the Talmud, where we read that circumcision, which "requires healing" (BT Megillah 17b), took place eight days after birth. It is preceded by the blessing of forgiveness, which is also consistent from a rabbinical perspective, since healing presupposes penance. The entire *Amidah* must be recited; the segment of the prayer relating to healing may not be recited alone. That, as already mentioned, is the purpose of the *Mi Sheberach* prayer.[77]

Praying is not limited to family members and friends. The sick person may also seek healing in prayer and request God's blessing. The Talmud stipulates, for example, that when a person is bled—one of the most widely used standard therapies until the nineteenth century—he must recite the following: "May it be Your will, O Lord my God, that this enterprise be for healing and that You should heal me. As You are a faithful God of healing and Your healing is truth" (BT Berakhot 60a). After surviving this somewhat risky procedure, the patient is to recite a short prayer of thanks. There is no consensus even today about whether this applies solely to the practice of bleeding, or if a patient is obliged to say the lines before any invasive medical procedure.[78]

Before taking medicine a person is likewise obliged to recite a blessing (*birkat hanehenim*), even if he is not expecting pleasure (as in the case of eating), but relief:

> One who has a sore throat should not, *ab initio*, gargle oil on Shabbat for medicinal purposes, as doing so would violate the decree prohibiting the use of medicine on Shabbat. However, he may, even *ab initio*, add a large amount of oil to the *anigeron* [a stew of beet greens and wine] and swallow it. . . . This is obvious that one must recite a blessing. . . . Lest you say: Since he intends to use it for medicinal purposes, let him not recite a blessing over it at all, as one does not recite a blessing before taking medicine. Therefore, it teaches us that, since he derived pleasure from it, he must recite a blessing over it. (BT Berakhot 36a)

In this case the appropriate blessing is required for the secondary substance of oil. But what about before ingesting a (usually plant-based) medicine if it is not really "enjoyable," but has a bitter taste, for example, and is hard to swallow? Here scholarly opinion is divided: some rabbis say "yes," the appropriate blessing is required even before taking bitter medicine,[79] while others say it is not. In the *Kitzur Shulchan Aruch*, for example, we read:

> If you eat or drink something for medicinal purposes, and it is tasteful and you enjoy it, you should recite the appropriate berachah before and after [taking it], even if it consists of forbidden food. Since under the present circumstances, the Torah permits it, you should say the berachah over it. However, if it has a bitter flavor and is distasteful to you, then do not say the berachah over it. If you drink a raw egg in order to make your voice clear, although you do not enjoy the taste, you do enjoy the nourishment it provides; and you should recite the berachah over it. (*Kitzur Shulchan Aruch* 50:8)

A religious Jew must recite an additional blessing as soon as he has recovered from an illness. The Talmud tells of how Rabbi Yehuda was visited by fellow rabbis after recovering from an illness. In his presence they said a prayer thanking God for saving this famous rabbi from death. Rabbi Yehuda responded: "You have exempted me from offering thanks, as your statement fulfilled my obligation to recite a blessing" (BT Berakhot 54b). This passage indicates that every Jew is bound by the obligation to give thanks and also that the prayer of thanks is not private, but should instead be recited before the gathered congregation, which means that a *minjan*, or quorum, is also necessary. Today, the blessing usually recited after the Torah reading is: "Blessed art thou, O Lord our God, King of the universe, who vouchsafest benefits unto the undeserving, who hast also vouchsafed all good unto me." All present then respond: "He who hath vouchsafed all good unto thee, may he vouchsafe all good unto thee for ever."[80] Scholarly opinion is divided only on the issue of how severe the illness needs to be in order to require a corresponding prayer of thanks. Some believe that the commandment applies only in the case of a life-threatening illness, while others feel it depends on whether the person was bedridden and for how long.[81] No distinction is made, however, between acute and chronic pain. In any case, the person must have made a complete recovery. Even though with certain illnesses (biliary colic, epileptic fits, and so on) the possibility of recurrence still exists, that is, the person is not completely cured, the obligation still holds. Once the patient has recovered, he should not delay too long before reciting the blessing. A thirty-day period is usually allowed, since there must be enough time to include a religious service and thereby obtain the necessary quorum. Jewish law also requires women to recite a prayer of thanks, though it is not customary in some congregations. A blessing is definitely required of a woman after the healthy delivery of a baby.

In contrast, a doctor does not have to recite a blessing before or after giving medical treatment. Jewish legal scholars explain this provision by noting that physicians are under an obligation to provide treatment and in some cases must also act quickly, so they can afford no delays. The doctor can only ask God for support, as we see in the prayer that a Jewish doctor is supposed to recite every day. The prayer, long falsely attributed to renowned Jewish philosopher and physician Maimonides, goes as follows: "Almighty God! Thou hast chosen me in Thy mercy to watch over the life and death of Thy creatures. I now apply myself to my profession. Support me in this great task so that it may benefit mankind, for without Thy help not even the least thing will succeed."[82] The text is now known to have come from Jewish doctor and Enlightenment thinker Marcus Herz.[83]

Chapter 7

The Mortal Body

Euthanasia and End-of-Life Care

The German language has almost no synonyms for the sick person whose death is imminent. Depending on context, expressions like *Sterbender* (the dying person), *Moribundus* (moribund), or *Todgeweihter* (doomed) are used. Hebrew, in contrast, has a considerable number of expressions for the different stages of the dying process.[1] The term *treifa* is used for both people and animals that will die within a short time (under a year). A *shechiv mera* is someone who, though on his deathbed, still has a chance of survival and is still capable of dictating a will, making a gift or donation, or requesting a divorce; in other words, this is a person who is still of sound mind. In the German translation of the corresponding Talmud passage (Bava Batra 135b), the term *Sterbenskranker*, or "terminally ill person," is used. *Gosses* refers to a critically ill person with an unfavorable prognosis who will die within several days. *Chayei sha'ah* (Hebrew for "hourly life"), in contrast, is used for a patient whose short time left to live is considerably less than a year.[2] *Note lamut* (Hebrew for "in the throes of death") refers to the final moments of life, and the final stage is called *yetziat neshamah*, or "departure of the soul."[3]

For interactions with the dying, Judaism places special emphasis on the term *gosses*, since it is decisive in a number of fundamental ethical issues including end-of-life care and euthanasia. In the halakhic literature, however, there is no consensus on how to recognize that a person has reached this stage of the dying process. The *Shulchan Arukh* defines *gosses* (גוסס) as a "person close to death who brings up liquid to his throat" (Even HaEzer 121.7). Moses Isserles added the important qualifier that the person must still be able to speak. In the twentieth century, following tremendous advances made in intensive care medicine, rabbinical authorities found themselves compelled to conceive the term more broadly. American rabbi J. David Bleich used it, for instance, to describe someone who is sure to die within seventy-two hours, even if that person is given life-prolonging medications.[4] This derives from the halakhic regulation: "one who is informed, 'we saw your relative in a dying position three days ago,' is bound to mourn for him" (*Shulchan Arukh*, Yoreh Deah 339.2). Conversely, this means that the critically ill person who does not die within three days is technically speaking not *gosses*.[5] However, the three-day rule only applies if the dying person is physically absent. If you are present when somone is dying, the length of time that the person is *gosses* may well be somewhat longer.[6] In view of all that today's intensive care medicine can achieve, Jewish legal scholars say that determining who belongs in the category of *gosses* depends on the doctor's prognosis; at the same time, they are all well aware that even in the case of someone who is critically ill, predictions about the end of life can be hard to make.

Halakhah gives detailed instructions about how to interact with someone who is *gosses*. When those present are convinced that death is imminent, they first encourage the dying person to confess his sins.[7] This appeal should be made very gently and not in the presence of those unfamiliar with the Torah, women, or minors, lest it break their hearts (*Shulchan Arukh*, Yoreh Deah 338.1). The dying person is then to recite these words: "I confess before Thee, O Lord, my God and the God of my fathers, that my healing and my death are in your hand. May it be Thy will to heal me completely, and if I die, my death should be an expiation of all sins, wrongs and rebellious acts, which I have committed sinfully, wrongfully and rebelliously before Thee, and grant me a share in Paradise, and favour me with the world to come which is stored away for the Righteous" (Yoreh Deah 338.2). This section of the *Shulchan Arukh* also includes the general provision that the dying person is still to be treated as "a living being in all respects," which means that he may not be washed or anointed with oil, nor is his lower jaw to be bound shut

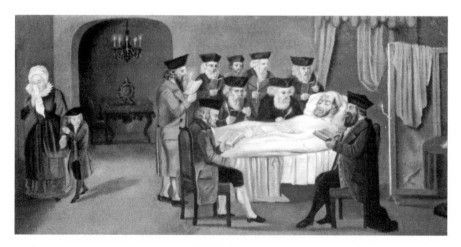

Figure 27. Members of the Prague *chevra kadisha* praying at a deathbed. Painting, late eighteenth century. © Jewish Museum Prague.

(like a dead person). Those present are also not allowed to show signs of mourning or "make lamentations" for the dying person.[8] Someone who is near death should not be left alone; it is important to provide him with spiritual comfort that will ease his passing. In his book on Jewish rites, Leon Modena writes that this was also the case in early seventeenth-century Venice: "When the Sick man is now at the point of Death, and that he perceiveth he cannot live long; he is not then to be left alone, without some company by him, and there is some one to be by his bedside, Night and Day: and they account it a very great Blessing to be present at the Departure of a Dying person, especially if it were a man of Learning."[9]

Not surprisingly, Modena adhered to this tradition himself: in his autobiography he describes keeping vigil at his aged father's bedside and receiving his father's blessing after the dying man makes his confession in the presence of ten men.[10]

We get a good sense of what end-of-life care actually looked like in a Jewish household from the early eighteenth-century memoirs of businesswoman Glückel of Hameln. Her husband Chayim had injured himself severely in a fall, and he "bade me send for the Sephardi Abraham Lopez, a physician and chirurgeon-barber. I had him fetched at once. . . . Thursday I brought in another rupture-cutter and two more physicians," but they were unable to provide much actual help.[11] In the five days between Chayim's fall and his death, his brother Joseph and Glückel's mother came to visit, and their son Loeb stayed with and cared for him the entire time. Chayim tried to hide the extent of his injuries from his wife, but with limited success. In the hours before his death he was still able to express his will and secure his children's future. After that, Glückel summoned Reb Feibisch and the family teacher to the house. Chayim asked the rabbi to bring him the *Shinei Luchot HaBrit* (Two Tablets of the Covenant), a then-popular work on Jewish laws and ethics by Frankfurt rabbi Isaiah ben Abraham Horowitz; after reading in it for about half an hour, he asked the rabbi to remove Glückel and their son Loeb, "whereupon Reb Feibisch thrust us by main force from the room."[12] This left only the rabbi, the teacher, and the doctor Abraham Lopez at his bedside. Chayim now began speaking softy to himself, and when the doctor leaned in closer, he could hear the man utter his dying words: "Hear, O Israel, the Lord our God, the Lord is One!"—the beginning of the Jewish profession of faith. "With that, his breath ceased and he had breathed away his pure soul. Thus he died in purity and holiness, and they saw from his end the man that he was."[13]

Especially when a dying person had no family members who might console him in his final hours, the burial society, or *chevra kadisha* (see Chapter 6), stepped in to take their place. The society members guaranteed the presence of the *minjan*, or quorum of ten men required for the communal prayer. According to the 1701 statutes of the Altona community's *chevra kadisha*, the ten members who kept vigil were tasked with encouraging the dying person to prepare a will, acknowledge his sins and repent. They were required to stay with the dying person until he had died and during this time were to act "as written in the two tablets of the Commandments,"[14] in other words, in accordance with the early modern guidelines for end-of-life care outlined above. In addition, they were not to engage in idle conversation with the sick person.

Just how detailed the guidelines are in Judaism concerning end-of-life care is clearly seen in Hebrew-language manuals that were usually entitled *Maabar Yabbok*. They go back to a work by Italian rabbi Aaron Berechja ben Moses ben Nechemja (d. 1639) from Modena, a text that was also translated into Judeo-German. This five-part work gives precise instructions on the treatment of the dying and the dead. The Jewish community of Fürth used the abridged version published in 1714 under the title *Refuat Neshama*, or "Medicine for the Soul."[15] Here we learn what *chevra kadisha* members were expected to do when summoned, but also what the dying person could do in his final hours to prepare for "a good death." The role played by the burial society is singled out for praise by Jewish physicians: "The scholars . . . make an effort to remind the sick man of his obligations, and if he is critically ill, they admonish him to pray, but they do this cautiously and with prudence; it is their duty not to be too forward in doing so, lest they upset the sick person, for an agitated mood could be detrimental and harm his chances of recovering."[16]

Here we find a Jewish *ars moriendi* that surpasses even the Christian version in both style and substance. If after multiple sickbed visits it becomes clear that the person is in danger of dying, then society members wash his hands, gird him, and clothe him in his prayer shawl. They encourage him to recite a special prayer (*mesirat moda'a*) requesting God's forgiveness in advance, since in his final hours, fear of dying might cause him to do something like renounce God, giving in to temptation by the devil. After the prayer requesting advance absolution, the profession of faith is said as corroboration. Finally the dying person is asked to acknowledge and express contrition for his sins. If he is unable to do so in Hebrew, he may do so in the vernacular. Several prayers for the final moments of life follow. One popular one is the *Ana BeKoach*, believed to have been written by Rabbi Nehunya ben HaKanah (first or second century CE). The Kabbalistic prayer, also known as the forty-two-letter name of God, consists of seven lines (corresponding to the seven days of the week), each composed of six words. In the second line, the first letters of the six words spell the protective formula *kera satan* (Hebrew for "tear Satan to pieces"). Incantations like this one were recited in the hope of securing a life in the hereafter for the person facing death and preserving him from hell.

A number of congregations also had and still have their own special prayers. In Fürth, for instance, it was common to recite the request for the annulment of vows (*hatarat nedarim*). When someone is about to face divine judgment, according to Jewish belief, he is released from all vows made during his lifetime both to other people and to God. All those present affirm this in set phrases containing the sick person's name. A more widespread practice is the recitation of certain psalms (Psalms 90, 91) or the Prophet Isaiah's hymn of praise, "Holy, holy, holy is the Lord of Hosts: the whole earth is full of his glory" (Isaiah 6:3). Prayers asking for the remission of sins alternate with ones asking for recovery, since until the very end, those attending to the sick person do not abandon hope that he might regain his health. In another ritual, one with many different local variations, all those present including family and *chevra kadisha* members walk solemnly around the the deathbed, which has been moved away from the wall. They are careful not to make any sounds or gestures that might distract or upset the dying person as he prepares for death. No one should ever stand at the foot of the bed, since there the gaze of the dreaded angel of death would fall on him. When the end is clearly imminent, those keeping vigil recite the profession of faith once more as candles are lit. Once signs of death as defined by Halakhah are observed (usually respiratory arrest), all windows in the room are opened to allow the soul an easier exit, and the well-known verse from Job is recited: "The Lord gives and the Lord takes away; blessed be the name of the Lord" (Job 1:21).

In Judaism, euthanasia is expressly forbidden.[17] This firm rejection is based on three fundamental principles: first, the general commandment against killing; second, the concept of life as a "loan" from God; and third, the high value placed on life. The *Kitzur Shulchan Aruch* summarizes what is repeatedly stressed already in the Talmud and other Jewish codicils, namely, that under no circumstances may death be hastened by external intervention:

> A person who is very near death is considered as a living being in every respect. It is, therefore, forbidden to touch him, for anyone who touches him is considered like one who sheds blood. To what can this be compared? To a dripping [flickering] candle, which becomes extinguished as soon as someone touches it. Even if he is critical over a long period, and he and his family are in great agony, it is, nevertheless, forbidden to hasten his death in any way. [It is forbidden] for example to remove a feathered pillow from under him, because some people say that feathers of certain birds defer death, or for example to place the keys to the synagogue under his head; all these things are forbidden. (*Kitzur Shulchan Aruch* 194:1)

In contrast, removing a sound that the dying person finds unpleasant is allowed, since doing so does not involve touching him. This example is found already in the late medieval *Book of the Pious*, which also mentions the custom of placing salt on the person's tongue, apparently to arouse his spirits.[18] Since this type of measure can also be seen as a possible impediment to death, it may be omitted without coming into conflict with the commandment against killing. A dying person's wish to be taken to a different location where he might die more readily may not be granted. It is, however, permissible to pray for a quick death, as Rabbi Nissim ben Reuben Gerondi (ca. 1310–76) explains, citing the excruciating death of renowned Jewish scholar Judah ha-Nasi. Even as his students and disciples continued to pray for his recovery, God listened to the requests of a pious maidservant for a quick end to his suffering (BT Ketubot 104a). This is why the Gemara say in a different passage that "it is sometimes necessary to pray for mercy that an ill person should die."[19]

Thus in Judaism even today there are strict limitations on passive euthanasia.[20] The sole exception: extending a dying person's life is forbidden if it will cause him additional pain and suffering. In contrast, what today is known as active euthanasia is absolutely forbidden, even though the Hebrew Bible mentions at least one incident of mercy killing (2 Samuel 1:5–16): during battle a young Amalekite finds the seriously wounded King Saul leaning on his spear, and when Saul learns who he is, he asks the enemy soldier to dispatch him. The Amalekite complies, then seeks out David to inform him. Deeply saddened by the news, David in turn has the messenger killed, since he had openly admitted to dealing Saul the death blow, and declares: "Your blood be on your own head; for out of your own mouth you condemned yourself when you said, 'I killed the LORD's anointed.'" This is not about revenge; it is a matter of atonement for having committed the sacrilege of laying a hand on God's anointed one—something that not even David had dared to do (1 Samuel 24:10), let alone would be acceptable from a stranger.[21]

The situation is somewhat different in the case described in the Talmud. The Romans condemned Rabbi Hanina ben Teradyon (second century CE) to be burned at the stake for being a law-abiding Jew. Damp tufts of wool were also placed over his heart so that the process would be even slower and more painful. When his students, who were forced to watch his martyrdom, called out to their beloved teacher that he should open his mouth wide so that he would suffocate more quickly, he answered them: "It is preferable that He who gave me my soul should take it away, and one should not harm onself to speed his death" (BT Avodah Zarah 18a). Here once again, the commandment against taking one's own life is invoked in dramatic fashion. The pious rabbi relented only when the executioner offered to stoke the flames and hasten his death, and declared he would jump into the flames himself, dying alongside the condemned man so that he might gain eternal life. This seemingly contradictory behavior has been discussed in many later Talmud commentaries, but as yet no completely persuasive interpretation has been offered.[22] Be that as it may, this passage is never invoked by Jewish scholars as a justification for mercy killing.

Just the opposite: in accordance with Jewish teachings, until the very end everything must be done—especially given the abilities of modern intensive care medicine—to see that a terminally ill person receives adequate food, artificial respiration, and pain relief.[23] It is for this reason that the 2014 Israeli film *Mita Tova* (literally, "good death") by Tal Granit and Sharon Maymon generated so much controversy. At the center of the tragicomic story is an inventor who builds a "mercy killing machine" for his friend who wishes to die, then cannot rid himself of the spirits he has summoned, since other world-weary people now also want to use his invention to gain release from their earthly existence.

Still, even Halakhah does not insist that treatment be continued if the doctors are unanimous that there is no prospect of success. In this case, a therapy that has already been started may not simply be discontinued, but no additional treatments need to be introduced, and no unneccesary diagnostic tests must be done. This, however, applies only to cases of chronic illness. If someone is suddenly facing a life-threatening situation, then everything possible must be done to save his life.

Death Criteria

According to the Talmud, there are 903 different types of death. The number reflects the numerical value $(400 + 6 + 90 + 1 + 6 + 400)$ of the Hebrew first letters (תוצאות, *totzaot*) in Psalm 68:20 (האל לנו אל למושעות וליהוה אדני למות תוצאות), "Our God is a God who saves us, in the LORD God's hand lies escape from death"). In addition, this passage indicates that not all ways to die have the same level of difficulty: "the most difficult of all these types of death is croup [*askara*], while the easiest of all is the kiss of death" (BT Berakhot 8a). The "kiss of death" image comes from the interpretation of the Bible passage about Aaron's gentle death at an advanced age on Mount Hor (Numbers 33:38). Taken literally, the Hebrew expression (על פי יהוה, "out of God's mouth") is understood as the announcement of imminent death.

Even more important than the manner of death is the issue of when someone is dead or, more precisely, is declared dead. In the age of intensive care medicine there are several different definitions of death: (1) *clinical death*, the cessation of heartbeat and breathing, a condition that may still be reversible if timely countermeasures are taken; (2) *cardiac death*, when the heart stops beating and circulation ceases, causing irreparable damage to the heart, and circulation alone is artificially maintained; (3) *brain death*, irreversible cessation of all brain stem function. Heart and circulatory system function are mainained only by means of artificial respiration and medication.

Judaism was occupied with the question of when a person is dead long before organ transplants became possible in the late 1960s.[24] In the Mishnah period we already find debate about whether it is permissible to violate the Sabbath in order to save someone buried by a rockslide or collapsed building (Mishnah Yoma 8:7).

If the victim still shows some sign of life, then efforts to save him may continue; otherwise he must be left in place until after the Sabbath. But how do we know in such cases if the person under the debris is even alive? "Until what point does one check to clarify whether the victim is still alive? . . . They [the Gemara] said: One clears until the victim's nose. . . . And some say: One clears until the victim's heart" (BT Yoma 85a). But who is right: those who rely on observing that breathing has ceased, or those who check for a heartbeat? Rav Papa in the Talmud offers this opinion: "The dispute with regard to how far to check for signs of life applies when the digger begins removing the rubble from below, starting with the feet, to above. In such a case it is insufficient to check until his heart; rather, one must continue removing rubble until he is able to check his nose for breath. But if one cleared the rubble from above to below, once he checked as far as the victim's nose he is not required to check further, as it is written: 'All in whose nostrils was the breath of the spirit of life' (Genesis 7:22)" (BT Yoma 85a).

With the Torah as its reference point ("Everything . . . that had the breath of life," Genesis 7:22), Judaism grants breathing a key role in defining death. Only a minority of scholars contend that digging must continue in order to determine that there is also no heartbeat. Maimonides, whose profession as a physician lent his philosophical views even greater heft, sides with the majority in his Talmud commentary: "If [in the process of clearing the debris] they [reached] his nose and saw that he was not breathing, he should be left there, for he has died already" (*Mishneh Torah*, Shabbat 2:19).[25] The later *Shulchan Arukh* also takes this position (see tractate Orach Chayim 329.4). Even so, both here and in Maimonides's commentary we also find contradictory passages: ones stating that the absence of breathing can also be of a temporary nature, and that a person is therefore not considered dead "until he dies" (Mishnah Oholot 1:6), that is, until his soul has been exhaled in the most literal sense of the word. In order to be sure, later generations of rabbis held that multiple conditions need to be met before someone is declared dead. According to one of the leading nineteenth-century Orthodox rabbis, Chatam Sofer (1762–1839), this is the case when "once [the patient] lies as an inanimate stone and there is no pulsation whatsoever, and if subsequently respiration ceases we have only the words of our holy Torah that he is dead" (Responsa: Yoreh Deah 338).[26] The halakhic view is thus that death may be assumed in all cases where someone is motionless, has no pulse, and is not breathing. Until well into the twentieth century, family members also took respiratory arrest as a clear sign that the person had died, as Jewish autobiographical accounts attest. Glückel of Hameln is not speaking metaphorically when she describes her husband's premature death as follows: "With that, his breath ceased and he had breathed away his pure soul."[27]

The contested issue of which indication of death takes precedence (respiratory or cardiac arrest) was not resolved until the twentieth century. One of the most prominent Orthodox Jewish legal scholars of his time, Rabbi Joseph Ber Soloveitchik (1903–93) argued that while death begins when breathing ceases, a person becomes a corpse only when all bodily functions have stopped.

This raises the question of where Judaism stands on brain death, the subject of a fairly recent debate that was sparked by new developments in intensive care medicine. Based on centuries of practical experience, people have an intuitive sense of how a deceased person looks: cold, with waxen-looking skin, not breathing, without a pulse or blood pressure, and not responding to external stimuli. Thanks to artificial respiration, however, a person who has been declared brain-dead still shows many of the usual signs of life, including reflex movements. To an outsider this person looks more like someone who is unconscious, even though his brain shows no activity whatsoever. Without the help of artificial respiration, cardiac death would soon take place.

For strictly observant Jews the case is therefore clear: anyone who is still breathing and has a pulse, even if this is only with the aid of intensive care medicine, can, strictly speaking, not be dead, at least according to the classic halakhic definition of death. At the same time, already in 1986 the Israeli Chief Rabbinate declared that heart transplant operations, which require the removal of an organ from a brain-dead donor, are permissible. Some rabbis admittedly do not recognize this criterion of death. Its proponents cite Maimonides: "A corpse does not impart ritual impurity until the person actually dies. Even if one's veins have been cut, or he is in his death-throes, even if his two vital signs have been slit, he does not impart ritual impurity until his soul expires. . . . If his backbone is broken together with most of the surrounding flesh, he was torn apart like a fish from his back, he was decapitated, or he was cut in half from his stomach, he imparts impurity, even though some of his limbs are still making convulsive movements" (*Mishneh Torah*, Sefer Taharah, Tum'at Met 1:15). But not even an experiment done in Israel in 1995, in which a pregnant sheep, decapitated but still on artificial respiration, delivered a lamb, convinced critics among the Orthodox rabbis. They maintain that brain death is not acceptable from a halakhic standpoint. In the words of the influential rabbi Shlomo Zalman Auerbach (1910–95): "Brain death as it is established by physicians today is not adequate to etablish the death of a person. Such an individual is legally like a *safek* (possible dead) and *safek gosses* (possibly terminally ill). Therefore, it is prohibited to hasten the death of such a person in any manner. It is also forbidden to to remove organs for transplantation as long as the heart is still beating for fear of hastening the death of the *gosses*. This act is forbidden even for the need to safe the life of another extant patient who would otherwise certainly die."[28]

Judaism remains divided even today over the question of when a person may be declared dead. Among Orthodox Jews the traditional concept of respiratory arrest, with its connection to the image of the human soul, still prevails.

Apparent Death

The resurrection of the dead has been a topic of enduring interest to Christians and Jews alike. The Jewish Enlightenment thus marked a noticeable break, since with Reform Judaism and secularly oriented Zionism, from the late eighteenth century onward greater emphasis was placed on the life of this world and traditional concepts were abandoned. But at the beginning of the modern period, another and completely different issue also occupied Judaism, namely, the fear that (overly) hasty burial in keeping with Halakhah regulations might result in burying someone alive. Up until this time, the deceased were treated as Ascher Levy (1598–1635) of Alsatia describes in the following account of his father's death on November 25, 1627: "I myself washed the body with spring water at his request, for people were afraid to go near him. This took place in my house, here in Reichshofen. And on that same Thursday [the day of his father's death] I transported him—miraculously, since at the time . . . the land was filled with the din of war—to give him an honorable burial, and I had ten people with me. He was buried in the cemetery of Ettendorf, in the uppermost row if you are taking a tour of the burial ground."[29] As the passage indicates, the burial took place on the same day that Levy's father died.

The so-called controversy concerning early burial was one of the most important debates on how to reform Judaism to emerge from the Haskalah movement.[30] Until the late eighteenth century, Jews did not question the commandment to bury someone if possible on the same day he died. This precept goes back to a biblical regulation, one that actually applied only to burying those who had been executed, but that in Talmudic interpretation became a general rule: "When a man is convicted of a capital offence and is put to death, you shall hang him on a gibbet; but his body shall not remain on the gibbet overnight; you shall bury it on the same day, for a hanged man is offensive in the sight of God. You shall not pollute the land which the LORD your God is giving you as your patrimony" (Deuteronomy 21:22–23).

If this was how to treat someone who had been sentenced to death, then the obligation must apply all the more to someone receiving an honorable burial—that was, in any case, how Jewish legal scholars saw it. Members of the Jewish Orthodoxy found themselves having to defend the practice only once the fear of being buried while still alive became rife—first among European Christians and then among Jews. Such fears had of course always existed, but with the 1748 publication of *Dissertation sur l'incertitude des signes de la mort . . . (The Uncertainty of the Signs of Death, and the Danger of Precipitate Interments and Dissections)* by French physician Jacques-Jean Bruhier d'Ablaincourt (1685–1756), also translated into German in 1754, apparent death became a central topic in Enlightenment medical literature.[31] This also affected Jewish physicians. One of their most prominent representatives was a student of Kant at the time, the Berlin physician and Enlightenment thinker Marcus Herz. We will return to him shortly.

The controversy concerning early burial began in Mecklenburg-Schwerin, where in 1772 the duke issued a rescript directing the Schwerin Jewish community to henceforth bury their dead three days after death had been determined. This was intended to offset fears of being buried alive. The duke's regulation represented more than a radical challenge to the community's autonomy; it also cast doubt on a centuries-old practice. The background for the decree was this: the practice of burying of a Jew within three hours of his death had become known in Christian circles and had prompted Oluf Gerhard Tychsen (1734–1815), a professor of Oriental languages, to send a memorandum to the duke. In it he explained that the custom of early burial in Judaism could be traced back to fears of rapid physical decay, which was to be expected in the climate "in Canaan, Babylon, and Egypt."[32] But since decay did not set in so quickly in "our colder regions," here the danger of burying someone who might only seem to be dead was considerably higher, according to Tychsen. He therefore recommended that the regional ruler pass legislation against such early burial, since "it would be pointless to try convincing the Jews of the error of their ways by using rational argument." In the spirit of enlightened absolutism, he urged that only a legal measure by the local ruler, who "bears such concern for their [the Jews'] lives," would prevent the burial of people who only appeared to be dead.

Not surprisingly, the Schwerin Jewish community did not immediately bend to the will of the sovereign, but sought reassurance from a Jewish authority instead. They turned to the prominent rabbi Jacob Emden of Altona, requesting a legal opinion that would confirm the halakhic obligation of early burial. Surmising the sensitive nature of the subject for Christian-Jewish relations, Emden asked his student Moses Mendelssohn to intercede. The renowned philosopher and Jewish scholar wrote two different letters in response, one to the duke of Schwerin and the other to the Jewish community. In his address to the duke, Mendelssohn stressed the halakhic obligation to bury the dead promptly, citing passages from the Talmud as support. He also included a reminder that the duke had promised to protect the Jews' right to religious freedom. In closing he suggested a compromise that he hoped would lead to a repeal of the decree: "So that we may have a clear conscience in all cases, and be absolutely certain that on the one hand no person is buried who still has some life in him, and on the other that no corpse is kept in the house any longer than necessary, henceforth we will no longer rely on our own judgment, but instead let the decision be based on the statement of a person with medical knowledge, and not bury the dead until an experienced doctor has examined the corpse and in accordance with the rules of his art judged that there can be no doubt about the death."[33]

In the other letter, he sought to convince his coreligionists in the Schwerin community that extending the waiting period between death and burial could certainly be reconciled with Jewish law. To do so he mentioned, among other things, the burial customs in ancient Israel:

> All deceased were kept in subterranean vaults or caverns; there, they were watched over for three days, in order to see whether they might by chance still be alive and give signs of coming awake. . . . Our teachers approved of the body's speedy removal from the family's dwelling because there was not the slightest danger that any sign of life might go undetected under the given circumstances. But we, whose present customs permit no such close observation of our deceased, should indeed delay their burial. For how could we ever justify our negligence if we were to realize too late (and such incidents do occur, and have been recorded) that what we judged to be a dead body was merely an inert one?[34]

Mendelssohn proceeded diplomatically, trying to get each party to understand the other's position and suggesting a compromise. But Emden, who had asked for his intercession, stood firm. In an address to the Schwerin Jewish community that became known to the government, he asserted that prompt burial was essential, since he understood death "as a form of judgment: whether one was to receive reward or punishment, the process could not begin until the body had been interred. The righteous are to be laid to rest on the same day so that they can enter paradise and enjoy their reward without delay. Sinners must be laid to rest so that they can begin their course of punishment."[35] Emden thus saw early burial as a biblical commandment that was nonnegotiable, as Mendelssohn himself soon learned. When he presented Emden with his opinion, he was accused by the Altona rabbi of promoting "idolatry."[36]

The dispute over early burial, initially a local matter that barely registered beyond the borders of Schwerin, became a broader debate over tradition and reform due to four anonymous articles, published in Hebrew between 1785 and 1787 in the journal *Hameasef* (Hebrew for "The Collector"), the organ of the Jewish Enlightenment, and apparently written by its editor Isaak Euchel. In 1786 Mendelssohn granted Euchel permission to print his previously unpublished correspondence on the Schwerin matter in his journal. With this, the local dispute became a test case for the Jewish population's willingness to reform as a whole—or at least that is how it was seen by the *maskilim*. They gave it ample space in the debate over reform within Judaism, and ultimately, the non-Jewish public was also drawn into the discussion. This was primarily the work of Marcus Herz, whose 1788 text *Über die frühe Beerdigung der Juden* (On the Early Burial of Jews) resonated deeply both in Jewish circles and beyond.[37] Herz writes as a physician and a representative of the Enlightenment. He claims that delaying burial is a prerequisite for Jewish emancipation: in their burial customs, Jews should "follow the example of our civilized and enlightened neighboring peoples."[38] Much of his text is therefore devoted to medical rather than religious matters. He devotes only a few lines to the issue of "religious, ethical reasons" for early burial. Since he can find none, he recommends that burial take place within three days after the pronouncement of death. He vehemently criticizes the "obstinacy and conceitedness" of the Orthodoxy in clinging to a centuries-old custom that medical advances have made obsolete.[39] In his view, the definition of death lies in the hands of the physician: "The question is not whether we should bury a dead person promptly, but whether the person we are promptly burying is actually dead."[40]

Not all Jewish doctors accepted Herz's critical stance on early burial. One who disagreed was Marx Jacob Marx (1743–89), the personal physician to the Cologne elector, who held that traditional Jewish burial practices were the ideal precaution against burying someone who might not actually be dead. Marx contended that the careful washing of the corpse and the painstaking death vigil provided good opportunities for detecting signs of life. He considered Jewish burial society members far more experienced in this regard than Christians, who perform these final services as relatives or in their capacity as gravediggers, keeping watch and preparing the corpse for burial. He therefore deemed the halakhic regulations medically sound. The ritual cleansing of the corpse "may have always been impressed on us as only a ceremonial law, but it has great medical value."[41] Hamburg Jewish physician Hirsch Wolf (1738–1820) likewise defended the ancient custom. He not only felt that the traditional determination of death in Judaism was a sure thing, but he also claimed that early burial was good for the spiritual health of the bereaved, since "the longer the burial is delayed, the more offensive and dangerous it is for the relatives."[42]

Herz came under even sharper critique from tradition-bound experts in Jewish law. These included Salomon Seligmann Pappenheimer (1740–1814), who worked in Breslau (Wrocław) as a rabbinate assessor. In his treatise *An die Barmherzigen zu En-Dor oder über die frühe Beerdigung bei den Juden* (To the Merciful of En-Dor; or, On Early Burial Among the Jews, 1798), Pappenheimer dismissed the medical reasons cited by Enlightenment thinkers. Instead, he, like Marx, focused on the benefits of early burial for the survivors, stressing that the process of physical decay that inevitably began if burial was delayed offended the dignity of the deceased.[43]

And how did Christian authorities react to this internal Jewish debate? In many territories they sided strongly with "reason," accepting the arguments of Englightenment thinkers. As in Mecklenburg-Schwerin, in Altona (1785) and Prague (1786) regulations were passed that allowed for a longer waiting period before burial. Even so, as we see in the example of the three congregations in Hamburg and Altona, in the late 1780s internal efforts at Jewish reform failed. Support from the *maskilim* was still minimal at best; government commitment to the effort was also lacking, and here respect for Jewish privileges—whatever its motivation—may have played a role.[44] Prussia introduced change only some years later (1798),[45] and it was not until the early nineteenth century that most other German states followed suit. From then on, the protests of the burial societies were ignored. Yet despite the threat of severe penalties, signs of local resistance to the new regulations can be found as late as the 1820s. In the Jewish cemetery of Schwäbisch Hall, for example, the remaining gravestones from between 1812 and 1828 show that the deceased were interred on the day of their death.[46] And even in Prussia we find instances around the mid-nineteenth century of reducing the prescribed three-day waiting period.[47] In some territories, it was possible to legally circumvent the required interval if a public health official had conducted a postmortem examination and issued a certificate to that effect. Examples of this type of document were discovered for instance in the Altenkunstadt (Upper Franconia) Jewish community, preserved in the *genizah*, or special depository for books and manuscripts in the attic of the synagogue. In one of these recently rediscovered texts, dated June 6, 1835, we read: "The body of Seeligman Siegmann of Altkundstadt [*sic*] can be duly buried once the judicial inspection has taken place."[48]

By the 1830s at the latest, the heated debate over early burial was over. In 1889, liberal rabbi Ludwig Geiger (1848–1919) already referred to it as a historical phenomenon.[49]

Today throughout the world, the practice of early burial is limited almost exclusively to ultra-Orthodox circles. Problems with the authorities are a thing of the past, since it is now easier to be sure that death has occurred. In Israel, a death certificate and corresponding burial permit from either a hospital or a health department must be procured before the burial can take place.

Autopsy

Orthodox Jewry even today remains fundamentally opposed to autopsies and allows very few exceptions.[50] The most important reason is that the honor of the dead must be preserved, and when an autopsy is done it "disfigures" the corpse and involves the removal of internal organs. A further argument is that performing an autopsy violates the commandment against benefiting from someone who has died. An autopsy also means delaying the burial, which is supposed to occur on the same day as death. And finally, an autopsy is problematic from the standpoint of the resurrection of the dead.

Whether an autopsy should be permitted in special cases has been the topic of debate in Judaism only since the eighteenth century. At that time a growing number of Jewish students were enrolling in anatomy courses, and medical faculties, especially in Poland, attached a new condition to enrollment: that Jewish cadavers were also to be dissected.[51] Two centuries earlier, Jewish students studying medicine at the University of Padua had already had the same experience. Following the construction of an anatomical theater in 1594, dissections performed there were supposed to include Jewish cadavers. However, the local Jewish community managed to get around the provision by agreeing to pay an annual fee. Occasional mishaps did still happen, though: in 1680, for example, it was only with great effort that a Jewish boy who had been the victim of a murder was removed from the dissection table at the very last minute.[52]

Even after Jewish emancipation had brought about some progress and Jews had become citizens of the state, government offices continued to respect their traditional ban on autopsy, as an example from Hesse shows. In 1857 there were protests in Hessian state hospitals against the ruling that all patient corpses should be delivered to the Marburg anatomy department, a measure meant to help ease the shortage of body donors at the time. Officials acknowledged that in principle, Jews and Christians should be treated alike, but they ultimately chose to respect the religious sentiments of the few Jewish hospital patients.[53] In 1774, the Jewish community of Dresden paid a large sum of money so that the corpse of a community member who had committed suicide in prison would not be sent to the anatomy department of the medical-surgical college.[54] In the early twentieth century in Eastern Europe but also Austria, Jewish communities' exemption from the obligation to send corpses to anatomy departments was used for political purposes by anti-Semitic groups of students and professors. In 1923, a handful of Viennese students declared it scandalous that given the general shortage of cadavers in the anatomy department, their Jewish fellow students were completing the anatomy course only thanks to "Aryan" corpses.[55] In Lviv (Lemberg) in 1926, a representative of the Catholic students demanded that Jews no longer be allowed to tamper with Christian cadavers and should instead kindly dissect their own coreligionists.[56]

In Israel, internal postmortem examination has been regulated since 1953 by an autopsy law that has seen multiple revisions.[57] According to this law, an autopsy is allowed only in the following cases: (1) to directly save another life; (2) if there is suspicion that a serious error in treatment was committed; (3) to solve a crime, by identifying the murderer and preventing additional crimes; (4) to avert harm to other family members (for instance, with indications of hereditary diseases). In Israel it was long debated whether an autopsy in these situations also required permission from the relatives of the deceased. Following changes to the law in 1980, this permission is explicity required.

If these exceptional circumstances apply, the examination must involve as little bodily tissue as possible.[58] Autopsy is thus restricted to the absolute minimum needed in the interest of scientific knowledge. Even the instruments used must be cleaned in a way that preserves the tiniest pieces of bodily tissue so that they, too, may ultimately be buried. As the dissection is being performed, respect for the dignity of the deceased must be shown at all times.

Adherence to these strict rules is admittedly possible only in a Jewish state, and even there, in the past repeated attempts were made to circumvent these provisions so as not to hinder the progress of medicine. Things look different in countries where Jews are in the minority and where religious laws are only partially recognized as an expression of religious freedom. In those cases, the maxim issued early on for the Diaspora applies: "the law of the kingdom is the law" (BT Nedarim 28a).[59] Even so, in Germany and elsewhere there have been any number of incidents when Jewish law came into conflict with government burial regulations, yet the state did not simply override religious provisions—even though, legally speaking, this would have been possible. This happened in 2005, for instance, when a mass grave was discovered on the grounds of the Stuttgart airport. In an interview with the *Stuttgarter Zeitung*, Ulrich Goll, then justice minister, explained his decision to forgo a forensic examination by pointing out that it was highly unlikely a DNA analysis would identify someone who could still be brought to justice for the crime. Why offend the Orthodox Jews with a postmortem examination when the prospect of finding the perpetrators was so small?[60]

Suicide

According to Jewish traditional thinking life is not owned by human beings, it is only on loan from God. Someone who commits suicide is appropriating what belongs to God, so to speak, and is thereby commiting an act of *Chillul Hashem* or "desecration of the name of God." This view is expressed in a well-known monologue on the pros and cons of heroic suicide by Jewish historian Flavius Josephus:

"It is noble to kill oneself," another will declare. Not at all, I say; it is most ignoble. I think there is no greater coward than the captain who, fearing the stormy sea, deliberately sinks his ship before the tempest. No; suicide is equally repugnant to the instincts shared by all living creatures, and a real act of impiety towards God who created us. Among all the animals there is not one that deliberately seeks death or kills itself; the will to live is a powerful law of nature rooted in all. . . . And do you not think that God is indignant when a man treats His gift with contempt? For it is from Him that we have received our being, and it is to Him we must leave the decision to take it away."[61]

A person who knowingly takes his own life should be buried (Deuteronomy 21:23), but most of the mourning rituals are omitted, since mourning is forbidden: God has not taken a life here, but rather, someone has stolen a life from God. Jacob ben Ascher (1283–1340) nonetheless maintained that this only applied to distant relatives, not immediate family members, who should be buried with the mourning rituals required of survivors (*Tur*, Yoreh Deah 345).[62] In actual practice up until today, however, the situation usually looks somewhat different: relatives do not tear their clothing, "one does not mourn for him, and no lamentation is made for him" (*Shulchan Arukh*, Yoreh Deah 245), but the suicide victim is washed, placed in a shroud, and buried. In accordance with Jewish religious law, the gravesite is at least eight cubits away from other graves. In Frankfurt am Main in 1695, a woman and her son, both suicides, were buried in a remote part of the Jewish cemetery under a pile of stones, and a fence was also built around the grave to separate it even more.[63] Normally, though, people who had killed themselves were buried with less effort. Those who had become dishonorable by taking their own lives were also denied headstones, which were normally erected to keep the memory of the deceased alive. In the Jewish cemetery in Berlin-Weißensee, a special field dating from a later time even has many headstones inscribed with the dates when deportations of Jews took place.[64]

After a suicide, no kaddish is said for the deceased, though opinions vary on this in rabbinical literature, and differences exist from one congregation to the next. There is, however, consensus on several things: family members are not to be considered *avelim*, or mourners, and shivah, the seven-day mourning period for immediate relatives, is not observed. Only the portion of the death ritual that serves the living is used, when for example people express their condolences to the family at the gravesite. Those who are still living are honored, in other words, but the person who raised a hand against himself is not mourned.

Unlike Christianity, Judaism has strict guidelines for when a self-inflicted death officially counts as suicide and correspondingly has social consequences, which are expressed in a special ritual. Not everything that criminal law categorizes as "suicide" corresponds to the halakhic definition of willful suicide, or *hameabed azmo lada'at*, that is, someone who publicly announces he will take his life and then immediately does so. As an example, the *Shulchan Arukh* (Yoreh Deah 245) cites the case of a visibly enraged man who says he is going up on the roof. If he falls from the roof and dies from the fall, then, according to Jewish legal tradition, it is case of willful suicide. But if someone is discovered dead hanging from a tree, he is treated like any other deceased person and buried with honor. The underlying principle is: "Without proof to the contrary, a man is not presumed to be wicked" (*Kitzur Shulchan Aruch* 201).

In some cases death is considered an accident or a normal death, and this includes even the death of children and elderly people who express a wish to die, since their free will is seen as limited. The Bible, Talmud, and Midrash contain many examples of people who take their lives for three main reasons: despair, guilt, or shame.[65] Despair was behind the suicides of Samson (Judges 16:23–31), Saul (1 Samuel 31:1–5), Ahitofel (2 Samuel 17:24), Simri (1 Kings 16:18), a girl (BT Bava Batra 3b), a Roman (BT Taanit 29a), a set of parents (BT Chullin 94a), and a group of abducted boys and girls who feared they would be abused (BT Gittin 57b). Pangs of guilt drove the executioner of Rabbi Hanina ben Teradyon to suicide (BT Avodah Zarah 18a). Examples of shame as a motivation for suicide include a man who offered guests "oil" that turned out to be wine (BT Chullin 94a) and a Talmudic student who threw himself off of a roof when people falsely suspected him of having had sex with a prostitue in a public bathroom (BT Berakhot 23a). Valeria, the wife of Rabbi Meir, is said to have hanged herself out of shame after having sex with one of her husband's pupils. Particularly memorable is the story of Yakim of Tzerorot, whose shame was so profound that he "subjected himself to . . . stoning, burning, decapitation, and strangulation. . . . He took a post and planted it in the earth, raised a wall of stones around it and tied a cord to it. He made a fire in front of it and fixed a sword in the middle [of the post]. He hanged himself on the post, the cord was burnt through and he was strangled. The sword caught him, while the wall [of stones] fell upon him and he was burnt" (*Midrash Rabbah Genesis* 65.22).

A special type of suicide, much-discussed in rabbinical literature, is the one commited in the name of faith that makes a person a martyr: *Kiddush Hashem*, or "sanctification of the name of God." The Hebrew expression has been used since the second century CE for a martyr's death. This noble-minded type of suicide is reflected in the Jewish liturgy.[66] The sanctity of God's name is commemorated in a general way, for example, during the kaddish prayer and in the *Kedushah* verse of the *Amidah* (Prayer of Eighteen Blessings). The commemorative formulas for martyrs are more specific on the Day of Atonement (Yom Kippur), the most important High Holy Day of the Jewish year. The same is true of the songs of lamentation, which describe the suffering of the Israelites from the destruction of the first temple up through the most recent events in the history of the people and are recited after the reading from the Torah on Tisha B'Av, when the destruction of both temples is commemorated. The Talmud itself recalls how Hananiah, Mishael, and Azaria (Daniel 3) "were led to deliver themselves to the fiery furnace for sanctification of the name of God" (BT Pesachim 53b).

A second-century rabbinical conference determined that *Kiddush Hashem* is required of an observant Jew in three different cases: if he would otherwise be forced into "idol worship, forbidden sexual relations, and bloodshed" (BT Sanhedrin 74a). Later commentators do not all agree on how strictly to apply this commandment, since, according to Halakhah, killing oneself is per se taboo. It could thus have exactly the opposite effect of what was intended, tarnishing the name of God instead of sanctifying it. The medieval rabbis known as Tosafists held that suicide was definitely preferable to idol worship, for example, but Maimonides urged caution before making that decision. If a Jew was forced to disobey a commandment on pain of death (eat something that is not kosher, for instance), he should choose the transgression, since the preservation of life is more important. But should a Jew find himself in a position where he would be forced to commit murder, perform heathen practices, or engage in forbidden sexual relations, then he should choose the martyr's death and thereby avoid commiting an act of *Chillul Hashem*, or desecrating God's name (*Mishneh Torah*, Yesodei Hatorah 5:4). More recent commentators, such as the influential rabbi Abraham Isaac Kook (1865–1935), find such action commendable but do not consider it mandatory.[67] While non-Jews were and still are bound by the so-called Noahide commandments, killing oneself in the spirit of *Kiddush Hashem*, or sanctifying God's name, is most definitely not among them (BT Sanhedrin 74b).

One role model cited repeatedly in Jewish lore as an example of *Kiddush Hashem* in a situation where faith is on the line is the highly respected scribe Eleazar:

There was Eleazar, one of the leading teachers of the law, a man of great age and distinguished bearing. He was being forced to open his mouth and eat pork, but preferring an honourable death to an unclean life, he spat it out and voluntarily submitted to the flogging, as indeed men should act who have the courage to refuse to eat forbidden food even for love of life. For old acquaintance' sake, the officials in charge of this sacrilegious feast had a word with Eleazar in private; they urged him to bring meat which he was permitted to eat and had himself prepared, and only pretend to be eating the sacrificial meat as the king had ordered. In that way he would escape death and take advantage of the clemency which their longstanding friendship merited. But Eleazar made an honourable decision, one worthy of his years and the authority of old age, worthy of the grey hairs he had attained to and wore with such distinction, worthy of his perfect conduct from childhood up, but above all, worthy of the holy and God-given law. So he answered at once: "Send me quickly to my grave. If I went through with this pretence at my time of life, many of the young might believe that at the age of ninety Eleazar had turned apostate. If I practiced deceit for the sake of a brief moment of life, I should lead them astray and bring stain and pollution on my old age. I might for the present avoid man's punishment, but, alive or dead, I shall never escape from the hand of the Almighty. So if I now die bravely, I shall show that I have deserved my long life and leave the young a fine example, to teach them how to die a good death, gladly and nobly, for our revered and holy laws."

When he had finished speaking, he was immediately dragged away to be flogged. Those who a little while before had shown him friendship now became his enemies because, in their view, what he had said was madness. When he was almost dead from the blows, Eleazar sighed deeply and said: "To the Lord belongs all holy knowledge. He knows what terrible agony I endure in my body from this flogging, though I could have escaped death; yet he knows also that in my soul I suffer gladly, because I stand in awe of him." (2 Maccabees 6:18–31)

The legend of Hannah (2 Maccabees 7:20–23), who encouraged her seven sons to choose martyrdom over breaking the commandment about eating pork, also belongs to this context. Equally famous is the heroic collective suicide of those defending the fort of Masada against the Romans. The steadfast bearing of Eleazar ben Simon, described by Flavius Josephus in his *History of the Jewish War*, is among the myths that continue to sustain the state of Israel today, even if in the meantime more critical, post-Zionist historiography has cast some doubt on this and other heroic tales: "Eleazar, however, intended neither to slip out nor to allow anyone else to do so. Seeing the wall go up in flames and being unable to devise any further means of escape or heroic resistance, he foresaw clearly what the Romans would do to the men, the women and children if they won, and he thought that death was preferable for all."[68]

In the further course of history, Jews faced situations time and time again when, for the sake of their faith, they chose either collective or individual suicide over conversion or idolatry. This was especially true during the Crusades, as memorialized in Jewish communities' memory books. These describe events like the following, which took place in 1096 in Wevelinghoven (Rhineland):

When the enemy approached the village, some of the pious men ascended the tower and cast themselves into the Rhine River, which flowed around the village, and perished by drowning. Only two young men were not able to die by drowning. . . . When they resolved to cast themselves into the water, they kissed each other, and held each other, and embraced each other around their shoulders, and wept to each other, saying: "Woe for our youth, for we were not given the privilege of seeing it produce off-spring, and we have not attained old age. Nevertheless, let us now fall into the hand of the Lord, Who is God, Trustworthy and Merciful King. It is better for us to die here for His Great Name and walk with the righteous in the Garden of Eden than to fall into the hands of these impure uncir-cumcised ones and be forcibly defiled by them with their evil water."[69]

Other chronicles tell of parents who killed their children to save them from being forcibly baptized. In Jewish historiography these actions were long cast as examples of the *Kiddush Hashem* tradition, but medieval historian Israel Yuval takes the controversial position that, with this terrible deed, the parents were trying to "stir up the wrath of the vengeful God" so that he would then take revenge on their enemies.[70] Yuval also suggests that, given the high value placed on life and the protection of children in Judaism, this act may well have contributed to the accusations of ritual murder made against the Jews: "The only difference between the ritual murder libel and martyrdom lies in the question of whom the Jews kill: their own children or those of the Christians."[71] In his view, this interrelation is key to reconstructing the logic of those who leveled such accusations at the Jews and, in doing so, unleashed yet another wave of persecution.[72]

During the first large wave of anti-Jewish persecution in Spain in 1391, cities like Barcelona and Madrid were the sites of massacres and individual cases in which Jews chose a martyr's death at their own hand. Their expulsion from Spain in 1492 and the forced baptisms that went with it led to similar acts of desperation that were interpreted accordingly in Jewish historiography.[73]

In the modern era this tradition at first seemed a relic of the past, since most of the repressive measures that could have driven Jews to such desperate acts disappeared with emancipation. But the memory of *Kiddush Hashem* as a possible course of action was kept alive by events including the persecution of Jews in Eastern Europe in the late nineteenth and early twentieth centuries. Responding to the pogroms in Ukraine, in 1919 the Yiddish-language author Sholem Asch (1880–1957) published a novel tellingly entitled *Kiddush ha-Shem*. The motif has also been used by Zionist writers such as Shaul Tchernichovsky (1875–1943). Literary historians see connections for instance between Tchernichovsky's poem "Baruch mi Magenza" (Baruch of Mainz), about a martyr from the First Crusade,[74] and the Kishinev pogrom of 1903.[75] Last but certainly not least, collective resistance to National Socialist terror was inspired in part by remembrance of the Maccabee Uprising.[76]

Belief in Resurrection

Belief in the resurrection of the dead is documented early on in Judaism.[77] This hope is expressed most clearly in the book of Daniel: "many of those who sleep in the dust of the earth will wake, some to everlasting life and some to the reproach of eternal abhorrence" (Daniel 12:2). In Maccabees, resurrection is mentioned in numerous passages.[78] When heathen talismans were found on the bodies of fallen soldiers in the army of Judas Maccabee, the army leader took up a collection for a sin offering and said a prayer for the dead whose purpose is described as follows:

"For if he had not been expecting the fallen to rise again, it would have been foolish and superfluous to pray for the dead. But since he had in view the wonderful reward reserved for those who die a godly death, his purpose was a holy and pious one. And this was why he offered an atoning sacrifice to free the dead from their sin" (2 Maccabees 12:44–45).

This is not an uncontested belief, however, as we see in the dispute between two schools of thought—the Sadducees and the Pharisees—in the Talmudic period:

> Heretics asked Rabban Gamliel: From where is it derived that the Holy One, Blessed be He, revives the dead? Rabban Gamliel said to them that this matter can be proven from the Torah, from the Prophets, and from Writings, but they did not accept the proofs from him. The proof from the Torah is as it is written: "And the Lord said to Moses, behold, you shall lie with your fathers and arise" (Deuteronomy 31:16). . . . The proof from the Prophets is as it is written: "Your dead shall live, my corpse shall arise" (Isaiah 16:19). . . . The proof from Writings is as it is written: "And your palate is like the best wine that glides down smoothly for my beloved, moving gently the lips of those that sleep" (Song of Songs 7:10). (BT Sanhedrin 90b)

Even so, at the latest by the time the Romans had destroyed the second temple and a new period of exile had begun, the belief in resurrection had become part of Jewish dogma: "And these are the ones who have no portion in the world to come: He who maintains that resurrection is not a biblical doctrine, that the torah was not divinely revealed" (Mishnah Sanhedrin 10:1b). Yet it remains unclear precisely how people imagined the afterlife.[79] The clearest notion we find is that resurrection is not so much the reunion of body and soul but, rather, the revival of the "shadow." Death, in other words, does not mean the end of the psychosomatic unity. Instead, resurrection is more often seen as an awakening. In the *Amidah* prayer, for example, we read: "Thou, O Lord, art mighty for ever, thou quickenest the dead, thou art mighty to save."[80] Yet a Talmud passage refers to the reunion of body and soul: "Blessed are You, O Lord, who restores souls to lifeless bodies" (BT Berakhot 60b).

The corporeality of the resurrected is another question that apparently required a decisive answer from rabbinical authorities. In *Emunot ve-Deot*, or *The Book of Beliefs and Opinions*, Jewish scholar Saadia ben Joseph Gaon (882–942 CE) specifically addresses how someone "who died blind or deprived of his limbs or smitten with other afflictions or defects" will experience resurrection: "he will first be resurrected with that blemish still adhering to him" and will then be cured by the Creator.[81] The afterlife is described almost tersely in the Mishnah as follows: "this world is like a vestibule before the world to come; prepare yourself in the vestibule, so that you may enter the banquet-hall" (Pirkei Avot 4:16). Only in later, post-Talmudic times do we find a more detailed concept of resurrection (for example, with regard to eating and drinking); this stands in sharp contrast to more spiritual notions, which are based on the idea that the world of resurrection cannot be described. The Aristotelian concept of the soul underlies the attempts to resolve these conflicting notions both in and outside Judaism. Saadia ben Joseph Gaon holds that there are two distinct stages of resurrection. In the *Book of Beliefs and Opinions* he differentiates between a Messianic era (material) and the one for the world to come (immaterial), and he answers the question that apparently occupied many of his Jewish contemporaries as follows: " 'Will the resurrected eat and drink and marry, and continue to live on in a normal fashion?' My reply hereto is: 'Yes, just as the son of the *Zarephite* woman, whom the Creator brought back to life through *Elijah*, and the son of the *Shunammite* woman, whom He revived through *Elisha*, ate and drank and conceivably also married.' "[82]

Abraham Geiger, himself quite critical of the Jewish belief in resurrection, notes that like Saadia Gaon, Maimonides distinguishes between a Messianic time and the future world: "It is commonly believed that the resurrection of the dead will take place in connection with the coming of the Messiah and the hereafter: the reawakened dead will then enjoy eternal life in their bodies. Maimonides, however, understands the hereafter as the afterlife of the spirit alone; he teaches that the Messianic time, in contrast, occurs in this life, and with it the resurrection of the dead, but those who are reawakened will die after a long and happy life."[83] This idea was not well received, especially among strictly observant French Talmud scholars in the late Middle Ages, as we read in a satirical verse passed down by Abraham Geiger:

If the arisen must once more die
for this fate I will never apply;
If the bands of the grave enfold them again
I'd prefer to stay where I've already been

(Wenn die Auferstand'nen wieder müssen sterben.
Will um solches Loos ich nimmer mich bewerben;
Wenn die Grabesbande nochmals sie umfangen.
Bleib' ich lieber, wo ich einmal hingegangen).[84]

In Kabbalistic mysticism, the idea that souls are reincarnated (*gilgul neshamot*, or "cycling of souls") predominates, even though there are no references to such a thing in the Torah itself.[85] In the definitive work of Kabbalah, the *Zohar* (Radiance), the mysteries of reincarnation are discussed in detail in *Parashat Mishpatim* (see *Zohar* 2:100a).[86] Isaac Luria developed the theme even further in his book *Shaar Hagilgulim* (Gate of Reincarnation), describing the reincarnation of five different parts of the soul that correspond to the higher spiritual limbs of being. These parts are no longer in order because of original sin, and, according to Luria, the confusion will only be resolved when the Messiah arrives. Until then, the soul cannot return to its original shape and be absolved; instead, it must undergo countless rebirths—and not just in human bodies, but also in animals, plants, and even inanimate objects like rivers, wood, and stone:

> If someone has died a sinner, he must endure the punishment of the transmigration of souls to various places. Very few people avoid taking on the form of an animal, a mineral, or a plant. . . . The soul of a person who has spilled blood enters the water and is ceaselessly buffeted about. If people knew of this pain, they would weep without end. The greatest torment is in a waterfall. Anyone who has committed a crime that was punishable by choking will be drowned repeatedly in his future lives. Adulterers and adultresses will be banished together inside the constantly turning waterwheel of a mill. Anyone who speaks ill of another and slanders will become a mute stone. Anyone who gives a Jew unclean food to eat will be turned into a windblown leaf. Anyone who does not wash his hands will become water. The same fate awaits anyone who does not recite the required prayers of thanks.[87]

The transmigration of souls was a popular belief in the early modern period, as we read in the following passage from Venetian rabbi Leon Modena's text on Jewish rites and customs: "There are many among the Jews, that are of that *Pythagorical Opinion* of the *Transmigration of souls*, and its passing from one Body into Another, believing, that after a man is departed, his soul returns again into the World, and informs other bodies: and this they call גלגול, *Ghilgul*, that is to say, *Revolutio*; a *Revolution*, or coming about in a Circle."[88]

Orthodox Jews to this day firmly believe in not only the immortality of the soul but also the hope of resurrection. Three times a day when saying the *Amidah*, an observant Jew praises God "who quickenest the dead."[89] God is also thanked for keeping faith with those who are "sleeping in dust," an obvious reference to the verse in Genesis, "Dust you are, to dust you shall return" (Genesis 3:19). Reflecting the notion that death and decay are not the final stage, the Hebrew expression for a Jewish cemetery still today is *Beit haChaim*, or "House of the Living" or "House of Life."

Reform Judaism in contrast, which developed in the nineteenth century, long recognized only the teaching on the immortality of soul. This reflects the influence of (among others) Jewish Enlightenment thinker Moses Mendelssohn, whose *Phaedon* revisits the Platonic dialogue of same name that developed the notion of the soul's immortality. In 1854 in Breslau (Wrocław), prominent Reform movement leader Abraham Geiger published a new prayer book in which he replaced the word "resurrection" in the Hebrew text with "eternal life."[90] At a conference of American Reform rabbis in 1869, one of the fundmental articles of faith is formulated as follows: "The belief in the bodily resurrection has no religious foundation, and the doctrine of immortality refers to the after-existence of souls only."[91] At another conference in Pittsburgh in 1885, this stance was reinforced and expanded upon: "We reassert the doctrine of Judaism that the soul is immortal, grounding the belief on the divine nature of the human spirit, which forever finds bliss in righteousness and misery in wickedness. We reject, as ideas not rooted in Judaism, the beliefs both in bodily resurrection and in Gehenna and Eden (Hell and Paradise) as abodes for everlasting punishment and reward."[92]

Every reference to resurrection was accordingly stricken from the prayer book used by Reform congregations. In the meantime, however, this position has relaxed somewhat, as seen in the 2007 prayer book *Siddur Mishkan T'filah*.[93] The decision to reinsert the prayer for the resurrection of the dead was a controversial one. Yet even those who supported the decision still fundamentally reject the idea of a resurrection in the literal sense of the word. Jonathan Sarna, professor of Jewish history, explains their struggle with the issue in this way: "Certainly to the 19th century reformers, the idea that Judaism believed in resurrection of the dead seemed to them the antithesis of the kind of rational Judaism that they thought most Jews wanted and expected."[94] In earlier Reform prayer books, the traditional praise of God as the one "who raises the dead" (*mechaje hametim*) was initially changed to "the source of all life" (*mechaye hakol*).[95] Now both formulations are printed side by side in an effort to accommodate those who see the concept of resurrection as more than a metaphor and who firmly believe that life after death must also be physical.

Burial

The preparation of a corpse today is no different from what it was in earlier times, at least in cases of traditional burial that are organized by a *chevra kadisha*.[96] Here is how the seventeenth-century rabbi Leon Modena of Venice describes the process: "When the Breath is now gone out of the Body, they take and lay the Corpse upon the ground, wrapping it about with a sheet, and covering the face, and so having placed the Feet of it toward the Chamber dore, they set up, at the Head, a Waxe Light, placed in an Earthen pitcher, or Vessel, full of Ashes."[97] Minor deviations may occur, depending on the *minhag*, or custom of a given congregation.[98] Furthermore, it is believed that the deceased should not be returned to the earth in an impure state. This is the purpose of the so-called *tahara*, or washing of the corpse, which takes place as soon as death has occurred. The body is first cleansed with water, then ritually purified. Afterward, it is dressed in hand-stitched white burial clothing (*tachrichim*) of pure linen: for men this is usually a cap, tunic, belt, and possibly a *kittel*, the ceremonial robe worn during life on occasions such as Yom Kippur; the *tachrichim* for women are a bonnet, dress, and belt. The body is placed in a plain coffin of rough wood, or, in Israel, simply wrapped in a shroud. A man's body is also covered with the prayer shawl he wore in life, with the knots on its fringes undone, making the shawl unusable.

Accompanying the coffin from the "House of Purification" (*Beth Tahara*) to the cemetery is considered a work of mercy. In some places, mourners sing songs of lamentation along the way. The funeral procession stops three times en route to the grave for the recitation of Psalm 91 ("You that live in the shelter of the Most High"). Before the body is interred, a small sack containing earth from the country of Israel is often placed beneath the head as a symbol of the person's connection to the Promised Land. As a sign of mourning, family members make a small tear in their clothing. As Modena noted already in the seventeenth century: "If he were a Person of Note, or Quality, they use to have one that makes a certain Funerall Oration in Praise of the Party deceased."[99] This is still the custom today. The corpse is then laid in the grave, and each person in attendance puts three shovelfuls of dirt into the open grave, the last honor that a person can be shown. Unlike in Christianity, no flowers or wreaths are placed on the fresh grave. The nearest relative of the deceased, usually his son, now says the kaddish in the presence of the community, which differs from the prayer of the same name recited in the regular Jewish liturgy.

Deviations from the ritual described here were and still are possible, as long as halakhic regulations set out in texts such as the *Shulchan Arukh* are still observed.[100] We learn additional details from accounts of the funerals of prominent Jews and from surviving wills. Leon Modena, for example, describes precisely what he would like for his own burial in his will of 1634, including the shape of the coffin and the wording of his epitaph. Modena says that "the coffin should be rectangular, instead of with a sloped top,"[101] hereby indicating his modesty, since men of his rank were usually honored with pointed coffin lids. All of his writings—published texts and manuscripts alike—are to be placed on the coffin and care should be taken that no one touches the manuscripts with his hands. During the funeral procession, the cantor is not to recite *Tochachot* ("Admonitions," allusions to the threat of curses in Leviticus 26:14–15) but *Ma'alot* (Psalms of Ascent 120 to 134) or other psalms. Further, Modena says that no funeral sermon should be given at his burial or in the thirty-day period to follow (known as *shloshim*). He merely wants it to be said that in life he had not been a hypocrite, that his deeds had been consistent with his beliefs. Modena even has specific wishes about where he would like to be buried in the cemetery on the

Lido: he wishes to be near the entrance, close to where his mother, sons, maternal grandfather, and uncle are also buried. Funeral attendees are to walk in a circle around his open grave, as was customary in Jewish communities of the Levant.

As we learn from Hamburg wills, many people there believed that torturing the corpse could reduce or even preempt the pain of purgatory. In 1746, for example, head of the Altona Jewish community Salomon Nehemias directs that "immediately following my death, I should be choked and thrown on the ground and laid on straw; my brothers and friends should accompany my corpse. I also command that no speech of praise or eulogy be given."[102] In a will written several decades later by another member of this community, Ascher Anselm Simon Segal gives these instructions: "right after my death, the burial society should do all manner of dishonorable things with my body, which should be tossed to the ground three times in succession from the cleansing table."[103]

The ritual purification of the deceased and subsequent burial are followed by the second phase of the mourning period. The sequence of events as described in the mid-seventeenth-century memoirs of Glückel of Hameln has remained virtually unchanged to this day.[104] Glückel writes that after the death of her husband Chayim, "with my children gathered around me, I sat upon the ground for the seven days of mourning, and a sad sight it must have been to see me sitting thus with my twelve fatherless children by my side."[105] She is also joined by fellow mourners in prayer, "and we engaged scholars to 'learn' Torah day and night through the whole year." She adds: "And there was not a man or woman who did not come, daily, to comfort the bereaved among us. And, alas, there was no dearth of tears."[106] In this seven-day period of sitting shivah, mourners stay at home. It is believed that during this period immediately following the burial, the soul of the deceased is still closely connected to his earthly home. Manual labor, finalizing business affairs, bathing, cosmetics, and the wearing of leather shoes are all to be avoided during these days of mourning. According to Jewish traditional beliefs, this is to help keep the deceased fresh in people's memory. Prayer and the study of holy scripture and the Mishnah reflect the belief that the living may still be able to influence the fate of the deceased. Glückel also writes of the mourning period of *shloshim* in her memoirs, saying that she did not look at her business register for thirty days following her husband's death.

The loss of a parent brings with it a particularly intense form of mourning, as we read in Glückel's description of her husband Chayim following the death of his father, Joseph Hameln: "Straight after the seven days of mourning he [Chayim] he engaged ten Talmud scholars, and fitted up a room in our house where services were held; and he devoted his days and nights to the Torah. He gave up his business travels throughout the whole year of mourning, in order not to miss a single *kaddish*."[107] Twelve weeks after Joseph's death, Chayim joined his brothers at their request in Hannover to visit their father's grave: "He took with him nine companions in order to hold daily prayers, and on the entire journey he did not once fail to say *kaddish*, even though it cost him a good sum of money."[108] To fully appreciate why the kaddish is so important in the mourning period, as Glückel emphasizes in this passage, it is necessary to know that in Judaism it has been believed for centuries that constant prayer for the deceased will cause his soul to ascend continually higher in heaven.[109]

Today the world over, the local *chevra kadisha* is still responsible for seeing that the traditional burial ritual is observed, though secularization and assimilation have altered a number of customs and in some cases even replaced them with Christian ones. In the Venetian Jewish cemetery on the Lido, for example, photos of the deceased and the occasional floral arrangement can be seen on some graves. In Israel, it is possible to be buried on kibbutz grounds even without a religious ceremony and to make individual decisions about tombstone design and the maintenance of the grave.

Cremation

Even cremation has long since ceased to be taboo.[110] Albert Einstein (1879–1955), who, though not religious, did see himself as a Jew, was by no means one of its first supporters among secular Jews when in the 1950s he stated in his will his wish to be cremated. Even so, his final wishes were not entirely respected. As is widely known, when Einstein died of a ruptured abdominal artery in Titusville, New Jersey, Princeton Hospital pathologist Dr. Thomas Stoltz Harvey (1912–2007) was apparently unable to accept that Einstein be cremated in accordance with his wishes and, without permission, removed the scientist's brain several hours after his death. He cut it into cubes and slices, which he kept presereved in formaldehyde for over forty years.[111] It was not until 1997 that Harvey could be persuaded to release them to Einstein's legal heirs. The recipient was his granddaughter Evelyn, who in turn bequeathed the remains to the National Museum for Health and Medicine in Chicago. Shortly thereafter, forty-six slices of the brain were purchased from a private owner by the Mütter Museum of the College of Physicians in Philadelphia, where they are now part of a permanent exhibit. Long-unknown images of Einstein's brain can now even be downloaded on an iPhone app.[112]

In the United States, the number of funerals with cremated remains at Jewish cemeteries has risen steadily in recent years.[113] Though Orthodox Jews reject cremation outright as a violation of Halakhah, it is permitted in Reform Jewish communities. The Conservative branch of American Judaism takes a middle position: while generally opposed to the practice, it allows rabbis to partipate in the memorial service held before the actual cremation. In view of the growing number of cremations, several years ago an umbrella organization of Jewish funeral organizations tried to repopularize traditional ground burial among American Jews, citing ecological reasons (burning pollutes the environment!) as part of its strategy. In Israel cremation is now allowed by the government, but in certain religious circles opposition can still be found. In 2015, an ultra-Orthodox family went to the Supreme Count to block the cremation of their thirty-one-year-old son who had undergone a sex-change operation and later committed suicide. The court ruled in favor of the deceased, whose will had clearly indicated the wish to be cremated.[114]

Embalming

Embalming was practiced already in ancient Egypt. As as we read in the Torah: "Then Joseph threw himself upon his father, weeping and kissing his face. He ordered the physicians in his service to embalm his father Israel, and they did so, finishing the task in forty days, which was the usual time for embalming" (Genesis 50:1–4). The reference requires some explanation, however, since according to Jewish custom, a corpse should "return to dust" as quickly as possible. In Jewish Bible exegesis we find different attempts to explain what is meant in the passage.[115] One suggests that the corpse was merely perfumed with pleasant-smelling herbs to keep it from drying out during transport and developing a strong odor. A different explanation was that Jacob might have been embalmed using the method then commonly used in Egypt. There were several established ways: either the internal organs, including the brain, could be removed from the corpse, or they could be temporarily conserved by means of pleasant-smelling essential oils absorbed through the skin. The second method would not be a violation of Jewish burial traditions. Those Torah scholars who assumed that the embalming method common at the time (one also described by Greek historian Herodotus) had been used for Jacob searched for an explanation for this unusual procedure involving organ removal. One midrash states that Joseph was later punished for his deed by not being allowed to reach the same age as his father, since he must have known that the body of a righteous man would not decay and that embalming was therefore unnecessary. A different line of argument states that embalming after removing organs was allowed in exceptional cases when it was a matter of preserving the dignity of a dead person and slowing the process of decay. In the seminal work of Kabbalah, the *Zohar*, we find the following speculation about how to imagine Jacob's embalming:

> "The embalming of Jacob—what is it?" . . . Come and see what is written: *Joseph ordered his servants the physicians to embalm his father, and the physicians embalmed Israel* (Genesis 50:2). Now, would you ever imagine that this embalming was like that of other people? If you say that it was done

because of the journey, look at what is written: *Joseph died, a hundred and
ten years old, and they embalmed him and he was placed in a plain coffin in
Egypt* (ibid., 26)! . . . This is customary for kings: in order to preserve their
bodies, they are embalmed with anointing oil—finest of all oils, blended
with spices—and they infuse the body with that excellent oil day after day
for forty days. . . . Once this is completed, the body perdures intact for a
long time. For the entire land of Canaan and the land of Egypt decay and
decompose the body in less time than any other land; so in order to
preserve the body, they do this. They perform this embalming both internally and externally. Internally, by placing that oil on the navel, through
which it enters within, absorbed by the entrails; so it preserves the body
within and without for a long time. (*Zohar* 1:251a)[116]

Thus according to the *Zohar*, in this special case the corpse was preserved with
balm, but the internal organs were left undisturbed; in other words, the commonly used method in Egypt was not used.

The description of King Asa's funeral should be interpreted in a similar way.
"He . . . was buried in the tomb which he had bought for himself in the city of
David, being laid on a bier which had been heaped with all kinds of spices skilfully
compounded; and they kindled a great fire in his honour" (2 Chronicles 16:13–
14). Here, too, the use of balms is not the same thing as the embalming that was
the norm in Egypt, and the fire mentioned in the passage presumably refers to the
burning of spices, not the king's corpse.[117] Support for this reading of the passage,
that is, as the description of something that deviated from Egyptian norms, is also
found in the Gospel of John, where we read the following about the death of
Christ: "So Joseph came and took the body away. He was joined by Nicodemus
(the man who had first visited Jesus by night), who brought with him a mixture of
myrrh and aloes, more than half a hundredweight. They took the body of Jesus
and wrapped it, with the spices, in strips of linen cloth according to Jewish burial
customs" (John 19:39–40).

The story of Lazarus in the New Testament likewise clearly indicates that it
was not the custom of the Jews to elaborately embalm the body of the deceased in
order to preserve it for a lengthy period. When Jesus says to remove the stone
from the entrance to the tomb, Lazarus's sister Martha responds: "Sir, by now
there will be a stench; he has been there four days" (John 11:39–40). Had Lazarus
been carefully embalmed, his sister's olfactory experience would surely have been
different. In addition, the condition of Israelite remains found by archaeologists
indicate that in ancient Israel it was generally not common to embalm the dead
(at least not in order to preserve them, as was the custom in Egypt).

For the same reasons, in Israel today a corpse is not preserved before the
funeral (for instance, by the injection of formaldehyde). In other countries, such

as France, however, such religious regulations are given little consideration when preparing a Jewish corpse for transport to the Holy Land, despite the protests from Orthodox quarters.[118] In Israel, where the *chevra kadisha* organizes both the funeral and the transport of the body, temporarily preserving the corpse by placing it on dry ice is all that is allowed.

In the early modern period sometimes an exception was made in the case of people with abnormalities, whose corpses were not buried but instead embalmed and put on display, a practice that existed both in and outside Judaism. On May 26, 1575, Siamese twins were born in the Venice ghetto.[119] The sensational news about the conjoined twins quickly made the rounds, and people streamed to the house of the Petachia family—apparently including many Christians. The only unusual thing seems to be that the place where they were displayed was the earliest Italian ghetto. The twins died only several days later, and, according to a Hebrew source, their father donated the corpse to a Jewish charitable organization (*gemilut chasadim*) as a gift of sorts. Its leader had the Siamese twins embalmed and put on exhibit to raise funds in Venice and beyond (the source says that "they went from city to city"). The Jewish brotherhood thereby turned a not inconsiderable profit. There are no exact figures on how many people paid to see this particular exhibit, but, generally speaking, at the time deceased conjoined twins were still a viable business proposition. It was usually embalmed corpses or dry specimens (following an anatomical dissection) that were exhibited to the paying public. Hebrew sources clearly indicate that the Siamese twins underwent an embalming process (*chanita*), though in the sixteenth century attempts were already being made to preserve with ethanol mixtures. Despite the fact that in this case the profits were going to a good cause, unease soon developed in the Jewish population of Venice, since Jewish law clearly mandates early burial of the deceased. Two leading rabbis protested especially loudly: Samuel Judah Katzenellenbogen and Raphael Joseph Treves (precise birth and death dates unknown), who was active for some time in Ferrara. In his detailed responsum, Katzenellenbogen invoked numerous halakhic authorities to support his argument that the conjoined twins had been a live birth and therefore a human existence (*bnei ke'ima*), which meant that the strict burial commandment applied. The exhibition could not be justified and was an insult to the deceased (*bisayon elu hametim*). An infant who dies within thirty days might be in some cases considered a stillborn (*nefel*), depending on the level of development in which the child was born. According to some *poskim* (legal scholars), a stillborn does not necessarily have to be buried; other rabbis, however, rule it is an obligation to bury, but the corpse of a *nefel* often does not receive full funeral rites.

How the dispute over the burial of the Siamese twins ended in 1575 we do not know. There are many indications that their preserved remains were buried at some undetermined later point in time, but without an actual funeral. In his autobiography, published three years after this event, Jewish natural philosopher Abraham Yagel writes of his astonishment when the souls of the Siamese twins came to him in a dream. His father, however, who was also in the dream, explained that there is a difference between Jewish and gentile souls: the Jewish soul is present already at the time of conception, though the spiritual potential that exists long before birth must still be developed. With this, Yagel's father shows himself to be a follower of the Aristotelian notion of entelechy, a way of thinking that was apparently also widespread among Jewish scholars.

The memory of this unique case was kept alive in rabbinical literature until the late eighteenth century. In *Bina Le'itim* (1796), renowned Moravian rabbi Jonathan Eybeschütz cited the Venetian rabbis' objections to support a decision of his own, namely, his refusal to allow the public exhibition of a misshapen infant born to a poor Jewish woman. As this excursus makes clear, imperfectly formed humans are also most definitely included in the burial regulations of Halakhah.

Notes

Introduction

1. Olsvanger (1931), 209–10 (no. 318).
2. Freud (2002).
3. On Shylock, see Feinberg (1995), 119ff.
4. Coryat (1905), 472.
5. Brett Hirsch (2009).
6. Robert Jütte (1993), 68ff.
7. Davidman (2011), 209ff.
8. McGuire (2008).
9. See among others Eckart and Jütte (2014), 222–40.
10. Lorenz (2000), 13.
11. See, among others, Gilman (1991); Eilberg-Schwartz (1992); Diemling and Veltri (2009); and the special issue of the *Jewish Quarterly Review* 95 (2005) with methodological essays by Kirshenblatt-Gimblett, Wolfson, Daniel Boyarin, Fonrobert, Gillerman, Hasan-Rokem, and Wieseltier.
12. Wieseltier (2005), 436.
13. See, among others, Fonrobert (2005), 466, in reference to the Talmud; and Wolfson (2005), 479, on the Kabbalah.
14. Mauss (1973), 70.
15. On the methodological problem, see Auslander (2009), 47ff.
16. On Christianity and Islam, see Asad (2003); and Hirschkind (2011).
17. Almog (1991).

Chapter 1

1. Goshen-Gottstein (1994), 171ff.
2. *Sefer Chasidim* (1997), no. 582.
3. Schack (1998), p. 57, no. 4.
4. See Preuss (1911/1992), 66ff.
5. Laqueur (1992), 117. For a critique of this model see among others Stolberg (2003).
6. Preuss (1911/1992), 67.
7. Quoted from Preuss (1911/1992), 68.
8. See Preuss (1911/1992), 67.
9. See Scholem (1977), 351ff. The number 612 is the sum of the Hebrew numerals ר (200) + ב (2) + א (1) + ב (2) + ר (200) + א (1) + ג (3) + ב (2) + ר (200) + א (1).
10. See Aryeh Kaplan (2007), n. 105.
11. Quoted from Weinstein (2009a), 90–91.
12. From Weinstein (2009b), 51.
13. See Scholem (1977), 96ff.
14. Scholem (1977), 131–32. See also Konner (2009), 76–77.
15. See Wolfson (1992), 143ff.; Wolfson (2005), 495.

16. Yagel (1999), 333.

17. Scholem (1977), 356–57.

18. Trachtenberg (1939), 169.

19. Teller (1988), 10.

20. See Zinger (2009b), 144–45; Zinger (2009/10), 82.

21. Allan (1984), 324ff.

22. Allan (1984), 327; Natalia Berger (1995), 8; Ruderman (1995), 220.

23. Lepicard (2008), 100–101.

24. *Midrash Rabbah Genesis* (1939).

25. Daniel Jütte (2016), 600–661.

26. Tobias Cohen (1708), 106a.

27. Debschitz and Debschitz (2009).

28. Borck (2007), 501–2.

29. Clendening (1943).

30. Gunkel (2010).

31. Grossgebauer (1711). See also Matteoni (2008), 193–94.

32. On this, see, among others, Gilman (1995b), 168ff.; Hödl (1997a), 212ff.

33. "Der *Character* aber oder merckliche Kennzeichen der Juden ist theils des Leibes / theils des Gemüths / theils der Lebens-Art / als an welchen ein Jud gar bald von einem Christen zu unterscheiden ist." Schudt (1714–17), pt. 2, bk. 6, chap. 21, p. 368. See also Diemling (2006), 79.

34. "Zu den Kennzeichen des Leibes will ich nicht eben bey den Männern zehlen die sonderbahre Ziehung des Barts / und bey denen Weibern die Verbergung deren Haupt-Haaren / . . . sondern daß sie in der Bildung ihres Angesichts so *formiret*; daß der Jud gleich hervorguckt / an der Nase / Lippen / Augen / auch der Farbe und der gantzen Leibes-*Positur*." Schudt (1714–17), pt. 2, bk. 6, chap. 21, p. 368.

35. See Andree (1881), 37.

36. Lavater (1787), 110.

37. Eilberg-Schwartz (1992).

38. On this, see Eilberg-Schwartz (1992), 5.

39. Resnick (2012), 33.

40. Drake (2013), 25ff.

41. On the issue of whether Judaism can be characterized as "carnal," see Daniel Boyarin (1993), 31ff.; also Wieseltier (2005), 439–40.

42. See Gilman (1997), 202–3.

43. Pardo Tomás (2003), 172–74.

44. Bhabha (1994), 70.

45. Bhabha (1994), 69.

46. Bhabha (1994), 66.

47. On this, see the seminal work by Moses Wiener (2006), unfortunately still available only in Hebrew.

48. From Erb (1985), 121.

49. Peter K. Klein (1999), 43–44.

50. Münster (1539), sig. A5v. See Resnick (2012), 300; also Diemling (2005), 402.

51. Fishberg (1911), 83.

52. Gilman (1991), 169ff. See also Goldblatt (2003), 565–66.

53. Personal communication in connection with the opening of the 1998 exhibit "Der schejne Jid" in the Jewish Museum in Vienna.

54. http://www.jmberlin.de/main/DE/Pdfs/Sonderausstellungen/gorelik.pdf, last retrieved March 24, 2016.

55. Erb (1985), 118.

56. Patton (2012), 73. See also Mirrer (1994), 18; and Lipton (2008), 141.

57. Peter K. Klein (1999), 44.

58. Peter K. Klein (1999), 47.
59. Peter K. Klein (1999), 47.
60. Resnick (2012), 269.
61. Lipton (2010), 262.
62. Lipton (2010), 262. See also Zafran (1973), 20.
63. Cecil Roth (1962), 23.
64. Blumenkranz (1963), 23.
65. Reprinted in German translation in Höxter (1983), 16.
66. See Robert Jütte (1993), esp. 68ff.
67. Groebner (2007), 87.
68. Rupert von Deutz (1854), bk. 5, chap. 31, col. 395. See Shaye J. D. Cohen (2005), 195.
69. On this see Scharff (2000), esp. 146.
70. In contrast, anti-Jewish visual propaganda in eighteenth-century England does not include "nose" as a characteristic. See Shahar (1975), 337.
71. Heinrich Heine (1879), 306.
72. See above all Gilman (1991), 179ff. For a contemporary source, see Beddoe (1861), 222.
73. Joseph Jacobs (1886), 37.
74. Hess (1935), 4th letter, pp. 25–26. Quoted from the translation by Rose (1990), 323.
75. Fishberg (1911), 79.
76. Hiemer (1938), n.p.: "Erstens erkennt man einen Juden an seiner Nase. Die jüdische Nase ist hakenförmig. Sie sieht aus wie die Form 6. Darum nennen wir sie 6er-förmig. Viel Nichtjuden haben genauso Hakennasen. Aber in ihrem Falle sind die Nasen dann nach oben krumm, nicht nach unten. Das hat nichts mit der jüdischen Nase zu tun."
77. Hiemer (1942), n.p.: "Es haben die Juden in Land und Straßen, nicht immer krause Haare und krumme Nasen. Die Schlimmsten sind die, die man nicht kann erkennen, und sich so gerne Deutsche nennen!"
78. Chamberlain (1910), 376.
79. Schleich (1927), 75.
80. Elsaghe (2004), 181.
81. See Goldblatt (2003), 563–64.
82. Philip Roth (2010), 100.
83. Joseph (1898).
84. See Zipes (1991), 87ff.; Jens Malte Fischer (1978), 93ff.; Gilman (1990), 1002–3.
85. Zipes (1991), 48.
86. Zipes (1991), 76.
87. See detailed discussion in Gilman (1991), 181ff.
88. Joseph (1898), 881.
89. Egon Erwin Kisch (1985), 332.
90. See Natvig (1982), 93–96. See also Gilman (1991), 187.
91. Roggenkamp (2012).
92. http://www.ruhrbarone.de/der-westen-judennase-lafontaine/4921, last retrieved March 24, 2016.
93. Peter K. Klein (1999), 48.
94. Schreckenberg (1996), p. 317, fig. 8.
95. Porta (2007), 1:131; Porta (1930), 396.
96. See Borrmann (1994), p. 72, fig. 38.
97. Lavater (1787), 260.
98. Lavater (1787), 110.
99. Quoted from Hein (1996), 145.
100. Quoted from Waitzbauer (2002), 251.
101. Bajohr (2003), p. 41, fig. 3.
102. Quoted from Bajohr (2003), 112.

103. Zweig (1920/21), 133.

104. Darmaun (2003), 26.

105. Dinter (1920), 55.

106. Kremer (1942), 31.

107. Günther (1925), 427.

108. Georg Diez, "Aus der Mitte entspringt der Hass," S.P.O.N.–Der Kritiker, *Spiegel Online*, February 28, 2014, http://www.spiegel.de/kultur/gesellschaft/antisemitische-sz-karikatur-kolumne-von-georg-diez-a-956296.html, last retrieved March 24, 2016.

109. See these and other examples in Gronemeyer (1987); and Solms (2008). See also Robert Jütte (1980).

110. *Zedlers Universal-Lexicon* (1732–50), vol. 62, col. 523.

111. Quoted in Balberg (2011), 342.

112. Quoted from David Berger (1979), 224 (English); *Sefer Nizzahon Yashan* (1978), 192 (Hebrew).

113. Quoted from Leo Wiener (1899), 59:

Schwarz bist du, schwarz, asō wie a Zigeuner,
Ich häb' gemeint, as du we'st sein meiner;
Schwarz bist du, aber mit Cheen,
Für wemen du bist mies, für mir bist du schoen.

See also Somogyi (1982), 92.

114. Somogyi (1982), 92.

115. Idelson-Shein (2014), 149.

116. Eybeschütz (1765), 58b–59a. My thanks to Iris Idelson-Shein for this reference. For commentary on this difficult textual passage, I thank David Stern (Harvard University).

117. Pinto (1762), 12.

118. Buffon (1797), 4:262. On this, see, among others, Schorsch (2005), 115.

119. Menasseh ben Israel (1651), p. 13, sect. 7. See also Melamed (2003), 211.

120. La Peyrère (1643), 81. On this, see Diemling (2005), 410.

121. Groebner (2007), 137.

122. *Groß Planeten Buch* (1590), fol. 7v. See Groebner (2007), 128.

123. Groebner (2007), 129.

124. See, among others, Gage (1978).

125. Voß (2011), 104.

126. Cited from Gow (1995), 184. On this, see Voß (2011), 103.

127. Diemling (2005), 404.

128. Fishberg (1911), 24.

129. See, among others, Hödl (2002), 51ff.

130. Fishberg (1913), 16.

131. Prichard (1813), 187. On this, see Efron (1994), 43.

132. See on this, among others, Gilman (1991), 174; Efron (1994), 47ff.

133. Knox (1850), 133.

134. Karl Marx (1979), 466ff.

135. Brocke and Laitko (1996), 397.

136. Hundt-Radowsky (1822/23), 2:443.

137. Günther (1925), 428, emphasis added.

138. Kirchhof (1563), no. 195.

139. See *Handwörterbuch des deutschen Aberglaubens* (2000), vol. 7, cols. 802–3. See also Mellinkoff (1991), 147ff.; Junkerjürgen (2009), 60.

140. Quoted in Felsenstein (1995), 163.

141. http://www.islaminstitut.de/Anzeigen-von-Fatawa.43 + M54e8cobcc61.0.htm, last retrieved March 24, 2016.

142. See *Sahih Muslim* (2000), 1156.

143. Gruner (1790), 169.

144. Pezzl (1923), 170f. Quoted from Gilman (1991), 172. See Oişteanu (2009), 45.

145. *Oekonomische Hauspostille* (1792), 399.

146. Shaye J. D. Cohen (1999), 28.

147. See Horowitz and Rozenbaumas (1994), esp. 1086.

148. Auzépy (2011), 79–87.

149. Preuss (1911/1992), 92. See also Broyde (2009).

150. Reprinted in original Hebrew and English translation in Finkelstein (1964), 225 (Hebrew), 234–35 (English). See also Aschoff (1993), 20.

151. See Horowitz (1994).

152. *Jüdisches Lexikon* (1927), vol. 1, col. 739.

153. On Kabbalah and beards, see Horowitz and Rozenbaumas (1994), 1068–69.

154. Maimon (2001), 99.

155. Maimon (2001), 261.

156. See the case of court cleric Ludwig the Pious in Aronius (1902), p. 44, no. 103.

157. Simcha Assaf (1921), 24, 112ff. See also Zimmels (1952), 48.

158. Horowitz and Rozenbaumas (1994), 1071.

159. Horowitz and Rozenbaumas (1994), 1079–80; Lipton (2014), 48–49.

160. Kühnel (1992), 25.

161. See, among others, *Lexikon des Mittelalters* (1980–98), vol. 1, col. 1490; Auzépy (2011), 78; Horowitz and Rozenbaumas (1994), 1076.

162. Magin (1999), 153; Horowitz and Rozenbaumas (1994), 1080.

163. Nübling (1896), 150.

164. Le Gall (2011), 30ff.

165. Quoted from Heyden (1889), 160.

166. Landucci (1978), 333.

167. Le Gall (2011), 241ff.

168. Kobolt (1738), 218–19.

169. Johann Peter Ludewig (1716–19), 1:864.

170. Casparson (1785), 284.

171. Municipal Archives of Münster, Acta criminalia no. 282, quoted from Aschoff (1993), 45.

172. Bericht der Niederösterreichischen Regierung an die Kaiserin, Wien, 1778 Januar 27, bzgl. Kleiderordnung der Juden, Konzept, in Niederösterreichisches Landesarchiv, Maria Theresianische Verwaltung und Varia, Hof Resoluta in Publ. (Monatsbuschen), Kart. 176, unfol., quoted from Wurzer (2008), 82.

173. The Municipal Archives of Freiburg im Breisgau, for example, contain a 1781 writing about the "organization of the Jewish nation in the Austrian Patrimonial Lands" that mentions the exemption from being identified as a Jew by means of signs, clothing, or beard (https://www.freiburg.de/pb/site/Freiburg/get/345189/C1%20Judensachen%201%20A.pdf, last retrieved February 4, 2020). On Central Austria, see Karniel (1981), 205.

174. See Zürn (2001), 150.

175. *Mein erstes Wort . . .* (1804).

176. Quoted from Ruth Gay (1992), 142.

177. Horowitz (2010), 2.

178. Dohrn (2008), 169.

179. Singer (2004), 49.

180. See Somogyi (1982), 88.

181. *Der Israelit* 12 (1871): 248.

182. Horowitz (2010), 2–3.

183. Joseph Roth (2001), 29.
184. http://orf.at/stories/2172493/2172524/, last retrieved February 4, 2020.
185. http://malkowsky.jimdo.com/jüdische-witze/, last retrieved May 19, 2016.
186. Kamczycki (2013).
187. Brod (1960), 48.
188. Gronemann (1984), 14.
189. Gronemann (1984), 13.
190. Illustrated in Gilman (1995b), 174.
191. See the illustration at Lebendiges Museum Online—Zeitstrahl Weimarer Republik, http://www.dhm.de/lemo/html/weimar/antisemitismus, last retrieved February 4, 2020.
192. Quoted from Leiser (1968), 68.
193. Walk (1996), chap. 4, no. 210.
194. Horkheimer and Adorno (2002), 153.
195. Klemperer (1999), 2:11.
196. Kulka and Jäckel (2004), 453.
197. Mallmann, Rieß, and Pyta (2003), 13.
198. Quoted from Christ (2008), 5.
199. Mallmann, Rieß, and Ptya (2003), 15.
200. Löw (2006), 71.
201. See Heer and Naumann (1996).
202. Horowitz (2010), 3.
203. Löw (2006), 71.
204. Tiedemann (2007), 107.
205. http://tachles.ch/news/der-streit-um-den-bart, last retrieved February 4, 2020.
206. http://www.gutefrage.net/frage/wieso-haben-juden-oft-dunkle-haare-ich-bin-kein-nazi, last retrieved February 4, 2020.
207. Haas (1861), 113.
208. Junkerjürgen (2009), 49.
209. See Kübler (2007), 265–66.
210. *Encyclopaedia Judaica* (1971/72), vol. 6, col. 379.
211. See Voß (2011); Gow (1995).
212. Junkerjürgen (2009), 60.
213. Wirnt von Grafenberg (1977), 136; Wirnt von Grafenberg (2005), 66:

im was der bart und dasz hâr
beidiu rôt, viurvar
von den selben hoere ich sagen,
dasz si valschiu herze tragen.
      (lines 2841–44)

214. Junkerjürgen (2009), 49.
215. See Quast (2012), 186.
216. Freytag (1863), 32.
217. Kemelman (1973), 82.
218. Chamberlain (1910), 385 with footnote.
219. Margaritha (1713), 12.
220. Felsenstein (1995), 50.
221. *Specification* (1715), nos. 31–38.
222. Friedrich Benjamin Osiander (1819), 652.
223. *Allgemeine Zeitung des Judenthums* 4 (1840), 587.
224. Virchow (1886–87), 298. See Lilienthal (1993), 181–82. On the use of these statistics in the so-called "Anti-Semitism Debate" in the empire, see Hacking (1990), 190; Zimmerman (1999), 409ff. On Virchow's position, see Efron (1994), 25–26.

225. See the overview in Fishberg (1911), 64.
226. Ruppin (1918), 169.
227. Schug (2004), 94.
228. Günther (1925), 429.
229. Kübler (2007), 266.
230. Wegener (2005), 52.
231. Torsten Schäfer (2007), 245.
232. Schmalhausen (1991), 67.
233. See, for example, Rubach (2010), 69; Tec (2013), 174.
234. Ringelblum (1967), 101.
235. Strobl (1989), 191.
236. Grube (2004), 240.
237. Janovskaja and Kriener (2001), 54.
238. Struminski (2007).
239. Weitz (2004), 21.
240. See Geller (1992).
241. See the examples in Wesselski (1934), 15.
242. Ammianus Marcellinus, *Res Gestae* 22.5, http://www.thelatinlibrary.com/ammianus.html, last retrieved February 4, 2020.
243. Cited from Schreckenberg (1982), 290.
244. Cited from Schreckenberg (1982), 332.
245. Cited from Schreckenberg (1982), 422.
246. Caesarius (2009), chap. 2.25. See also Biller (1992), 188.
247. Cited from Güdemann (1966), 1:145:

ez wart sô grôz nie ein stat
sie waer von drîzec juden sat
stankes unde unglouben.

248. Cited from Trachtenberg (1983), 227 n. 15: "dye Juden, dye sneiden, hartneckygen, stink-unden Gotis verreter."
249. Reprinted in Schöner (2002), p. 196, fig. 55: "vm dz wir nit essen swinin brotten / dar vmb sind wir gel vnd stinckt vnß der oten."
250. *Zedlers Universal-Lexicon* (1732–50), vol. 14, col. 1500.
251. Schudt (1714–17), pt. 2, bk. 6, chap. 20, p. 344.
252. Schudt (1714–17), pt. 2, bk. 6, chap. 20, p. 349.
253. See Diemling (2004), 215ff.
254. Browne (1672), bk. 4, chap. 10, p. 241.
255. Trachtenberg (1983), 50.
256. See Lévi (1890), 249ff.
257. *On the Eve of the Reformation* (1964), 156–57.
258. Trachtenberg (1983), 116. See also Hsia (1988), 21.
259. Morosini (1683), 251. See Toaff (1996), 103–4.
260. "Davening while sweating," *Dinonline*, June 10, 2012, http://www.dinonline.org/2012/06/10/davening-while-sweaty, last retrieved February 4, 2020.
261. Efron (1998), 76.
262. Günther (1925), 428.
263. Hiemer (1942). On proverbs of this type in Eastern Europe, see Oişteanu (2009), 66–67.
264. Hitler (1939), 61–62.

Chapter 2

1. Böhme (2003), 63.
2. Hitzler (2002), 71.

3. Hitzler (2002), 71.
4. Scholem (2001), 17.
5. Somogyi (1982), 84.
6. Gilman, Jütte, and Kohlbauer-Fritz (1998).
7. See, among others, Greg Kaplan (2003); Zimmermann (2006), 15.
8. See, among others, Presner (2007), 1ff.
9. Nordau (1980), 434.
10. Freud (1939), 147.
11. Wildmann (2009), 221ff.
12. See, among others, Presner (2007), 46ff.
13. Buchholz et al. (2001), 55–56.
14. Nordau (1980), 435.
15. Nordau (1980), 435.
16. Cited in Besser (1910), 4.
17. Cited in Besser (1910), 4.
18. Besser (1910), 4.
19. *Jüdische Turnzeitung* 10, no. 1 (1909), 14.
20. Cited in Gluzman (2004), 232.
21. See Haumann (1998), 43.
22. *Jüdische Turnzeitung* 1, no. 1 (1900), 1.
23. See, among others, *Jüdische Turnzeitung* 9, no. 6 (1908), 115–17.
24. See, among others, Wildmann (2009), 250.
25. Auerbach (1908), 189.
26. Wildmann (2009), 269.
27. See, among others, Presner (2007), 126ff.
28. Mandelstamm (1900), 63.
29. Mandelstamm (1900), 75.
30. Cited in Heid (1986), 341.
31. Cited in Heid (1986), 347–48.
32. See Lüthi (2009), 239–40.
33. Bayor (2014), 61.
34. Fairchild (2003), 168.
35. Cited in Lüthi (2009), 239–40.
36. Lüthi (2009), 287.
37. Cited in Horowitz (2002b), 31.
38. Isidor Wolff (1906), 182.
39. *Jüdische Turnzeitung* 9, no. 7 (1908), 140.
40. See Wildmann (2009), 149.
41. See Blecking (2008), esp. 38ff.
42. Blecking (2008), 21.
43. *Jüdische Turnzeitung* 10, no. 9 (1909), 158.
44. See Wildmann (2009), 152.
45. *Jüdische Turnzeitung* 9, no. 4 (1908), 67.
46. Wildmann (2009), 169.
47. Gillerman (2011), 42ff.
48. Wildmann (2009), 228.
49. *Jüdische Turnzeitung* 11, no. 1 (1910), 11.
50. *Jüdische Turnzeitung* 8, no. 7 (1907), 131.
51. See Wildmann (2009), 199.
52. Wildmann (2009), 211.
53. See Burstyn (2002).
54. See Ungar (2010), 143.

55. Cited in Ungar (2010), 142.

56. Ungar (2010), 143.

57. See, among others, Horowitz (2006), 203ff.; Bodner (2011); Dee (2012).

58. Peter Levine (1992), 16.

59. Klemperer (1999), 1:71–72.

60. Reprinted in Aly and Gruner (2008), 280.

61. Kraus (2009).

62. Moll (2015), 3.

63. Haft (2009).

64. Sacken (1855), 244.

65. Ginsburger (1929), 164.

66. Blum and Lamm (1916), 14. See also Wenninger (2003), 52.

67. Kirchhof (1563), no. 266.

68. Taken from the 1898/99 semester bulletin of a Jewish dueling fraternity; cited in Rürup (2008), 206.

69. Levinas (2003), 64.

70. Duerr (1988).

71. See Robert Jütte (1992).

72. Duerr (1988), 80ff.

73. See Crane (2011), 63ff.

74. Benedict (2005), 268.

75. Maimonides (1956), 263 (pt. 3, chap. 8).

76. See Chapman (2008), 143.

77. See Louis M. Epstein (1948), 26.

78. A similar passage is found in BT Niddah, 16b.

79. https://archive.org/stream/BeweisantragImJudaisumus-prozess/Beweisantrag_djvu.txt, last retrieved March 31, 2016.

80. Philo (1993), p. 612, no. 176.

81. Clark (1956), 5.

82. On this general topic see Robert Jütte (1992).

83. *Sefer Chasidim* (1864), p. 269, no. 1060.

84. *Shulchan Arukh*, Orach Chayim 75.9.

85. *Brantspiegel* (1596), chap. 46, cited in Browning and Bunge (2009), 39.

86. Ruth Berger (2003), 284.

87. Aleichem (1987), 5.

88. See Crane (2011), 66.

89. See Satlow (1997), 440; Crane (2011), 68; Le (2012), 55.

90. Zinberg (1975), 144.

91. Lesses (2013), 285.

92. Louis M. Epstein (1948), 30. Also see Horowitz (2002a), 577.

93. Allendorf (1535).

94. See Leviticus 18:6. For an interpretation, see, among others, Maimonides (1956), 264 (pt. 3, chap. 8).

95. Shalev-Eyni (2014), p. 22, fig. 7 (Darmstadt University and State Library, Cod. Or. 8, fol. 58r).

96. Preuss (1911/1992), 147.

97. See David Biale (1992a), 51–52.

98. See Ruth Berger (2003), 231.

99. Baskin (2007).

100. Shalev-Eyni (2009).

101. Hamburg, State and University Library, Cod. Hebr. 37, fol. 79v, reprinted also in Metzger and Metzger (1982), fig. 106.

102. Buxtorf (1657), 300.

103. Gorsetman and Sztokman (2013), 178.

104. Shalev-Eyni (2014), 6.

105. Preuß (2005), 127.

106. Graupe (1973), 1:280, nos. 73–74.

107. Finkelstein (1964), 317–18 (Hebrew), 323 (English).

108. On this, see Louis M. Epstein (1948), 36.

109. I am grateful to Martha Keil (St. Pölten) for this reference. See Keil (2009), 38.

110. See Ruth Berger (2003), 115.

111. Kaidanover (1799), chap. 82.

112. See Katz (1994), 258.

113. Schudt (1714–17), pt. 4, contin. 3, p. 102.

114. Kafka (1954), 132–33.

115. Esquirol (1838), 205.

116. Thanks to Ruth von Bernuth (Chapel Hill) for this reference.

117. François Guesnet (2013), 148. I thank François Guesnet for the reference.

118. Nahshon (2008), 10.

119. Pollack (1971), 195f.

120. Zinger (2011), 67.

121. On this topic, see Bauks (2011), 28–29; Eilberg-Schwartz (1994), 86–87; Ranke-Graves and Patai (1986), 148ff.

122. Duerr (1988), 38ff.

123. Suslin (1571), fol. 163b.

124. See Louis M. Epstein (1948), 33.

125. Andy Newman and Sharon Otterman, "Debate over the Rabbi and the Sauna," *New York Times*, May 29, 2015, http://www.nytimes.com/2015/05/31/nyregion/fresh-debate-over-whether-a-rabbi-acted-inappropriately.html?_r = o, last retrieved March 31, 2016.

126. Börner-Klein (2007), 6–7.

127. *Evel Rabati* (1949), chap. 12, verse 10, p. 73.

128. Preuß (2007), 60.

129. Schur (2008), 215.

130. Graus (1988), 184.

131. Cited in Feiner (2011), 64. See also Maciejko (2011), 27.

132. See Schuchard (2009), 260.

133. Friedländer (2010), 57.

134. Gay (1998), 85.

135. Keller (1853), p. 183, lines 21–25:

Ich urtail, das man sie alle jar
Ganz ploß und nacket ziehe auß,
Setz jeden unter ein scheißhaus
Und ließ ein tag auf sie schmaliern
Und darnach gar rein uberfriren.

On this, see Rommel (2002), 187.

136. Liss (2004), 193.

137. Kamen (2014), 82.

138. Kobler (1952), 2:500.

139. See Duerr (1993), 310.

140. Jakob Jaffé (1916), 16.

141. See Duerr (1993), 312.

142. Cited from Wolfram Wette, "Nur seine Pflicht getan," *Die Zeit,* January 26, 2012, https://www.zeit.de/2012/05/SS-Jaeger, last retrieved February 15, 2020.

143. Grobman (1983), 249.

144. See, among others, Prescott (2010), 40ff.

145. His work was shown in Germany in 2014 at the NS Documentation Center of Cologne (August 27–November 2) in an exhibit called "KZ—Kampf—Kunst. Boris Lurie: NO!Art" (Concentration Camp—Struggle—Art. Boris Lurie: NO!Art).

146. Kramer (2003), 225ff.

147. See David Assaf (1995).

148. Rosenbach (2002), 45.

149. David Biale (1992b), 301.

150. Schwarz (2005), 38.

151. Wachstein (2006), 146.

152. See Yaron (2012).

153. Zimmer (1992), p. 342, n. 72.

154. See, among others, Pollack (1971), 94–95.

155. Brenner and Ullmann (2013), 246.

156. Przyrembel (2003), 70.

157. Cited from the "Judenhut" entry in *Deutsches Rechtswörterbuch*, http://www.rzuser.uni-heidelberg.de/~cd2/drw/e/ju/denh/judenhut.htm, last retrieved March 31, 2016.

158. See, among others, Robert (1891); Rezasco (1888/89); Guido Kisch (1957); Kriegel (1976); Ravid (1992).

159. Lubrich (2015).

160. Latin text in Aronius (1902), p. 301, no. 724. On this, also see Straus (1942), 60.

161. Cited from the "Judenhut" entry in *Deutsches Rechtswörterbuch*, http://www.rzuser.uni-heidelberg.de/~cd2/drw/e/ju/denh/judenhut.htm, last retrieved March 31, 2016.

162. See Zimmer (1992), 332–33.

163. See Zimmer (1992), 329.

164. https://www.chabad.org/library/article_cdo/aid/920167/jewish/Tefilah-and-Birkat-Kohanim-Chapter-Five.htm.

165. See Zimmer (1992), 330–31.

166. Maharam (1957–62), 1:1 Pesakim 150, no. 65.

167. See Rabinowitz (2007), 223 with references.

168. See Zimmer (1992), 336.

169. See Zimmer (1992), 337.

170. Modena (1650), 14.

171. Modena (2007), 10.

172. Seligmann (1922), 125–26.

173. See, among others, Rabinowitz (2007), 227.

174. Jick (1976), 182–83.

175. Saphra (1916), cols. 125–26.

176. Zimmer (1992), 349.

177. Rahe (1999), 42.

178. See, among others, Silverman (2013), 91–95.

179. Brüll (1887); Salomon Carlebach (1914), 454ff.; Abrahams (1932), 303–4.

180. See the controversy between Broyde (2010) and Shulman (2010).

181. Tertullian (1842), 166 (*De corona*, chap. 4).

182. See Louis M. Epstein (1948), 53.

183. http://www.sefaria.org/Shulchan_Arukh,_Orach_Chayim.75, last retrieved March 31, 2016.

184. Louis M. Epstein (1948), 54.

185. Quoted in Lowenstein (2003), 203.

186. Reissner (1965), 12.
187. Quoted in Lowenstein (2003), 203.
188. Louis M. Epstein (1948), 59.
189. Ben Joez (1837), 361.
190. Rappaport (1921/22), 413.
191. See Hertz (2007), p. 104, fig. 4.4.
192. See Rainer Schmitz (2013), 35.
193. See Gotzmann (2008), 361.
194. Wengeroff (2014), 117.
195. *Der Israelit* 12 (1871): 248.
196. Schwara (1999), 284.
197. Somogyi (1982), 231.
198. Zadoff (2012), 86.
199. Marperger (1708), 960.
200. *Patriotisches Tageblatt* 2 (1801): 509.
201. Jakobovits (1936), 115.
202. Rosin (2005), 34.
203. Hampel (2010).
204. Mostegel (2014).
205. Glückel (1977), 266.
206. Schudt (1714–17), pt. 4, contin. 3, p. 102.
207. Mendelssohn (1975), 60–61.
208. Haasis (1998), 270, 244. Also see Gerber (1990), 256.
209. Richarz (1974), 173. See also Rubens (1967), 174.
210. Schudt (1714–17), pt. 4, contin. 3, p. 171.
211. Euchel (2004), 40.
212. See Meyer (2000), 223.
213. Siegmund A. Wolf (1956), no. 5351.
214. Kirchschlager (2005), 81.
215. Westermann (1955), 19; Sandra Jacobs (2014), 7.
216. Schorsch (2004), 262.
217. See, among others, Dalman (1893), 46.
218. Peter Schäfer (2007), 15ff.
219. Axelrod (2010), 54.
220. On this, see Kohlbach (1910), 237.
221. See Kohlbach (1910), 237ff.
222. See Wachten (2006), fig. 2.
223. https://www.chabad.org/library/article_cdo/aid/912371/jewish/Avodat-Kochavim-Chapter-Twelve.htm, last retrieved January 12, 2020.
224. See Jachter (2008), 68ff.
225. Schwartz (2014).
226. See, among others, Dorff and Newman (2008), 16; Torgovnick (2008); Zivotofsky (2010).
227. Oshry (1959–74), 4:22.
228. See, among others, Weiss and Brackman (2013).
229. Levi (2015), 1:23–24.
230. Levi (2015), 3:2497.
231. Améry (1980), 94.
232. *Dayton Daily News*, March 26, 2010, http://www.eliewieseltattoo.com/the-evidence/the-tattoo/where-is-elies-tattoo/, last retrieved April 5, 2016.
233. Klüger (2008), 28. See Morewedge (2010), 175.
234. Apel (2001), 308.
235. Jachter (2008), 76.

236. Lapidoth and Aharonowitz (2004), 906ff.

237. Brawer (2010).

238. See, among others, Knobel (1857), 214; Brooks (1922), 80ff.

239. Houtman (1997), 92.

240. Lucas (1997), 119.

241. See Andree (1881), 216.

242. Graetz (1874), 345.

243. Antoine Guesnet (1773), 113.

244. Towiah Friedman (1997), 7, 11.

245. Toaff (1991), 277.

246. Hughes (1986), 24.

247. Farrell (2013), 16.

248. Hughes (1986), 24.

249. Simonsohn (1982), 1450–51.

250. Häberlein and Zürn (2001), 251.

251. Schwenken (1820), 348.

252. Adler (1931), 230.

253. Somogyi (1982), 241.

254. Somogyi (1982), 241.

255. Somogyi (1982), 179.

256. Wengeroff (2014), 2:53.

257. Goitein (1999), 4:214–15.

258. Shilo (2005), 74.

259. See, among others, Dorff (2003), 270.

260. Ross (2009).

261. Frübis (2013), 43.

Chapter 3

1. Schudt (1714–17), pt. 1, bk. 4, chap. 26, p. 11.

2. "Siddur Ashkenaz: Weekday, Shacharit, Preparatory Prayers, Morning Blessings," https://www.sefaria.org/Siddur_Ashkenaz%2C_Weekday%2C_Shacharit%2C_Preparatory_Prayers%2C_Yigdal?lang=bi, last retrieved May 15, 2019.

3. Yitzchak Yaacov Fuchs (1985), 29ff. On the ostensibly patriarchal character of Jewish prayers, see Cantor (1995), 437ff; Adelman (2001), 53; Shaye J. D. Cohen (2005), 120.

4. See, among others, Rachel Biale (1995); Brayer (1986); and Herweg (1994).

5. See, among others, Kratz-Ritter (1995).

6. Kay (2004), 129.

7. See Weissler (1998), 67.

8. *Midrash Tanhuma-Yelammedenu* (1996), 40, commentary on Genesis 6. See Fonrobert (2000), 31.

9. See Fonrobert (2000), 44.

10. Wagenseil (1681), 471. See also Shaye J. D. Cohen (2005), 49.

11. Baader (2006), 218–19.

12. Abraham Geiger (1837), 7.

13. Abraham Geiger (1837), 13.

14. Abraham Geiger (1837), 6.

15. *Protokolle* (1847), 265.

16. Fränkel (1806), 479.

17. Lewin (1909), 331.

18. Philo (1993), p. 857, no. 47. On this, see, among others, Neutel and Anderson (2014), 235.

19. Bekhor Shor (1994), 29. See the translation in Shaye J. D. Cohen (2005), 129.

20. David Berger (1979), 192.

21. Bettelheim (1954), 116.

22. See Shaye J. D. Cohen (2005), 112.

23. See Shaye J. D. Cohen (2005), 114.

24. Lipman-Mühlhausen (1681), sect. 21. See the English translation of the *Sefer Nizzahon* in Shaye J. D. Cohen (2005), 186.

25. Justin (2003), p. 38 (23:4–5).

26. Brinks (2009), 97.

27. Hildegard (1990), p. 177 (2.3.21).

28. Hundt-Radowsky (1822/23), 2:76.

29. Richter (1841), 263.

30. Klüber (1834), x.

31. See Güdemann (1966), 2:76.

32. See, among others, Grab (1989), 323.

33. Cited in Broder (1996), 37.

34. See, among others, Anderson (1996).

35. Weininger (2003), 320.

36. See, among others, Hödl (1997b), 164ff.

37. Gilman (1993b), 8.

38. On this, see Hoberman (1995), 143.

39. Gilman (1993b), 103.

40. John Chrysostom, *Against the Jews*, Homily 2, http://www.tertullian.org/fathers/chrysostom_adversus_judaeos_02_homily2.htm, last retrieved August 15, 2019.

41. Drake (2008), 204.

42. See Mosse (1985), 6.

43. See Feuer (1963), 305.

44. See Baader (2006), 217–18.

45. Samson Raphael Hirsch (1858), 182.

46. Jellinek (1869), 89.

47. See Gilman (1993b), 42.

48. David Biale (2007), 106.

49. Daniel Boyarin (1997), 10ff.; Daniel Boyarin (1995), 41ff.

50. See also Graybill (2012), 12ff.

51. Daniel Boyarin (1997), 10–11.

52. On this, see Kosman (2009), 19.

53. Benor (2004/5), 147ff.

54. Eilberg-Schwarz (1994), 144.

55. See Dafna Hirsch (2009), 582–83.

56. See, among others, Harrowitz and Hyams (1995); Boyarin and Boyarin (1997); Frankel (2000); Tova Rosen (2003); Dorff and Newman (2008); Kaplan and Moore (2011).

57. Weiss (2005), 18ff.

58. http://www.haaretz.com/news/features/word-of-the-day/word-of-the-day-rosh-gadol-what-sort-of-head-do-you-have-1.463372, last retrieved April 5, 2016.

59. See, among others, Barilan (n.d.); Unterman (1995); Mark Solomon (1995); Mariner (1995).

60. See, among others, Sarah (1995).

61. http://www.sefaria.org/Sifra_Acharei_Mot,_Section_8, last retrieved April 7, 2016.

62. Rashi on BT Yevamot 76a; see Steinberg (2003), 937.

63. https://www.chabad.org/library/article_cdo/aid/960669/jewish/Issurei-Biah-Chapter-Twenty-One.htm, last retrieved August 10, 2019.

64. Boswell (1980), 81ff.

65. Gotzmann (2008), 797.

66. Walzer (2000), 90.

67. Sparr (1996), 269.
68. For an early exception in Orthodox Judaism, see Halper (2011), 225ff.
69. On the early history, see Cooper (1989/90).
70. English translation in Rosner (1994), 17–40 ("Treatise on Cohabitation").
71. Boteach (1999).
72. Rosner (1994), 42ff.; Ackermann (1983), 86–90.
73. David Biale (1992a), 95–96.
74. See the English translation of 1993, *The Holy Letter*.
75. Biale (1992), 144.
76. Foucault (1980), 33.
77. Foucault (1980), 67.
78. See, among others, Hohmann (1985).
79. Iwan Bloch (1937), xix.
80. See, among others, Herzer (1992).
81. Hohmann (1987), 40.
82. Robert Jütte (2001), v.
83. On the Jewish background of many sex researchers, see Sigusch and Grau (2009).
84. See, among others, Louis M. Epstein (1948), 157.
85. Maimonides (1956), 373 (pt. 3, chap. 49).
86. Louis M. Epstein (1948), 166.
87. American Standard Version wording; see https://www.biblegateway.com/passage/?search = Proverbs + 5&version = ASV, last retrieved August 15, 2019.
88. Preuss (1911/1992), 564.
89. See, among others, Nirenberg (2002), 1075.
90. Schuster (1992), 116.
91. On the incidence of sexual offenses involving Jewish men and Christian women, including prostitutes, in medieval and early modern Italy, see Toaff (1998), 8ff.; Bonfil (2012), 101ff.
92. Butzer, Hüttnmeister, and Treue (2005), 27.
93. See, for example, Weihns (1899).
94. Glickman (2000); Bristow (1982).
95. See Hödl (1997b), 190ff.
96. Wuliger (2012). See also Stratenwerth (2012).
97. Lavaud (2015), 223.
98. Nathans (2004), 104. My thanks to Oleksiy Salivon (Stuttgart) for this reference.
99. On forced prostitution in general, see Sommer (2009).
100. Cziborra (2010), 176.
101. Brayer (1986), 177–78.
102. On this, see, among others, Ruth Berger (2003), 247ff.
103. *Sefer Chasidim* (1997), no. 408.
104. *Sefer Chasidim* (1997), no. 404.
105. See David Biale (1992a), 54ff.
106. *Sefer Chasidim* (1997), no. 501.
107. Papo (1924/25), 214.
108. See Robert Jütte (2010), 531. On the ruling about this sexual position in rabbinical literature, see Satlow (1995), 239ff.
109. Eduard Fuchs (1909), 208.
110. See Daniel Boyarin (1993), 142ff.
111. Steinberg (2003), 928.
112. On this, see *The Holy Letter* (1993), 102, for the detailed discussion in the late medieval tractate *Iggeret Hakodesh*.
113. See, among others, Satlow (1995), 296–97.
114. Fraenkel-Goldschmidt (2006), 306–7.

115. Satlow (1995), 285; David Biale (1992a), 147.

116. Schubert and Huttner (1999), 518.

117. See Satlow (1995), 298.

118. See Steinberg (2003), 931.

119. Morgenstern (2014), 43–44.

120. See Ritter (2003), 156–57.

121. See Rosner (1994).

122. *Nimmukei Yosef*, cited in Feldman (1974), 68.

123. See Satlow (1995), 232ff.

124. *Tos'fot RiD*, the Tosafot of Isaiah di Trani, cited in Feldman (1974), 103.

125. "Reasons for the Commandments Concerning 'Be Fruitful and Multiply': Ta'amei ha-Mitsvot, Parashat Bereshit," by Hayyim Vital (1570s), trans. Lawrence Fine, http://wesscholar.wesleyan.edu/emw/emw2006/emw2006/15/, last retrieved April 7, 2016.

126. See Riddle (1997), 73–74.

127. On this, see Feldman (1974), 297ff.; Schachter (1982), 32.

128. Tendler (1988), 12.

129. Okun (2000), table 2.

130. Cited from Robert Jütte (2008), 198.

131. See Robert Jütte (2008), 198.

132. Schellekens and Anson (2007), 176.

133. Adelman (2009), 188.

134. See, among others, Louis M. Epstein (1948), 155–56.

135. Davidovich-Eshed (2014), iii.

136. For cases in medieval and early modern legal contexts, see Ruth Berger (2003), 219.

137. Adelman (2009), 187–88.

138. See the examples in Malkiel (2006); Adelman (2009), 189.

139. Malkiel (2006), 111.

140. Malkiel (2006), 113.

141. Steinberg (2003), 1116–17. On sexual abstinence during menstruation, see Marienberg (2004), 8–9; Koren (2004), 325.

142. Adelman (2009), 193.

143. Wild, Poulin, and Biller-Andorno (2009).

144. See Natalia Berger (1995), 53–54.

145. Elisheva Carlebach (2006), fol. 4a.

146. According to Durex Global Sex Survey 2005, http://www.data360.org/pdf/20070416064139.Global%20Sex%20Survey.pdf, last retrieved February 16, 2020.

Chapter 4

1. "Abi gesunt," http://www.klesmer-musik.de/abi_gesunt.htm, last retrieved February 7, 2020.

a bisl zun a bisl regn, a ruik ort dem kop tsu legn,
abi gezunt, ken men gliklekh zayn. A shukh
a sok, a kleyd on lates, in khashene dray fir
tslotez, abi gezunt, ken men gliklekh zayn.

di luft iz fray, far yedn glaykh, di zun zi sheynt
far yedn eynem orem oder raykh.

2. "Aj-lju-lju" (Yiddish lullaby), http://www.holger-saarmann.de/texte_aj_lju_lju.htm, last retrieved February 7, 2020.

3. Michels (2013), 330.

4. See Preuss (1911/1992), 85.

5. "Oath and Prayer of Maimonides," https://dal.ca.libguides.com/c.php?g=256990&p =1717827, last retrieved August 10, 2019.

6. Hogan (1992), 302ff.; Isaacs (1998), 49ff; Kaiser (2002), 11–12.

7. Kaiser (2002), 33.

8. See the research overview in Levin and Prince (2011), 567–68.

9. Tacitus (1931), p. 185 (*Histories* 5.6).

10. Buxtorf (1657), 303.

11. See Baneth (1912), esp. 83ff. See also Wiesemann (1993).

12. Quoted in Grunwald (1912), 299.

13. See Ephraim M. Epstein (1874); Gilman (1995c), 110.

14. Krauskopf (1889), 7. See Gilman (1995c), 109.

15. See, among others, Susser and Watson (1972), 75; Josef Schuster (1980), 63–64.

16. See Hart (2007), 18.

17. Nossig (1894), 32.

18. Nossig (1894), 33. See Hart (1995), 79.

19. Williams (1882), 8; also cited in Hart (2007), 181.

20. *Kitzur Schulchan Aruch* 31:7.

21. See, among others, Grunwald (1912); Preuss (1911/1992).

22. Steinberg (2003), 834, with references to pertinent responsa.

23. Grunwald (1912), 5–6.

24. Tobel (1836), 8.

25. Tobel (1836), 9.

26. See Schlich (1996).

27. See Wenger (1998/99), 181ff.

28. Mombert (1830), 286; Mombert (1828), 53.

29. Schlich (1996), 180.

30. Mombert (1830), 277.

31. *Encyclopädisches Wörterbuch der Staatsarzneikunde* (1872), 209.

32. See Weissenberg (1912), 38–39.

33. *Jüdisches Lexikon* (1927), 4.1:178.

34. See Schüler-Springorum (2014), 46.

35. Report from 1882 cited in Großherzoglich Badischer Oberrat (1897), 31. On preventing masturbation, see also Julius Jaffé (1886), 8.

36. Gollaher (2000), 149ff.

37. Gollaher (2000), 158.

38. Isaacs (2008), 130–31; Dorff (2003), 120–21.

39. On this issue from a medical and Jewish perspective, see, among others, Deusel (2012).

40. Kaiser (2015), 144–46.

41. Philo (1993), 534.

42. Maimonides (1956), 378 (pt. 3, chap. 49). See Trusen (1853), 121.

43. Darby (2005), 262.

44. Bamberger (1912a).

45. Gilman (1993b), 66.

46. Eberhard Wolff (2002), 147.

47. See Judd (2007), 37.

48. Kafka (1976), 147–48, December 24, 1911.

49. Franz (2012), 7. On this, see multiple essays in the volume by Franz (2014).

50. Cited from Gilman (1993b), 87.

51. Freud (1953–74), 10:36, n. 1.

52. Silverman (2006), 219–20.

53. Gilman (1993b), 60. On Wolfers, see also Storz (2005), 139.

54. See Gilman (1993b), 59.

55. See Judd (2007), 22–23.

56. Philippson (1838), 53.

57. See Judd (2007), 39.

58. Interview with Frank Ulrich Montgomery, *Der Tagesspiegel*, July 17, 2012. On the debate over the Cologne decision, see Heil and Kramer (2012).

59. "Beleuchtung der Protokolle" (1847), 209.

60. Goldman (n.d.).

61. See the detailed description in Lipschutz (1995).

62. Heinrich Heine (1986), pp. 79–80 (chap. 22).

63. *Protokolle* (1847), 6 and 32.

64. Quoted from Adolf Wiener (1895), 492.

65. Quoted from Holdheim (1847), 41.

66. Holdheim (1847), 59–60.

67. Deutsch (1855), 62.

68. See, among others, Wiese (2009), 363ff.

69. Samuel Hirsch (1843), 179.

70. Adolf Wiener (1895), 484.

71. On this, see Judd (2007), 86ff.

72. Knobel (1857), 441.

73. Nicolai (1835), 318.

74. Adolf Wiener (1895), 420.

75. Adolf Wiener (1895), 427.

76. Adolf Wiener (1895), 480.

77. Grunwald (1912), 37.

78. Grunwald (1912), 36.

79. Daniel Jütte (2002).

80. "Study Finds Kosher Chicken Less Safe," https://jewishweek.timesofisrael.com/study-finds-kosher-chicken-less-saf, last retrieved February 7, 2020.

81. http://www.kosherzert.de, last retrieved February 7, 2020.

82. Aiken (2009), 16. On health routines of Orthodox Jews, see Coleman-Brueckheimer and Dein (2011), 425ff.; on the findings of empirical social research in the United States, see Levin (2011), 866.

83. On their early history during the Hellenistic period, see Dvorjetski (2007).

84. Schudt (1714–17), pt. 4, bk. 6, chap. 19, p. 159.

85. Schudt (1714–17), pt. 4, appendix, p. 47.

86. Schudt (1714–17), pt. 4, cont. 3, p. 104, which also includes the Hebrew text of the ordinance.

87. Schudt (1714–17), pt. 4, cont. 3, p. 104.

88. Schnapper-Arndt (1915), 330. On the popularity of mineral water among Jews in Prague and elsewhere, see Pollack (1971), 144, including references to Eger and Bad Ems.

89. Fenner (1807), 41.

90. Castle (1952), 612.

91. Albrecht (2010).

92. Brenner (2001), 119.

93. See Zadoff (2012).

94. See Heidel (2008).

95. See, among others, Fritzen (2006).

96. Robert Jütte (2002).

97. Binder (1979), 412.

98. Kafka (1976), 478 (July 9, 1912).

99. Kafka (1976), 477–78 (July 9, 1912).

100. Kafka (1976), 477 (July 8, 1912).

101. Kafka (1976), 479 (July 11, 1912).

102. Kafka (1976), 478 (July 9, 1912).

103. Pouzarová (1995), 63.

104. Cited in Pawel (1985), 171.

105. Hetkamp (1994).

106. See Walk (1996), pt. 3, no. 205, 295.

107. Jim G. Tobias, "Schwäbisches Sanatorium verwandelte sich in Kibbuz: Jüdische Kinder und Jugendliche im DP-Camp Jordanbad," 2009, http://www.hagalil.com/archiv/2009/08/23/jordan bad, last retrieved February 7, 2020.

108. Landau (2008).

109. Bajohr (2003).

110. Kriechbaumer (2002), 53.

111. Appelfeld (1980), 148.

112. "Idylle mit braunen Tropfen," 2016, http://www.sueddeutsche.de/reise/serfaus-in-tirol -idylle-mit-braunen-tupfen-1.441364, last retrieved February 7, 2020.

113. See Kupferberg (2011), 23.

114. Zweig (2004), 120–21.

115. On this stereotype, see Lathers (2000). On the German literature, see Anna-Dorothea Ludewig (2008).

116. See Standhartinger (1995), 137.

117. Quoted in Ruth Berger (2003), 141.

118. Guido Kisch (1978), 140. I would like to thank Cornelia Aust for this reference.

119. From an interview with an Eastern Jew in Somogyi (1982), 101.

120. See Somogyi (1982), 99.

121. Rhoda Rosen (1998), 12.

122. Uta Klein (2001), 84.

123. Quoted in Yiddish and German in Somogyi (1982), 101:

Dain Gestalt wi a schain Waksfigur
Un daine Liplach zucker siss
Daine Eigelach wi schwarze Karschen
Oj wu nemt noch dain Kisch

Daine Bekelech wie rozewe Blumen
Un daine Herelach koiln schwarz
Daine Hentelach wie waiss gefallen Schnai
Oj wi s'ziet zu dir main Harz.

124. Schack (1998), p. 64, no. 67.

125. See, among others, Präger and Schmitz (1964), 61–62.

126. See Efron (2016), 100.

127. Fishberg (1911), 109–10.

128. Spiegel (2013), 30–31.

129. Angel (1991), 177.

Chapter 5

1. "Ehec ist ne Judenkrankheit," June 13, 2011, https://dieaktuelleantimobbingrundschau.word press.com/tag/ehec-ist-ne-judenkrankheit/, last retrieved February 9, 2020.

2. Josephus (1926), 285–86.

3. See, among others, Cardoso (1679), 347. On medieval Jewish sources, see Shoham-Steiner (2003), 244–45.

4. Tacitus (1931), 179.

5. Cited in Ulrich (1998), 233.

6. On Piacenza as a person, see Chwolson (1901), 207; Poliakov (1965), 103. Contrary to what has been claimed (see, for instance, Efron 1994, 6), Piacenza did not write a work on "Jewish diseases." He instead merely drew up a list of penalties or curses incurred by the Jewish people's alleged crimes against the Son of God that includes diseases. On this genre (list of curses), see Soyer (2014), 242.

7. Dudulaeus (ca. 1635), sig. Eii (v). The name of the author is apparently a pseudonym; see Frey (2002), 216–17.

8. Buxtorf (1657), 303.

9. Margaritha (1713), 133.

10. Cited from Friedenwald (1967), 2:527.

11. Cited from Friedenwald (1967), 2:527.

12. See Koren (2009), 45ff.; Koren (2011), 144ff.

13. Thomas de Cantimpré (1605), 305–6. See, among others, Trachtenberg (1983), 148; Gilman (1993a), 97–98.

14. On this, see, among others, Resnick (2000), 242ff.; Resnick (2012), 200.

15. Johnson (1998), 275ff.

16. See, among others, Kassouf (1998), 101ff.; Katz (1999), 448ff.; Pomata (2001); Horowitz (2001), 346–47; Smith (2010).

17. Beusterien (1999), 447ff.

18. Cited from Yerushalmi (1981), 128.

19. See Höfler (1899), 4; Pomata (2001), 109ff.; Smith (2010), 27ff.

20. See Yerushalmi (1981), 436.

21. On this, see, among others, Trachtenberg (1983), 51–52; Chwolson (1901), 207ff.

22. See, among others, Kornmann (1694), 128; Schudt (1714–17), pt. 2, bk. 4, chap. 31, p. 345.

23. Abraham a Sancta Clara (1721), 33.

24. Andreas Osiander (1893), 15.

25. Rau (1821), 54.

26. Elcan Isaac Wolf (1777), 50. On Wolf, see, among others, Efron (1995), 349ff.

27. Gilman (1993b), 57.

28. Friedenwald (1967), 2:528.

29. Abramovitsh (1996), 33.

30. Althaus (2003), 157.

31. Gilman (1991), 100–101.

32. See Präger and Schmitz (1964), 158–59.

33. Schudt (1714–17), pt. 4, bk. 6, chap. 13, p. 47.

34. Ramazzini (1705), 196–97.

35. Lobes (1791), 37.

36. Elcan Isaac Wolf (1777), 25.

37. Friese (1836), 722.

38. See Mehler (2001), 205.

39. Ostermann (1836), 263.

40. See among others Wenck (2000), 236.

41. Grüner (2008), 259 n. 105.

42. Vaynig (1938), 22ff.

43. "Parekh-lid," May 5, 2010, https://yiddishsong.wordpress.com/tag/parekh/, last retrieved February 9, 2020.

Ale parches hobn zikh arumgenemen in a reydl,
hobn getontst funem hekdesh bizn beydl.
Hey-hu, parkhenyu,
gib zikh a krots in kepenyu.

44. Thanks to François Guesnet (London) for this information.

45. See, among others, Bauer (2004).

46. Schwimmer (1888), 624.

47. Hamburger (1861), 4.

48. Jesionek (1921), 524.

49. La Fontaine (1792), 11.

50. Beschorner (1843), 16.

51. See La Fontaine (1792), 30.

52. Rosenberg (1839), 58.

53. Cress (1682), 4.

54. Scheiba (1717/1739). Seven years later at a different German university, a doctoral student from Köslin in Pomerania also wrote a thesis on this topic, and the title of his dissertation likewise contains the term *Judenzopf*.

55. Eilenburg (1755), 35.

56. Dietmar Müller (2005), 171–72.

57. Rohrer (1804), 27.

58. Maximilian Heine (1853), 17.

59. See the statistics in Tschoetschel (1990), 177.

60. Rigter (1996), 620.

61. Markel (2000), 544.

62. Reinecke (2010), 48.

63. Markel (2000), 544.

64. Boldt (1904), 50.

65. Markel (2000), 540.

66. Markel (2000), 545.

67. Sandler (1904), 165.

68. Reifler (2015), 198.

69. Fishberg (1911), 296.

70. Freud (2015), 147.

71. Quoted from Gans (2013), 90. I thank Evelien Gans (Amsterdam) for this reference.

72. Seegen (1870), 65.

73. Tschoetschel (1990), 121.

74. Theilhaber and Auerbach (1909), 10.

75. Engländer (1902), 38–39. See also Fishberg (1911), 301.

76. Eisenstadt (1916/19), 137–38.

77. Tschoetschel (1990), 134–35.

78. Frerichs (1884), 185.

79. Pollatschek (1902), 478.

80. Kalter-Leibovici et al. (2012).

81. Zung et al. (2004).

82. *Südhessisches Wörterbuch*, vol. 3, col. 999 (http://www.lagis-hessen.de/de/subjects/rsrec/sn/shwb/entry/Juden-krankheit, last retrieved April 21, 2016); vol. 3, col. 1376 (http://woerterbuchnetz.de/PfWB/, last retrieved April 21, 2016).

83. See, among others, Gilman (1993b), 173.

84. Collin (1842), 9–10.

85. Hoppe (1903), 42–43.

86. See Sauerteig (1999), 392; Michl (2007), 148.

87. Wolf (1777), 7.

88. Wolf (1777), 93–94.

89. La Fontaine (1792), 147.

90. La Fontaine (1792), 151.

91. Schneider (1825), 274–75.

92. On this, see the foundational overview in Tschoetschel (1990).

93. See Efron (2001), 126ff.

94. Tschoetschel (1990), 1–2.
95. See Turmann (1968), 11ff.
96. See Oller (1984), 182ff.
97. See Pollak (2011), 798ff. For an ethical perspective, see Schell-Apacik (2007), 99ff.
98. Reuter (2006), 291ff.
99. Goodman (1979), 468.
100. Freud (1999), 83.
101. Wynn (2007), 100; Dorman (2007).
102. See Preuss (1911/1992), 267–68.
103. See Olyan (2011), 102ff.
104. Hödl (1997b), 140; Julia Schäfer (2005), 257.
105. See Schüler-Springorum (2014), 105.
106. Eduard Fuchs (1921), 118.
107. Gilman (1991), 38ff.
108. Grillparzer (1953), 31; Grillparzer (1992), p. 20, lines 485–87:

Ich selber lieb es nicht dies Volk, doch weiß ich,
Was sie verunziert, es ist unser Werk;
Wir lähmen sie und grollen, wenn sie hinken.

109. Gilman (1991), 54.
110. Fishberg (1911), 327.
111. Kroll (1929), 140–41.
112. Heinrich Singer (1904), 125.
113. See Preuss (1911/1992), 313ff.; Steinberg (1986), 284.
114. Hentrich (2007), 81–82.
115. Steinberg (1986), 287.
116. See Belser (2011), 19ff.
117. Zimmels (1952), 88, 155.
118. Tschoetschel (1990), 218ff.
119. *Zedaka* (1992). On the Middle Ages, see Mark R. Cohen (2005), 169–72.
120. Shoham-Steiner (2007), 76–77.
121. See Preuss (1911/1992), 318; Steinberg (1986), 287–88.
122. Daniel S. Nevins (2006), 39ff.
123. Abrams (1998), 104.
124. Walk (1996), no. 392.
125. "Das Israelitische Blindeninstitut," October 14, 2002, https://www.wienerzeitung.at/nach
richten/chronik/oesterreich/177058_Das-Israelitische-Blindeninstitut.html?em_cnt_page = 2, last
retrieved February 9, 2020.
126. Hillenbrand (1995), 78, no. 58.
127. Preuss (1911/1992), 337–38.
128. Gracer (2006), 85ff.
129. Steinberg (2003), 283–84, with individual references.
130. Steinberg (2003), 288, with individual references.
131. Söderfeldt (2014), 211.
132. Söderfeldt (2014), 213.
133. Zaurov (2003), 73.
134. Julius Wolffreim in 1896, quoted in Söderfeldt (2014), 218; emphasis in original.
135. Tschoetschel (1990), 224.
136. Bell (1883), 4.
137. Waldenburg (1902), 40. See Lipphardt (2008), 109–10.
138. Fishberg (1911), 336.

139. Muhs (2002), 80.

140. Sonke (1993), 76.

141. Muhs (2002), 92.

142. Schack (1998), p. 60, no. 29: "A kaljokégit men gicher a nédowe, wi a tálmid chóchem."

143. See Weiss (2005), 90.

144. On the Middle Ages, see Shoham-Steiner (2014).

145. *Sefer Chasidim* (1997), no. 309.

146. *Sefer Chasidim* (1997), no. 312.

147. Mor (n.d.), 27–28; Sufian (2007).

148. Weiss (2005), 88.

149. Avrami and Rimmerman (2005).

150. Barnartt and Rotman (2007).

151. See Steinberg (2003), 355.

152. See, among others, Daniel Schäfer (2004), 34ff.

153. Sedley (2012), sect. 4a.

154. See, among others, Dayle A. Friedman (2008), 5–6.

155. See Sedley (2012), n. 102.

156. Philo (1993), p. 746, 11.13.

157. See Steinberg (2003), 356.

158. Lange (2010), 162ff.

159. Lavaud (2015), 134.

160. "Mitglieder jüdischer Gemeinden in Deutschland 1955–2016," April 26, 2017, https://fowid.de/meldung/mitglieder-juedischer-gemeinden-deutschland-1955–2016, last retrieved February 9, 2020.

Chapter 6

1. Kohnen (2003), 72.

2. Berthold B. Wolff (1985), 23; cited in Rollman (1998), 267.

3. See Suchman (1964), 319; Goldstein, Watkins, and Spector (1994), 57.

4. Berthold B. Wolff (1985), 27.

5. Rollman (1998), 273.

6. This was found already in the 1920s with regard to Jewish immigrants to England (Woolf 1928). See the overview in Wolff and Langley (1968), 495–96.

7. Zborowski (1969), 101.

8. Zborowski (1969), 114.

9. Zborowski (1969), 135.

10. "Anzahl der ambulanten Arztkontakte je Person in Deutschland nach Geschlecht in den Jahren 2004 bis 2017," *Statista* 2020, https://de.statista.com/statistik/daten/studie/75866/umfrage/arztkontakte-in-deutschland-nach-geschlecht-seit-2004, last retrieved February 10, 2020.

11. "Health Care Utilization: Consultation," November 15, 2019, https://stats.oecd.org/index.aspx?queryid = 30161, last retrieved February 10, 2020.

12. Mitchell and Kottek (1993), 255.

13. Novak and Waldoks (1981), 48.

14. Maimonides (2019a), 70.

15. Leibowitz (1969), 39.

16. Probst (2016).

17. Tilevitz (1993), 58.

18. See Steinberg (2003), 797.

19. Preuss (1911/1992), 27.

20. See, among others, Sinclair (1998/99).

21. United States Conference of Catholic Bishops, "Exodus, Chapter 21," http://www.usccb.org/bible/exodus/21, last retrieved February 10, 2020.

22. Probst (2016), 21.
23. *Midrash Shmuel* (1893), 4:52a; see Preuss (1911/1992), 29.
24. Kaiser (2002), 33.
25. Abraham P. Bloch (1984), 129.
26. See Preuss (1911/1992), 25.
27. Kottek (1996), 172.
28. See Teter (2006), 74.
29. Shatzmiller (1994), 122.
30. *Sefer Chasidim* (1997), no. 586.
31. Shatzmiller (1994), 123.
32. *Sefer Chasidim* (1864), no. 1352.
33. Shoham-Steiner (2006), 375f.
34. Preuss (1911/1992), 21.
35. See, among others, Cecil Roth (1953), 834ff.
36. Marcus (1947), 27.
37. Marcus (1947), 34.
38. Litt (2008), 167.
39. Robert Jütte (1996).
40. Shatzmiller (1994); Efron (2001); Eberhard Wolff (2014).
41. Robert Jütte et al. (2011), 83ff.
42. Gaster (1968), p. 97, no. 197.
43. See Aaron Levine (1987).
44. Buber (1948), 87.
45. http://www.chabad.org/library/article_cdo/aid/1181895/jewish/Avel-Chapter-14.htm, last retrieved August 10, 2019.
46. *Sefer Chasidim* (1997), no. 587.
47. For his biography, see Kämpf (1838).
48. Modena (1988), 89.
49. Modena (1988), 142.
50. Glückel (1977), 265.
51. Marcus (1947), 262ff.
52. Marcus (1947), 12.
53. Marcus (1947), p. 15, n. 15.
54. Zürn (2001), 97–98.
55. Zürn (2001), 98–99.
56. Marcus (1947), 129. On Breslau, see Reinke (1999), 36–37.
57. Glückel (1977), 177.
58. Glückel (1977), 66.
59. Mendelssohn (1793), 120–21.
60. "Letter from a woman to the chief rabbi of Trieste Raffael Natan Tedesco," January 24, 1794, trans. Lois C. Dubin, http://wesscholar.wesleyan.edu/emw/emw2006/emw2006/14, last retrieved February 10, 2020.
61. Zürn (2001), 190.
62. Zürn (2001), 191.
63. Lavaud (2015), 189.
64. Marcus (1947), 144; Eberhard Wolff (2014), 196ff.
65. Baader (2006), 165.
66. "Rule for the Care of the Sick," Fuerth, 1786 (Judaeo-German) in Marcus (1947), 281–82.
67. Stricker (1847), 165.
68. Baader (2006), 167–68.
69. Stricker (1847), 165.
70. Zürn (2001), 193ff.

71. Zürn (2001), 195.
72. Modena (2007), p. 180, n. 433.
73. Marcus (1947), 130.
74. Elbogen (1967), 201ff.
75. See in detail Steinberg (2003), 97.
76. "What Is a Mi Sheberach?," https://www.chabad.org/library/article_cdo/aid/2903187/jewish/Mi-Sheberach, last retrieved February 10, 2020.
77. Steinberg (2003), 96–97.
78. Steinberg (2003), 97.
79. Steinberg (2003), 98.
80. *Authorised Daily Prayer Book* (1912), 69.
81. Steinberg (2003), 99.
82. Maimonides, "Oath and Prayer."
83. Leder (2007), 238ff.

Chapter 7

1. See Steinberg (2003), 1046; Kinzbrunner (2004), 562–63; Figdor (2015), 29ff.
2. Feinstein (1996), 63.
3. Bleich (2002), 187.
4. Bleich (2002), 142; Nordmann (1999), 51.
5. Yaakov Friedman (1993), 106.
6. Abraham S. Abraham (1993), 118.
7. See the example from Verona in Horowitz (2000), 171. See also Horowitz (1982) for additional examples.
8. On mourning in Judaism, see Kidorf (1963), 250.
9. Modena (1650), 232.
10. Modena (1988), 93.
11. Glückel (1977), 148.
12. Glückel (1977), 151. On this custom, see Goldberg (1996), 106.
13. Glückel (1977), 152. On praying together at the bedside of a sick or dying person, see, among others, Zinger (2009a), 69.
14. Quoted from Zürn (2001), 99.
15. The following from Marcus (1947), 262ff.
16. Marx Jacob Marx (1784), 228.
17. See, among others, Kinzbrunner (2004), 565–66.
18. *Sefer Chasidim* (1997), no. 595.
19. Crane (2015), 18.
20. For Israel, see Ravitzky and Prawer (2008). See also Steinberg and Sprung (2007), 550ff.
21. Bar-Efrat (2009), 14. See also Rosner (1972), 117.
22. Noam Zohar (1997), 53.
23. See, among others, Steinberg (2003), 1067ff.; Barilan (2003), 141ff.; Dorff (2003), 176ff.; Kinzbrunner (2004), 558ff.
24. See, among others, Rosner (1972), 127ff.
25. https://www.chabad.org/library/article_cdo/aid/935201/jewish/Shabbat-Chapter-Two.htm, last retrieved August 11, 2019.
26. Bleich (2013), 181.
27. Glückel (1977), 152.
28. Cited in Steinberg (2003), 710.
29. Levy (1913), 34.
30. See, among others, Eberhard Wolff (2014), 166ff.; Zürn (2001), 129ff.; Krochmalnik (1997); Wiesemann (1992).
31. See, among others, Rüve (2008).

32. Cited in Silberstein (1929), 279.

33. Mendelssohn's letter is reprinted in Silberstein (1929), 284–85, here 285.

34. Mendelssohn (1975), 103.

35. Emden's letter as paraphrased by Sorkin (1996), 100; for the entire letter, see Silberstein (1929), 282–83.

36. See Krochmalnik (1997), 133.

37. See Eberhard Wolff (2014), 179ff.

38. Herz (1788), 7.

39. Herz (1788), 41.

40. Herz (1788), 39.

41. Marx Jacob Marx (1788), 5.

42. Cited in Eberhard Wolff (2014), 189–90.

43. See Eberhard Wolff (2014), 192.

44. Zürn (2001), 147.

45. Reinke (1999), 101.

46. Schlich (1998), 154.

47. Eberhard Wolff (2014), 173.

48. Reprinted in Müller and Rudolf (2015), 98.

49. Ludwig Geiger (1889), 211.

50. Steinberg (2003), 79ff.; Rosner (1986), 321–22.

51. See in general Steinberg (2003), 73–90; Rosner, Bleich, and Brayer (1999), 363ff.; Rosner (1972), 132.

52. Cecil Roth (1930), 287.

53. Sahmland (2008), 88.

54. Kästner and Pawlowitsch (2011), 1.

55. Aleksiun (2012), 8.

56. Aleksiun (2012), 331.

57. On this, see Ettinger (2006).

58. Steinberg (2003), 84. See also the detailed list of measures to be taken in a pamphlet of the Jewish burial societies in America: "Traditional Jewish Autopsy Procedure," http://www.shemayisrael .co.il/burial/autopsy.htm, last retrieved February 10, 2020.

59. See, for example, the rulings of various U.S. courts: Kohn v. United States, 591 F. Supp. 568 (E.D.N.Y. 1984); Montgomery v. County of Clinton, Michigan, 743 F. Supp. 1253 (D. Mich. 1990), aff'd 940 F.2d 661 (6th Cir. 1991).

60. See Faltin (2008), 201.

61. Josephus (1982), 240.

62. See Böckler (2014).

63. Gotzmann (2008), 776.

64. Anna Fischer (2009).

65. For a comparative perspective, see Dietrich (2016).

66. Bammel (1986), 84ff.

67. Lamm and Ben-Sasson (2007).

68. Josephus (1982), 492.

69. Eidelberg (1977), 51. See also Neubauer and Stern (1892), 118.

70. Yuval (2006), 154.

71. Yuval (2006), 164.

72. See also Yuval (1999). On the controversy, see Raspe (2006), 181ff.

73. Wenzel (2013), 72–73.

74. Bahat (1963).

75. Penkower (2004).

76. See, among others, Huberband (1987), x and the following pages.

77. See, among others, Wahle (1972), 291ff.; Gillman (1997); Setzer (2009).

78. Barbara Schmitz (2009), 110.

79. Avery-Peck (2009), 243.

80. *Authorised Daily Prayer Book* (1912), 44.

81. Saadia Gaon (1948), 432.

82. Saadia Gaon (1948), 432.

83. Abraham Geiger (1857), 42.

84. Abraham Geiger (1857), 43.

85. See, among others, Schröder (1851), 393ff.; Goldberg (1996), 88–89.

86. See Werner (2002), 140.

87. Quoted in Werner (2002), 200–201.

88. Modena (1650), 245.

89. *Authorised Daily Prayer Book* (1912), 44.

90. Stemberger (2002), 174.

91. Norman Solomon (2015), 521.

92. Norman Solomon (2015), 523.

93. Sarason (2006).

94. Quoted in Ben Harris, "Reform Siddur Revives Resurrection Prayer," *Jewish Telegraphic Agency*, September 19, 2007, https://www.jta.org/2007/09/19/united-states/reform-siddur-revives -resurrection-prayer, last retrieved August 19, 2019.

95. *Mishkan T'filah* (2007), 78.

96. On the history of this institution in Central Europe (Ashkenazim), see, among others, Marcus (1947), 63ff.; for Hamburg, see Zürn (2001), 104ff.

97. Modena (1650), 233.

98. For Frankfurt am Main, see Gotzmann (2008), 716.

99. Modena (1650), 236.

100. Goldberg (1996), 114.

101. Modena (1988), 177.

102. Quoted in Zürn (2001), 213.

103. Quoted in Zürn (2001), 213.

104. See Goldberg (1996), 122ff.

105. Glückel (1977), 152.

106. Glückel (1977), 152–53.

107. Glückel (1977), 131.

108. Glückel (1977), 131.

109. Zürn (2001), 206.

110. See Rosner (1985), 232ff.

111. See Carolyn Abraham (2002).

112. "Einstein Brain Atlas," https://itunes.apple.com/app/id555722456, last retrieved February 10, 2020.

113. Fishkoff (2010).

114. *Frankfurter Allgemeine Zeitung*, November 25, 2015; "Supreme Court upholds transgender activist's cremation request," *Times of Israel*, November 25, 2015, http://www.timesofisrael.com/ supreme-court-upholds-transgender-activists-cremation-request, last retrieved February 10, 2020.

115. See, among others, Preuss (1911/1992), 602–3; Rosner (1985), 220ff.; Citron (2015); Ranke-Graves and Patai (1986), 348.

116. *Zohar* (2006), 3:543–44.

117. See Rosner (1985), 227.

118. Golan (2011).

119. See Robert Jütte (2010), including bibliography.

Bibliography

Abraham, Abraham S. "The Goses." In *Medicine and Jewish Law*, ed. Fred Rosner, 2:117–19. Northvale, NJ: Jason Aronson, 1993.

Abraham, Carolyn. *Possessing Genius: The Bizarre Odyssey of Einstein's Brain*. New York: St. Martin's, 2002.

Abraham a Sancta Clara. *Abrahamische Lauber-Hütt* . . . . Vienna: Lehmann, 1721.

Abrahams, Israel. *Jewish Life in the Middle Ages*. London: E. Goldston, 1932.

Abramovitsh, S. Y. (Mendele Moykher Sforim). *Tales of Mendele the Book Peddler: Fishke the Lame and Benjamin the Third*. Ed. Dan Miron and Ken Frieden. Trans. Ted Gorelick and Hillel Halkin. New York: Schocken, 1996.

Abrams, Judith Z. *Judaism and Disability: Portrayals in Ancient Texts from the Tanach Through the Bavli*. Washington, DC: Gallaudet University Press, 1998.

Ackermann, Hermann. "Die Gesundheitslehre des Maimonides: Medizinische, ethische und religionsphilosophische Aspekte." Med. diss., Heidelberg, 1983.

Adelman, Howard Tzvi. "Italian Jewish Women at Prayer." In *Judaism in Practice: From the Middle Ages to the Early Modern Period*, ed. Lawrence Fine, 52–60. Princeton, NJ: Princeton University Press, 2001.

Adelman, Howard Tzvi. "Virginity: Women's Body as a State of Mind: Destiny Becomes Biology." In *The Jewish Body*, ed. Maria Diemling and Giuseppe Veltri, 179–214. Leiden: Brill, 2009.

Adler, Simon. "Das älteste Judicial-Protokoll des jüdischen Gemeinde-Archives in Prag (1662)." *Jahrbuch der Gesellschaft für die Geschichte der Juden in der Čechoslovakischen Republik* 3 (1931): 217–56.

Aiken, Lisa. *The Baal Teshuva Survival Guide*. Beverly Hills: Rossi Publications, 2009.

Albrecht, Joachim. "Der umstrittene Aufenthalt der Juden im Linckeschen Bad in Dresden um 1800." *Medaon: Magazin für jüdisches Leben in Forschung und Bildung* 4, no. 7 (2010): 1–6.

Aleichem, Sholem. *Tevye the Dairyman and the Railroad Stories*. Trans. and introd. Hillel Halkin. New York: Schocken, 1987.

Aleksiun, Natalia. "Jewish Students and Christian Corpses in Interwar Poland: Playing with the Language of Blood Libel." *Jewish History* 26 (2012): 327–42.

Aleksiun, Natalia. "Pleading for Cadavers: Medical Students at the University of Vienna and the Study of Anatomy." *S:I.M.O.N.—Shoah: Intervention, Methods, Documentation* 2 (2015): 4–10.

Allan, Nigel. "A Jewish Physician in the Seventeenth Century." *Medical History* 28 (1984): 324–28.

Allendorf, Philipp von. *Der Juden Badstub: Ein Anzeygung irer manigfeltigen schedlichen Hendel zu Warnung allen Christen iren trieglichen Listigkeyten zu entweychen und zuvermeyden; wer wissen wil was Schand und Schad entspringet auß dem Juden Bad der selb durchleß mich biß zum Endt von in wir sehend sind verblendt*. S.l., s.n., 1535.

Almog, Shmuel. " 'Judentum als Krankheit': Antisemitisches Stereotyp und Selbstdarstellung." *Tel Aviver Jahrbuch für deutsche Geschichte* 20 (1991): 215–35.

Althaus, Hans Peter. *Kleines Lexikon deutscher Wörter jiddischer Herkunft*. Munich: C. H. Beck, 2003.

Aly, Götz, and Wolf Gruner, eds. *Die Erfolgung und Ermordung der europäischen Juden durch das nationalsozialistische Deutschland, 1933–1945*. Munich: C. H. Beck, 2008.

Améry, Jean. *At the Mind's Limits: Contemplations by a Survivor of Auschwitz and Its Realities.* Trans. Sidney Rosenfeld and Stella P. Rosenfeld. Bloomington: Indiana University Press, 1980.

Anderson, Susan C. "Otto Weininger's Masculine Utopia." *German Studies Review* 19 (1996): 433–53.

Andree, Richard. *Zur Volkskunde der Juden.* Bielefeld: Velhagen & Klasing, 1881.

Angel, Marc D. *Voices in Exile: A Study in Sephardic Intellectual History.* Hoboken, NJ: Ktav, 1991.

Apel, Dana. "The Tattooed Jew." In *Visual Culture and the Holocaust,* ed. Barbie Zelizer, 300–322. New Brunsick, NJ: Rutgers University Press, 2001.

Appelfeld, Aharon. *Badenheim 1939.* Trans. Dalya Bilu. Boston: Godine, 1980.

Aronius, Julius, ed. *Regesten zur Geschichte der Juden im fränkischen und deutschen Reiche bis zum Jahre 1273.* Berlin: Leonhard Simeon, 1902.

Asad, Talal. *Formations of the Secular: Christianity, Islam, Modernity.* Stanford, CA: Stanford University Press, 2003.

Aschoff, Diethard. "Judenkennzeichnung und Judendiskriminierung in Westfalen bis zum Ende des Alten Reiches." *Aschkenas* 1 (1993): 15–47.

Assaf, David. "Erinnerungsräuber" (Hebr.). *Ha'aretz,* February 17, 1995.

Assaf, Simcha. *Ha-'onasin 'ahare hatimat ha-talmud* (Hebr.) [Punishment After the Conclusion of the Talmud]. Jerusalem: Y. Yunoviz, 1921.

Auerbach, Elias. "Ueber die Militärtauglichkeit der Juden." *Jüdische Turnzeitung* 9, no. 10/11 (1908): 187–89.

Augusti, Friedrich Albrecht. *Geheimnisse der Jüden von dem Wunder-Fluß Sambathjon, wie auch von denen rothen Juden, in einem Brief-Wechsel mit denen heutigen Jüden, zur Erläuterung 2 Reg. 17,6 abgehandelt, und dem Druck überlassen.* Erfurt: Jungnicol, 1748.

Auslander, Leora. "The Boundaries of Jewishness, or When Is a Cultural Practice Jewish?" *Journal of Modern Jewish Studies* 8 (2001): 47–64.

The Authorised Daily Prayer Book of the United Hebrew Congregations of the British Empire. Trans. Rabbi Simeon Singer. 9th ed. London: Eyre and Spottiswoode, 1912.

Auzépy, Marie-France. "Tonsure des clercs, barbe des moines et barbe du Christ." In *Histoire du poil,* ed. Marie-France Auzépy and Joël Cornette, 71–92. Paris: Belin, 2011.

Avery-Peck, Alan J. "Resurrection of the Body in Early Modern Rabbinic Judaism." In *The Human Body in Death and Resurrection,* ed. Tobias Nicklas, Friedrich v. Reiterer, and Joseph Verheyden, 243–66. Berlin: Walter de Gruyter, 2009.

Avrami, Shirley, and Arie Rimmerman. "Voting Intentions of Israeli Legislators Regarding Proposed Disability and Social Welfare Laws." *Journal of Comparative Policy Analysis* 7 (2005): 221–32.

Axelrod, David B. "Jews Don't Get Tattoos." *Mnemosyne* 32 (2010): 54.

Baader, Benjamin Maria. *Gender, Judaism, and Bourgeois Culture in Germany, 1800–1870.* Bloomington: Indiana University Press, 2006.

Babylonian Talmud. https://www.sefaria.org/texts/Talmud.

Bacher, Wilhelm. *Die Agada der Tannaiten.* Vol. 1, *Von Hillel bis Akiba: Von 30 vor bis 135 nach d.g.Z.* Strasbourg: Karl J. Trübner, 1884.

Bahat, Yaakov. "Kiddusch haschem bejezirato schel Tchernichovsky" (Hebr.) [Suicide in the Work of Tchernichovsky]. *Moznayim* 17 (1963): 432–37.

Bajohr, Frank. *"Unser Hotel ist judenfrei": Bäder-Antisemitismus im 19. und 20. Jahrhundert.* Frankfurt/ M.: Fischer Taschenbuch, 2003.

Balberg, Mira. "Rabbinic Authority, Medical Rhetoric, and Body Hermeneutics in Mishnah Nega'im." *AJS Review* 35 (2011): 323–46.

Bamberger, M. L. "Die Hygiene der Beschneidung." In *Die Hygiene der Juden: Im Anschluß an die Internationale Hygiene-Ausstellung Dresden 1911,* ed. Max Grundwald, 103–12. Dresden: Verlag der Historischen Abteilung der Internationalen Hygiene-Ausstellung, 1912a.

Bamberger, M. L. "Die Hygiene des Schulchan Arukh." In *Die Hygiene der Juden: Im Anschluß an die Internationale Hygiene-Ausstellung Dresden 1911,* ed. Max Grunwald, 231–41. Dresden: Verlag der Historischen Abteilung der Internationalen Hygiene-Ausstellung, 1912b.

Bammel, Ernst. *Judaica: Kleine Schriften.* Tübingen: Mohr Siebeck, 1986.

Baneth, B. "Das jüdische Ritualgesetz in hygienischer Beleuchtung." In *Die Hygiene der Juden: Im Anschluß an die Internationale Hygiene-Ausstellung Dresden 1911*, ed. Max Grunwald, 43–102. Dresden: Verlag der Historischen Abteilung der Internationalen Hygiene-Ausstellung, 1912.

Bar-Efrat, Shimon. *Das Zweite Buch Samuel: Ein narratologisch-philologischer Kommentar*. Trans. Johannes Klein. Stuttgart: Kohlhammer, 2009.

Barilan, Y. Michael. "Revisiting the Problem of Jewish Bioethics: The Case of Terminal Care." *Kennedy Institute of Ethics Journal* 13 (2003): 141–68.

Barilan, Y. Michael. "Beyond Consent: Homosexuality Through the Prism of Jewish Sexual Ethics." Unpublished MS, n.d.

Barnartt, Sharon, and Rachel Rotman. "Disability Policies and Protests in Israel." *Disability Studies Quarterly* 27 (Fall 2007). http://dsq-sds.org/article/view/42/42. Last retrieved February 22, 2020.

Baskin, Judith Reesa. "Male Piety, Female Bodies: Men, Women, and Ritual Immersion in Medieval Ashkenaz." *Jewish Law Association Studies* 17 (2007): 11–30.

Bauer, Axel W. "Der 'Weichselzopf' in medizinhistorischer Perspektive: Eigenständige Hautkrankheit oder mythologisches Konstrukt?" *Aktuelle Dermatologie* 30 (2004): 218–22.

Bauks, Michaela. "Nacktheit und Scham in Genesis 2–3." In *Zur Kulturgeschichte der Scham*, ed. Michaela Bauks and Martin Meyer, 17–34. Hamburg: Felix Meiner, 2011.

Bayor, Ronald H. *Encountering Ellis Island: How European Immigrants Entered America*. Baltimore: Johns Hopkins University Press, 2014.

Beddoe, John. "On the Physical Characteristics of the Jews." *Transactions of the Ethnological Society of London* 1 (1861): 222–37.

Bekhor Shor, Yosef. *Perusche Rabbi Yosef Bechor Schor Al Hatorah* (Hebr.) [Commentary on the Torah by Rabbi Joseph Bekhor Schor]. Ed. Yehoshafat Nevo. Jerusalem: Mosad ha-Rav Kuk, 1994.

"Beleuchtung der Protokolle der dritten Versammlung deutscher Rabbinen." *Der treue Zions-Wächter* 3 (1847): 201–3, 209–10, 217–18.

Bell, Alexander Graham. *Memoir upon the Formation of a Deaf Variety of the Human Race*. Washington, DC: National Academy of Sciences, 1883.

Belser, Julia Watts. "Reading Talmudic Bodies: Disability, Narrative, and the Gaze in Rabbinic Judaism." In *Disability in Judaism, Christianity and Islam: Sacred Texts, Historical Traditions, and Social Analysis*, ed. Darla Schumm and Michael Stoltzfus, 5–28. New York: Palgrave Macmillan, 2011.

Ben-Chorin, Schalom. *Jüdischer Glaube*. Tübingen: Mohr Siebeck, 1975.

Ben Joez, Schelomo. "Zwei die Frauen betreffende Gebräuche." *Wissenschaftliche Zeitschrift für jüdische Theologie* 3 (1837): 354–74.

Benedict, Ruth. *The Chrysanthemum and the Sword: Patterns of Japanese Culture*. New York: Houghton Mifflin, 2005. (Orig. pub. 1946.)

Benor, Sarah Bunin. "Talmid Chachams and Tsedeykeses: Language, Learnedness, and Masculinity Among Orthodox Jews." *Jewish Social Studies* 11, no. 1 (2004): 147–70.

Berger, David. *The Jewish-Christian Debate in the High Middle Ages: A Critical Edition of the Nizzahon Vetus with an Introduction, Translation and Commentary*. Philadelphia: Jewish Publication Society of America, 1979.

Berger, Natalia, ed. *Jews and Medicine: Religion, Culture and Science*. Tel Aviv: Beit Hatefutsoth, 1995.

Berger, Ruth. *Sexualität, Ehe und Familienleben in der jüdischen Moralliteratur (900–1900)*. Wiesbaden: Harrassowitz, 2003.

Bernfield, Tirtsah Levie. *Poverty and Welfare Among the Portuguese Jews in Early Modern Amsterdam*. Oxford: Littman Library of Jewish Civilization, 2012.

Beschorner, Friedrich. *Der Weichselzopf: Nach statistischen und physiologischen Beziehungen dargestellt*. Breslau: Ferdinand Hirt, 1843.

Besser, Max. "Das Hamburger Schauturnen." *Jüdische Turnzeitung* 1, no. 1 (1910): 2–5.

Bettelheim, Bruno. *Symbolic Wounds: Puberty Rites and the Envious Male*. Glencoe, IL: Free Press, 1954.

Beusterien, John. "Jewish Male Menstruation in Seventeenth-Century Spain." *Bulletin of the History of Medicine* 73 (1999): 447–56.

Bhabha, Homi K. *The Location of Culture.* London: Routledge, 1994.

Biale, David. *Eros and the Jews: From Biblical to Contemporary America.* New York: Basic Books, 1992a.

Biale, David. "Zionism as an Erotic Revolution." In *People of the Body: Jews and Judaism from an Embodied Perspective,* ed. Howard Eilberg-Schwartz, 283–306. Albany: State University of New York Press, 1992b.

Biale, David. *Blood and Belief: The Circulation of a Symbol Between Jews and Christians.* Berkeley: University of California Press, 2007.

Biale, Rachel. *Women and Jewish Law: The Essential Texts, Their History, and Their Relevance for Today.* New York: Schocken Books, 1995.

Biller, Peter. "Views of Jews from Paris around 1300: Christian or 'Scientific'?" In *Christianity and Judaism,* ed. Diana Wood, 187–208. Oxford: Blackwell, 1992.

Binder, Hartmut, ed. *Kafka-Handbuch.* Vol. 1. Stuttgart: J. B. Metzler, 1979.

Blecking, Diethelm. "Marxismus versus Muskeljudentum: Die jüdische Sportbewegung in Polen von den Anfängen bis nach dem Zweiten Weltkrieg." *SportZeit* 1 (2001): 1–52.

Blecking, Diethelm. "Jews and Sport in Poland Before the Second World War." In *Jews and the Sporting Life,* ed. Ezra Mendelsohn, 17–35. Oxford: Oxford University Press, 2008.

Bleich, J. David. *Judaism and Healing: Halakhic Perspectives.* Jersey City, NJ: Ktav, 2002.

Bleich, J. David. *Contemporary Halakhic Problems.* Vol. 3. New York: Ktav, 2013.

Bloch, Abraham P. *A Book of Jewish Ethical Concepts: Biblical and Postbiblical.* New York: Ktav, 1984.

Bloch, Iwan. *The Sexual Life of Our Time: A Complete Encyclopedia of the Sexual Sciences in Their Relation to Modern Civilization.* Trans. M. Eden Paul. New York: Falstaff, 1937.

Blum, Richard, and Louis Lamm. "Jüdische Kraft im Mittelalter." In *Makkabäa: Jüdisch-literarische Sammlung,* ed. Louis Lamm, 8–15. Berlin: Louis Lamm, 1916.

Blumenkranz, Bernhard. *Juden und Judentum in der mittelalterlichen Kunst.* Stuttgart: Kohlhammer, 1963.

Böckler, Annette M. "Mein Tod gehört nicht mir: Sich das Leben zu nehmen, ist im Judentum nicht erlaubt—denn über das Ende entscheidet Gott allein." *Jüdische Allgemeine,* January 23, 2014. http://www.juedische-allgemeine.de/article/view/id/18148. Last retrieved May 3, 2016.

Bodner, Allen. *When Boxing Was a Jewish Sport.* Albany: State University of New York Press, 2011.

Böhme, Gernot. *Leibsein als Aufgabe: Leibphilosophie in pragmatischer Hinsicht.* Kusterdingen: Graue Edition, 2003.

Boldt, Julius. *Trachoma.* Trans. J. Herbert Parsons. London: Hodder and Stoughton, 1904.

Bonfil, Robert. "Jews, Christians, and Sex in Renaissance Italy: A Historiographical Problem." *Jewish History* 26 (2012): 101–11.

Book of Jubilees. https://www.sefaria.org/Book_of_Jubilees?lang=bi. Last retrieved August 13, 2019.

Borck, Cornelius. "Communicating the Modern Body: Fritz Kahn's Popular Images of Human Physiology as an Industrialized World." *Canadian Journal of Communication* 32 (2007): 495–520.

Börner-Klein, Dagmar. *Das Alphabet des Ben Sira: Hebräisch-deutsche Textausgabe mit einer Interpretation.* Wiesbaden: Marix Verlag, 2007.

Borrmann, Norbert. *Kunst und Physiognomik: Menschendeutung und Menschendarstellung im Abendland.* Cologne: DuMont, 1994.

Bos, Gerrit. *Novel Medical and General Hebrew Terminology from the 13th Century: Translations by Hillel (Ben Samuel of Verona), Moses Ben Samuel Ibn Tibbon, Shem Tov Ben Isaac of Tortosa, and Zerahyah Ben Isaac Ben She'altiel Hen.* Oxford: Oxford University Press, 2011.

Boswell, John. *Christianity, Social Tolerance, and Homosexuality: Gay People in Western Europe from the Beginning of the Christian Era to the Fourteenth Century.* Chicago: University of Chicago Press, 1980.

Boteach, Shmuley. *Kosher Sex.* New York: Crown, 1999.

Boyarin, Daniel. *Carnal Israel: Reading Sex in Talmudic Culture.* Berkeley: University of California Press, 1993.

Boyarin, Daniel. "Homotopia: The Feminized Jewish Man and the Lives of Women in Late Antiquity." *Differences* 7 (1995): 41–81.

Boyarin, Daniel. *Unheroic Conduct: The Rise of Heterosexuality and the Invention of the Jewish Man*. Berkeley: University of California Press, 1997.

Boyarin, Daniel. "Response to Leon Wieseltier." *Jewish Quarterly Review* 95 (2005): 443–46.

Boyarin, Jonathan, and Daniel Boyarin, eds. *Jews and Other Differences: The New Jewish Cultural Studies*. Minneapolis: University of Minnesota Press, 1997.

Brawer, Naftali. "What Should I Do About My Tattoos Before Converting?" TheJC.com, June 3, 2010. http://www.thejc.com/judaism/rabbi-i-have-a-problem/32459/what-should-i-do-about-my -tattoos-converting. Last retrieved April 5, 2016.

Brayer, Menachem M. *The Jewish Woman in Rabbinic Literature: A Psychohistorical Perspective*. Hoboken, NJ: Ktav, 1986.

Brenner, Michael. "Zwischen Marienbad und Norderney: Der Kurort als 'Jewish Space.'" In *Jüdischer Almanach*, 119–37. Frankfurt/M.: Suhrkamp, 2001.

Brenner, Michael, and Sabine Ullmann, eds. *Die Juden in Schwaben*. Munich: Walter de Gruyter, 2013.

Brinks, Michael J. "The *Altercatio Ecclesiae et Synagogae* as a Late Antique Anti-Jewish Polemic." Master's thesis, Western Michigan University, 2009. https://scholarworks.wmich.edu/masters_ theses/248/. Last retrieved May 16, 2019.

Bristow, E. J. *Prostitution and Prejudice: The Jewish Fight Against White Slavery, 1870–1939*. Oxford: Oxford University Press, 1982.

Brocke, Bernhard vom, and Hugo Laitko, eds. *Die Kaiser-Wilhelm-/Max-Planck-Gesellschaft und ihre Institute: Studien zu ihrer Geschichte: Das Harnack-Prinzip*. Berlin: Walter de Gruyter, 1996.

Brod, Max. *Streitbares Leben*. Munich: Kindler, 1960.

Broder, Henry M. "Die schöne Wehrlosigkeit." *Der Spiegel*, no. 1 (1996): 36–37.

Brooks, Beatrice Allard. "The Babylonian Marking of Slaves." *Journal of the American Oriental Association* 42 (1922): 80–90.

Browne, Thomas. *Pseudoxia Epidemica*. 6th ed. London: Nath. Ekins, 1672. http://penelope.uchic ago.edu/pseudodoxia/pseudo410.html. Last retrieved August 13, 2014.

Browning, Don S., and Marcia J. Bunge, eds. *Children and Childhood in World Religions: Primary Sources and Texts*. New Brunswick, NJ: Rutgers University Press, 2009.

Broyde, Michael J. "Hair Covering and Jewish Law." *Tradition* 42, no. 3 (2009): 97–179.

Broyde, Michael J. "Hair Covering and Jewish Law: A Response." *Tradition* 43, no. 2 (2010): 89–108.

Brüll, N. "Die Haarbedeckung der jüdischen Frau." *Jahrbücher für Jüdische Geschichte und Litteratur* 8 (1887): 51–52.

Buber, Martin. *Tales of the Hasidim: The Later Masters*. Trans. Olga Marx. New York: Schocken, 1948.

Buchholz, Kai, Rita Latocha, Hilke Peckmann, and Klaus Wolbert, eds. *Die Lebensreform: Entwürfe zur Neugestaltung von Leben und Kunst um 1900*. Vol. 1. Darmstadt: H. J. Häußer, 2001.

Buffon, Georges-Louis Leclerc, comte de. *Buffon's Natural History, Containing a Theory of the Earth. . . .* Trans. J. S. Barr. 10 vols. London: H. D. Symonds, 1797–1807.

Burstyn, Shai. "Jewish Singing and Boxing in Georgian England." In *Studies in Honour of Israel Adler*, ed. Eliyahu Schleifer and Edwin Seroussi, 425–41. Jerusalem: Magnes Press, 2002.

Butzer, Evi, Nathanja Hüttenmeister, and Wolfgang Treue. "'Ich will euch sagen von einem bösen Stück . . .': Ein jiddisches Lied über sexuelle Vergehen und deren Bestrafung aus dem frühen 17. Jahrhundert." *Aschkenas* 15 (2005): 25–53.

Buxtorf, Johann. *The Jewish Synagogue*. London: T. Roycroft, 1657.

Caesarius of Heisterbach. *Dialogus miraculorum*. Vol. 1. Ed. Horst Schneider. Turnhout: Brepols, 2009.

Cantor, Aviva. *Jewish Women / Jewish Men: The Legacy of Patriarchy in Jewish Life*. San Francisco: HarperSanFrancisco, 1995.

Cardoso, Isaac. *Las excelencias de los Hebreos*. Amsterdam: David de Castro Tartas, 1679.

Carlebach, Elisheva. "Pinkas Shamash Altona (1766–1767)." Early Modern Workshop: Resources in Jewish History, 2006. http://wesscholar.wesleyan.edu/emw/emw2006/emw2006/6/. Last retrieved February 10 , 2020.

Carlebach, Salomon. "Haarverhüllung des jüdischen Weibes." In *Festschrift zum 70. Geburtstag David Hoffmanns*, ed. Simon Eppenstein, Meier Hildesheimer, and Joseph Wohlgemuth, 454–59 (German), 218–47 (Hebrew). Berlin: Louis Lamm, 1914.

Casparson, Johann Wilhelm Christian Gustav. "Von deutscher Policey und der Hessischen insbesondere." *Journal von und für Deutschland* 2, no. 4:1 (1785): 281–97.

Castle, Eduard. *Der große Unbekannte: Das Leben von Charles Sealsfield (Karl Postl); Briefe und Aktenstücke*. Vienna: Manutiuspresse, 1952.

Chamberlain, Houston Stewart. *Foundations of the Nineteenth Century*. Trans. John Lees. New York: J. Lane, 1910.

Chapman, David W. *Ancient Jewish and Christian Perceptions of Crucifixion*. Tübingen: Mohr Siebeck, 2008.

Christ, Michaela. "(Un-)sichtbare Körper: Über die Wirkungsmacht von jüdischen Körperbildern während des Nationalsozialismus." *Medaon. Magazin für Jüdisches Leben in Forschung und Bildung* 2 (2008): 1–15.

Chrysostom, John. *Against the Jews*. Homily 2. http://www.tertullian.org/fathers/chrysostom_adversus_judaeos_02_homily2.htm. Last retrieved August 9, 2019.

Chwolson, Daniil Abramovic. *Die Blutanklage und sonstige mittelalterliche Beschuldigungen der Juden*. Frankfurt/M.: J. Kaufmann, 1901.

Citron, Aryeh. "Embalming and Autopsies in Jewish Law." *Parsha*, January 2, 2015. http://yeshivah college.com/?p = 1178. Last retrieved May 5, 2016.

Clark, Kenneth. *The Nude: A Study in Ideal Form*. New York: Pantheon, 1956.

Clendening, Logan. "Guide and Chart for the Human Interior." Review of *Man in Structure and Function*, by Fritz Kahn. *New York Times*, April 4, 1943.

Cohen, Mark R. *The Voice of the Poor in the Middle Ages: An Anthology of Documents from the Cairo Geniza*. Princeton, NJ: Princeton University Press, 2005.

Cohen, Shaye J. D. *The Beginnings of Jewishness: Boundaries, Varieties, Uncertainties*. Berkeley: University of California Press, 1999.

Cohen, Shaye J. D. *Why Aren't Jewish Women Circumcised? Gender and Covenant in Judaism*. Berkeley: University of California Press, 2005.

Cohen, Tobias. *Maase Towia* (Hebr.) [The Work of Tobias]. Venice: Nella Stamperia Bragadina, 1708. http://www.hebrewbooks.org/19607. Last retrieved August 20, 2019.

Coleman-Brueckheimer, Kate, and Simon Dein. "Health Care Behaviours and Beliefs in Hasidic Jewish Populations: A Systematic Review of the Literature." *Journal of Religion and Health* 50 (2011): 422–36.

Collin, Elias. *Die Beschneidung der Israeliten und ihre Nachbehandlung*. Leipzig: Ludwig Schreck, 1842.

Cooper, Aaron. "No Longer Invisible: Gay and Lesbian Jews Build a Movement." *Journal of Homosexuality* 18 (1989/90): 83–94.

Coryat, Thomas. *Coryat's Crudities....* Vol. 1. Glasgow: J. MacLehose and Sons, 1905.

Crane, Jonathan K. "Shameful Ambivalences: Dimensions of Rabbinic Shame." *AJS Review* 35 (2011): 61–84.

Crane, Jonathan K. "Praying to Die: Medicine and Liturgy." *Journal of Religious Ethics* 43 (2015): 1–27.

Cress, Sebastian. *Dissertatio inauguralis medica de plica German: Wichtel-Zopff*. Heidelberg: Ammonius, 1682.

Cziborra, Pascal. *Frauen im KZ*. Bielefeld: Lorbeer Verlag, 2010.

Dalman, Gustaf. *Jesus Christ in the Talmud, Midrash, Zohar, and the Liturgy of the Synagogue*. Cambridge: Deighton, Bell, 1893.

Darby, Robert. *A Surgical Temptation: The Demonization of the Foreskin and the Rise of Circumcision in Britain*. Chicago: University of Chicago Press, 2005.

Das Groß Planeten Buch, sampt der Geomanci, Physiognomi vnd Chiromanci.... Straßburg: Josiam Rihel, 1590.

Darmaun, Jacques. *Thomas Mann, Deutschland und die Juden*. Tübingen: Max Niemeyer, 2003.

Davidman, Lynn. "The Transformation of Bodily Practices Among Religious Defectors." In *Embodied Resistance: Challenging the Norms, Breaking the Rules*, ed. Chris Bobel and Samantha Kwan, 209–19. Nashville: Vanderbilt University Press, 2011.

Davidovich-Eshed, Avital. " 'How Then Could I Gaze at a Virgin?' The Concept of Virginity in Medieval Ashkenazi-Jewish Culture in Christendom." PhD diss., Tel Aviv University, 2014. https://www.academia.edu/9621330. Last retrieved December 28, 2015.

Debschitz, Uta von, and Thilo von Debschitz. *Fritz Kahn: Man Machine / Maschine Mensch*. New York: Springer, 2009.

Dee, David. " 'The Hefty Hebrew': Boxing and British-Jewish Identity, 1890–1960." *Sport in History* 32 (2012): 361–81.

Deusel, Antje Yael. *Mein Bund, den ihr bewahren sollt: Religionsgesetzliche und medizinische Aspekte der Beschneidung*. Freiburg/Brsg.: Herder, 2012.

Deutsch, Israel. *Zer'a yisrael: . . . Proben aus dem literarischen Nachlasse*. Ed. Abraham Deutsch and David Deutsch. Gleiwitz: V. Troplowitz, 1855.

Diemling, Maria. " 'As the Jews Like to Eat Garlick': Garlic in Christian-Jewish Polemical Discourse in Early Modern Germany." In *Food and Judaism*, ed. Leonard J. Greenspoon, Ronald A. Simkins, and Gerald Shapiro, 215–34. Omaha, NE: Creighton University Press, 2004.

Diemling, Maria. "Mit Leib und Seele? Überlegungen zum Körperbild jüdischer Konvertiten in der Frühen Neuzeit." *Aschkenas* 15 (2005): 399–418.

Diemling, Maria. " 'Daß man unter so viel tausend Menschen so fort einen Juden erkennen kann': Johann Jacob Schudt und der jüdische Körper." In *Die Frankfurter Judengasse: Jüdisches Leben in der Frühen Neuzeit*, ed. Fritz Backhaus, Gisela Engel, Robert Liberles, and Margarete Schlüter, 77–89. Frankfurt/M.: Societätsverlag, 2006.

Diemling, Maria, and Giuseppe Veltri, eds. *The Jewish Body: Corporeality, Society, and Identity in the Renaissance and Early Modern Period*. Leiden: Brill, 2009.

Dietrich, Jan. *Der Tod von eigener Hand: Studien zum Suizid im Alten Testament, Alten Ägypten und Alten Orient*. Tübingen: Mohr Siebeck, 2016.

Dinter, Artur. *Die Sünde wider das Blut*. 10th ed. Leipzig: Matthes & Thost, 1920.

Dohrn, Verena. *Jüdische Eliten im Russischen Reich: Aufklärung und Integration im 19. Jahrhundert*. Cologne: Böhlau, 2008.

Dorff, Elliot N. *Matters of Life and Death: A Jewish Approach to Modern Medical Ethics*. Philadelphia: Jewish Publication Society, 2003.

Dorff, Elliot N., and Louis E. Newman, eds. *Jewish Choices, Jewish Voices: Body*. Philadelphia: Jewish Publication Society, 2008.

Dorman, Johanna. *The Blemished Body: Deformity and Disability in the Qumran Scrolls*. Groningen: Rijksuniversiteit Groningen, 2007.

Drake, Susanna. "Sexing the Jew: Early Christian Constructions of Jewishness." PhD diss., Duke University, 2008.

Drake, Susanna. *Slandering the Jew: Sexuality and Difference in Early Christian Texts*. Philadelphia: University of Pennsylvania Press, 2013.

Dudulaeus, Chrysostomus. *Gründliche und warhafftige Relation, Von einem Juden, Namens Ahasvero Von Jerusalem; Der, von der Zeit deß gecreutzigten Herrn Jesu Christi, durch sonderbare Schickung, zu einem lebendigen Zeugnuß in der Welt herum gehen muß. . . .* Nuremberg: Fürst, n.d. [ca. 1635].

Duerr, Hans Peter. *Nacktheit und Scham*. Frankfurt/M.: Suhrkamp, 1988.

Duerr, Hans Peter. *Obszönität und Gewalt*. Frankfurt/M.: Suhrkamp, 1993.

Dvorjetski, Estée. *Leisure, Pleasure and Healing: Spa Culture and Medicine in Ancient Eastern Mediterranean*. Leiden: Brill, 2007.

Eckart, Wolfgang U., and Robert Jütte. *Medizingeschichte: Eine Einführung*. 2nd rev. ed. Cologne: Böhlau, 2014.

Efron, John M. *Defenders of the Race: Jewish Doctors and Race Science in Fin-de-Siècle Europe*. New Haven, CT: Yale University Press, 1994.

Efron, John M. "Images of the Body: Three Medical Views from the Jewish Enlightenment." *Bulletin for the History of Medicine* 69 (1995): 349–66.

Efron, John M. "Der reine und der schmutzige Jude." In *"Der schejne Jid": Das Bild des "jüdischen Körpers" in Mythos und Ritual*, ed. Sander L. Gilman, Robert Jütte, and Gabriele Kohlbauer-Fritz, 75–85. Vienna: Picus, 1998.

Efron, John M. *Medicine and the German Jews: A History.* New Haven, CT: Yale University Press, 2001.

Efron, John M. *German Jewry and the Allure of the Sephardic.* Princeton, NJ: Princeton University Press, 2016.

Eidelberg, Shlomo. *The Jews and the Crusaders: The Hebrew Chronicles of the First and Second Crusades.* Madison: University of Wisconsin Press, 1977.

Eilberg-Schwartz, Howard, ed. *People of the Body: Jews and Judaism from an Embodied Perspective.* Albany: State University of New York Press, 1992.

Eilberg-Schwartz, Howard. *God's Phallus and Other Problems for Men and Monotheism.* Boston: Beacon Press, 1994.

Eilenburg, Christian Heinrich. *Kurzer Entwurf der königlichen Naturalienkammer zu Dresden.* Dresden: Waltherische Buchhandlung, 1755.

Eisenstadt, H. Ludwig. "Methoden und Ergebnisse der jüdischen Krankheitsstatistik." *Zeitschrift für Psychotherapie und medizinische Psychologie* 7 (1916/19): 128–54.

Elbogen, Ismar. *Der jüdische Gottesdienst in seiner geschichtlichen Entwicklung.* 3rd ed. Frankfurt/M.: J. Kauffmann, 1931. Reprint, Hildesheim: G. Olms, 1967.

Elsaghe, Yahya. *Thomas Mann und die kleinen Unterschiede: Zur erzählerischen Imagination des Anderen.* Cologne: Böhlau, 2004.

Encyclopädisches Wörterbuch der Staatsarzneikunde. Ed. Gottlieb Kraus and W. Pichler. Vol. 1. Erlangen: Ferdinand Enke, 1872.

Engländer, Martin. *Die auffallend häufigen Krankheitserscheinungen der jüdischen Rasse.* Vienna: J. L. Pollak, 1902.

Epstein, Ephraim M. "Have the Jews Any Immunity from Certain Diseases?" *Medical and Surgical Reporter* 30 (1874): 342–44.

Epstein, Louis M. *Sex Laws and Customs in Judaism.* New York: Bloch, 1948.

Erb, Rainer. "Die Wahrnehmung der Physiognomie der Juden: Die Nase." In *Das Bild des Juden in der Volks- und Jugendliteratur vom 18. Jahrhundert bis 1945*, ed. Heinrich Pleticha, 107–26. Würzburg: Königshausen & Neumann, 1985.

Esquirol, Jean Étienne Dominique. *Die Geisteskrankheiten: In Beziehung zur Medizin und Staatsarznei-kunde.* Trans. W. Bernhard. Vol. 1. Berlin: Voss'sche Buchhandlung, 1838.

Ettinger, Yair. "Hitpatchut chadascha bemavak charedi neged nituach gufot" (Hebr.) [New Development in Religious Opposition to Dissection]. *Ha'aretz*, June 21, 2006.

Euchel, Isaak. *Reb Henoch; oder, Woß tut me damit: Eine jüdische Komödie der Aufklärungszeit.* Ed. Marion Aptroot and Roland Gruschka. Hamburg: Buske, 2004.

Evel Rabati (Hebr.). Ed. Ephraim Kaminka. Tel Aviv: Hoza'at ha-oved ha-dati, 1949. http://www.he-brewbooks.org/38248. Last retrieved March 31, 2016.

Eybeschütz, Jonathan. *Ahawat Jonathan* (Hebr.) [The Love of Jonathan]. Hamburg: Conrad Jacob, 1765.

Fairchild, Amy L. *Science at the Borders: Immigrant Medical Inspection and the Shaping of the Modern Industrial Labor Force.* Baltimore: Johns Hopkins University Press, 2003.

Faltin, Thomas. *Im Angesicht des Todes: Das KZ-Außenlager Echterdingen 1944/45 und der Leidensweg der 600 Häftlinge.* Filderstadt: Stadtarchiv Leinfelden-Echterdingen, 2008.

Farrell, Jennifer. "An Examination of Sumptuary Laws, Presentation of Costume, and Jewish Identities in Renaissance Italy." 2014. https://www.academia.edu/5793953/An_Examination_of_Sump tuary_Laws_Presentation_of_Costume_and_Jewish_Identities_in_Renaissance_Italy. Last retrieved April 5, 2016.

Feinberg, Anat. "Shylock." In *Antisemitismus: Vorurteile und Mythen*, ed. Julius H. Schoeps and Joachim Schlör, 119–26. Munich: Piper, 1995.

Feiner, Shmuel. *The Origins of Jewish Secularization in Eighteenth-Century Europe.* Trans. Chaya Naor. Philadelphia: University of Pennsylvania Press, 2011.

Feinstein, Moshe. *Responsa of Rav Moshe Feinstein.* Vol. 1, *Care of the Critically Ill.* Trans. and commentary Moshe Dovid Tendler. Hoboken, NJ: Ktav, 1996.

Feldman, David M. *Marital Relations, Birth Control, and Abortion in Jewish Law.* New York: Schocken, 1974.

Felsenstein, Frank. *Anti-Semitic Stereotypes: A Paradigm of Otherness in English Popular Culture, 1660–1830.* Baltimore: Johns Hopkins University Press, 1995.

Fenner, Justus. *Freimüthige Briefe über Schwalbach, dessen Quellen und Umgebung: Zur Unterhaltung für Ärzte und Laien.* Frankfurt/M.: Jägersche Papier-, Buch- und Landkartenhandlung, 1807.

Feuer, Lewis S. *The Scientific Intellectual: The Psychological and Sociological Origins of Modern Science.* New York: Basic Books, 1963.

Figdor, Moritz. "Halacha und Fragen am Ende des Lebens Anwendung der traditionellen jüdischen Lehre auf moderne Fragestellungen am Beispiel des terminalen Patienten in Justiz und Legislative im Staat Israel." Med. diss., LMU Munich, 2015.

Finkelstein. Louis. *Jewish Self-Government in the Middle Ages.* 2nd ed. New York: P. Feldheim, 1964.

Fischer, Anna. *Erzwungener Freitod: Spuren und Zeugnisse von in den Freitod getriebener Juden der Jahre 1938–1945 in Berlin.* Berlin: Text-Verlag, 2009.

Fischer, Jens Malte. "Deutschsprachige Phantastik zwischen Décadence und Faschismus." In *Phaïcon 3, Almanach der phantastischen Literatur,* ed. Rein A. Zondergeld, 93–130. Frankfurt/M.: Insel, 1978.

Fishberg, Maurice. *Die Rassenmerkmale der Juden.* Munich: E. Reinhardt, 1913.

Fishberg, Maurice. *The Jews: A Study of Race and Environment.* London: Walter Scott; New York: Scribner's, 1911.

Fishkoff, Sue. "Erde statt Asche: Immer mehr Menschen lassen sich nach dem Tod verbrennen: Rabbiner versuchen, diesem Trend entgegenzusteuern." *Jüdische Allgemeine,* May 12, 2010. http://www.juedische-allgemeine.de/article/view/id/7417. Last retrieved June 10, 2015.

Fonrobert, Charlotte Elisheva. *Menstrual Purity: Rabbinic and Christian Reconstructions of Biblical Gender.* Stanford, CA: Stanford University Press, 2000.

Fonrobert, Charlotte Elisheva. "On 'Carnal Israel' and the Consequences: Talmudic Studies Since Foucault." *Jewish Quarterly Review* 95 (2005): 462–69.

Foucault, Michel. *The History of Sexuality.* Vol. 1, *An Introduction.* Trans. Robert Hurley. New York: Vintage (Random House), 1980.

Fraenkel-Goldschmidt, Chava, ed. *The Historical Writings of Joseph of Rosheim: Leader of Jewry in Early Modern Germany.* Trans., introd., and commentary Naomi Schendowich. English edition ed. and afterword Adam Shear. Leiden: Brill, 2006.

Fränkel, David. "Über die religiöse Bildung der Frauenzimmer jüdischen Glaubens (Fragment aus einer freundschaftlichen Korrespondenz)." *Sulamith* 1 (1806): 473–88.

Frankel, Jonathan. *Jews and Gender: The Challenge to Hierarchy.* New York: Oxford University Press, 2000.

Franz, Matthias. "Ritual, Traum, Kindeswohl." *Frankfurter Allgemeine Zeitung,* July 9, 2012:7.

Franz, Matthias, ed. *Die Beschneidung von Jungen: Ein trauriges Vermächtnis.* Göttingen: Vandenhoeck & Ruprecht, 2014.

Frerichs, Friedrich Theodor von. *Über den Diabetes.* Berlin: A. Hirschwald, 1884.

Freud, Sigmund. *Moses and Monotheism.* Trans. Katherine Jones. New York: Vintage Books (Knopf), 1939.

Freud, Sigmund. *The Standard Edition of the Complete Psychological Works of Sigmund Freud.* Trans. and ed. James Strachey, in collaboration with Anna Freud, assisted by Alix Strachey, Alan Tyson, and Angela Richards. 24 vols. London: Hogarth Press and the Institute of Psycho-Analysis, 1953–74.

Freud, Sigmund. *Wit and Its Relation to the Unconscious.* Trans. A. A. Brill. London: Routledge, 1999.

Freud, Sigmund. *The Joke and Its Relation to the Unconscious.* Trans. Joyce Crick and Adam Philipps. London: Penguin, 2002.

Freud, Sigmund. *The Interpretation of Dreams*. Trans. A. A. Brill. Mineola: Dover, 2015.

Frey, Winfried. "Ein geborner Jud von Jerusalem: Überlegungen zur Entstehung der Ahasver-Figur." In *Von Enoch bis Kafka: Festschrift für Karl E. Grözinger zum 60. Geburtstag*, ed. Manfred Voigts, 207–17. Wiesbaden: Harrassowitz, 2002.

Freytag, Gustav. *Debit and Credit*. Trans. L. C. C. New York: Harper and Brothers, 1863.

Friedenwald, Harry. *The Jews and Medicine: Essays*. 2 vols. Baltimore: Johns Hopkins University Press, 1944. Reprint, Hoboken, NJ: Ktav, 1967.

Friedlaender, Salomo / Mynona. *Grotesken (Teil 1)*. Ed. Detlef Thiel and Hartmut Geerken. Herrsching: Waitawhile, 2008.

Friedländer, Saul. *Das Dritte Reich und die Juden: 1933–1945*. Trans. Martin Pfeiffer. Munich: C. H. Beck, 2010.

Friedman, Dayle A. *Jewish Visions for Aging: A Professional Guide for Fostering Wholeness*. Woodstock, VT: Jewish Lights, 2008.

Friedman, Towiah. *Das Vermögen der ermordeten Juden Europas: Dokumentensammlung*. Haifa: Institute of Documentation in Israel for the Investigation of Nazi War Crimes, 1997.

Friedman, Yaakov. "Defining a Goses." In *Medicine and Jewish Law*, ed. Fred Rosner, 2:105–15. Northvale, NJ: Jason Aronson, 1993.

Friese, [?]. "Über die Entstehung der Krätze in den verschiedenen Gewerben." *Wochenschrift für die gesammte Heilkunde* 46 (1836): 721–29.

Fritzen, Florentine. *Gesünder leben: Die Lebensreformbewegung im 20. Jahrhundert*. Stuttgart: Franz Steiner, 2006.

Frübis, Hildegard. "Porträt und Typus: Repräsentationen 'der' Jüdin in der Moderne." In *Bilder des Jüdischen: Selbst- und Fremdzuschreibungen im 20. und 21. Jahrhundert*, ed. Juliane Sucker and Lea Wohl von Haselberg, 33–56. Berlin: Walter de Gruyter, 2013.

Fuchs, Eduard. *Illustrierte Sittengeschichte vom Mittelalter bis zur Gegenwart: Renaissance*. Munich: Albert Langen, 1909.

Fuchs, Eduard. *Die Juden in der Karikatur: Ein Beitrag zur Kulturgeschichte*. Munich: Albert Langen, 1921.

Fuchs, Yitzchak Yaacov. *Halichos Bas Yisrael: A Woman's Guide to Jewish Observance*. Oak Park, MI: Targum, 1985.

Gage, John. "Colour in History: Relative and Absolute." *Art History* 1 (1978): 104–30.

Gans, Evelien. "'Hamas, Hamas, All Jews to the Gas': The History and Significance of an Antisemitic Slogan in the Netherlands, 1945–2010." In *Perceptions of the Holocaust in Europe and Muslim Communities: Sources, Comparisons and Educational Challenges*, ed. Günther Jikeli and Joëlle Allouche-Benayoun, 85–103. Dordrecht: Springer, 2013.

Gaster, Moses. *The Exempla of the Rabbis*. New York: Ktav, 1968.

Gay, Peter. *My German Question: Growing Up in Nazi Berlin*. New Haven, CT: Yale University Press, 1998.

Gay, Ruth. *The Jews of Germany: A Historical Portrait*. New Haven, CT: Yale University Press, 1992.

Geiger, Abraham. "Die Stellung des Weibes in dem Judenthume unserer Zeit." *Wissenschaftliche Zeitschrift für jüdische Theologie* 3 (1837): 1–14.

Geiger, Abraham. *Jüdische Dichtungen der spanischen und italienischen Schule*. Leipzig: Oskar Leiner, 1857.

Geiger, Ludwig. "Vor hundert Jahren: 4 Aktenstücke über die frühe Beerdigung der Todten." *Zeitschrift für die Geschichte der Juden in Deutschland* 3 (1889): 211–23.

Geller, Jay. "(G)nos(e)logy: The Cultural Structure of the Other." In *People of the Body: Jews and Judaism from an Embodied Perspective*, ed. Howard Eilberg-Schwartz, 234–82. New York: State University of New York Press, 1992.

Gerber, Barbara. *Jud Süß: Aufstieg und Fall im frühen 18. Jahrhundert; Ein Beitrag zur Historischen Antisemitismus- und Rezeptionsforschung*. Hamburg: Hans Christians, 1990.

Gillerman, Sharon. "More Than Skin Deep: Histories of the Modern Jewish Body." *Jewish Quarterly Review* 95 (2005): 470–78.

Gillerman, Sharon. "Samson in Wien: Die theatralische Inszenierung jüdischer Männlichkeit." In *Sport: Jüdischer Almanach*, ed. Gisela Dachs, 42–57. Berlin: Suhrkamp, 2011.

Gillman, Neill. *The Death of Death: Resurrection and Immortality in Jewish Thought*. Woodstock, VT: Jewish Lights, 1997.

Gilman, Sander L. *Sexuality: An Illustrated History*. New York: Wiley, 1989.

Gilman, Sander L. "Anti-Semitism and the Body in Psychoanalysis." *Social Research* 57 (1990): 993–1017.

Gilman, Sander L. *The Jew's Body*. New York: Routledge, 1991.

Gilman, Sander L. "The Jewish Body: A Foot-Note." In *People of the Body: Jews and Judaism from an Embodied Perspective*, ed. Howard Eilberg-Schwartz, 223–41. Albany: State University of New York Press, 1992.

Gilman, Sander L. *The Case of Sigmund Freud*. Baltimore: Johns Hopkins University Press, 1993a.

Gilman, Sander L. *Freud, Race and Gender*. Princeton, NJ: Princeton University Press, 1993b.

Gilman, Sander L. "Der jüdische Körper." In *Antisemitismus: Vorurteile und Mythen*, ed. Julius H. Schoeps and Joachim Schlör, 167–79. Munich: Piper, 1995a.

Gilman, Sander L. "Der jüdische Körper: Gedanken zum physischen Anderssein der Juden." In *Die Macht der Bilder: Antisemitische Vorurteile und Mythen*, ed. Elisabeth Klamper et al., 168–79. Vienna: Jüdisches Museum der Stadt Wien, 1995b.

Gilman, Sander L. *Picturing Health and Illness: Images of Identity and Difference*. Baltimore: Johns Hopkins University Press, 1995c.

Gilman, Sander L. "Decircumcision: The First Aesthetic Surgery." *Modern Judaism* 17 (1997): 201–10.

Gilman, Sander L., Robert Jütte, and Gabriele Kohlbauer-Fritz, eds. *"Der schejne Jid": Das Bild des "jüdischen Körpers" in Mythos und Ritual*. Vienna: Picus, 1998.

Ginsburg, Christian David. *The Kabbalah: Its Doctrines, Development, and Literature*. 2nd ed. London: G. Routledge & Sons, 1920.

Ginsburger, Moses. "Les juifs et l'art militaire au moyen âge." *Revue des études juives* 88 (1929): 156–66.

Glickman, Nora. *Jewish White Slave Trade and the Untold Story of Raquel Liberman*. New York: Garland, 2000.

Glückel of Hameln. *The Memoirs of Glückel of Hameln*. Trans. and notes Marvin Lowenthal. Introd. Robert R. Rosen. New York: Schocken, 1977.

Gluzman, Michael. "Verwirrung der Geschlechter auf Jüdisch: Der Zionismus und das Schauspiel des grotesken Leibes." In *Der Differenz auf der Spur: Frauen und Gender in Aschkenas*, ed. Christiane E. Müller and Andrea Schatz, 231–58. Berlin: Metropol Verlag, 2004.

Goitein, S. D. *A Mediterranean Society: The Jewish Communities of the World Portrayed in the Documents of the Cairo Geniza*. 5 vols. Berkeley: University of California Press, 1999.

Golan, Serge. "Le scandale dans les transports funéraires vers Israël!" *HaModia*, June 22, 2011. http://www.hamodia.fr/article.php?id=2217. Last retrieved May 5, 2016.

Goldberg, Sylvie-Anne. *Crossing the Jabbok: Illness and Death in Ashkenazi Judaism in Sixteenth-Through Nineteenth-Century Prague*. Berkeley: University of California Press, 1996.

Goldblatt, Roy. "As Plain as the Nose on Your Face: The Nose as Organ of Othering." *Amerikastudien/American Studies* 48 (2003): 563–76.

Goldenberg, David M. *The Curse of Ham: Race and Slavery in Early Judaism, Christianity, and Islam*. Princeton, NJ: Princeton University Press, 2003.

Goldman, Yossy. "Warum wir koscher bleiben." Jüdische.info, n.d. http://www.de.chabad.org/library/article_cdo/aid/656527/jewish/Warum-wir-koscher-bleiben.htm. Last retrieved February 10, 2020.

Goldstein, Alice, Susan Cotts Watkins, and Ann Rosen Spector. "Childhood Health-Care Practices Among Italians and Jews in the United States, 1910–1940." *Health Transition Review* 4 (1994): 45–62.

Gollaher, David L. *Circumcision: A History of the World's Most Controversial Surgery*. New York: Basic Books, 2000.

Goodman, Richard M. *Genetic Disorders Among the Jewish People.* Baltimore: Johns Hopkins University Press, 1979.

Gorsetman, Chaya Rosenfeld, and Elana Maryles Sztokman. *Educating in the Divine Image: Gender Issues in Orthodox Jewish Day Schools.* Waltham, NH: Brandeis University Press, 2013.

Goshen-Gottstein, Alon. "The Body as Image of God in Rabbinic Literature." *Harvard Theological Review* 87 (1994): 171–95.

Gotzmann, Andreas. *Jüdische Autonomie in der Frühen Neuzeit: Recht und Gemeinschaft im deutschen Judentum.* Göttingen: Vandenhoeck & Ruprecht, 2008.

Gow, Andrew Colin. *The Red Jews: Antisemitism in the Apocalyptic Age, 1200–1600.* Leiden: Brill, 1995.

Grab, Walter. " 'Jüdischer Selbsthaß' und jüdische Selbstachtung in der deutschen Literatur und Publizistik 1890 bis 1933." In *Conditio Judaica: Judentum, Antisemitismus und deutschsprachige Literatur vom 18. Jahrhundert bis zum Ersten Weltkrieg,* ed. Horst Denkler and Hans Otto Horch, 313–36. Tübingen: Niemeyer, 1989.

Gracer, Bonnie. "What the Rabbis Heard: Deafness in the *Mishnah.*" In *Jewish Perspectives on Theology and the Human Experience of Disability,* ed. Judith Z. Abrams and William C. Gaventa, 85–99. Binghamton, NY: Haworth Pastoral Press 2006.

Graetz, Heinrich. *Geschichte der Juden.* Vol. 1. Leipzig: O. Leiner, 1874.

Graupe, Heinz Mosche. *Die Statuten der drei Gemeinden Altona, Hamburg und Wandsbek: Quellen zur jüdischen Gemeindeorganisation im 17. und 18. Jahrhundert.* 2 vols. Hamburg: Hans Christians, 1973.

Graus, František. *Pest—Geissler—Judenmorde: Das 14. Jahrhundert als Krisenzeit.* 2nd rev. ed. Göttingen: Vandenhoeck & Ruprecht, 1988.

Graybill, Cristina Rhiannon. "Men in Travail: Masculinity and the Problems of the Body in the Hebrew Prophets." PhD diss., University of California, Berkeley, 2012.

Grillparzer, Franz. *The Jewess of Toledo; Esther.* Trans. Arthur Burkhard. Yarmouth Port, MA: Register Press, 1953.

Grillparzer, Franz. *Die Jüdin von Toledo: Historisches Trauerspiel in fünf Aufzügen.* Stuttgart: Reclam, 1992.

Grobman, Alex. "Attempts at Resistance in the Camps." In *Genocide: Critical Issues of the Holocaust,* ed. Alex Grobman, Daniel Landes, and Sybil Milton, 243–55. Los Angeles: Simon Wiesenthal Center, 1983.

Groebner, Valentin. *Who Are You? Identification, Deception, and Surveillance in Early Modern Europe.* Trans. Mark Kyburz and John Peck. New York: Zone Books, 2007.

Gronemann, Samuel. *Hawdoloh und Zapfenstreich: Erinnerungen an die ostjüdische Etappe, 1916–1918.* Königstein/Ts.: Athenäum, 1984.

Gronemeyer, Reimer. *Zigeuner im Spiegel früher Chroniken und Abhandlungen: Quellen vom 15. bis 18. Jahrhundert.* Gießen: Focus, 1987.

Grossgebauer, Philipp. *De Judaeo male foetente: Von dem stinkenden Jüden . . . .* Weimar: Müller, 1711.

Großherzoglich Badischer Oberrat der Israeliten, ed. *Dienstvorschriften für Mohelim.* Karlsruhe: Malsch & Vogel, 1897.

Grözinger, Karl-Erich. *Jüdisches Denken: Theologie, Philosophie, Mystik.* Vol. 2. Frankfurt/M.: Campus, 2006.

Grube, Norbert. "Westdeutsche Haarmoden und Haarpflege der 50er und 60er Jahre im Spiegel demoskopischer Daten." In *Haar Tragen: Eine kulturwissenschaftliche Annäherung,* ed. Christian Janecke, 233–50. Cologne: Böhlau, 2004.

Gruner, Christian Gottfried. *Almanach für Ärzte und Nichtärzte auf das Jahr 1790.* Jena: Christian Heinrich Cuno, 1790.

Grüner, Frank. *Patrioten und Kosmopoliten: Juden im Sowjetstaat, 1941–1953.* Cologne: Böhlau, 2008.

Grunwald, Max, ed. *Die Hygiene der Juden: Im Anschluß an die Internationale Hygiene-Ausstellung Dresden, 1911.* Dresden: Verlag der Historischen Abteilung der Internationalen Hygiene-Ausstellung, 1912.

Güdemann, Moritz. *Geschichte des Erziehungswesens und der Cultur der abendländischen Juden während des Mittelalters und der Neueren Zeit.* 2nd ed. Amsterdam: Philo Verlag, 1966. (Reprint of Vienna: Alfred Hölder, 1880–88.)

Guesnet, Antoine. *Briefe einiger portugiesischen und deutschen Juden an den Herrn von Voltaire über verschiedene seiner Schriften.* Danzig: Wedel, 1773.

Guesnet, François. "Der angestupste Sohn des Vorstehers: Jüdische Lebenswelt, Recht und Geschlecht in einer jiddischen Komödie des 19. Jahrhunderts." In *Lesestunde/Lekcja czytania,* ed. Ruth Leiserowitz and Stephan Lehnstaedt, 139–54. Warsaw: Wydawnictwo NERITON, 2013.

Gunkel, Christoph. "Körper-Erklärer Fritz Kahn." *Spiegel Online,* October 8, 2010. http://www.spiegel.de/einestages/koerper-erklaerer-fritz-kahn-a-946748.html. Last retrieved July 3, 2015.

Günther, Hans F. K. *Rassenkunde des deutschen Volkes.* 7th ed. Munich: Lehmanns, 1925.

Haas, Carl, trans. *Augustinus-Postille: Eine Auswahl aus den Reden des heiligen Augustin auf das Kirchenjahr verteilt und aus dem Lateinischen übersetzt für Prediger und zur Privaterbauung.* Tübingen: H. Laupp, 1861.

Haasis, Hellmut G. *Joseph Süß Oppenheimer, genannt Jud Süß: Financier, Freidenker, Justizopfer.* Reinbek: Rowohlt, 1998.

Häberlein, Mark, and Martin Zürn, eds. *Minderheiten, Obrigkeit und Gesellschaft in der Frühen Neuzeit: Integrations- und Abgrenzungsprozesse im süddeutschen Raum.* St. Katharinen: Winkel Stiftung, 2001.

Hacking, Ian. "A Chapter from Prussian Statistics." In *The Taming of Chance,* ed. Ian Hacking, 189–99. Cambridge: Cambridge University Press, 1990.

Haft, Alan S. *Eines Tages werde ich alles erzählen: Die Überlebensgeschichte des jüdischen Boxers Hertzko Haft.* Göttingen: Die Werkstatt, 2009.

Halper, Shaun Jacob. "Coming Out of the Hasidic Closet: Jiří Mordechai Langer (1894–1943) and the Fashioning of Homosexual-Jewish Identity." *Jewish Quarterly Review* 101 (2011): 189–231.

Hamburger, E[manuel]. *Über die Irrlehre von der Plica polonica.* Berlin: August Hirschwald, 1861.

Hampel, Lea. "Perücken als Kopfbedeckung: Jüdische Frauen wollen's modisch." *Panorama,* n-tv, March 4, 2010. http://www.n-tv.de/panorama/Juedische-Frauen-wollens-modisch-article758827 .html. Last retrieved February 10, 2020.

Handwörterbuch des deutschen Aberglaubens. Ed. Hanns Bächtold-Stäubli with Eduard Hoffmann-Krayer. 9 vols. 3rd ed. Berlin: Walter de Gruyter, 2000.

Harrowitz, Nancy A., and Barbara Hyams, eds. *Jews & Gender: Responses to Otto Weininger.* Philadelphia: Temple University Press, 1995.

Hart, Mitchell. "Moses the Microbiologist: Judaism and Social Hygiene in the Work of Alfred Nossig." *Jewish Social Studies* 2 (1995): 72–97.

Hart, Mitchell B. *The Healthy Jew: The Symbiosis of Judaism and Modern Medicine.* New York: Cambridge University Press, 2007.

Hasan-Rokem, Galit. "Between Narrating Bodies and Carnal Knowledge." *Jewish Quarterly Review* 95 (2005): 501–7.

Haumann, Heiko. *Der Traum von Israel: Die Ursprünge des modernen Zionismus.* Weinheim: Beltz, 1998.

Haverkamp, Eva, ed. *Hebräische Berichte über die Judenverfolgungen während des Ersten Kreuzugs.* Hannover: Hahnsche Buchhandlung, 2005.

Heer, Johannes, and Klaus Naumann, eds. *Vernichtungskrieg: Verbrechen der Wehrmacht, 1941–1944.* Exhibition catalog. Hamburg: Hamburger Institut für Sozialgeschichte, 1996.

Heid, Ludger. " 'Mehr Intelligenz als körperliche Kraft': Zur Sozialgeschichte ostjüdischer Proletarier an Rhein und Ruhr 1914–1923." *Jahrbuch des Instituts für Deutsche Geschichte (Tel Aviv)* 15 (1986): 337–62.

Heidel, Caris-Petra, ed. *Naturheilkunde und Judentum.* Frankfurt/M.: Mabuse Verlag, 2008.

Heil, Johannes, and Stephan J. Kramer, eds. *Beschneidung: Das Zeichen des Bundes in der Kritik Zur Debatte um das Kölner Urteil.* Berlin: Metropol, 2012.

Hein, Annette. *"Es ist viel 'Hitler' in Wagner": Rassismus und Antisemitische Deutschtumsideologie in den "Bayreuther Blättern" (1878–1938).* Tübingen: Niemeyer, 1996.

Heine, Heinrich. *Pictures of Travel*. Trans. Charles Godfrey Leland. 8th rev. ed. Philadelphia: Schaefer & Koradi, 1879.

Heine, Heinrich. *Briefe, 1815–1831*. Säkularausgabe, vol. 20. Berlin: Walter de Gruyter, 1970.

Heine, Heinrich. *Deutschland: A Winter's Tale*. Trans., introd., and notes T. J. Reed. London: Angel Books, 1986.

Heine, Maximilian. *Über die Conjunctivitis granulosa in Rußland*. St. Petersburg: s.n., 1853.

Hentrich, Thomas. "Masculinity and Disability in the Bible." In *This Abled Body: Rethinking Disabilities in Biblical Studies*, ed. Hector Avalos, Sarah J. Melcher, and Jeremy Schipper, 73–87. Atlanta: Society of Biblical Literature, 2007.

Hertz, Deborah Sadie. *How Jews Became Germans: The History of Conversion and Assimilation in Berlin*. New Haven, CT: Yale University Press, 2007.

Herweg, Monika Rachel. *Die jüdische Mutter: Das verborgene Matriarchat*. Darmstadt: Wissenschaftliche Buchgesellschaft, 1994.

Herz, Marcus. *Über die frühe Beerdigung der Juden: An die Herausgeber des hebräischen Sammlers*. 2nd ed. Berlin: Voß, 1788.

Herzer, Manfred. *Magnus Hirschfeld: Leben und Werk eines jüdischen, schwulen und sozialistischen Sexologen*. Frankfurt/M.: Bibliothek rosa Winkel, 1992.

Hess, Moses. *Rom und Jerusalem: Die letzte Nationalitätenfrage*. Vienna: R. Löwith, 1935. (Orig. pub. 1862.)

Hetkamp, Jutta. *Die jüdische Jugendbewegung in Deutschland von 1913–1933*. Münster: Lit Verlag, 1994.

Heyden, A. von. *Die Tracht der Kulturvölker Europas vom Zeitalter Homers bis zum Beginne des XIX. Jahrhunderts*. Leipzig: E. A. Seemann, W. H. Kühl, 1889.

Hiemer, Ernst. *Der Giftpilz: Ein Stürmerbuch für Jung und Alt*. Nuremberg: Der Stürmer, 1938.

Hiemer, Ernst. *Der Jude im Sprichwort der Völker*. Nuremberg: Der Stürmer, 1942.

Hildegard of Bingen. *Scivias*. Trans. Columba Hart and Jane Bishop; introd. Barbara J. Newman; preface Caroline Walker Bynum. New York: Paulist Press, 1990.

Hillenbrand, F. K. M. *Underground Humour in Nazi Germany, 1933–1945*. London: Routledge, 1995.

Hirsch, Brett. "Counterfeit Professions: Jewish Daughters and the Drama of Failed Conversion in Marlowe's *The Jew of Malta* and Shakespeare's *The Merchant of Venice*." *Early Modern Literary Studies*, special issue 19, no. 4 (2009): 1–37. https://extra.shu.ac.uk/emls/si-19/hirscoun.html. Last retrieved March 15, 2016.

Hirsch, Dafna. "'We Are Here to Bring the West, Not Only to Ourselves': Zionist Occidentalism and the Discourse of Hygiene in Mandate Palestine." *International Journal of Middle East Studies* 41 (2009): 577–94.

Hirsch, Samson Raphael. "Teweth, der Fasttag." *Jeschurun* 4 (1858): 171–83.

Hirsch, Samuel. *Die Messiaslehre der Juden in Kanzelvorträgen zur Erbauung denkender Leser*. Leipzig: Heinrich Hunger, 1843.

Hirschkind, Charles. "Is There a Secular Body?" *Cultural Anthropology* 26 (2011): 633–47.

Hitler, Adolf. *Mein Kampf*. Trans. James Murphy. London: Hurst and Blackett, 1939.

Hitzler, Roland. "Der Körper als Gegenstand der Gestaltung: Über physische Konsequenzen der Bastelexistenz." In *Körperrepräsentationen*, ed. Kornelia Hahn and Michael Meuser, 71–85. Konstanz: UVK, 2002.

Hoberman, John M. "Otto Weininger and the Critique of Jewish Masculinity." In *Jews & Gender: Responses to Otto Weininger*, ed. Nancy Harrowitz and Barbara Hyams, 141–53. Philadelphia: Temple University Press, 1995.

Hödl, Klaus. "Der 'jüdische Körper' als Stigma." *Österreichische Zeitschrift für Geschichtswissenschaft* 8 (1997a): 212–30.

Hödl, Klaus. *Die Pathologisierung des jüdischen Körpers: Antisemitismus, Geschlecht und Medizin im Fin de siècle*. Vienna: Böhlau, 1997b.

Hödl, Klaus. *Gesunde Juden—kranke Schwarze: Körperbilder im medizinischen Diskurs*. Innsbruck: Studien Verlag, 2002.

Höfler, Max. *Deutsches Krankheitsnamen-Buch*. Munich: Piloty & Loehle, 1899.

Hogan, Larry P. *Healing in the Second Temple Period*. Fribourg: Universitätsverlag, 1992.

Hohmann, Joachim S. *Geschichte der Sexualwissenschaft in Deutschland, 1886–1933*. Berlin: Foerster Verlag, 1985.

Hohmann, Joachim S. *Sexualforschung und –aufklärung in der Weimarer Republik*. Berlin: Foerster Verlag, 1987.

Holdheim, Samuel. "Die Speisegesetze." *Wissenschaftliche Zeitschrift für jüdische Theologie* 6 (1847): 41–63.

The Holy Bible [and] Apocrypha. American Standard Version [Revised Standard Version]. New York: Nelson, 1946–57.

The Holy Letter: A Study in Jewish Sexual Morality. Trans. and introd. Seymour J. Cohen. Northvale, NJ: Jason Aronson, 1993.

Hoppe, Hugo. *Krankheiten und Sterblichkeit bei Juden und Nichtjuden*. Berlin: S. Calvary, 1903.

Horkheimer, Max, and Theodor W. Adorno. *Dialectic of Enlightenment: Philosophical Fragments*. Ed. Gunzelin Schmid Noerr; trans. Edmund Jephcott. Stanford, CA: Stanford University Press, 2002.

Horowitz, Elliott. "Jewish Confraternities in Seventeenth-Century Verona: A Study in the Social History of Piety." PhD diss., Yale University, 1982.

Horowitz, Elliott. "The Early Eighteenth Century Confronts the Beard: Kabbalah and Jewish Self-Fashioning." *Jewish History* 8 (1994): 95–115.

Horowitz, Elliott. "The Jews of Europe and the Moment of Death in Medieval and Modern Times." *Judaism* 44 (1995): 271–81.

Horowitz, Elliott. "Jewish Confraternal Piety in Sixteenth-Century Ferrara: Continuity and Change." In *The Politics of Ritual Kinship: Confraternities and Social Order in Early Modern Italy*, ed. Nicholas Terpstra, 150–71. Cambridge: Cambridge University Press, 2000.

Horowitz, Elliott. "A 'Dangerous Encounter': Thomas Coryate and the Swaggering Jews of Venice." *Journal of Jewish Studies* 52 (2001): 341–53.

Horowitz, Elliott. "Families and Their Fortunes: The Jews in Early Modern Italy." In *Cultures of the Jews: A New History*, ed. David Biale, 573–638. New York: Schocken Books, 2002a.

Horowitz, Elliot. " 'They Fought Because They Were Fighters and They Fought Because They Were Jews': Violence and the Construction of Modern Jewish Identity." In *Jews and Violence: Images, Ideologies, Realities*, ed. Peter Y. Medding, 23–42. Oxford: Oxford University Press, 2002b.

Horowitz, Elliott. *Reckless Rites: Purim and the Legacy of Jewish Violence*. Princeton, NJ: Princeton University Press, 2006.

Horowitz, Elliott. "Beards." In *YIVO Encyclopedia of Jews in Eastern Europe* (2010). http://www .yivoencyclopedia.org/article.aspx/Beards. Last retrieved March 24, 2016.

Horowitz, Elliott, and Isabelle Rozenbaumas. "Visages du judaïsme: De la barbe en monde juif et de l'élaboration de ses significations." *Annales: Histoire, Sciences Sociales* 49 (1994): 1065–90.

Höxter, Julius. *Quellenlesebuch zur jüdischen Geschichte und Literatur*. Vol. 3. Reprint, Zurich: Morascha, 1983.

Houtman, Cornelis. *Das Bundesbuch: Ein Kommentar*. Leiden: Brill, 1997.

Hsia, R. Po-chia. *The Myth of Ritual Murder: Jews and Magic in Reformation Germany*. New Haven, CT: Yale University Press, 1988.

Huberband, Shimon. *Kiddush Hashem: Jewish Religious and Cultural Life in Poland During the Holocaust*. New York: Yeshiva University Press, 1987.

Hughes, Diane Owen. "Distinguishing Signs: Ear-Rings, Jews and Franciscan Rhetoric in the Italian Renaissance City." *Past & Present* 112 (1986): 3–59.

Hundt-Radowsky, Hartwig. *Die Judenschule, oder gründliche Anleitung, in kurzer Zeit ein vollkommener schwarzer oder weißer Jude zu werden*. 3 vols. [Stuttgart?]: s.n., 1822/23.

Idelson-Shein, Iris. *Difference of a Different Kind: Jewish Construction of Race During the Long Eighteenth Century*. Philadelphia: University of Pennsylvania Press, 2014.

Iggers, Wilma Abeles, ed. *The Jews of Bohemia and Moravia: A Historical Reader*. Detroit: Wayne State University Press, 1992.

Isaacs, Ronald H. *Judaism, Medicine and Healing*. Northvale, NJ: Jason Aronson, 1998.

Isaacs, Ronald H. *Bubbe Meises: Jewish Myths, Jewish Realities.* Jersey City, NJ: Ktav, 2008.

Jachter, Chaim. *Gray Matter.* Vol. 3. Teaneck, NJ: Jachter, 2008.

Jacobs, Joseph. "On the Racial Characteristics of Modern Jews." *Journal of the Anthropological Institute of Great Britain and Ireland* 15 (1886): 23–62.

Jacobs, Sandra. "The Body Inscribed: A Priestly Initiative?" In *The Body in Biblical, Christian and Jewish Texts,* ed. Joan E. Taylor, 1–16. London: Bloomsbury, 2014.

Jaffé, Jakob. *Ursachen und Verlauf der Juden-Pogrome in Russland im Oktober 1905.* Bern: Drechsel, 1916.

Jaffé, Julius. *Die rituelle Circumcision im Lichte der antiseptischen Chirurgie mit Berücksichtigung der religiösen Vorschriften.* Leipzig: Gustav Fock, 1886.

Jakobovits, Tobias. "Die jüdischen Zünfte in Prag." *Jahrbuch der Gesellschaft für Geschichte der Juden in der Čechoslovakischen Republik* 8 (1936): 57–145.

Janovskaja, Natascha, and Katja Kriener, eds. *Wir melden uns zu Wort: Interviews mit Frauen aus der Jüdischen Gemeinde Düsseldorf.* Düsseldorf: Presseverband der Evangelischen Kirche im Rheinland, 2001.

Jellinek, Adolf. *Predigten.* 3 vols. Vienna: Carl Gerold's Sohn, 1862–66.

Jellinek, Adolf. *Der jüdische Stamm: Ethnographische Studien.* Vienna: Herzfeld Bauer, 1869.

Jesionek, Albert. "Die Pediculidae." In *Lehrbuch der Haut-und Geschlechtskrankheiten,* ed. Erhard Riecke, 523–24. 6th ed. Jena: Gustav Fischer, 1921.

Jick, Leon. *The Americanization of the Synagogue, 1820–1870.* Waltham, MA: Brandeis University Press, 1976.

Johnson, Willis. "The Myth of Jewish Male Menses." *Journal of Medieval History* 24 (1998): 273–95.

Joseph, Jacques. "Über die operative Verkleinerung einer Nase (Rhinomios)." *Berliner Klinische Wochenschrift* 40 (1898): 881–86.

Josephus, Flavius. *The Life; Against Apion.* Trans. H. St. J. Thackeray. Cambridge, MA: Harvard University Press; London: W. Heinemann, 1926.

Josephus, Flavius. *The Jewish War.* Ed. Gaalya Cornfeld. Grand Rapids, MI: Zondervan, 1982.

Judd, Robin. *Contested Rituals: Circumcision, Kosher Butchering, and Jewish Political Life in Germany, 1843–1933.* Ithaca, NY: Cornell University Press, 2007.

Jüdisches Lexikon. Ed. Bruno Kirchner. 4 vols. Berlin: Jüdischer Verlag, 1927.

Junkerjürgen, Ralf. *Haarfarben: Eine Kulturgeschichte in Europa seit der Antike.* Cologne: Böhlau, 2009.

Justin Martyr. *Dialogue with Trypho.* Trans. Thomas B. Falls; rev. and with new introd. Thomas P. Halton; ed. Michael Slusser. Washington, DC: Catholic University of America Press, 2003.

Jütte, Daniel. "Schächtet für Deutschland: Als Muslime schon einmal rituell schlachten durften." *Frankfurter Allgemeine Zeitung,* January 17, 2002, 44.

Jütte, Daniel. "Living Stones: The House as Actor in Early Modern Europe." *Journal of Urban History* 42 (2016): 659–87.

Jütte, Robert. "Vagantentum und Bettlerwesen bei Hans Jacob Christoffel von Grimmelshausen." *Daphnis: Zeitschrift für mittlere Deutsche Literatur* 9 (1980): 109–31.

Jütte, Robert. "Der anstößige Körper: Anmerkungen zu einer Semiotik der Nacktheit." In *Gepeinigt, begehrt, vergessen: Symbolik und Sozialbezug des Körpers im späten Mittelalter und in der frühen Neuzeit,* ed. Klaus Schreiner and Norbert Schnitzler, 109–29. Munich: Wilhelm Fink, 1992.

Jütte, Robert. "Stigma-Symbole: Kleidung als identitätsstiftendes Merkmal bei spätmittelalterlichen und frühneuzeitlichen Randgruppen (Juden, Dirnen, Aussätzige, Bettler)." In *Zwischen Sein und Schein. Kleidung und Identität in der ständischen Gesellschaft,* ed. Neithard Bulst and Robert Jütte (= *Saeculum* 44, no. 1), 66–90. Freiburg/Brsg.: Karl Alber, 1993.

Jütte, Robert. "Contacts at the Bedside: Jewish Physicians and Their Christian Patients." In *In and Out of the Ghetto: Jewish-Gentile Relations in Late Medieval and Early Modern Germany,* ed. Hartmut Lehmann and Ronnie Po-chia Hsia, 137–50. New York: Cambridge University Press, 1995.

Jütte, Robert. "Zur Funktion und sozialen Stellung jüdischer 'gelehrter' Ärzte im spätmittelalterlichen und frühneuzeitlichen Deutschland." In *Gelehrte im Reich,* ed. Rainer Christoph Schwinges, 159–79. Berlin: Duncker & Humblot, 1996.

Jütte, Robert. "Einleitung: Sexualwissenschaft in der Weimar Republik." In *Handwörterbuch der Sexualwissenschaft*, ed. Max Marcuse, v–xvi. Berlin: Walter de Gruyter, 2001.

Jütte, Robert. "'Übrigens weiß ich schon aus meiner Naturheilkunde, daß alle Gefahr von der Medicin herkommt . . .': Franz Kafka als Medizinkritiker und Naturheilkundiger." In *Von Enoch bis Kafka: Festschrift für Karl E. Grözinger zum 60. Geburtstag*, ed. Manfred Voigts, 421–35. Wiesbaden: Harrassowitz, 2002.

Jütte, Robert. *Contraception: A History*. Cambridge: Polity, 2008.

Jütte, Robert. "Im Wunder vereint: Eine spektakuläre Missgeburt im Ghetto 1575." In *Interstizi: Culture ebraico-cristiane a Venezia e nei suoi domini dal medioevo all'età' moderna*, ed. Uwe Israel, Robert Jütte, and Reinhold C. Mueller, 517–40. Rome: Storia e Letteratura, 2010.

Jütte, Robert, Wolfgang U. Eckart, Hans-Walter Schmuhl, and Winfried Süß. *Medizin und Nationalsozialismus: Bilanz und Perspektiven der Forschung*. Göttingen: Wallstein, 2011.

Kafka, Franz. *Dearest Father: Stories and Other Writings*. Trans. Ernst Kaiser and Eithne Wilkins. New York: Schocken, 1954.

Kafka, Franz. *The Diaries of Franz Kafka, 1910–1923*. Ed. Max Brod. Trans. Joseph Kresh (1910–13), Martin Greenberg and Hannah Arendt (1914–23). New York: Schocken, 1976.

Kaidanover, Tzvi Hirsch. *Sefer Kav ha-yashar* (Hebr.) [The Just Measure]. Sulzbach: Aharon Zekl, 1799.

Kaiser, Otto. "Krankheit und Heilung nach dem Alten Testament." *Medizin, Gesellschaft und Geschichte* 20 (2002): 9–43.

Kaiser, Otto. *Philo von Alexandrien: Denkender Glaube—eine Einführung*. Göttingen: Vandenhoeck & Ruprecht, 2015.

Kalter-Leibovici, O., et al. "Adult-Onset Diabetes Among Arabs and Jews in Israel: A Population-Based Study." *Diabetic Medicine* 29 (2012): 748–54.

Kamczycki, Artur. "Orientalisms: Herzl and His Beard." *Journal of Modern Jewish Studies* 12 (2013): 90–116.

Kamen, Henry. *The Spanish Inquisition: A Historical Revision*. 4th ed. New Haven, CT: Yale University Press, 2014.

Kämpf, S. I. *Biographie des hochberühmten hochseligen Herrn Akiva Eger Oberrabinen zu Posen, Verfasser einer Sammlung von Rechtsgutachten, nebst einem hebräischen Trauergedicht auf sein Hinscheiden*. Salzuflen: Lissa, 1838.

Kaplan, Aryeh. *Sefer Jezira. Das Buch der Schöpfung in Theorie und Praxis*. Grevenbroich: Ruther, 2007.

Kaplan, Greg. "Germanising the Jewish Male: Military Masculinity as the Last Stage of Acculturation." In *Towards Normality? Acculturation and Modern German Jewry*, ed. Rainer Liedtke and David Rechter, 159–85. Tübingen: Mohr Siebeck, 2003.

Kaplan, Marion A., and Deborah Dash Moore, eds. *Gender and Jewish History*. Bloomington: Indiana University Press, 2011.

Karniel, Josef. "Zur Auswirkung der Toleranzpatente für die Juden in der Habsburgermonarchie im josephinischen Jahrzehnt." In *Im Zeichen der Toleranz: Aufsätze zur Toleranzgesetzgebung des 18. Jahrhunderts in den Reichen Joseph II., ihren Voraussetzungen und Folgen*, ed. Peter F. Barton, 203–21. Vienna: Institut für protestantische Kirchengeschichte, 1981.

Kassouf, Susan. "The Shared Pain of the Golden Vein: The Discursive Proximity of Jewish and Scholarly Diseases in the Late Eighteenth Century." *Eighteenth-Century Studies* 32 (1998): 101–10.

Kästner, Alexander, and Claudia Pawlowitsch. "Vor dem Zerstückeln bewahrt: Die außergewöhnliche Geschichte des Leichnams von Judas Pollack." *Medaon—Magazin für jüdisches Leben in Forschung und Bildung* 5, no. 8 (2011): 1–5. http://medaon.de/pdf/M_Pawlowitsch + Kaestner-8-2011 .pdf. [1.5.2011]. Last retrieved May 3, 2016.

Katz, David S. *The Jews in the History of England, 1485–1850*. Oxford: Clarendon Press, 1994.

Katz, David S. "Shylock's Gender: Jewish Male Menstruation in Early Modern England." *Review of English Studies*, n.s., 50 (1999): 440–62.

Kay, Devra, ed., trans., and commentary. *Seyder Tkhines: The Forgotten Book of Common Prayer for Jewish Women*. Philadelphia: Jewish Publication Society, 2004.

Keil, Martha. "Verfall der Sitten—Schuld der Frauen? Geschlecht und Moral in jüdischen Quellen aus Eisenstadt und Deutschkreutz (1700–1900)." In *Das Judentum im pannonischen Raum vom 16. Jahrhundert bis zum Jahr 1914*, ed. Sándor Bösze, 35–45. Kaposvár: Somogy M. Közgyűlés, 2009.

Keller, Adelbert von, ed. *Fastnachtspiele aus dem fünfzehnten Jahrhundert*. Stuttgart: Litterarischer Vereins, 1853.

Kemelman, Harry. *Tuesday the Rabbi Saw Red*. Greenwich, CT: Fawcett, 1973.

Kidorf, Irwin W. "Jewish Tradition and the Freudian Theory of Mourning." *Journal of Religion and Health* 2 (1963): 248–52.

Kinzbrunner, Barry M. "Jewish Medical Ethics and the End-of-Life Care." *Journal of Palliative Medicine* 7 (2004): 558–73.

Kirchhof, Hans Wilhelm. *Wendunmuth, darinnen fünff hundert und fünfftzig höflicher, züchtiger, und lustiger historien, schimpffreden, und gleichnüssen begriffen und gezogen seyn auß alten und ietzigen scribenten; item den Facetiis deß berümpten und wolgelehrten Henrici Bebelii . . . / beschrieben und zusammen gebracht. . . .* Frankfurt/M.: Georg Raben und Weygand Hans Erben, 1563.

Kirchschlager, Michael, ed. *Mörder/Räuber/Menschenfresser: Einhundert Biografien und Merkwürdigkeiten deutscher Verbrecher des 15. bis 18. Jahrhunderts*. Leipzig: Festa, 2005.

Kirshenblatt-Gimblett, Barbara. "The Corporeal Turn." *Jewish Quarterly Review* 95 (2005): 447–61.

Kisch, Egon Erwin. "Das Haus zu den veränderten Nasen." In *Gesammelte Werke in Einzelausgaben*, vol. 10, *Läuse auf dem Markt: Vermischte Prosa*, ed. Bodo Uhse and Gisela Kisch, 331–33. Berlin: Aufbau Verlag, 1985.

Kisch, Guido. "The Yellow Badge in History." *Historia Judaica* 19 (1957): 89–146.

Kisch, Guido. *Forschungen zur Rechts- und Sozialgeschichte der Juden in Deutschland während des Mittelalters*. Sigmaringen: Thorbecke, 1978.

Kitzur Schulchan Aruch. https://www.sefaria.org/Kitzur_Shulchan_Aruch?lang = bi&p2 = Kitzur_Shulchan_Aruch.50.8&lang2 = bi. Last retrieved August 20, 2019.

Klein, Peter K. " 'Jud, Dir kuckt der Spitzbub aus dem Gesicht!' Traditionen antisemitischer Bildstereotype oder die Physiognomie des 'Juden' als Konstrukt." In *Abgestempelt: Judenfeindliche Postkarten*, ed. Helmut Gold and Georg Heuberger, 43–78. Heidelberg: Umschau Braus, 1999.

Klein, Uta. *Militär und Geschlecht in Israel*. Frankfurt/M.: Campus, 2001.

Klemperer, Victor. *I Will Bear Witness: A Diary of the Nazi Years*. Trans. Martin Chalmers. 2 vols. New York: Random House, 1999.

Klüber, Johann Salomon. *Interessante Rechts-Verhältnisse zwischen Christen und Juden als Religions-Partheien betrachtet. . . .* Dinkelsbühl: Fr. Walthr'sche Buchhandlung, 1834.

Klüger, Ruth. *Unterwegs verloren: Erinnerungen*. Vienna: Paul Zsolnay Verlag, 2008.

Knobel, August. *Kurzgefasstes exegetisches Handbuch zum Alten Testament: Die Bücher Exodus und Leviticus*. Leipzig: S. Hirzel, 1857.

Knox, Robert. *The Races of Men: A Fragment*. Philadelphia: Lea & Blanchard, 1850.

Kobler, Franz, ed. *A Treasury of Jewish Letters: Letters from the Famous and the Humble*. 2 vols. London: East and West Library, 1952.

Kobolt, Willibald. *Die Groß- und Kleine Welt, Natürlich- Sittlich- und Politischer Weiß zum Lust und Nutzen vorgestellt. . . .* Augsburg: Martin Veith, 1738.

Kohlbach, Berthold. "Spuren der Tätowierung im Judentum." *Globus* 97 (1910): 237–41.

Kohnen, Norbert. *Von der Schmerzlichkeit des Schmerzerlebens: Wie fremde Kulturen Schmerzen wahrnehmen, erleben und bewältigen*. Ratingen: Alfred Preuß, 2003.

Konner, Melvin. *The Jewish Body*. New York: Nextbook / Schocken, 2009.

Koren, Sharon Faye. "Kabbalistic Physiology: Isaac the Blind, Nahmanides, and Moses de Leon on Menstruation." *AJS Review* 28 (2004): 317–39.

Koren, Sharon Faye. "The Menstruant as 'Other' in Medieval Judaism and Christianity." *Nashim: A Journal of Jewish Women's Studies & Gender Issues* 17 (2009): 33–59.

Koren, Sharon Faye. *Forsaken: The Menstruant in Medieval Jewish Mysticism*. Waltham, MA: Brandeis University Press, 2011.

Kornmann, Heinrich. *Opera curiosa in tractatus quatuor distributa: Quorum I. Miracula vivorum; II. Miracula mortuorum, opus novum & admirandum in decem partes distributum. III. Templum naturae historicum, in quo de natura & miraculis elementorum ignis, aeris, aquae & terrae disseritur. IV. Quaestiones enucleatae de virginum statu ac jure: Ex optimis tum sacris, tum prophanis authoribus jurisbusque natur. Divin. Canonic. civil desumpta, atq[ue]* . . . *pertractata* . . . . Frankfurt/M.: Officina Genschiana, 1694.

Kosman, Admiel. *Men's World: Reading Masculinity in Jewish Stories in a Spiritual Context.* Trans. Edvard Levin. Würzburg: Ergon Verlag, 2009.

Kottek, Samuel S. "Medical Practice and Jewish Law: Nahmanides's Sefer Torat Haadam." In *Medicine and Medical Ethics in Medieval and Early Modern Spain: An Intercultural Approach,* ed. Samuel S. Kottek and Luis García-Ballester, 163–72. Jerusalem: Magnes Press, 1996.

Krahl, Vanessa. "Das Selbstverständnis der Reformrabbiner und die Entwicklung der deutsch-jüdischen Reformbewegung bis 1848." PhD diss., TU Berlin, 2011.

Kramer, Sven. "Nacktheit in Holocaust-Fotos und -Filmen." In *Die Shoah im Bild,* ed. Sven Kramer, 225–48. Munich: Edition text + kritik, 2003.

Kratz-Ritter, Bettina. *Für "fromme Zionstöchter" und "gebildete Frauenzimmer."* Hildesheim: Olms, 1995.

Kraus, Martin. "Fünf Minuten mit Yuri Foreman über Profiboxen und Torastudium." *Jüdische Allgemeine,* September 17, 2009. https://www.juedische-allgemeine.de/allgemein/fuenf-minuten-mit -yuri-foreman-ueber-profiboxen-und-torastudium/. Last retrieved February 22, 2020.

Krauskopf, Samuel. *Sanitary Science: A Sunday Lecture.* Philadelphia: S. W. Goldman, 1899.

Kremer, Hannes. *Gottes Rune: Ein Buch von Glaube und Treue.* 6th ed. Munich: Zentralverlag der NSDAP, 1942.

Kriechbaumer, Robert, ed. *Der Geschmack der Vergänglichkeit: Jüdische Sommerfrische in Salzburg.* Vienna: Böhlau, 2002.

Kriegel, Maurice. "Un trait de psychologie sociale dans les pays méditerranéens du bas moyen âge: Le juif comme intouchable." *Annales: Economies, sociétés, civilisations* 31 (1976): 326–30.

Kritz, Reuven. *Die Krankheit der Dichter oder Hoffmanns Erzählungen.* Norderstedt: Book on Demand, 2008.

Krochmalnik, Daniel. "Scheintod und Emanzipation: Der Beerdigungsstreit in seinem historischen Kontext." *Trumah: Zeitschrift der Hochschule für Jüdische Studien Heidelberg* 6 (1997): 107–49.

Kroll, M[ichael]. *Die neuropathologischen Syndrome zugleich Differentialdiagnostik der Nervenkrankheiten.* Berlin: Julius Springer, 1929.

Kübler, Mirjam. *Judas Iskariot: Das abendländische Judasbild und seine antisemitische Instrumentalisierung im Nationalsozialismus.* Kamen: Hartmut Spenner, 2007.

Kühnel, Harry, ed. *Bildwörterbuch der Kleidung und Rüstung.* Stuttgart: Kröner, 1992.

Kulka, Otto Dov, and Eberhard Jäckel, eds. *Die Juden in den geheimen NS-Stimmungsberichten, 1933–1945.* Düsseldorf: Droste Verlag, 2004.

Kupferberg, Yael. *Dimensionen des Witzes um Heinrich Heine: Zur Säkularisation der poetischen Sprache.* Würzburg: Königshausen & Neumann, 2011.

La Fontaine, Franz Leopold de. *Chirurgisch-medicinische Abhandlungen verschiedenen Inhalts Polen betreffend.* Breslau and Leipzig: Korn, 1792.

Lamm, Norman, and Haim Hillel Ben-Sasson. "Kiddush ha-Shem and hillul ha-Shem." In *Encylopedia Judaica* 12:139–45. 2nd ed. Detroit: Macmillan Reference, 2007.

Landau, Ernest. "Purim in Elmau—Um die jüdische Zukunft: Texte jüdischen Überlebens." *Dachauer Hefte* 24 (2008): 236–51.

Landucci, Luca. *Ein florentinisches Tagebuch: 1450–1516; Nebst einer anonymen Fortsetzung, 1516–1542.* Trans., introd., and commentary Marie Herzfeld. Jena: Diederichs, 1912/13. Reprint, Düsseldorf: Diederichs, 1978.

Lange, Alissa. "Das jüdische Altenhaus am Grindel in Hamburg." In *Jüdische Wohlfahrtsstiftungen: Initiativen jüdischer Stifterinnen und Stifter zwischen Wohltätigkeit und sozialer Reform,* ed. Andreas Ludwig and Kurt Schilde, 159–72. Frankfurt/M.: Fachhochschulverlag, 2010.

La Peyrère, Isaac de. *Du rappel des Juifs.* S.l., s.n., 1643.

Lapidoth, M[oshe] and G[ali] Aharonowitz. "Tattoo Removal Among Ethiopian Jews in Israel: Tradition Faces Technology." *Journal of the American Academy of Dermatology* 51 (2004): 906–9.

Laqueur, Thomas. *Making Sex: Body and Gender from the Greeks to Freud.* Cambridge, MA: Harvard University Press, 1990.

Lathers, Marie. "Posing the 'Belle Juive': Jewish Models in 19th-Century Paris." *Woman's Art Journal* 21 (2000): 27–32.

Lavater, Johann Caspar. *Physiognomische Fragmente zur Beförderung der Menschenkenntniß und der Menschenliebe.* Vol. 3. Winterthur: Heinrich Steiners und Compagnie, 1787.

Lavaud, Simona. *Gleichberechtigung und Gleichwertigkeit? Jüdische Wohlfahrt in der Weimarer Republik zwischen privaten Initiativen und öffentlichem Engagement der Berliner Gemeinde.* Frankfurt/ M.: Peter Lang, 2015.

Le, Dan. *The Naked Christ: An Atonement Model for a Body-Obsessed Culture.* Eugene, OR: Pickwick Publications, 2012.

Leder, Christoph Maria. *Die Grenzgänge des Marcus Herz: Beruf, Haltung und Identität eines jüdischen Arztes gegen Ende des 18. Jahrhunderts.* Münster: Waxmann Verlag, 2007.

Le Gall, Jean-Marie. *Un idéal masculin: Barbes et moustaches XVe–XVIIIe siècles.* Paris: Payot, 2011.

Leibowitz, Joshua O. *Some Aspects of Biblical and Talmudic Medicine.* Jerusalem: Division of the History of Medicine, Hebrew University, 1969.

Leiser, Erwin. *"Deutschland, erwache!": Propaganda im Film des Dritten Reiches.* Reinbek: Rowohlt, 1968.

Lenhard, Philipp. *Volk oder Religion? Die Entstehung moderner jüdischer Ethnizität in Frankreich und Deutschland, 1782–1848.* Göttingen: Vandenhoeck & Ruprecht, 2014.

Lepicard, Etienne. "An Alternative to the Cosmic and Mechanic Metaphors for the Human Body? The House Illustration in *Ma'aseh Tuviyah* (1708)." *Medical History* 52 (2008): 93–105.

Lesses, Rebecca. "Women and Gender in the Hekhalot Literature." In *Hekhalot Literature in Context: Between Byzantium and Babylonia*, ed. Ra'anan Boustan, Martha Himmelfarb, and Peter Schäfer, 279–312. Tübingen: Mohr Siebeck, 2013.

Lévi, Israel. "L'odeur des Juifs." *Revue des études juives* 20 (1890): 249–52.

Levi, Primo. *The Complete Works of Primo Levi.* Ed. Ann Goldstein. Trans. Stuart Woolf (*If This Is a Man*), Michael F. Moore (*The Drowned and the Saved*), et al. 3 vols. New York: Liveright, 2015.

Levin, Jeff. "Health Impact of Jewish Religious Observance in the USA: Findings from the 2000–01 National Jewish Population Survey." *Journal of Religion and Health* 50 (2011): 852–68.

Levin, Jeff, and Michele F. Prince. "Judaism and Health: Reflections on an Emerging Field." *Journal of Religion and Health* 50 (2011): 565–77.

Levin, Jeffrey S., and Preston L. Schiller. "Is There a Religious Factor in Health?" *Journal of Religion and Health* 26 (1987): 9–36.

Levinas, Emmanuel. *On Escape.* Trans. Bettina Bergo. Stanford, CA: Stanford University Press, 2003.

Levine, Aaron. *How to Perform the Great Mitzvah of Bikkur Cholim, Visiting the Sick.* Toronto: Zichron Meir, 1987.

Levine, Peter. *Ellis Island to Ebbets Field: Sport and the American Jewish Experience.* New York: Oxford University Press, 1992.

Levy, Ascher. *Die Memoiren des Ascher Levy aus Reichshofen im Elsaß (1598–1635).* Ed. Moses Ginsburger. Berlin: Lamm, 1913.

Lewin, Adolf. *Geschichte der badischen Juden seit der Regierung Karl Friedrichs, 1739–1909.* Karlsruhe: Komissionsverlag der G. Braunschen Hofdruckerei, 1909.

Lexikon des Mittelalters. 9 vols. Munich: Artemis, 1980–98.

Lilienthal, Georg. "Die jüdischen 'Rassenmerkmale': Zur Geschichte der Anthropologie der Juden." *Medizinhistorisches Journal* 28 (1993): 173–98.

Lipman-Mühlhausen, Yom Tov. "Liber Nizachon." In *Tela ignea Satanae*, ed. Johann Christoph Wagenseil, 1–260. Frankfurt/M.: Zunner, 1681.

Lipphardt, Veronika. *Biologie der Juden: Jüdische Wissenschaftler über "Rasse" und Vererbung, 1900–1935.* Göttingen: Vandenhoeck & Ruprecht, 2008.

Lipschutz, Yacov. *Kashruth: A Comprehensive Background and Reference Guide to the Principles of Kashruth*. Brooklyn, NY: Mesorah Publications, 1995.

Lipton, Sara. "Where Are the Gothic Jewish Women? On the Non-Iconography of the Jewess in the *Cantigas de Santa Maria*." *Jewish History* 22 (2008): 139–77.

Lipton, Sara. "The Jew's Face: Vision, Knowledge, and Identity in Medieval Anti-Jewish Caricature." In *Late Medieval Jewish Identities: Iberia and Beyond*, ed. Carmen Caballero-Navas and Esperanza Alfonso, 259–87. New York: Palgrave Macmillan, 2010.

Lipton, Sara. *Dark Mirror: The Medieval Origin of Anti-Jewish Iconography*. New York: Metropolitan Books, 2014.

Liss, Peggy K. *Isabel the Queen: Life and Times*. 2nd rev. ed. Philadelphia: University of Pennsylvania Press, 2004.

Litt, Stefan. *Pinkas, Kahal, and the Mediene: The Records of Dutch Ashkenazi Communities in the Eighteenth Century as Historical Sources*. Leiden: Brill, 2008.

Lobes, Edmund-Vincenz Guldener von. *Beobachtungen über die Krätze, gesammelt in dem Arbeitshause zu Prag*. Prague: Calve, 1791.

Lorenz, Maren. *Leibhaftige Vergangenheit. Einführung in die Körpergeschichte*. Tübingen: Edition Diskord, 2000.

Löw, Andrea. *Juden im Ghetto Litzmannstadt: Lebensbedingungen, Wahrnehmung, Verhalten*. Göttingen: Vandenhoeck & Ruprecht, 2006.

Lowenstein, Steven M. "Anfänge und Integration." In *Geschichte des jüdischen Alltags*, ed. Marion Kaplan, 125–224. Munich: C. H. Beck, 2003.

Lubrich, Naomi. "The Wandering Hat: Iterations of the Medieval Jewish Pointed Cap." *Jewish History* 29 (2015): 203–44.

Lucas, Alan B. "Tattooing and Body Piercing." YD 180 (1997). https://www.rabbinicalassembly.org/sites/default/files/public/halakhah/teshuvot/19912000/lucas_tattooing.pdf. Last retrieved April 5, 2016.

Ludewig, Anna-Dorothea. "'Schönste Heidin, süßeste Jüdin!' Die 'Schöne Jüdin' in der europäischen Literatur zwischen dem 17. und 19. Jahrhundert—ein Querschnitt." *Medeaon* 2, no. 3 (2008). http://www.medaon.de/. Last retrieved February 10, 2020.

Ludewig, Johann Peter. *Vollständige Erläuterung der Güldenen Bulle*. 2 pts. Frankfurt/M.: Fritsch, 1716–19.

Lüthi, Barbara. *Invading Bodies: Medizin und Immigration in den USA, 1880–1920*. Frankfurt/M.: Campus, 2009.

Lüttcke, Michael. *Dissertatio inauguralis medica de plica, vom Juden-Zopff*. Erfurt: Groschian, 1724.

Das Ma'assebuch: Altjiddische Erzählkunst. Trans. (German), ed., and commentary Ulf Diederichs. Munich: dtv, 2003.

Maciejko, Pawel. *The Mixed Multitude: Jacob Frank and the Frankist Movement, 1755–1816*. Philadelphia: University of Pennsylvania Press, 2011.

Magin, Christine. *"Wie es um der iuden recht stet": Der Status der Juden in den mittelalterlichen deutschen Rechtsbüchern*. Göttingen: Wallstein, 1999.

Magonet, Jonathan, ed. *Jewish Explorations of Sexuality*. Oxford: Berghahn Books, 1995.

Maharam [Meir Ben Baruch von Rothenburg]. *Teshuvot Pesakim Uminhagim* (Hebr.) [Responsa]. Ed. Isak Z Cahana. 3 vols. Jerusalem: Mossad Harav Kook, 1957–63.

Maimon, Salomon. *An Autobiography*. Trans. J. Clark Murray; introd. Michael Shapiro. Urbana: University of Illinois Press, 2001.

Maimonides, Moses. *The Guide for the Perplexed*. Trans. M. Friedländer. 2nd rev. ed. New York: Dover, 1956.

Maimonides, Moses. *On the Regimen of Health* [*Fī tadbīr al-sihhah*]. Trans. Gerrit Bos. Medical Works of Maimonides, vol. 12. Leiden: Brill, 2019a.

Maimonides, Moses. "Oath and Prayer of Maimonides." https://dal.ca.libguides.com/c.php?g=256990&p=1717827. Last retrieved August 10, 2019b.

Malkiel, David Joshua. "Manipulating Virginity: Digital Defloration in Midrash and History." *Jewish Studies Quarterly* 13 (2006): 105–27.

Mallmann, Klaus-Michael, Volker Rieß, and Wolfram Pyta, eds. *Deutscher Osten 1939–1945: Der Weltanschauungskrieg in Photos und Texten.* Darmstadt: Wissenschaftliche Buchgesellschaft, 2003.

Mandelstamm, Max. "Die Frage der körperlichen Hebung der osteuropäischen Juden [excerpts]." *Jüdische Turnzeitung* 1, no. 5 (1900): 51–53; no. 6 (1900): 62–67, 75–79.

Marcus, Jacob R. *Communal Sick-Care in the German Ghetto.* Cincinnati: Hebrew Union College Press, 1947.

Margaritha, Antonius. *Der gantze Jüdische Glaube . . . .* Leipzig: Lanckisch, 1713.

Marienberg, Evyatar. "Menstruation in Sacred Spaces: Medieval and Early Modern Jewish Women in the Synagogue." *Nordisk Judaistik* 25 (2004): 7–16.

Mariner, Rodney. "The Jewish Homosexual and the Halakhic Tradition: A Suitable Case for Treatment." In *Jewish Explorations of Sexuality,* ed. Jonathan Magonet, 83–93. Oxford: Berghahn Books, 1995.

Markel, Howard. "'The Eyes Have It': Trachoma, the Perception of Disease, the United States Public Health Service, and the American Jewish Immigration Experience, 1897–1924." *Bulletin of the History of Medicine* 74 (2000): 525–60.

Marperger, Paul Jacob. *Das in Natur- und Kunst-Sachen neu-eröffnete Kauffmanns-Magazin . . . .* Hamburg: Christian Albert Pfeiffer, 1708.

Marx, [Jacob Marx]. "Genaue Prüfung der frühen Beerdigung bei den Todten bey den Juden." *Journal von und für Deutschland* 1 (1784): 227–34.

Marx, Jacob Marx. *Über die Beerdigung der Todten.* Hannover: Schmidt, 1788.

Marx, Karl. *The Letters of Karl Marx.* Trans. Saul K. Padover. Englewood Cliffs, NJ: Prentice-Hall, 1979.

Matteoni, Francescal. "The Jew, the Blood and the Body in Late Medieval and Early Modern Europe." *Folklore* 119 (2008): 182–200.

Mauss, Marcel. "Techniques of the Body." *Economy and Society* 2, no.1 (1973): 70–88.

McGuire, Meredith B. *Lived Religion: Faith and Practice in Everyday Life.* Oxford: Oxford University Press, 2008.

Mehler, Richard. "Die Entstehung eines Bürgertums unter den Landjuden in der bayerischen Rhön vor dem Ersten Weltkrieg." In *Juden, Bürger, Deutsche: Zur Geschichte von Vielfalt und Differenz, 1800–1933,* ed. Andreas Gotzmann, Rainer Liedtke, and Till van Rahden, 193–216. Tübingen: Mohr Siebeck, 2001.

Melamed, Abraham. *The Image of the Black in Jewish Culture: A History.* London: RoutledgeCurzon, 2003.

Mellinkoff, Ruth. *Outcasts: Signs of Otherness in Northern European Art of the Late Middle Ages.* Berkeley: University of California Press, 1991.

Mein erstes Wort wider die Juden mit und ohne Bart. Berlin, 1804.

Menasseh ben Israel. *The Hope of Israel.* London: R. I[bbitson] for Livewell Chapman at the Crown in Popes-Head Alley, 1651.

Mendelssohn, Moses. *Ritualgesetze der Juden: Betreffend Erbschaften, Vormundschaftssachen, Testamente und Ehesachen, in so weit sie das Mein und Dein angehen.* 3rd ed. Berlin: Vossische Buchhandlung, 1793.

Mendelssohn, Moses. *Selections from His Writings.* Ed. and trans. Eva Jospe. New York: Viking, 1975.

Metzger, Thérèse, and Mendel Metzger. *Jewish Life in the Middle Ages: Illuminated Hebrew Manuscripts of the Thirteenth to the Sixteenth Centuries.* Secaucus, NJ: Chartwell, 1982.

Meyer, Michael A. *Antwort auf die Moderne: Geschichte der Reformbewegung im Judentum.* Trans. Marie-Therese Pitner and Susanne Grabmayr. Cologne: Böhlau, 2000.

Michels, Evi. *Jiddische Handschriften der Niederlande.* Leiden: Brill, 2013.

Michl, Susanne. *Im Dienste des "Volkskörpers": Deutsche und französische Ärzte im Ersten Weltkrieg.* Göttingen: Vandenhoeck & Ruprecht, 2007.

Midrash. https://www.sefaria.org/texts/Midrash. Last retrieved August 23, 2019.

Midrasch Ruth Rabba: Das ist die haggadische Auslegung des Buches Ruth. Trans. (German) August Wünsche. Leipzig: Schulze, 1883.

Midrash Rabbah Genesis. Trans. Rabbi Dr. H. Freedman and Maurice Simon. 2 vols. London: Soncino, 1939.

Midrash Rabbah HaMavo: Sefer Bereshit (Hebr.). Vols. 1–2. Jerusalem: Magnes Press, 1983.

Midrash Shmuel (Hebr.). Ed. Salomon Buber. Cracow: Josef Fischer, 1893.

Midrash Tanhuma-Yelammedenu: An English Translation of Genesis and Exodus. Ed. Samuel A. Berman. Hoboken, NJ: Ktav, 1996.

Mirrer, Louise. "The Jew's Body in Medieval Iberian Literary Portraits and Miniatures: Examples from the *Cantigas de Santa Maria* and the *Cantar de mio Cid*." *Shofar* 12 (1994): 17–30.

Mishnah. https://www.sefaria.org/texts/Mishnah. Last retrieved August 23, 2019.

Mishkan T'filah: A Reform Siddur: Weekdays, Shabbat, Festivals, and Other Occasions of Public Worship. Ed. Elyse D. Frishman. New York: CCAR Press, 2007.

Mitchell, Harvey, and Samuel S. Kottek. "An Eighteenth-Century Medical View of the Diseases of the Jews in Northeastern France: Medical Anthropology and the Politics of Jewish Emancipation." *Bulletin for the History of Medicine* 67 (1993): 248–81.

Modena, Leo[n]. *The History of the Rites, Customes, and Manner of Life, of the Present Jews Throughout the World.* London: J. L. and to be sold by Jo. Martin and Jo. Ridley, at the Castle in Fleet Street, by Ram Alley, 1650.

Modena, Leon. *The Autobiography of a Seventeenth-Century Venetian Rabbi: Leon Modena's Life of Judah.* Trans. and ed. Mark R. Cohen. Princeton, NJ: Princeton University Press, 1988.

Modena, Leon. *Jüdische Riten, Sitten und Gebräuche.* Ed., trans., and commentary Rafael Arnold. Wiesbaden: Marix Verlag, 2007.

Moll, Sebastian. "Der boxende Rabbi." *Stuttgarter Zeitung,* December 5, 2015, 3.

Mombert, Moritz. *Das gesetzlich verordnete Kellerquellenbad der Israelitinnen: Dient es zur Gesundheit und Reinigung des Körpers oder ist es als eine bis jetzt unbekannt gebliebene Quelle unzähliger Krankheiten zu betrachten, etc.* Mühlhausen: Heinrichshofen, 1828.

Mombert, Moritz. "Das gemeinschaftliche Bad der jüdischen Frauen in Kellern, ein Gegenstand für die medicinische Polizei und für practische Ärzte." *Zeitschrift für Staatsarzneikunde* 10 (1830): 274–94.

Mor, Sagit. "Hierarchies of Disability in Israeli-Zionist Collective Ethos and Public Policy." Draft, n.d. http://weblaw.haifa.ac.il/he/Faculty/Mor/Publications/Hierarchies%20Disability%20in%20Israeli%20Collective%20Ethos%20-%20final%20for%20web.pdf. Last retrieved April 26, 2016.

Morewedge, Rosemarie Thee. "'Geschichte einer Nummer': Das Motiv der Tätowierung in Ruth Klügers Erinnerungen *Unterwegs verloren*." In *Literatur—Universalie und Kulturenspezifikum*, ed. Andreas Kramer and Jan Röhnert, 175–89. Göttingen: Universitätsverlag, 2010.

Morgenstern, Matthias. *Judentum und Gender.* Münster: LIT Verlag, 2014.

Morosini, Giulio. *Via della fede mostrata a'gli ebrei.* Rome: Nella La stamparia della Sacra Congregazione de Propaganda Fide, 1683.

Moryson, Fynes. *Shakespeare's Europe: Unpublished Chapters of Fynes Moryson's Itinerary, being a survey of the condition of Europe at the end of the 16th century.* London: Sherratt & Hughes, 1903.

Mosse, George L. "Jewish Emancipation: Between Bildung and Respectability." In *The Jewish Response to German Culture: From the Enlightenment to the Second World War*, ed. Jehuda Reinharz and Walter Schatzberg, 1–16. Hanover, NH: University Press of New England, 1985.

Mostegel, Iris. "Die Scheitelmacherin: Daniela Kaner betreibt in Wien ein Studio für koschere Perücken." *Jüdische Allgemeine,* July 1, 2014. https://www.juedische-allgemeine.de/juedische-welt/die-scheitelmacherin/. Last retrieved February 22, 2020.

Muhs, Jochen. "Deaf People as Eyewitnesses of National Socialism." In *Deaf People in Hitler's Europe*, ed. Donna F. Ryan and John S. Schuchman, 78–97. Washington, DC: Gallaudet University Press, 2002.

Müller, Dietmar. *Staatsbürger auf Widerruf: Juden und Muslime als Alteritätspartner im rumänischen und serbischen Nationscode; Ethnonationale Staatsbürgerschaftskonzepte, 1878–1941.* Wiesbaden: Harrassowitz, 2005.

Müller, Monika, and Gabi Rudolf. "Von tödlichen Krankheiten. Leichenblätter aus der Altenkunstadter Genisa." In *Genisa-Blätter*, ed. Rebekka Denz and Gabi Rudolf, 95–101. Potsdam: Universitätsverlag, 2015. https://publishup.uni-potsdam.de/frontdoor/index/index/docId/7731. Last retrieved May 3, 2016.

Münster, Sebastian. *Meshiah = Messias Christianorum et Iudaeorum Hebraicè & Latinè*. Basel: Apud Henricum Petrum, 1539.

Nahshon, Edna, ed. *Jews and Shoes*. London: Berg, 2008.

Nathans, Benjamin. *Beyond the Pale: The Jewish Encounter with Late Imperial Russia*. Berkeley: University of California Press, 2004.

Natvig, Paul. *Jacques Joseph: Surgical Sculptor*. Philadelphia: Saunders, 1982.

Naveh, Joseph. "Illnesses and Amulets in Antiquity." In *Illness and Healing in Ancient Times*, ed. Ofra Rimon, 24–28. Haifa: University of Haifa Press, 1996.

Neubauer, Adolf, and Moritz Stern, eds. *Hebräische Berichte über die Judenverfolgungen während der Kreuzzüge*. Berlin: Leonard Simion, 1892.

Neutel, Karin B., and Matthew R. Anderson. "The First Cut Is the Deepest: Masculinity and Circumcision in the First Century." In *Biblical Masculinities Foregrounded*, ed. Ovidiu Creanga and Peter-Ben Smit, 228–44. Sheffield: Sheffield Phoenix Press, 2014.

Nevins, Daniel S. "The Participation of Jews Who Are Blind in the Torah Service." In *Jewish Perspectives on Theology and the Human Experience of Disability*, ed. Judith Z. Abrams and William C. Gaventa, 27–52. Binghamton, NY: Haworth Pastoral Press, 2006.

Nevins, Michael. *The Jewish Doctor: A Narrative History*. Northvale, NJ: Jason Aronson, 1996.

The New English Bible with the Apocrypha. New York: Oxford University Press, 1971.

Nicolai, Johann A. *Grundriß der Sanitäts-Polizey mit besonderer Beziehung auf den preußischen Staat*. Vol 1. Berlin: Nicolaische Buchhandlung, 1835.

Nirenberg, David. "Conversion, Sex, and Segregation: Jews and Christians in Medieval Spain." *American Historical Review* 107 (2002): 1065–93.

Nordau, Max. "Jewry of Muscle." In *The Jew in the Modern World: A Documentary History*, ed. Paul R. Mendes-Flohr and Jehuda Reinharz, 434–35. New York: Oxford University Press, 1980.

Nordmann, Yves. *Zwischen Leben und Tod: Aspekte jüdischer Medizinethik*. Bern: Peter Lang, 1999.

Nossig, Albert. *Die Sozialhygiene der Juden und des altorientalischen Völkerkreises*. Stuttgart: Deutsche Verlags-Anstalt, 1894.

Novak, William, and Moshe Waldoks, eds. *The Big Book of Jewish Humor*. New York: Harper & Row, 1981.

Nübling, Eugen. *Die Judengemeinde des Mittelalters: Insbesondere die Judengemeinde der Reichsstadt Ulm*. Ulm: Nübling Verlag, 1896.

Oehl, Benedikt. *Die Altercatio Ecclesiae et Synagogae: Ein antijudaistischer Dialog der Spätantike*. PhD diss., Bonn, 2012.

Oekonomische Hauspostille, oder Sammlung der bewährtesten Mittel und Vorteile. . . . 2nd ed. Vienna: Christoph Rehm, 1792.

Oişteanu, Andrei. *Inventing the Jew: Antisemitic Stereotypes in Romanian and Other Central East-European Cultures*. Trans. Mirela Adăscăliţei. Lincoln: University of Nebraska Press, 2009.

Okun, B. S. "Religiosity and Contraceptive Method Choice: The Jewish Population of Israel." *European Journal of Population* 16 (2000): 109–32.

Oller, Dale Tobin. "Jewish Genetic Diseases and Jewish Illness Behavior: A Review of Selected Sociocultural Literature." *Jewish Social Studies* 46 (1984): 177–87.

Olsvanger, Immanuel. *Rosinkess mit Mandlen: Schwänke, Erzählungen, Sprichwörter, Rätsel aus der Volksliteratur der Ostjuden*. 2nd rev. ed. Basel: Schweizerische Gesellschaft für Volkskunde, 1931.

Olyan, Saul M. *Disability in the Hebrew Bible: Interpreting Mental and Physical Differences*. Cambridge: Cambridge University Press, 2001.

On the Eve of the Reformation: "Letters of Obscure Men." Trans. Francis Griffin Stokes. Introd. Hajo Holborn. New York: Harper Torchbooks, 1964.

Oshry, Ephraim. *She'elot u-Teshuvot mi-Ma'amakim* (Hebr.) [Responsa]. New York: Ephraim Oshry, 1959–74.

Osiander, Andreas. *Andreas Osianders Schrift über die Blutbeschuldigung (Ob es war und glaublich sey, dass die Juden der Christen kinder heimlich erwürgen und jr blut gebrauchen)*. Ed. Moritz Stern. Kiel: Sinai Verlag, 1893.

Osiander, Friedrich Benjamin. *Handbuch der Entbindungskunst*. Vol. 1. Tübingen: Christian Friedrich Osiander, 1819.

Ostermann, Heinrich. *Die gesammte Polizei-, Militair-, Steuer- und Gemeinde-Verwaltung in den Königl. Preuss. Staaten . . . .* Vol 1. Coesfeld: Verlag der Rieseschen Buchhandlung, 1836.

Papo, Manfred. "Die sexuelle Ethik im Qorân in ihrem Verhältnis zu seinen jüdischen Quellen." *Mitteilungen zur jüdischen Volkskunde* 26/27 (1924/25): 171–291.

Pardo Tomás, José. "Physicians' and Inquisitors' Stories? Circumcision and Crypto-Judaism in Sixteenth-Eighteenth-Century Spain." In *Bodily Extremities: Preoccupations with the Human Body in Early Modern European Culture*, ed. Florika Egmond and Robert Zwijnenberg, 168–94. Aldershot: Ashgate, 2003.

Patton, Pamela A. *Art of Estrangement: Redefining Jews in Reconquest Spain*. University Park: Pennsylvania State University Press, 2012.

Pawel, Ernst. *The Nightmare of Reason: A Life of Franz Kafka*. New York: Vintage, 1985.

Penkower, Monty Noam. "The Kishinev Pogrom of 1903: A Turning Point in Jewish History." *Modern Judaism* 24 (2004): 187–225.

Pezzl, Johann. *Skizze von Wien: Ein Kultur- und Sittenbild aus der josefinischen Zeit*. Ed. Gustav Gugitz and Anton Schlossar. Graz: Leykam, 1923.

Philippson, Ludwig. *Der Geist des Judenthums immer derselbe*. Nuremberg: Friedrich Campe, 1838.

Philo. *The Works of Philo*. Trans. C. D. Yonge. Peabody, MA: Hendrickson, 1993.

Pinto, Isaac de. *Apologie pour la nation juive, ou Réflexions critiques sur le premier chapitre du VII. tome des Oeuvres de monsieur de Voltaire, au sujet des juifs*. Amsterdam: J. Joubert, 1762.

Poliakov, Leon. *The History of Anti-Semitism*. Vol. 1. New York: Vanguard Press, 1965.

Pollack, Herman. *Jewish Folkways in Germanic Lands (1648–1806): Studies in Aspects of Daily Life*. Cambridge, MA: Harvard University Press, 1971.

Pollak, Shulamis Juni. "Correlates of Genetic Counseling and Testing." *Journal of Religion and Health* 50 (2011): 796–805.

Pollatschek, Arnold. "Zur Aetiologie des Diabetes mellitus." *Zeitschrift für klinische Medizin* 42 (1902): 478–82.

Pomata, Gianna. "Menstruating Men: Similarity and Difference of the Sexes in Early Modern Medicine." In *Generation and Degeneration: Tropes of Reproduction in Literature and History from Antiquity to Early Modern Europe*, ed. Valeria Finucci and Kevin Brownlee, 109–52. Durham, NC: Duke University Press, 2001.

Porta, Giambattista della [Johannes Baptista Porta]. *Die Physiognomie des Menschen: Vier Bücher*. Introd. Theodor Lessing; trans., introd., foreword, and commentary Will Rink. Dresden: Madaus, 1930.

Porta, Giambattista della [Giovan Battista Della Porta]. *Fisiognomía*. Trans. Miguel A. González Manjarrés. 2 vols. Madrid: Asociación Española de Neuropsiquiatría, 2007.

Pouzarová, Anna. "Als Erzieherin in der Familie Kafka." In *"Als Kafka mir entgegenkam . . ."*: *Erinnerungen an Franz Kafka*, ed. Hans-Gerd Koch, 55–65. Berlin: Wagenbach, 1995.

Präger, Max, and Siegfried Schmitz, eds. *Jüdische Schwänke: Eine volkskundliche Studie*. Wiesbaden: Rheinische Verlagsanstalt, 1964.

Prescott, Deborah Lee. *Imagery from Genesis in Holocaust Memoirs: A Critical Study*. Jefferson, NC: McFarland, 2010.

Presner, Todd Samuel. *Muscular Judaism: The Jewish Body and the Politics of Regeneration*. London: Routledge, 2007.

Preuss, Julius. *Biblisch-talmudische Medizin: Beiträge zur Geschichte der Heilkunde und der Kultur überhaupt*. 1911. Reprint, Wiesbaden: Fourier, 1992.

Preuß, Monika. ". . . aber die Krone des guten Namens überragt sie": Jüdische Ehrvorstellungen im 18. Jahrhundert im Kraichgau. Stuttgart: Kohlhammer, 2005.

Preuß, Monika. Gelehrte Juden: Lernen als Frömmigkeitsideal in der frühen Neuzeit. Göttingen: Wallstein, 2007.

Prichard, James Cowles. Researches into the Physical History of Man. London: Houlston & Stoneman, 1813.

Probst, Stephan M. "Mehr als Gotteslohn: Arzthonorare." Jüdische Allgemeine, February 1, 2016. https://www.juedische-allgemeine.de/religion/mehr-als-gotteslohn/. Last retrieved February 22, 2020.

Protokolle der dritten Versammlung deutscher Rabbiner: Abgehalten zu Breslau 13. bis 24. Juli 1846. Breslau: F. E. C. Leuckart, 1847.

Przyrembel, Alexandra. "Rassenschande": Reinheitsmythos und Vernichtungslegitimation im Nationalsozialismus. Göttingen: Vandenhoeck & Ruprecht, 2003.

Quast, Bruno. "Monochrome Ritter: Über Farbe und Ordnung in höfischen Erzähltexten des Mittelalters." In Die Farben imaginierter Welten: Zur Kulturgeschichte ihrer Codierung in Kunst und Literatur vom Mittelalter bis zur Gegenwart, ed. Monika Schausten, 169–200. Berlin: Oldenbourg Akademieverlag, 2012.

Rabinowitz, Dan. "Yarmulke: A Historic Cover-Up?" Hakirah 4 (2007): 221–38.

Rahe, Thomas. "Höre Israel": Jüdische Religiosität in nationalsozialistischen Konzentrationslagern. Göttingen: Vandenhoeck & Ruprecht, 1999.

Ramazzini, Bernardino. A Treatise of the Diseases of Tradesmen. London: Andrew Bell et al., 1705.

Ranke-Graves, Robert, and Raphael Patai. Hebräische Mythologie: Über die Schöpfungsgeschichte und andere Mythen aus dem Alten Testament. Trans. Sylvia Höpfert. Reinbek: Rowohlt, 1986.

Rappaport, Samuel. "Aus dem religiösen Leben der Ostjuden." Der Jude 7 (1921/22): 410–16.

Raspe, Julia. Jüdische Hagiographie im mittelalterlichen Aschkenas. Tübingen: Mohr Siebeck, 2006.

Rau, Gottlieb Ludwig. Ueber die Erkenntniß und Heilung der gesammten Hämorrhoidialkrankheit. Gießen: Heyer, 1821.

Ravid, Benjamin. "From Yellow to Red: On the Distinguishing Head-Covering of the Jews of Venice." Jewish History 6 (1992): 179–210.

Ravitsky, Vardit and Michael Prawer, Michael. "The Dying Patient Law, 2005." Jewish Medical Ethics and Halacha 6 (2008): 13–29.

Reifler, David. Days of Ticho: Empire, Mandate, Medicine and Art in the Holy Land. Jerusalem: Gefen Publishing House, 2015.

Reinecke, Christiane. Grenzen der Freizügigkeit: Migrationskontrolle in Großbritannien und Deutschland, 1880–1930. Munich: Oldenbourg, 2010.

Reinke, Andreas. Judentum und Wohlfahrtspflege in Deutschland: Das jüdische Krankenhaus in Breslau, 1726–1944. Hannover: Verlag Hahnsche Buchhandlung, 1999.

Reissner, Hanns Günther. Eduard Gans: Ein Leben im Vormärz. Tübingen: Mohr Siebeck, 1965.

Resnick, Irven M. "Medieval Roots of the Myth of Jewish Male Menses." Harvard Theological Review 93 (2000): 241–63.

Resnick, Irven M. Marks of Distinction: Christian Perceptions of Jews in the High Middle Ages. Washington, DC: Catholic University of America Press, 2012.

Reuter, Shelley Z. "The Genuine Jewish Type: Racial Ideology and Anti-Immigrationism in Early Medical Writing About Tay-Sachs Disease." Canadian Journal of Sociology / Cahiers canadiens de sociologie 31 (2006): 291–323.

Rezasco, Giulio. "Del segno degli ebrei." Giornale Ligustico di Archeologia, Storia e Belle Arti 15 (1888): 241–66, 321–51; and 16 (1889): 31–61.

Richarz, Monika. Der Eintritt der Juden in die akademischen Berufe: Jüdische Studenten und Akademiker in Deutschland, 1678–1848. Preface Adolf Leschnitzer. Tübingen: Mohr Siebeck, 1974.

Richter, Jean Paul. Sämtliche Werke. Vol. 4. Berlin: Reimer, 1841.

Riddle, John M. Eve's Herbs: A History of Contraception and Abortion in the West. Cambridge, MA: Harvard University Press, 1997.

Rigter, R. B. M. "Geschiedenis van het genezen; trachoom, de gesel van de Amsterdamse jodenbuurt" [History of Healing; Trachoma, the Scourge of the Jewish District in Amsterdam]. *Nederlands Tijdschrift voor Geneeskunde* 140 (1996): 616–20.

Ringelblum, Emanuel. *Ghetto Warschau: Tagebücher aus dem Chaos.* Stuttgart: Seewald Verlag, 1967.

Ritter, Christine. *Rachels Klage im Antiken Judentum und frühen Christentum: Eine auslegungsgeschichtliche Studie.* Leiden: Brill, 2003.

Robert, Ulysse. *Les signes dInfamie.* Paris: Librairer Honoré Champion, 1891.

Roggenkamp, Viola. "Immer der Nase nach: Anmerkungen zu einem jüdischen Alleinstellungsmerkmal." *Jüdische Allgemeine,* July 3, 2012. https://www.juedische-allgemeine.de/kultur/immer-der-nase-nach-2/. Last retrieved February 22, 2020.

Rohrer, Joseph. *Versuch über die jüdischen Bewohner der österreichischen Monarchie.* Vienna: Im Verlage des Kunst-und Industrie-Comptoirs, 1804.

Rollman, Gary B. "Culture and Pain." In *Cultural Clinical Psychology: Theory, Research, and Practice,* ed. S. S. Kazarian and D. R. Evans, 267–86. New York: Oxford University Press, 1998.

Rommel, Florian. "Judenfeindliche Vorstellungen im Passionsspiel des Mittelalters." In *Juden in der deutschen Literatur des Mittelalters: Religiöse Konzepte—Feindbilder—Rechtfertigungen,* ed. Ursula Schulze, 183–208. Tübingen: Niemeyer, 2002.

Rose, Paul Lawrence. *Revolutionary Antisemitism in Germany from Kant to Wagner.* Princeton, NJ: Princeton University Press, 1990.

Rosen, Rhoda. "Die Inszenierung des jüdischen Körper: Zwischen Identifikation und Projektion." In *"Der schejne Jid": Das Bild des "jüdischen Körpers" in Mythos und Ritual,* ed. Sander L. Gilman, Robert Jütte, and Gabriele Kohlbauer-Fritz, 11–22. Vienna: Picus Verlag, 1998.

Rosen, Tova. *Unveiling Eve: Reading Gender in Medieval Hebrew Literature.* Philadelphia: University of Pennsylvania Press, 2003.

Rosenbach, Detlev. *Lesser Ury: Das druckgraphische Werk.* Hannover: Gr. Mann, 2002.

Rosenberg, Heinrich. *Der Weichselzopf, eine theoretisch-practische Abhandlung sammt einer pragmatischen Geschichte desselben . . . .* Munich: Georg Franz, 1839.

Rosin, Josef. *Preserving our Litvak Heritage: A History of 31 Jewish Communities in Lithuania.* Ed. Joel Halpert. League City, TX: JewishGen, 2005.

Rosner, Fred. *Modern Medicine and Jewish Laws.* New York: Yeshiva University, 1972.

Rosner, Fred. "Embalming and Cremation in Judaism." *Korot* 8, no. 11/12 (1985): 218–35.

Rosner, Fred. "The Jewish Patient in a Non-Jewish Hospital." *Journal of Religion and Health* 25 (1986): 316–24.

Rosner, Fred. *Sex Ethics in the Writings of Moses Maimonides.* New York: Bloch, 1994.

Rosner, Fred, David J. Bleich, and Menachem M. Brayer, eds. *Jewish Bioethics.* Hoboken, NJ: Ktav, 1999.

Ross, Joshua. "Body Piercing in Judaism." 2009. http://blog.webyeshiva.org/body-piercing-in-judaism-by-rabbi-joshua-ross/. Last retrieved April 5, 2016.

Roth, Cecil. *Venice.* Philadelphia: Jewish Publication Society, 1930.

Roth, Cecil. "The Qualification of Jewish Physicians in the Middle Ages." *Speculum* 28 (1953): 834–84.

Roth, Cecil. *Essays and Portraits in Anglo-Jewish History.* Philadelphia: Jewish Publication Society, 1962.

Roth, Joseph. *The Wandering Jews.* Trans. Michael Hofmann. New York: Norton, 2001.

Roth, Philip. *Goodbye, Columbus.* Boston: Houghton Mifflin Harcourt, 1959.

Roth, Philip. *Nemesis.* Boston: Houghton Mifflin Harcourt, 2010.

Rubach, Leon. *The Autobiography of Leon Rubach: The First Twenty Years.* Bloomington: Indiana University Press, 2010.

Rubens, Alfred. *A History of Jewish Costume.* London: Valentine, Mitchell, 1967.

Ruderman, David B. *Jewish Thought and Scientific Discovery in Early Modern Europe.* New Haven, CT: Yale University Press, 1995.

Rupert von Deutz. "De Trinitate." In *Patrologia Cursus Completus,* Series Latina 167, ed. Jacques Paul Migne, cols. 394–97. Paris: Garnier Frères, 1854.

Ruppin, Arthur. *Die Juden der Gegenwart: Eine sozialwissenschaftliche Studie.* Berlin: Calvary, 1918.

Rürup, Miriam. *Ehrensache: Jüdische Studentenverbindungen an deutschen Universitäten, 1886–1937.* Göttingen: Vandenhoeck & Ruprecht, 2008.

Rüve, Gerlind. *Scheintod: Zur kulturellen Debatte der Schwelle zwischen Leben und Tod um 1800.* Bielefeld: Transcript Verlag, 2008.

Saadia Gaon. *The Book of Beliefs and Opinions.* Trans. Samuel Rosenblatt. New Haven, CT: Yale University Press, 1948.

Sacken, Eduard von. *Die K.K. Ambraser Sammlung.* Pt. 2. Vienna: Verlag Braunmüller, 1855.

Sahih Muslim: Being Traditions of the Sayings and Doings of the Prophet Muhammad as Narrated by His Companions and Compiled Under the Title Al Jami-Us-Sahih. Vol. 3. New Delhi: Kitab Bhavan, 2000.

Sahmland, Irmgard. "Verordnete Körperspende—Das Hospital Haina als Bezugsquelle für Anatomieleichen (1786–1855)." In *An der Wende zur Moderne: Die hessischen Hospitäler im 18. und 19. Jahrhundert,* ed. Arnd Friedrich, Irmtraud Sahmland, and Christina Vanja, 65–106. Petersberg: Imhof, 2008.

Sandler, Aaron. "Das Trachom in Palästina." *Altneuland* 1 (1904): 161–70.

Saphra, B. "Jüdische Kämpfe um Freiheit und Recht." 2nd ser. *Ost und West* 15/16 (1916): cols. 123–38.

Sarah, Elizabeth. "Judaism and Lesbianism: A Tale of Life on the Margins of the Text." In *Jewish Explorations of Sexuality,* ed. Jonathan Magonet, 95–102. Oxford: Berghahn Books, 1995.

Sarason, Richard. "To Rise from the Dead? Mishkan T'filah and a Reform Liturgical Conundrum." *Ten Minutes of Torah,* February 2006. https://www.ccarpress.org/content.asp?tid = 456. Last retrieved February 10, 2020.

Satlow, Michael L. *Tasting the Dish: Rabbinic Rhetorics of Sexuality.* Atlanta: Scholars Press, 1995.

Satlow, Michael L. "Jewish Constructions of Nakedness in Late Antiquity." *Journal of Biblical Literature* 116 (1997): 429–54.

Sauerteig, Lutz. *Krankheit, Sexualität, Gesellschaft: Geschlechtskrankheiten und Gesundheitspolitik in Deutschland im 19. und 20. Jahrhundert.* Stuttgart: Franz Steiner Verlag, 1999.

Saxonia, Herculis. *De plica quam poloni gwozdzec, roxolani koltunum vocant: Liber nunc primu[m] in luce[m] editus.* Padua: Laurentius Pasquatus, 1600.

Schachter, Herschel. "Halachic Aspects of Family Planning." *Journal of Halacha and Contemporary Society* 6 (1982): 5–32.

Schack, Ingeborg-Liane. *Die jiddische Sprache: Das jiddische Sprichwort.* Wiesbaden: VMA-Verlag, 1998.

Schäfer, Daniel. *Alter und Krankheit in der Frühen Neuzeit: Der ärztliche Blick auf die letzte Lebensphase.* Frankfurt/M.: Campus, 2010.

Schäfer, Julia. *Vermessen—gezeichnet—verlacht: Judenbilder in populären Zeitschriften 1918–1933.* Frankfurt/M.: Campus, 2005.

Schäfer, Peter. *Jesus in the Talmud.* Princeton, NJ: Princeton University Press, 2007.

Schäfer, Torsten. *"Jedenfalls habe ich auch mitgeschossen": Das NSG-Verfahren gegen Johann Josef Kuhr und andere ehemalige Angehörige des Polizeibataillons 306, der Polizeireiterabteilung 2 und der SD-Dienststelle von Pinsk beim Landgericht Frankfurt am Main 1962–1973; eine textanalytische Fallstudie zur Mentalitätsgeschichte.* Hamburg: LIT Verlag, 2007.

Scharff, Thomas. "Der Körper der Ketzer im hochmittelalterlichen Häresiediskurs." In *Körper mit Geschichte,* ed. Clemens Wischermann and Stefan Haas, 133–49. Stuttgart: Franz Steiner Verlag, 2000.

Scheiba, Michael. *Dissertatio inauguralis medica, sistens quaedam plicae pathologicae: Germ. Juden-Zopff, Polon. Kołtun. . . .* (1717). Königsberg: Litteris Reusnerianis, 1739.

Schell-Apacik, Chayim. "Genetische Untersuchungen und Schwangerschaftsabbruch im Kontext jüdischer Ethik am Beispiel der Tay-Sachs-Erkrankung." *PaRDeS: Zeitschrift der Vereinigung für Jüdische Studien e.V.* 13 (2007): 99–110.

Schellekens, Jona, and Jon Anson, eds. *Israel's Destiny: Fertility and Mortality in a Divided Society.* New Brunswick, NJ: Transaction Publishers, 2007.

Schleich, Carl Ludwig. *Aus dem Nachlaß*. Berlin: Ernst Rowohlt Verlag, 1927.

Schlich, Thomas. "Die Medizin und der Wandel der jüdischen Gemeinde: Das jüdische rituelle Bad im Hygienediskurs des 19. Jahrhunderts." In *Jüdische Gemeinden und Organisationsformen von der Antike bis zur Gegenwart*, ed. Robert Jütte and Abraham P. Kustermann, 173–94. Vienna: Böhlau, 1996.

Schlich, Thomas. "Der lebende und der tote Körper." In *"Der schejne Jid": Das Bild des "jüdischen Körpers" in Mythos und Ritual*, ed. Sander L. Gilman, Robert Jütte, and Gabriele Kohlbauer-Fritz, 147–57. Vienna: Picus Verlag, 1998.

Schmalhausen, Bernd. *Berthold Beitz im Dritten Reich: Mensch in unmenschlicher Zeit*. Essen: Pomp Verlag, 1991.

Schmitz, Barbara. "Auferstehung und Epiphanie: Jenseits- und Körperkonzepte im Zweiten Makkabäerbuch." In *The Human Body in Death and Resurrection*, ed. Tobias Nicklas, Friedrich V. Reiterer, Joseph Verheyden, and Heike Braun, 105–42. Berlin: Walter de Gruyter, 2009.

Schmitz, Rainer, ed. *Henriette Herz in Erinnerungen, Briefen und Zeugnissen*. Berlin: Die Andere Bibliothek, 2013.

Schnapper-Arndt, Gottlieb. *Studien zur Geschichte der Lebenshaltung in Frankfurt a. M. während des 17. und 18. Jahrhunderts*. Ed. Karl Bräuer. Pt. 1. Frankfurt/M.: Joseph Baer, 1915.

Schneider, Peter Joseph. "Medizinisch-polizeiliche Würdigung einiger Religionsbräuche und Sitten des israelitischen Volkes rücksichtlich ihres Einflusses auf den Gesundheitszustand desselben." *Zeitschrift für die Staatsarzneikunde* 10 (1825): 213–301.

Scholem, Gershom. *Kabbalah*. Jerusalem: Keter Publishing House, 1977.

Scholem, Gershom. *Ursprung und Anfänge der Kabbala*. 2nd ed. Berlin: Walter de Gruyter, 2001.

Schöner, Petra. *Judenbilder im deutschen Einblattdruck der Renaissance*. Baden-Baden: Valentin Koerner, 2002.

Schorsch, Jonathan. *Jews and Blacks in the Early Modern World*. Cambridge: Cambridge University Press, 2004.

Schorsch, Jonathan. "Blacks, Jews and the Racial Imagination in the Writings of Sephardim in the Long Seventeenth Century." *Jewish History* 19 (2005): 109–35.

Schreckenberg, Heinz. *Die christlichen Adversus-Judaeos-Texte und ihr literarisches und historisches Umfeld (1.–11. Jh.)*. Frankfurt/M.: Peter Lang, 1982.

Schreckenberg, Heinz. *Die Juden in der Kunst Europas: Ein historischer Bildatlas*. Göttingen: Vandenhoeck & Ruprecht, 1996.

Schröder, Johann Friedrich. *Satzungen und Gebräuche des talmudisch-rabbinischen Judenthums: Ein Handbuch für Juristen, Staatsmänner, Theologen und Geschichtsforscher, sowie für alle, welche sich über diesen Gegenstand belehren wollen*. Bremen: A. D. Geisler, 1851.

Schubert, Charlotte and Ulrich Huttner. *Frauenmedizin in der Antike: Griechisch, lateinisch, deutsch*. Düsseldorf: Artemis & Winkler, 1999.

Schuchard, Martha Keith. "From Poland to London: Sabbatean Influences on the Mystical Underworld of Zinzendorf, Swedenborg, and Blake." In *Holy Dissent: Jewish and Christian Mystics in Eastern Europe*, ed. Glenn Dynner, 250–80. Detroit: Wayne State University Press, 2011.

Schudt, Johann Jakob. *Jüdische Merckwürdigkeiten. . . .* 4 pts. Frankfurt/M.: Laim, 1714–17.

Schug, Alexander. " 'Immer frisch frisiert'—das gestaltete Kopfhaar als Requisite moderner Selbstinszenierung in der Weimarer Republik." In *Haar Tragen: Eine kulturwissenschaftliche Annäherung*, ed. Christian Janecke, 83–98. Cologne: Böhlau, 2004.

Schüler-Springorum, Stefanie. *Geschlecht und Differenz*. Paderborn: Ferdinand Schöningh, 2014.

Schur, Yechiel Y. "The Care of the Dead in Medieval Ashkenaz, 1000–1500." PhD diss., New York University, 2008.

Schuster, Josef, *Zur Sterblichkeit jüdischer und nicht-jüdischer Säuglinge*. Med. diss., University of Würzburg, 1980.

Schuster, Peter *Das Frauenhaus: Städtische Bordelle in Deutschland (1350–1600)*. Paderborn: Ferdinand Schöningh, 1992.

Schwara, Desanka."*Ojfn weg schtejt a bojm*": *Jüdische Kindheit und Jugend in Galizien, Kongresspolen, Litauen und Russland, 1881–1939.* Cologne: Böhlau, 1999.

Schwartz, Yardena. "Tattoos Reign in Israel—Jewish Law or No." *Forward*, February 19, 2014. http://forward.com/articles/193019/tattoos-reign-in-israel-jewish-law-or-no/?p = all. Last retrieved April 5, 2016.

Schwarz, Moshe. *Versteinertes Herz: Ein jüdisches Überlebensschicksal aus Buczacz/Polen unter dem Naziregime und in Israel 1936 bis 2004.* Konstanz: Hartung-Gorre, 2005.

Schwenken, Karl Philipp Theodor. *Notizen über die berüchtigsten jüdischen Gauner und Spitzbuben, welche sich gegenwärtig in Deutschland und an dessen Gränzen umhertreiben.* Marburg: Johann Christian Krieger, 1820.

Schwimmer, Ernst Ludwig. "Plica Polonica." In *Realencyclopädie der gesammten Heilkunde*, ed. Albert Eulenburg, 15:624–26. 2nd ed. Vienna: Urban & Schwarzenberg, 1888.

Sedley, David. "Jewish Perspectives on Ageing Enrichment." February 2012. http://www.rabbisedley.com/audio/Jewish_Aging.pdf. Last retrieved April 26, 2016.

Seegen, Josef. *Der Diabetes Mellitus auf Grundlage zahlreicher Beobachtungen.* Leipzig: T. O. Weigel, 1870.

Sefer Chasidim (Hebr.) Lemberg: B. L. Nechales, 1864. http://www.hebrewbooks.org/38069. Last retrieved March 31, 2016.

Sefer Chasidim: The Book of the Pious. Cond., trans., and annotations Avraham Yaakov Finkel. Northvale, NJ: Jason Aronson, 1997.

Sefer Maharil: Minhagim (Hebr.). Ed. Shlomo Spitzer. Jerusalem: Mifal Torat Hakhme Ashkenaz, 1989.

Sefer Nizzahon Yashan (Hebr.). Ed. Mordechai Breuer. Ramat Gan: Bar-Ilan University Press, 1978.

Sefer Yetzirah: The Book of Creation in Theory and Practice. 2nd rev. ed. Trans. Aryeh Kaplan. Newburyport: Samuel Weiser, 2005.

Sefer Yosef ha-Meqanne. Introd., trans., and commentary Luca Benotti. 1987. http://hdl.handle.net/10579/8829. Last retrieved August 24, 2019.

Seligmann, Caesar. *Geschichte der jüdischen Reformbewegung von Mendelssohn bis zur Gegenwart.* Frankfurt/M.: Kauffmann Verlag, 1922.

Setzer, Claudia. "Ressurection of the Body in Early Judaism and Christianity." In *The Human Body in Death and Resurrection*, ed. Tobias Nicklas, Friedrich V. Reiterer, and Joseph Joseph, with Heike Braun, 1–12. Berlin: Walter de Gruyter, 2009.

Shahar, Isaiah. "The Emergence of the Modern Pictorial Stereotype of the Jew in England: Studies in the Cultural Life of the Jews in England." *Folklore Research Center Studies* 5 (1975): 331–65.

Shakespeare, William. *The Merchant of Venice.* Ed. Leah S. Marcus. New York: W. W. Norton, 2006.

Shalev-Eyni, Sarit. "Purity and Impurity: The Naked Woman Bathing in Jewish and Christian Art." In *Between Judaism and Christianity Art: Historical Essays in Honor of Elisheva (Elisabeth) Revel-Neher*, ed. Katrin Kogman-Appel and Mati Meyer, 109–213. Leiden: Brill, 2009.

Shalev-Eyni, Sarit. "The Bared Breast in Medieval Ashkenazi Illumination: Cultural Connotations in a Heterogeneous Society." *Different Visions* 6 (2014): 1–39. http://differentvisions.org/articles-pdf/five/shalev-eyni-final.pdf. Last retrieved March 31, 2016.

Shatzmiller, Joseph. *Jews, Medicine and Medieval Society.* Berkeley: University of California Press, 1994.

Shilo, Margarit. *Princess or Prisoner? Jewish Women in Jerusalem, 1840–1914.* Waltham, MA: Brandeis University Press, 2005.

Shoham-Steiner, Ephraim. "An Ultimate Pariah? Jewish Social Attitudes Towards Jewish Lepers in Medieval Western Europe." *Social Research* 70 (2003): 237–68.

Shoham-Steiner, Ephraim. " 'For a Prayer in That Place Would Be Most Welcome': Jews, Holy Shrines and Miracles—a New Approach." *Viator* 37 (2006): 369–95.

Shoham-Steiner, Ephraim. "Poverty and Disability: The Medieval Jewish Perspective." In *The Sign Languages of Poverty*, ed. Gerhard Jaritz, 75–94. Vienna: Verlag der österreichischen Akademie der Wissenschaften, 2007.

Shoham-Steiner, Ephraim. *On the Margins of a Minority: Leprosy, Madness and Disability Among the Jews of Medieval Europe.* Trans. Haim Waltzman. Detroit: Wayne State University Press, 2014.

Shulchan Arukh. https://www.sefaria.org/texts/Halakhah/Shulchan%Arukh. Last retrieved August 24, 2019.

Shulman, Eli Baruch. "Hair Covering and Jewish Law: A Response." *Tradition* 43, no. 2 (2010): 73–88.

Shupak, Nili. "'And Joseph Commanded His Servants the Physicians to Embalm His Father' (Genesis 50:2): The Physicians רופאים in the Joseph Story." In *Illness and Healing in Ancient Times*, ed. Ofra Rimon, 6–7. Haifa: University of Haifa Press, 1996.

Siddur Ashkenaz. https://www.sefaria.org/Siddur_Ashkenaz?lang = bi. Last retrieved August 24, 2019.

Siddur Schma Kolenu. Trans. (German) Rav Joseph Scheuer. Basel: Morascha, 1997.

Sidur Sefat Emet. With German trans. Rabbi Dr. S. Bamberger. Basel: Victor Goldschmidt Verlag, 1995.

Sifrei Devarim. https://www.sefaria.org/Sifrei_Devarim?lang = bi. Last retrieved August 15, 2019.

Sigusch, Volkmar, and Günter Grau, eds. *Personenlexikon der Sexualforschung.* Frankfurt/M.: Campus, 2009.

Silberstein, Siegfried. "Mendelssohn und Mecklenburg." *Zeitschrift für die Geschichte der Juden in Deutschland,* Neue Folge, 1 (1929): 233–44, 275–90.

Silverman, Eric. *From Abraham to America: A History of Jewish Circumcision.* Lanham, MD: Rowman & Littlefield, 2006.

Silverman, Eric. *A Cultural History of Jewish Dress.* London: Bloomsbury, 2013.

Simonsohn, Shlomo. *Jews in the Duchy of Milan.* Vol. 3. Jerusalem: Israel Academy of Sciences and Humanities, 1982.

Sinclair, Daniel. "The Obligation to Heal and Patient Autonomy in Jewish Law." *Journal of Law and Religion* 13 (1998/99): 351–77.

Singer, Heinrich. *Allgemeine und spezielle Krankheitslehre der Juden.* Leipzig: Benno Konegen Verlag, 1904.

Singer, Isaac B. *The Manor and the Estate.* Madison: University of Wisconsin Press, 2004.

Singermann, Felix. *Die Kennzeichnung der Juden im Mittelalter.* Berlin: Paul Funk, 1915.

Smith, Lisa Wynnne. "The Body Embarrassed? Rethinking the Leaky Male Body in Eighteenth-Century England and France." *Gender & History* 23 (2010): 26–46.

Söderfeldt, Ylva. "Jüdische Gehörlose in Deutschland, 1800–1933: Blicke in die Geschichte einer doppelten Minderheit." *Medizin, Gesellschaft und Geschichte* 32 (2014): 207–30.

Solms, Wilhelm. *Zigeunerbilder: Ein dunkles Kapitel der deutschen Literaturgeschichte.* Würzburg: Königshausen & Neumann, 2008.

Solomon, Mark. "A Strange Conjunction." In *Jewish Explorations of Sexuality,* ed. Jonathan Magonet, 75–82. Oxford: Berghahn Books, 1995.

Solomon, Norman. *Historical Dictionary of Judaism.* 3rd ed. Lanham, MD: Rowman and Littlefield, 2015.

Sommer, Robert. *Das KZ-Bordell: Sexuelle Zwangsarbeit in nationalsozialistischen Konzentrationslagern.* Paderborn: Ferdinand Schöningh, 2009.

Somogyi, Tamar. *Die Schejnen und die Prosten: Untersuchungen zum Schönheitsideal der Ostjuden in Bezug auf Körper und Kleidung unter besonderer Berücksichtigung des Chassidismus.* Berlin: Dietrich Reimer Verlag, 1982.

Sonke, Monika. "Die Israelitische Taubstummen-Anstalt in Berlin-Weißensee: Von der Gründung 1873 bis zur Vernichtung 1942." In *"Öffne deine Hand für die Stummen": Die Geschichte der Israelitischen Taubstummen-Anstalt Berlin-Weissensee, 1873–1942,* ed. Vera Bendt and Nicola Galliner, 43–76. Berlin: Transit, 1993.

Sorkin, David. *Moses Mendelssohn and the Religious Enlightenment.* Berkeley: University of California Press, 1996.

Soyer, François. *Popularizing Anti-Semitism in Early Modern Spain and Its Empire: Francisco de Torrejoncillo and the "Centinela contra Judíos" (1674).* Leiden: Brill, 2014.

Sparr, Thomas. "Die Erfindung des Homosexuellen: Ein Motiv der Wissenschaft und Literatur des 19. Jahrhunderts." In *Nachmärz: Der Ursprung der ästhetischen Moderne in einer nachrevolutionären*

Konstellation, ed. Thomas Koebner and Sigrid Weigel, 256–72. Opladen: Westdeutscher Verlag, 1996.

Specification Derer in der Gegend Heydelberg/ Wormbs/ Darmstadt/ Franckfurt/ Hanau/ Friedberg/ Meyntz/ Coblentz und der Gegend herum vagierenden Diebs- und Spitzbubenrotte.... [Darmstadt]: s.n., 1715.

Spiegel, Nina S. *Embodying Hebrew Culture: Aesthetics, Athletics, and Dance in the Jewish Community of Mandate Palestine.* Detroit: Wayne State University Press, 2013.

Standhartinger, Angela. *Das Frauenbild im Judentum der hellenistischen Zeit: Ein Beitrag anhand von "Joseph" und "Asneth."* Leiden: Brill, 1995.

Steinberg, Avraham. "The Blind in the Light of Jewish Thought and Law." In *Tradition and Transition: Essays Presented to Chief Rabbi Sir Immanuel Jakobovits to Celebrate Twenty Years in Office*, ed. Jonathan Sacks and Immanuel Jakobovits, 283–93. London: Jew's College Publications, 1986.

Steinberg, Avraham. *Encyclopedia of Jewish Medical Ethics: A Compilation of Jewish Medical Law on All Topics of Medical Interest....* Trans. and ed. Fred Rosner. Jerusalem: Feldheim, 2003.

Steinberg, Avraham, and Charles L. Sprung. "The Dying Patient Act, 2005: Israeli Innovative Legislation." *Israel Medical Association Journal* 9 (2007): 550–52.

Stemberger, Günter. *Einführung in die Judaistik.* Munich: C. H. Beck, 2002.

Stolberg, Michael. "A Woman Down to Her Bones: The Anatomy of Sexual Difference in the Sixteenth and Early Seventeenth Centuries." *Isis* 94 (2003): 274–99.

Storz, Harald. *Als aufgeklärter Israelit wohlthätig wirken: Der jüdische Arzt Philipp Wolfers (1796–1832).* Bielefeld: Verlag für Regionalgeschichte, 2005.

Stratenwerth, Irene. *Der gelbe Schein: Mädchenhandel 1860 bis 1930.* Bremerhaven: Deutsches Auswandererhaus, 2012.

Straus, Raphael. "The 'Jewish Hat' as an Aspect of Social History." *Jewish Social Studies* 4 (1942): 59–72.

Stricker, Wilhelm Friedrich Karl. *Die Geschichte der Heilkunde und der verwandten Wissenschaften in der Stadt Frankfurt a. M.* Frankfurt/M.: Hermann Johann Keßler, 1847.

Strobl, Ingrid. *Sag nie, du gehst den letzten Weg: Frauen im bewaffneten Widerstand gegen Faschismus und deutsche Besatzung.* Frankfurt/M.: Fischer Taschenbuch, 1989.

Struminski, Wladimir. "Blondinen bevorzugt." *Jüdische Allgemeine*, May 24, 2007. https://www.juedische-allgemeine.de/allgemein/blondinen-bevorzugt/. Last retrieved February 22, 2020.

Suchman, Edward A. "Sociomedical Variations Among Ethnic Groups." *American Journal of Sociology* 70 (1964): 319–31.

Sufian, Sandy. "Mental Hygiene and Disability in the Zionist Project." *Disability Studies Quarterly* 27 (Fall 2007). http://dsq-sds.org/article/view/42/42. Last retrieved December 8, 2015.

Suslin ha-Kohen, Alexander. *Sefer Haagudah* (Hebr.). Cracow: Isaac Prostitz, 1571. http://www.hebrewbooks.org/45022. Last retrieved March 31, 2016.

Susser, Mervyn W., and William Watson. *Sociology in Medicine.* 2nd ed. New York: Oxford University Press, 1972.

Tacitus, Publius Cornelius. *Histories, Books 4–5; Annals, Books 1–3.* Trans. Clifford H. Moore and John Jackson. Loeb Classical Library 249. Cambridge, MA: Harvard University Press, 1931.

Tec, Nechama. *Resistance: Jews and Christians Who Defied the Nazi Terror.* Oxford: Oxford University Press, 2013.

Teller, Issachar Bär. *The Wellspring of Living Waters.* Trans., introd., and notes Arthur Teller. New York: Tal Or Oth, 1988.

Tendler, Moshe David. *Pardes Rimonim: A Manual for the Jewish Family.* New York: Ktav, 1988.

Tertullian, Quintus Septimius Florens. *Book 1: Apologetic and Practical Treatises.* Trans. C. Dodgson. Oxford: John Henry Parker, 1842.

Teter, Magda. *Jews and Heretics in Catholic Poland: A Beleaguered Church in the Post-Reformation Era.* Cambridge: Cambridge University Press, 2006.

Die Texte aus Qumran: Hebräisch und Deutsch. Ed. Eduard Lohse. 4th ed. Darmstadt: Wissenschaftliche Buchgesellschaft, 1986.

Die Texte aus Qumran II: Hebräisch/Aramäisch und Deutsch. Ed. Annette Steudel et al. Darmstadt: Wissenschaftliche Buchgesellschaft, 2001.

Theilhaber, Felix A., and Elias Auerbach. "Zur Sterblichkeit der Juden." *Zeitschrift für Demographie und Statistik der Juden* 5 (1909): 9–12.

Thomas de Cantimpré. *Miraculorum et exemplorum memorabilium sui temporis, libri duo.* Douai: Bellerus, 1605.

Tiedemann, Nicole. *Haar-Kunst: Zur Geschichte und Bedeutung eines menschlichen Schmuckstücks.* Cologne: Böhlau, 2004.

Tilevitz, Sarah Laidlaw. "Jews, Christians and Lion Pendants: Philosophical and Theological Aspects of Folk Cures as Reflected in Medieval Christian and Jewish Sources." PhD diss., Jewish Theological Seminary of America, 1993.

Toaff, Ariel. "The Jewish Badge in Italy During the 15th Century." In *Die Juden in ihrer mittelalterlichen Umwelt,* ed. Alfred Ebenbauer and Klaus Zatloukalm, 275–80. Cologne: Böhlau, 1991.

Toaff, Ariel. *Mostri giudei: L'immaginario ebraico dal Medievo alla prima età moderna.* Bologna: Il Mulino, 1996.

Toaff, Ariel. *Love, Work and Death: Jewish Life in Medieval Umbria.* Trans. Judith Landray. London: Littman Library of Jewish Civilization, 1998.

Tobel, [Dr. zum]. "Mittheilungen über einige unter den hiesigen Israeliten häufiger vorkommende Krankheiten." *Medicinisches Correspondenzblatt für Württemberg* 6 (1836): 8–11.

Torgovnick, Kate. "For Some Jews, It Only Sounds Like 'Taboo.'" *New York Times,* July 16, 2008. https://www.nytimes.com/2008/07/16/style/16iht-17skin.14532182.html. Last retrieved August 24, 2019.

Trachtenberg, Joshua. *Jewish Magic and Superstition: A Study in Folk Religion.* New York: Behrman's Jewish Book House, 1939.

Trachtenberg, Joshua. *The Devil and the Jews: The Medieval Conception of the Jew and Its Relation to Modern Anti-Semitism.* Philadelphia: Jewish Publication Society, 1983.

Trusen, Johann Peter. *Die Sitten, Gebräuche und Krankheiten der alten Hebräer: Nach der heiligen Schrift historisch und kritisch dargestellt.* Breslau: Wilhelm G. Korn, 1853.

Tschoetschel, Michael. "Die Diskussion über die Häufigkeit von Krankheiten bei den Juden bis 1920." Med. diss., University of Mainz, 1990.

Turmann, Marianne. "Jüdische Krankheiten: Historisch-kritische Betrachtungen zu einem medizinischen Problem." Med. diss., University of Kiel, 1968.

Ulrich, Jörg. *Euseb von Caesarea und die Juden: Studien zur Rolle der Juden in der Theologie des Eusebius von Caesarea.* Berlin: Walter de Gruyter, 1998.

Ungar, Ruti. "The Boxing Discourse in Late Georgian England, 1780–1820: A Study in Civic Humanism, Gender, Class and Race." PhD diss., Humboldt University of Berlin, 2010. http://edoc.hu-berlin.de/dissertationen/ungar-ruti-2010-02-10/PDF/ungar.pdf. Last retrieved March 29, 2016.

Unterman, Alan. "Judaism and Homosexuality: Some Orthodox Perspectives." In *Jewish Explorations of Sexuality,* ed. Jonathan Magonet, 67–73. Oxford: Berghahn Books, 1995.

Vaynig, Naftale. "Parekh-krankkayt in yidishn folklor" (Yidd.) [The *Parech* Ailment in Yiddish Folklore]. *Sotsyale Meditsin* 11 (1938): 22–27.

Virchow, Rudolf. "Gesamtbericht ueber die von der deutschen anthropologischen Gesellschaft veranlassten Erhebungen ueber die Farbe der Haut, der Haare und der Augen der Schulkinder in Deutschland." *Archiv für Anthropologie* 16 (1886–87): 275–475.

Voß, Rebekka. *Umstrittene Erlöser: Politik, Ideologie und jüdisch-christlicher Messianismus in Deutschland, 1500–1600.* Göttingen: Vandenhoeck & Ruprecht, 2011.

Wachstein, Sonia. *Hagenberggasse 49: Erinnerungen an eine Wiener jüdische Kindheit und Jugend.* Vienna: Böhlau, 2006.

Wachten, Johannes. "Körperbilder im Judentum." *journal-ethnologie.de.,* 2006. http://www.journal-ethnologie.de/Deutsch/Schwerpunktthemen/Schwerpunktthemen_2006/Hautzeichen_-_Koerperbilder/Koerperbilder_im_Judentum/index.phtml. Last retrieved May 4, 2016.

Wagenseil, Johann Christoph. *Tela Ignea Satanae: Hoc est, Arcani, & horribiles Judaeorum adversus Christum Deum, & Christianam Religionem Libri Anekdotoi.* . . . Altdorf: Schönnerstaedt, 1681. http://reader.digitale-sammlungen.de/de/fs1/object/goToPage/ bsb11069793.html?pageNo = 486. Last retrieved April 5, 2016.

Wahle, Hedwig. "Die Lehren des rabbinischen Judentums über das Leben nach dem Tode." *Kairos* 14 (1972): 291–309.

Waitzbauer, Harald. "'San die Juden scho' furt?' Salzburg, die Festspiele und das jüdische Publikum." In *Der Geschmack der Vergänglichkeit: Jüdische Sommerfrische in Salzburg,* ed. Robert Kriechbaumer, 249–58. Vienna: Böhlau, 2002.

Waldenburg, Alfred. *Das isocephale blonde Rassenelement unter Halligfriesen und jüdischen Taubstummen.* Berlin: Calvary, 1902.

Walk, Joseph, ed. *Das Sonderrecht für die Juden im NS-Staat.* 2nd ed. Heidelberg: C. F. Müller, 1996.

Walzer, Lee. *Between Sodom and Eden: A Gay Journey Through Today's Changing Israel.* New York: Columbia University Press, 2000.

Wegener, Franz. *Weishaar und der Bund der Guoten: Ariosophie und Kabbala.* Gladbeck: Kulturförderverein Ruhrgebiet, 2005.

Weidinger, Erich. *Die Apokryphen: Verborgene Bücher der Bibel.* Augsburg: Bechtermünz, 1999.

Weihns, W. *Bordell-Juden und Mädchenhandel: Ergänzung zu der Schrift "Juden- Bordelle."* Berlin: Heichen, 1899.

Weininger, Otto. *Sex and Character.* New York: Fertig, 2003.

Weinstein, Roni. *Juvenile Sexuality, Kabbalah, and Catholic Reformation in Italy: Tiferet Bahurim by Pinhas Barukh ben Pelatiyah Monselice.* Leiden: Brill, 2009a.

Weinstein, Roni. "The Rise of the Body in Early Modern Jewish Society: The Italian Case Study." In *The Jewish Body: Corporeality, Society, and Identity in the Renaissance and Early Modern Period,* ed. Maria Diemling and Giuseppe Veltri, 15–56. Leiden: Brill, 2009b.

Weiss, Meira. *The Chosen Body: The Politics of the Body in Israeli Society.* Stanford, CA: Stanford University Press, 2005.

Weiss, Ruchama and Levi Brackman. "Shoah Memories Live on Through Tattos." 2013. http://www.ynetnews.com/articles/0,7340,L-4368025,00.html. Last retrieved April 5, 2016.

Weissenberg, S. "Hygiene in Brauch und Sitte der Juden." In *Die Hygiene der Juden: Im Anschluß an die Internationale Hygiene-Ausstellung Dresden 1911,* ed. Max Grunwald, 29–43. Dresden: Verlag der Historischen Abteilung der Internationalen Hygiene-Ausstellung, 1912.

Weissler, Chavah. *Voices of the Matriarchs: Listening to the Prayers of Early Modern Jewish Women.* Boston: Beacon Press, 1998.

Weitz, Rose. *Rapunzel's Daughters: What Women's Hair Tells Us About Women's Lives.* New York: Farrar, Straus & Giroux, 2004.

Wenck, Alexandra-Eileen. *Zwischen Menschenhandel und "Endlösung": Das Konzentrationslager Bergen-Belsen.* Paderborn: Ferdinand Schöningh, 2000.

Wenger, Beth S. "Medicine: Gender, Assimilation, and the Scientific Defense of 'Family Purity.'" *Jewish Social Studies* 5 (1998/99): 177–202.

Wengeroff, Pauline. *Memoirs of a Grandmother.* 2 vols. Trans., introd., notes, and commentary Shulamit S. Magnus. Stanford, CA: Stanford University Press, 2010 (vol. 1); 2014 (vol. 2).

Wenninger, Markus J. "Von jüdischen Rittern und anderen waffentragenden Juden im mittelalterlichen Deutschland." *Aschkenas* 13 (2003): 35–82.

Wenzel, Jürgen. *Die Vertreibung der Juden aus Spanien im Jahr 1492: Vorgeschichte und Vergleich mit der Stellung anderer Minderheiten im christlichen Teil Spaniens (1369–1516).* Norderstedt: Books on Demand, 2013.

Werner, Helmut. *Kabbala.* Frechen: Komet, 2002.

Wesselski, Albert. *Der Sinn der Sinne: Ein Kapitel der Ältesten Menschheitsgeschichte.* Prague: Ústav, 1934.

Westermann, William L. *The Slave Systems of Greek and Roman Antiquity.* Philadelphia: American Philosophical Society, 1955.

Wiener, Adolf. *Die jüdischen Speisegesetze nach ihren verschiedenen Gesichtspunkten: Zum ersten Male wissenschaftlich-methodisch geordnet und kritisch beleuchtet*. Breslau: Schlesische Buchdruckerei, Kunst- und Verlagsanstalt, 1895.

Wiener, Leo. *The History of Yiddish Literature in the Nineteenth Century*. New York: Scribner's, 1899.

Wiener, Moses. *Hadrat panim zaken: Giluach wegidul hazakan leor hahalacha* (Hebr.) [Growing and Trimming a Beard from a Halakhic Perspective]. 3rd ed. New York: Moses Wiener, 2006.

Wiese, Christian. "Von Dessau nach Philadelphia: Samuel Hirsch als Philosoph, Apologet und radikaler Reformer." In *Jüdische Bildung und Kultur in Sachsen-Anhalt von der Aufklärung bis zum Nationalsozialismus*, ed. Giuseppe Veltri and Christian Wiese, 363–410. Berlin: Metropol, 2009.

Wieseltier, Leon. "Jewish Bodies, Jewish Minds." *Jewish Quarterly Review* 95 (2005): 435–42.

Wiesemann, Falk. "Jewish Burials in Germany—Between Tradition, the Enlightenment and the Authorities." *Leo Baeck Institute Yearbook* 37, no. 1 (1992): 17–31.

Wiesemann, Falk. "'Hygiene der Juden' auf der Düsseldorfer GESOLEI 1926: Jüdische Kulturleistungen in der Weimarer Republik." *Geschichte im Westen* 8 (1993): 24–37.

Wild, Verina, Hinda Poulin, and Nikola Biller-Andorno. "Rekonstruktion des Hymens: Zur Ethik eines tabuisierten Eingriffs." *Deutsches Ärzteblatt* 106 (2009): 340–41.

Wildmann, Daniel. *Der veränderbare Körper: Jüdische Turner, Männlichkeit und das Wiedergewinnen von Geschichte in Deutschland um 1900*. Tübingen: Mohr Siebeck, 2009.

Williams, Edward T. "Moses as a Sanitarian." *Boston Medical and Surgical Journal* 106 (1882): 6–8.

Wirnt von Grafenberg. *Wigalois: The Knight of Fortune's Wheel*. Trans. and introd. J. W. Thomas. Lincoln: University of Nebraska Press, 1977.

Wirnt von Grafenberg. *Wigalois: Text der Ausgabe von J. M. N. Kapteyn*. Ed., German trans., and notes Sabine Seelbach and Ulrich Seelbach. Berlin: Walter de Gruyter, 2005.

Wolf, Elcan Isaac. *Von den Krankheiten der Juden*. Mannheim: Schwan, 1777.

Wolf, Siegmund A. *Wörterbuch des Rotwelschen: Deutsche Gaunersprache*. Mannheim: Bibliographisches Institut, 1956.

Wolff, Berthold B. "Ethnocultural Factors Influencing Pain and Illness Behavior." *Clinical Journal of Pain* 1 (1985): 23–30.

Wolff, Berthold B., and Sarah Langley. "Cultural Factors and the Response to Pain: A Review." *American Anthopologist* 70 (1968): 494–501.

Wolff, Eberhard. "Medizinische Kompetenz und talmudische Autorität: Jüdische Ärzte und Rabbiner als ungleiche Partner in der Debatte um die Beschneidungsreform zwischen 1830 und 1850." In *Judentum und Aufklärung: Jüdisches Selbstverständnis in der bürgerlichen Öffentlichkeit*, ed. Arno Herzig, Hans-Otto Horch, and Robert Jütte, 119–49. Göttingen: Vandenhoeck & Ruprecht, 2002.

Wolff, Eberhard. *Medizin und Ärzte im deutschen Judentum der Reformära: Die Architektur einer modernen jüdischen Identität*. Göttingen: Vandenhoeck & Ruprecht, 2014.

Wolff, Isidor. "Über den Wellen." *Jüdische Turnzeitung* 7, no. 10 (1906): 180–82.

Wolfson, Elliot R. "Images of God's Feet: Some Observations of the Divine Body in Judaism." In *People of the Body: Jews and Judaism from an Embodied Perspective*, ed. Howard Eilberg-Schwartz, 143–81. Albany: State University of New York Press, 1992.

Wolfson, Elliot R. "The Body in the Text: A Kabbalistic Theory of Embodiment." *Jewish Quarterly Review* 95 (2005): 479–500.

Wolfthal, Diane. *Picturing Yiddish: Gender, Identity, and Memory in the Illustrated Yiddish Books of Renaissance Italy*. Leiden: Brill, 2004.

Wood, Percival. *Moses, the Founder of Preventive Medicine*. New York: Macmillan, 1920.

Woolf, L. S. "The Jewish Patient." *British Medical Journal* 2 (1928): 916.

Wuliger, Michael. "Vom Schtetl ins Bordell." *Jüdische Allgemeine*, August 13, 2012. https://www.juedische-allgemeine.de/kultur/vom-schtetl-ins-bordell/. Last retrieved August 24, 2019.

Wurzer, Lisa. "Akkulturation der Oberschicht: Die Annäherung der jüdischen an die christliche Welt im 18. Jahrhundert am Beispiel Wiens." Master's thesis, University of Vienna, 2008. http://othes.univie.ac.at/680/1/05–23–2008_0106135.pdf. Last retrieved March 24, 2016.

Wynn, Kerry H. "The Normate Hermeneutic and Interpretations of Disability Within the Yahwistic Narratives." In *This Abled Body: Rethinking Disabilities in Biblical Studies*, ed. Hector Avalos, Sarah J. Melcher, and Jeremy Schipper, 91–101. Atlanta: Society of Biblical Literature, 2007.

Yagel, Abraham ben Hananiah. *A Valley of Vision*. Trans., introd., and commentary David B. Ruderman. Philadelphia: University of Pennsylvania Press, 1999.

Yagod, Leon J. "Worms Jewry in the Seventeenth Century." PhD diss., Yeshiva University, 1967.

Yaron, Gil. "Der Hut, das Statussymbol der Ultraorthodoxen." *Berliner Morgenpost*, January 24, 2012. http://www.morgenpost.de/reise/article105919866/Der-Hut-das-Statussymbol-der-Ultraorthodoxen.html. Last retrieved March 31, 2016.

Yerushalmi, Yosef Hayim. *From Spanish Court to Italian Ghetto: Isaac Cardoso; A Study in Seventeenth-Century Marranism and Jewish Apologetics*. Seattle: University of Washington Press, 1981.

Yuval, Israel Jacob. "Christliche Symbolik und jüdische Martyrologie zur Zeit der Kreuzzüge." In *Juden und Christen zur Zeit der Kreuzzüge*, ed. Alfred Haverkamp, 87–106. Sigmaringen: Thorbecke, 1999.

Yuval, Israel Jacob. *Two Nations in Your Womb: Perceptions of Jews and Christians in Late Antiquity and the Middle Ages*. Trans. Barbara Harshav and Jonathan Chipman. Berkeley: University of California Press, 2006.

Zadoff, Mirjam. *Next Year in Marienbad: The Lost Worlds of Jewish Spa Culture*. Trans. William Templer. Philadelphia: University of Pennsylvania Press, 2012.

Zafran, Eric M. *The Iconography of Antisemitism: A Study of the Representation of the Jews in the Visual Arts of Europe, 1400–1600*. Ann Arbor, MI: UMI Dissertation Services, 1973.

Zaurov, Mark. *Gehörlose Juden: Eine doppelte kulturelle Minderheit*. Frankfurt/M.: Peter Lang, 2003.

Zborowski, Mark. *People in Pain*. San Francisco: Jossey-Bass, 1969.

Zborowski, Mark, and Elizabeth Herzog. *Life Is With People: The Culture of the Shtetl*. Introd. Margaret Read. New York: Schocken Books, 1962.

Zedaka: Jüdische Sozialarbeit im Wandel der Zeit; 75 Jahre Zentralwohlfahrtsstelle der Juden in Deutschland, 1917–1992. Hg. im Auftr. d. Dezernats für Kultur u. Freizeit, Amt für Wiss. u. Kunst d. Stadt Frankfurt am Main, Jüd. Museum, u. d. Zentralwohlfahrtsstelle d. Juden in Deutschland e.V. Frankfurt/M.: Jüdisches Museum Frankfurt/M., 1992.

Zias, Joe. "Health and Healing in the Land of Israel—A Paleopathological Perspective." In *Illness and Healing in Ancient Times*, ed. Ofra Rimon, 13–19. Haifa: Haifa University Press, 1996.

Zimmels, Hirsch Jacob. *Magicians, Theologians and Doctors: Studies in Folk-Medicine and Folk-Lore as Reflected in Rabbinical Responsa (12th–19th Centuries)*. London: E. Goldston & Son, 1952.

Zimmer, Eric. "Men's Headcovering: The Metamorphosis of a Practice." In *Reverence, Righteousness and Rahamanut: Essays in Memory of Rabbi Dr. Leo Jung*, ed. Jacob Schacter, 325–52. Northvale, NJ: Jason Aronson, 1992.

Zimmerman, Andrew. "Anti-Semitism as Skill: Rudolf Virchow's 'Schulstatistik' and the Racial Composition of Germany." *Central European History* 32 (1999): 409–29.

Zimmermann, Moshe. "Muscle Jews Versus Nervous Jews." In *Emancipation Through Muscles: Jews and Sports in Europe*, ed. Michael Brenner and Gideon Reuveni, 13–26. Lincoln: University of Nebraska Press, 2006.

Zinberg, Israel. *A History of Jewish Literature: Old Yiddish Literature from Its Origins to the Haskalah Period*. Trans. Bernard Martin. Jerusalem: Ktav, 1975.

Zinger, Nimrod. "'Our Hearts and Spirits Were Broken': The Medical World from the Perspective of German Jewish Patients in the Seventeenth and Eighteenth Centuries." *Leo Baeck Institute Yearbook* 54 (2009a): 59–91.

Zinger, Nimrod. "'Who Knows What the Cause Is?': 'Natural' and 'Unnatural' Causes for Illness in the Writings of Ba'alei Shem, Doctors and Patients Among German Jews in the Eighteenth Century." In *The Jewish Body: Corporeality, Society, and Identity in the Renaissance and Early Modern Period*, ed. Maria Diemling and Giuseppe Veltri, 127–58. Leiden: Brill, 2009b.

Zinger, Nimrod. "'Unto Their Assembly, Mine Honor, Be Not Thou United': Tuviya Cohen and the Medical Marketplace in the Early Modern Period." *Korot* 20 (2009/10): 67–95.

Zinger, Nimrod. "Away from Home: Travelling and Leisure Activities Among German Jews in the Seventeenth and Eighteenth Centuries." *Leo Baeck Institute Yearbook* 56 (2011): 53–78.

Zipes, Jack. *The Operated Jew: Two Tales of Anti-Semitism.* London: Routledge, 1991.

Zivotofsky, Ari. "Tzarich Iyun: Jews with Tattoos." OU Torah.org, 2010. http://www.ou.org/torah/machshava/tzarich-iyun/tzarich_iyun_jews_with_tattoos/. Last retrieved April 5, 2016.

Zohar, Noam J. *Alternatives in Jewish Bioethics.* Albany: State University of New York Press, 1997.

The Zohar. Trans. Maurice Simon and Harry Spering. Vol. 5. London: Soncino, 1934.

The Zohar. Pritzker edition. Vol. 3. Trans. and commentary Daniel C. Matt. Stanford, CA: Stanford University Press, 2006.

Zung, A., et al. "Type 1 Diabetes in Jewish Ethiopian Immigrants in Israel: HLA Class II Immunogenetics and Contribution of New Environment." *Human Immunology* 65 (2004): 1463–68.

Zürn, Gabriele. *Die Altonaer Jüdische Gemeinde (1611–1873): Ritus und soziale Institutionen des Todes im Wandel.* Münster: Waxmann, 2001.

Zweig, Arnold. "Der heutige Antisemitismus. Teil 2: Der Antisemitismus als jüdische Angelegenheit." *Der Jude* 5, no. 3 (1920/21): 129–39.

Zweig, Arnold. *The Face of Eastern European Jewry.* Ed., trans., and introd. Noah Isenberg. Berkeley: University of California Press, 2004.

Index

Acknowledgments

Prominent Yiddish researcher Jechiel Bin-Nun (1911–83) once wrote that emotions are best expressed in Yiddish. But since that language is not *mammeloschn*, my first language, I will have to do it in English.

This book has a long prehistory. It goes back to the 1990s, when, with the assistance of Julius H. Schoeps and together with Sander L. Gilman and Gabriele Kohlbauer-Fritz, I curated an exhibit on the history of the Jewish body ("*Der schejne Jid*—The Image of the 'Jewish Body' in Myth and Ritual") for the Jewish Museum in Vienna. The essay collection published in conjunction with the exhibit (Picus-Verlag) grew out of a July 1997 conference at the Institute for the History of Medicine of the Robert Bosch Foundation in Stuttgart. Here I would like to once again express my gratitude to the Robert Bosch Foundation for its support at the time, especially since the topic is a sensitive one that can give rise to misunderstandings and provoke strong reactions. I still fondly recall the positive and productive collaboration with the authors from Germany, Austria, and the United States.

The greatest benefit for me came from the stimulating discussions with the pioneer in this field, my friend and colleague Sander L. Gilman, who has since left Chicago to make his academic home in Atlanta, Georgia. Our lively exchange of ideas continues to this day. In 2015 we spent several days together with fifteen other colleagues from Germany and elsewhere in Europe, and the United States at a conference in the Villa La Collina on Lake Como, discussing the latest research on the history of the Jewish body. I owe any number of references in this book to papers presented and informal conversations there. Where these involve published materials, this cornucopia of information is reflected in the bibliography. In addition, some conference participants are thanked in the pertinent chapter notes, since I have benefited in particular from their help. The same applies to the conference "Bella figura Judaica?" (Stuttgart, 2016), where I likewise received many suggestions from presenters and audience members alike.

Institutions whose material and financial support have made this work possible include the Robert Bosch Foundation, whose Institute for the History of Medicine (IGM) has provided me with such outstanding conditions for writing and pursuing research for over twenty-five years. I also thank the Herbert D.

Katz Center for Advanced Judaic Studies in Philadelphia, where as a fellow two different times (2011 and 2014) I enjoyed the highly stimulating atmosphere in a circle of brilliant fellow grant recipients and was able to channel it into my own research. In this connection I owe special thanks to former center director David Ruderman, who is not only a brilliant host but also an inspiring soul. His research on the Jewish history of science in early modern Italy has given me any number of helpful pointers. Regarding medical-ethical aspects of several topics in this book, I am indebted to Y. Michael Barilan (Tel Aviv), who graciously allowed me access to even his unpublished work. My heartfelt thanks to David Stern (Cambridge, Massachusetts) for his expertise in interpreting Hebrew texts. François Guesnet (London) also deserves thanks, and not just in connection with his current research project on *plica polonica*. I have also profited from the work done on Jewish physicians in the Haskalah by my former research assistant Eberhard Wolff (Zurich and Basel). Valuable source references were provided by Stefanie Budmiger (Heidelberg), Evelien Gans (Amsterdam), Stephan Probst (Bielefeld), Iris Idelson-Shein (Frankfurt am Main and Tel Aviv), Rebekka Voß (Frankfurt am Main), and Falk Wiesemann (Düsseldorf). Judith Wetzka from the library of the College for Jewish Studies in Heidelberg helped me to obtain Hebrew texts. Interlibrary loan support was provided by IGM academic librarians Helene Korneck and Beate Schleh.

Over the years I was able to present various aspects of my research on the Jewish body in professional circles. I thank these colleagues for inviting me to deliver lectures on the topic: Cornelia Aust (Mainz), Renate Breuninger (Ulm), Edna Brocke (Essen), Joel Cahen (Amsterdam), Alfred Haferkamp (Trier), Margarete Krumpholz (Bonn), Vivian Liska (Antwerp), Michael Niemetz (Laupheim), Monika Renninger (Stuttgart), Rotraut Ries (Würzburg), Miriam Rürup (Hamburg), Matthias Schönewald (Laupheim), David Wertheim (Amsterdam). My thanks also to those who participated in the "Male History" panel organized by Martin Dinges at the 41st German Historians' Conference in Munich (1996) for their critical discussion of my paper on the Jewish man and their useful suggestions.

My deepest thanks, however, are to those who have read the manuscript from beginning to end; they include Heinrich Kohring (Tübingen), whose erudition and universal knowledge saved me from any number of errors, and my son Daniel, who has followed in his father's professional footsteps. I also thank my German publisher Thomas Sparr, who accepted the book project immediately and with great enthusiasm and whose informed comments and suggestions helped to shape the final product in significant ways. Thanks to Oliver Hebestreit (Stuttgart) for his careful editing. Any remaining errors are entirely my own. Special thanks must go to my translator, Elizabeth Bredeck, who has produced an excellent English version of the German text. She not only plumbed the nuances of the original and endured with patience and understanding my requests for finding English translations of halakhic texts and other sources but also turned out to be a reader with a remarkable eye for details and inconsistencies. I also wish to offer heartfelt thanks to my editor at the University of Pennsylvania Press, Jerry Singerman, for his amiable encouragement and support throughout the publication process. Much appreciation goes to managing editor Erica Ginsburg and copy editor Jennifer Shenk, whose efforts have improved this translation. I owe a debt of gratitude to the German Publishers & Booksellers Association for funding the English translation through its special program for German works in the humanities and social sciences. Finally, I am indebted to my wife, Anat Feinberg, for her many critical comments, even if her question of why a book like this needs to be written at all is one that I have probably never answered to her complete satisfaction.